Armstrong's Handbook of Management and Leadership for HR

Also available by Michael Armstrong

Armstrong's Handbook of Strategic Human Resource Management
Armstrong's Handbook of Human Resource Management Practice
Armstrong's Essential Human Resource Management Practice
Armstrong's Handbook of Reward Management Practice
Armstrong's Handbook of Performance Management
How to Manage People
How to be an Even Better Manager
Human Capital Management (with Angela Baron)
The Reward Management Toolkit (with Ann Cummins)
Evidence-Based Reward Management (with Duncan Brown
    and Peter Reilly)

www.koganpage.com

Fourth edition

Armstrong's Handbook of Management and Leadership for HR

Developing effective people skills for better leadership and management

Michael Armstrong

Kogan Page

LONDON PHILADELPHIA NEW DELHI

Publisher's note

Every possible effort has been made to ensure that the information contained in this book is accurate at the time of going to press, and the publishers and authors cannot accept responsibility for any errors or omissions, however caused. No responsibility for loss or damage occasioned to any person acting, or refraining from action, as a result of the material in this publication can be accepted by the editor, the publisher or the author.

First published as *The Handbook of Management and Leadership* in Great Britain and the United States in 2005 by Kogan Page Limited
Second edition published as *Armstrong's Handbook of Management and Leadership* in 2009
Third edition published in 2012
Fourth edition published as *Armstrong's Handbook of Management and Leadership for HR* in 2016

2nd Floor, 45 Gee Street	1518 Walnut Street	4737/23 Ansari Road
London	Suite 900	Daryaganj
EC1V 3RS	Philadelphia PA 19102	New Delhi 110002
United Kingdom	USA	India

www.koganpage.com

ISBN   978 0 7494 7815 5
E-ISBN   978 0 7494 7816 2

British Library Cataloguing-in-Publication Data

A CIP record for this book is available from the British Library.

Library of Congress Cataloging-in-Publication Data
Names: Armstrong, Michael, 1928–
Title: Armstrong's handbook of management and leadership for HR : developing effective people skills for better leadership and management / Michael Armstrong.
Other titles: Handbook of management and leadership
Description: Fourth edition. | Philadelphia, PA : Kogan Page, 2016.
Identifiers: LCCN 2016023687 (print) | LCCN 2016033428 (ebook) | ISBN 9780749478155 (paperback) | ISBN 9780749478162 (eISBN) | ISBN 9780749478162 (ebook)
Subjects: LCSH: Management–Handbooks, manuals, etc. | Leadership–Handbooks, manuals, etc. | BISAC: BUSINESS & ECONOMICS / Leadership. | BUSINESS & ECONOMICS / Management. | BUSINESS & ECONOMICS / Human Resources & Personnel Management.
Classification: LCC HD38.15 .A76 2016 (print) | LCC HD38.15 (ebook) | DDC 658.3–dc23
LC record available at https://lccn.loc.gov/2016023687

Typeset by SPi Global
Print production managed by Jellyfish
Printed and bound by CPI Group (UK) Ltd, Croydon, CR0 4YY

CONTENTS

List of figures and tables xii
Preface xiv
Alignment of text with CIPD modules xvi

PART ONE   Leading, managing and developing people fundamentals 1

01   Leadership 3

Introduction 4
Leadership defined 4
Leadership theories 5
What leaders do 11
Leadership style 14
Types of leaders 15
Leadership development 20

02   Management 27

Introduction 28
Management defined 28
The role of the management of an organization 28
The role of the manager 29
The characteristics that managers need 29
Strategic management 30
Leadership and management compared 33
Managing virtual teams 34
Effective managers 36

03   Developing people 41

Introduction 41
How people learn 42
The motivation to learn 42
Learning theory 43

Learning styles 43
Lessons from neuroscience 44

PART TWO   Human resource management
and learning and development 49

04   **The essence of human resource management** 51

Introduction 52
The concept of HRM 52
HRM defined 53
The goals of HRM 53
The philosophy of HRM 54
Underpinning theories of HRM 54
Models of HRM 54
Strategic HRM 57
The HR architecture 57
The context of HRM 63
HRM today 66

05   **The practice of HRM** 71

Work, organization and job design 72
People resourcing 76
Performance management 89
Reward management 97
Managing the employment relationship 100

06   **The practice of learning and development** 107

Introduction 108
Identifying learning needs 110
The process of L&D 111
Evaluation of learning 123
The role of L&D 125

07   **The contribution of HRM and L&D in different types
of organizations** 133

Introduction 134
The overall contribution of HR 134

The contribution of learning and development 135
The impact of HR 136
HRM in different contexts 141
International HRM 150

08 The professional and ethical approach to HRM and L&D 159

Introduction 160
Professionalism in HR 160
Codes of professional conduct 161
Professional ethical standards 162
Organizational codes of practice (ethics policies) 163
The meaning and nature of ethics 167
The nature of ethical decisions and judgements 168
Ethical theories 168
Ethical concepts 169
The ethical dimension of HRM 171
HRM ethical guidelines 172
Ethical dilemmas 177
Managing within the expectations of the law 179

PART THREE   People management processes 185

09 Motivation 187

Introduction 188
The meaning of motivation 188
Types of motivation 188
Motivation theory 189
Conclusions 198

10 Commitment 201

Introduction 202
The importance of commitment 202
Commitment and engagement 203
Critical evaluation of the concept of commitment 204
Factors affecting commitment 205
Developing a commitment strategy 206

11   Employee engagement 211

Introduction 212
The meaning of employee engagement 212
The components of employee engagement 213
Drivers of employee engagement 215
Outcomes of engagement 216
Enhancing employee engagement 216
Measuring engagement 222
Critical evaluation of the concept of employee
    engagement 223

12   Change management 227

Introduction 228
Types of change 228
The change process 229
Change models 230
Resistance to change 234
Implementing change 236
Organizational transformation 238
The role of HR in managing change 240

13   Flexible working 251

Introduction 251
The flexible firm 252
Operational flexibility 254
Flexible working arrangements 254

14   Managing diversity and inclusion 261

Introduction 261
The meaning and significance of managing diversity
    and inclusion 262
The rationale for managing diversity and inclusion 263
How to manage diversity and inclusion 263

PART FOUR   Leadership, management and learning and development skills 271

15   **Leadership skills** 273

Introduction 273
The skills required by effective leaders 274
The qualities of a good leader 274
How to motivate people 276

16   **Management skills** 279

Introduction 279
Effective supervision: providing direction 280
Delegating 280
Influencing people 284
How to make an effective presentation 288
Chairing meetings 291
Facilitating and coordinating discussions 293
Project management 294

17   **People management skills** 299

Introduction 299
How to conduct a selection interview 300
How to conduct a performance review meeting 304
Providing feedback 304
How to conduct a discipline meeting 306
How to manage poor performance 307

18   **Learning and development skills** 315

Introduction 315
Defining role profiles 316
Induction training 316
Personal development plans 316
Coaching 317
Mentoring 319
Job instruction 320

19   Managing interpersonal relationships at work 323

Introduction 324
Characteristics of effective teams and team-building 324
Assertiveness 326
Interpersonal communication 326
Handling emotional behaviour 329
Handling conflict 331
Handling challenging conversations 335
Networking 336
Negotiating 337
Organizational politics 339
Meeting HR aims in a politically astute and ethical
    manner 341
Liaising with customers 342

20   Managing oneself 349

Introduction 349
Individual differences 350
Dimensions of personality 352
Self-awareness 355
Time management 358
Personal organizing skills 361
Managing stress 363
Principles of continuous professional development 366
Professional and ethical approaches to self-management
    at work 366

21   Problem solving and decision making 373

Introduction 374
Problem solving 374
Decision making 377

22   Analytical, critical and consultancy skills 385

Introduction 385
Evidence-based management 386
Analytical skills 387
Logical reasoning 387

Critical thinking 389
Critical evaluation 389
Developing and justifying original arguments 391
Consulting skills 392

23   Information handling skills 395

Introduction 396
Handling information 396
HR analytics 397
Using statistics 399
HR information systems 404

24   Business and financial skills 413

Introduction 414
Business skills 415
Financial skills 415

25   Postgraduate study skills 425

Introduction 426
Effective learning 426
Study skills 427
Essay and report writing 434

Index 441

LIST OF FIGURES AND TABLES

Figures

FIGURE 1.1   John Adair's model of leadership 12
FIGURE 3.1   The Kolb learning cycle 44
FIGURE 4.1   The HRM system 59
FIGURE 5.1   The CEMEX model of talent management 82
FIGURE 5.2   The process of talent management 83
FIGURE 5.3   The performance management cycle 90
FIGURE 5.4   A reward system 98
FIGURE 6.1   Components of learning and development 109
FIGURE 6.2   Formal and informal learning 112
FIGURE 6.3   Systematic training model 119
FIGURE 7.1   The black box phenomenon 140
FIGURE 7.2   Impact of HRM on organizational performance 142
FIGURE 9.1   The process of motivation according to content theory 190
FIGURE 11.1   IES model of employee engagement 213
FIGURE 11.2   How reward policies influence performance through engagement 219
FIGURE 13.1   The core-periphery model 253
FIGURE 16.1   The sequence of delegation 283
FIGURE 20.1   Example of a daily organizer 361
FIGURE 20.2   How pressure becomes stress 364
FIGURE 23.1   Examples of charts 400
FIGURE 23.2   A scattergram with regression (trend) line 402

Tables

TABLE 7.1   Research on the link between HRM and firm performance 137
TABLE 9.1   Summary of motivation theories 195
TABLE 11.1   Employee engagement management competency framework 217

TABLE 17.1   The dos and don'ts of selection interviewing 303

TABLE 19.1   Industrial and commercial negotiations compared 338

TABLE 20.1   Self-assessment questionnaire 356

TABLE 25.1   The dos and don'ts of revision 430

TABLE 25.2   The dos and don'ts of taking exams 432

TABLE 25.3   The dos and don'ts of writing 437

PREFACE

The aim of this book is to explore the key concepts of leadership, management and development as they affect the work of everyone involved in management but with special reference to those concerned with human resource management. The book takes account of the learning objective stated by the CIPD in its description of its Leadership, Management and Development module. This is to help those studying the subject to 'become effective managers as well as effective HR specialists, managing others fairly and effectively and increasing levels of engagement, commitment, motivation and performance'.

A recurring theme in the book is that in order to make an effective contribution HR specialists have to be good at management, leadership and developing themselves and others, but, in addition, they need to be aware of the management and business considerations that affect their work. They function alongside line managers as part of the management of the organization and can only do that well if they understand what managers do, the leadership and development activities managers carry out and how they, as HR professionals, provide guidance, support and services to managers in the performance of the latter's roles. However, although the business dimension of management, leadership and development is important, there is also an ethical dimension. This too is emphasized throughout the book.

The final part of the book is concerned with enhancing HR skills for business leadership. It concentrates on people management skills and the aim, in the words of the CIPD module, is to:

> develop and improve a range of definable skills that are pivotal to successful management practice and to effective leadership. These include leadership, management, and learning and development skills, thinking and decision-making skills, the management of financial information, managing budgets, a range of team working and interpersonal skills and others associated with developing personal effectiveness and credibility at work.

The CIPD states that its module for Leadership, Management and Development:

> seeks to familiarise learners with major contemporary research evidence on employment and effective approaches to human resource (HR) and learning and

development (L&D) practice. Research focusing on the links between people management practices and positive organisational outcomes is covered, as is research that highlights major contemporary changes and developments in practice.

References to research are made frequently in the main parts of this book; in addition, summaries of the findings from a number of recent research studies are provided in the web-based supporting material.

This new edition of the book includes a completely revised and extended chapter on the practice of HRM and new chapters on the practice of learning and development and the management of diversity and inclusion. Other chapters have been revised to reflect the latest thinking, practice and research. A number of new case studies have also been included in the text.

The alignments between the main provisions of the CIPD Leading, Managing and Developing People and Developing Skills for Business Leadership modules and the relevant sections of this book are contained in the section following this preface.

ALIGNMENT OF TEXT WITH CIPD MODULES

Leading, managing and developing people: indicative module content

1 Review and critically evaluate major contemporary research and debates in the fields of HRM and HRD

	Page(s)
• Major research studies on contemporary developments in the HRM and HRD fields published in the UK and overseas, including those carried out or sponsored by the CIPD	(see index and support material)
• Evidence on links between HR practice and business outcomes	136–41
• Measuring the value of the HR function	59, 134–35, 344–45
• HRM and HRD practices in the most successful organisations	72–103, 108–27
• Developing an effective interface between HR and line management through partnership working	61

2 Evaluate major theories relating to motivation, commitment and engagement at work and how these are put into practice by organisations

• Understand, explain and evaluate major theories relating to motivation, commitment and engagement at work and how these are put into practice by organisations	188–98 202–07 212–23, 276
• Major motivation theories and their critics	188–98
• The significance of effective leadership, reward, performance management and career development opportunities	11–13, 81–84, 89–96, 218

3 Debate and critically evaluate the characteristics of effective leadership and the methods used to develop leaders in organisations

- Types of leadership and management styles and their impact — 7–11, 14–15
- Characteristics of successful and unsuccessful leaders — 11–13, 14, 16–19
- Developing effective leaders in organisations — 121–23

4 Contribute to the promotion of flexible working and effective change management in organisations

- Understand and contribute to the promotion of flexible working and effective change management in organisations — 228–47
- The growing significance of flexibility — 251–52
- Different types of flexibility — 254–57
- The contribution made by HRM and HRD specialists to the promotion of flexible working — 252
- Effective approaches to change management and major theories in the field — 228–47
- The central role played by people management practices in the effective management of change — 240–44

5 Critically discuss the aims and objectives of the HRM and HRD functions in organisations and how these are met in practice

- Organisation and job design — 73–75
- Attracting and retaining people — 78, 84–86
- Motivating and managing performance — 89–96
- Efficient administration of the employment relationship — 100
- Managing employee relations — 100–02
- Training and developing people — 108–25
- Rewarding people — 97–99

6 Assess the contribution made by HRM and HRD specialists in different types of organisation

- Major contemporary developments in HRM and HRD practice in larger private sector companies, small and medium-sized enterprises, public sector — 134–36, 141–49

organisations, voluntary sector organisations and
international corporations

7 Promote professionalism and an ethical approach to HRM and HRD
practice in organisations

- Major debates about professionalism and ethics in   161
  organisations
- Common ethical dilemmas faced by managers and   177–78
  ways of resolving these
- Equity and fair-dealing   170–71
- Managing within the expectations of the law   179

Developing skills for business leadership: indicative module content

1 Manage themselves more effectively at work or in another
professional context

- Self-awareness   355–58
- Dimensions of personality and individual   350–54
  differences
- Time management   358–59
- Personal organising skills   359–63
- Stress management   363–65
- Principles of continuous professional development   366
- Professional and ethical approaches to self-   366–69
  management at work

2 Manage interpersonal relationships at work more effectively

- Characteristics of effective teams and team-building   275, 325
- Assertiveness   326
- Interpersonal communication   326–29
- Effective negotiation   337–38
- Handling emotion and conflict   329, 335
- Written, verbal and non-verbal communication   326–29
- Networking   336–37

- Negotiating 337–38
- Organisational politics and the need to act in a 339–41
  politically astute and ethical manner to secure HR objectives
- Liaising with customers 342–45

3 Make sound and justifiable decisions and solve problems more effectively

- Systematic and evidence-based decision making 375, 377
- Testing ideas 376
- Creative and team-based decision making 377–80
- Evaluating evidence and options 376,
  378–79
- Ethical decision making 380
- Communicating and justifying decisions 380
- Proactive approaches to problem-solving 374
- Consulting skills 392

4 Lead and influence others more effectively

- Effective supervision and team leadership 373–76,
  280
- Coaching and mentoring 317–20
- Effective delegation 280–84
- Resolving conflict between team members 334–35
- Positively motivating others to raise their level of 276
  performance
- Chairing meetings and coordinating discussions 291–94
- Leading and facilitating change 242–44
- Providing direction 280
- Influencing thinking and decision making on the 284–88
  part of others

5 Interpret financial information and manage financial resources

- Structure, content and interpretation of simple 415–18
  balance sheets, profit and loss accounts and trading
  statements
- Ratio analysis 418
- Basic costing concepts and techniques 420

- Cash flow and cash budgets   419–20
- Budgetary planning and control   419

6 Demonstrate enhanced IT proficiency

- Information-handling skills   396–97
- Commonly used IT applications and software packages   404–07
- Statistical techniques and the presentation of statistical data   399–404

7 Demonstrate an essential people management skill-set

- Selection interviewing   79–80, 300–03
- Appraisal interviewing   304
- Disciplinary interviewing   306
- Delivering training   118–20
- Making presentations   288–91
- Project management   294–96
- Managing poor performance (including absence, lateness and incompetence)   307–10

8 Demonstrate competence in postgraduate study skills

- Accessing and evaluating published research evidence   390–91
- Critical thinking   389
- Developing and justifying original arguments   391–92
- Referencing the work of others   438
- Effective essay and report-writing   434–37
- Effective revision and examination preparation   430–33

PART ONE
Leading, managing and developing people fundamentals

Leadership

01

KEY CONCEPTS AND TERMS

Authentic leaders

Charismatic leaders

Contingent leadership

Distributed leadership

Emotional intelligence

Leader–member exchange theory

Leadership

Leadership development

Path-goal model

Situational leadership

Social exchange theory

Trait

Transactional leaders

Transformational leaders

Visionary leaders

LEARNING OUTCOMES

On completing this chapter you should be able to define these key concepts. You should also know about:

- The meaning of leadership
- The main leadership theories
- What leaders do
- The main leadership styles
- The qualities of a good leader
- The process of leadership development
- What makes an effective leader

Introduction

To lead people is to inspire, influence and guide. The significance of leadership in achieving results was established in research conducted by the consulting firm Hay/McBer as reported by Goleman (2000). This study of 3,871 executives, selected from a database of more than 20,000 executives worldwide, found that leadership had a direct impact on organizational climate, and that climate in turn accounted for nearly one third of the financial results of organizations. The conclusion from research conducted by Higgs (2006) was that leadership behaviour is responsible for almost 50 per cent of the difference between change success and failure. Research by Northouse (2006) into 167 US firms in 13 industries established that over a 20-year period leadership was the cause of more variations in performance than any other variable.

This chapter is concerned with the concept of leadership and starts with definitions of leadership. However, even if the essence of leadership can be defined quite simply it has to be recognized that in practice it is a complex affair that takes place in all sorts of ways. To understand it fully it is necessary to know more about:

- the underpinning theories that explain the process of leadership;
- what leaders do;
- how they do it;
- the different types of leaders;
- the various styles that leaders can adopt;
- the qualities that good leaders possess.

These aspects of leadership are considered in turn in this chapter. Leadership skills are dealt with in Chapter 15.

Leadership defined

Leadership is the process of getting people to do their best to achieve a desired result. It can be described as the ability to persuade others willingly to behave differently. Leadership involves developing and communicating a vision for the future, motivating people and securing their engagement to the task they are expected to do. Other definitions (there are many) include:

- Stodgill (1950: 3) Leadership is an 'influencing process aimed at goal achievement'.

- Bennis and Nanus (1985: 17) Leadership is: 'The capacity to translate intentions into reality and sustain it.'

- Dixon (1994: 214) 'Leadership is no more than exercising such an influence upon others that they tend to act in concert towards achieving a goal which they might not have achieved so readily had they been left to their own devices.'

- Buchanan and Huczynski (2007: 696) Leadership is: 'The process of influencing the activities of an organized group in its efforts toward goal-setting and goal-achievement.'

- Goleman (2000: 78) 'A leader's singular job is to get results.'

Leadership theories

Leadership is a complicated notion and a number of theories have been produced to explain it. These theories have developed over the years and explore a number of different facets of leadership and leadership behaviour. In many ways they complement one another and together they help to gain a comprehensive understanding of what the process of leadership is about.

The development of leadership theories

Trait theory, which explains leadership by reference to the qualities leaders have, is the basic and for many people the most familiar theory. But it has its limitations, as explained later, and pragmatic research was carried out to identify what types of behaviour characterized leadership rather than focusing on the personalities of leaders. The key leadership behaviour studies conducted by the Universities of Michigan and Ohio State led respectively to the identification of employee-centred as distinct from job-centred behaviour and the leadership processes of consideration and initiating structure.

The next step in the development of leadership theory was the recognition by researchers that what leaders did and how they did it was dependent or contingent on the situation they were in. Different traits became important; different behaviours or styles of leadership had to be used to achieve effectiveness in different situations. These studies resulted in the theories of contingent and situational leadership.

However, the evolution of thinking about leadership still had some way to go. Researchers began to dig more deeply into what went on when people exercised leadership. This led to the path-goal and leader–member exchange theories. At the same time it was recognized that leaders could not exist or succeed without followers and that the role of the latter therefore deserved consideration. Next, trait theory was in effect revived by Goleman (2001) in the notion of emotional intelligence as a necessary attribute of leaders. Most recently Ulrich put his oar in alongside his colleague Smallwood (2007) with the notion of the leadership brand as a comprehensive approach to leadership by organizations.

Trait theory

Trait theory, which defines leadership in terms of the traits (enduring characteristics of behaviour) all leaders are said to possess, was amongst the earliest approaches to describing leaders and leadership. In its initial form it provided an easy explanation for the complex set of individual characteristics that together form a leader. As a way of describing the qualities required of leaders it still persists in some quarters. However, its limitations were exposed long ago by Stogdill (1948: 64) whose research found that a person does not become a leader by virtue of the possession of some combination of traits.

Trait theorists have generated dozens of lists. The research by Stogdill (1948) revealed 79 unique traits but only four (extroversion, humour, intelligence and initiative) appeared in five or more studies. Research conducted by Perren and Burgoyne (2001) identified over 1,000 traits distilled to 83 more or less distinct attributes. The following list of qualities produced by Adair (1973) is fairly typical:

- *enthusiasm* – to get things done, which they can communicate to other people;
- *confidence* – belief in themselves, which again people can sense (but this must not be over-confidence, which leads to arrogance);
- *toughness* – resilient, tenacious and demanding high standards, seeking respect but not necessarily popularity;
- *integrity* – being true to oneself: personal wholeness, soundness and honesty, which inspire trust;
- *warmth* – in personal relationships, caring for people and being considerate;
- *humility* – willingness to listen and take the blame; not being arrogant and overbearing.

Yet, as Levine (2008: 165) observed: 'It is clear that traits alone are not sufficient to explain or to give rise to successful leadership… More importantly, there is no agreement about what mix of traits really distinguishes leaders from others.' Adair (1973: 13) argued that the study of leadership in terms of the qualities that one person has to a greater degree than his or her fellows is still relevant, but it is far from being the whole story. The later leadership theories discussed below showed this to be the case.

Leadership behaviour studies

The conclusion that trait theory was too vague, inconsistent and generalized to help in understanding the process of leadership (and therefore the identification, selection and training of leaders) led to a shift of focus by researchers to how leaders behaved and the leadership styles they adopted. The studies at the Survey Research Centre in Michigan (Katz *et al*, 1950) identified two dimensions of leadership behaviour: 1) *employee-centred behaviour*, focusing on relationships and employee needs, and 2) *job-centred behaviour*, focusing on getting the job done.

Similar results were obtained by the Ohio State University research (Stogdill, 1950), which revealed two categories of leadership behaviour: 1) *consideration* (concern for people) and 2) *initiating structure* (getting the job done). In both cases, the researchers stressed that the two types of behaviour did not represent the extremes of a continuum. A leader can emphasize one or other of them or both to different degrees.

The problem with the leadership behaviour approach is that it did not take sufficient account of the effect of the situation in which leadership took place. This gap was filled by the contingent and situational theories described below.

Contingent leadership

The theory of contingent leadership developed by Fiedler (1967) states that the type of leadership exercised depends to a large extent on the situation and the ability of the leader to understand it and act accordingly. Fiedler wrote:

> Leadership performance… depends as much on the organization as on the leader's own attributes. Except perhaps for the unusual case, it is simply not meaningful to speak of an effective leader or an ineffective leader. We can only speak of a leader who tends to be effective in one situation and ineffective in another. (*ibid*: 261)

The performance of a group, as Fiedler pointed out, is related both to the leadership style and the degree to which the situation provides the leader with the opportunity to exert influence. He referred to the leadership behaviour studies of Ohio State and established through his research that an initiating structure approach worked best for leaders in conditions where the leader has power, formal backing and a relatively well-structured task. Considerate leaders do better in unstructured or ambiguous situations or where their power as a leader is restricted.

Situational leadership

The notion of situational leadership is an extension of contingency theory. As described by Hersey and Blanchard (1974), leaders move between four different styles – directing, coaching, supporting and delegating – in ways that depend on the situation in terms of the development level of the subordinate and their own competence and commitment. A later version of the model (Hersey *et al*, 2001) identified the four main styles as telling, selling, participating and delegating. This is an intuitively appealing approach that has been popular with practitioners.

The path-goal model

Based on expectancy theory (see Chapter 9), the path-goal model developed by House (1971) states that leaders are there to define the path that should be followed by their team to achieve its goals. A leader's behaviour is acceptable to subordinates when viewed as a source of satisfaction, and it is motivational when need satisfaction is contingent on performance, and the leader facilitates, coaches and rewards effective performance. Leaders have to engage in different types of behaviour depending on the nature and the demands of a particular situation. It is the leader's job to assist followers in attaining goals and to provide the direction and support needed to ensure that their goals are compatible with the organization's goals. Path-goal theory identifies four leadership styles: achievement-oriented, directive, participative, and supportive.

Leader/follower theory

Leader/follower theory states that, ultimately, leaders depend on the followers they lead. The originator of leader/follower theory, Kelley (1988: 142), argued that:

Leaders matter greatly. But in searching so zealously for better leaders we tend to lose sight of the people these people will lead... Organizations stand or fall partly on the basis of how well their leaders lead, but partly also on the basis of how well their followers follow.

He suggested that the role of the follower should be studied as carefully as that of the leader. Dixon (1994: 215) observed that: 'Leadership depends upon a proper understanding of the needs and opinions of those one hopes to lead.' Hesketh and Hird (2010: 104) emphasized that:

Leadership is not reducible simply to what leaders do, or in fact, who they are or even the capabilities they possess. We should focus instead on whom leaders do leadership with, and how they achieve together what they cannot achieve alone.

Leaders need effective followers. Successful leaders depend on followers who want to feel that they are being led in the right direction. Followers need to know where they stand, where they are going and what is in it for them. They want to feel that it is all worthwhile. Grint (2005) observed that what leaders have to do is to develop followers who can privately resolve the problems leaders have caused or cannot resolve. Leaders need to learn what the role of their followers is and how to enable them to perform that role effectively.

A report on the poet Robert Graves by his CO in World War I said that, 'The men will follow this young officer if only to know where he is going.' This is a good start but it is not enough. Followers want to feel that they are being led in the right direction. They need to know where they stand, where they are going and what is in it for them. They want to feel that it is all worthwhile. They have three requirements of their leaders:

1 *Leaders must fit their followers' expectations* – they are more likely to gain the respect and cooperation of their followers if they behave in ways that people expect from their leaders. These expectations will vary according to the group and the context but will often include being straight, fair and firm – as a 19th century schoolboy once said of his headmaster: 'He's a beast but a just beast.' They also appreciate leaders who are considerate, friendly and approachable but don't want them to get too close – leaders who take too much time courting popularity are not liked.

2 *Leaders must be perceived as the 'best of us'* – they have to demonstrate that they are experts in the overall task facing the group. They need not

necessarily have more expertise than any members of their group in particular aspects of the task, but they must demonstrate that they can get the group working purposefully together and direct and harness the expertise shared by group members to obtain results.

3 *Leaders must be perceived as 'the most of us'* – they must incorporate the norms and values that are central to the group. They can influence these values by visionary powers but they will fail if they move too far away from them.

Leader–member exchange theory

The leader–member exchange (LMX) theory of leadership as formulated by Graen (1976) focuses on the two-way (dyadic) relationship between leaders and the people they lead. It is linked to social exchange theory, which explains social change and stability as a process of negotiated exchanges between parties.

LMX theory suggests that effective leaders develop exchange relationships with each of their subordinates based on trust and respect, and that the quality of these exchanges favourably influences the decisions and performance of their team members.

Leadership and emotional intelligence

According to Goleman (2001), emotional intelligence (the capacity of leaders to understand the emotional makeup of people in order to relate to them effectively), is a critical ingredient in leadership. He claimed that good leaders are alike in one crucial way: they have a high degree of emotional intelligence, which plays an increasingly important part at higher levels in organizations where differences in technical skills are of negligible importance.

Leadership brand

Ulrich and Smallwood (2007) stressed that businesses are responsible for establishing a leadership brand as an organizational capability by introducing and maintaining processes that help leaders to grow and develop. Leadership brand is pervasive through all levels of leadership in the organization. Every leader must contribute to the creation of this leadership brand, which defines their identity as leaders, translates customer expectations into employee behaviours and outlasts them.

Social intelligence

The theory of social intelligence was developed by Gardner (2011), who defined it as the capacity to get along well with others, and to get them to cooperate with you. It requires the use of a set of abilities and skills needed to understand social situations and a knowledge of interaction styles and strategies that can help a person achieve his or her objectives in dealing with others. Leaders are constantly in social situations when they are involved with their teams, and social intelligence is therefore an important attribute for them to have.

The problem with leadership theories

In spite of all the research and theorizing, the concept of leadership is still problematic. As Meindl *et al* (1985: 78) commented: 'It has become apparent that, after years of trying, we have been unable to generate an understanding of leadership that is both intellectually compelling and emotionally satisfying. The concept of leadership remains elusive and enigmatic.'

These problems may arise because, as a notion, leadership is difficult to pin down. There are many different types of situations in which leaders operate, many different types of leaders and many different leadership styles. Producing one theory that covers all these variables is difficult if not impossible. All that can be done is to draw on the various theories that exist to explain different facets of leadership without necessarily relying on any one of them for a comprehensive explanation of what is involved. Perhaps leadership is best defined by considering what leaders do and how they do it (the different styles they adopt), examining what sort of leaders carry out these activities and practise these styles, and looking at any empirical evidence available on what makes them good leaders. These are all covered in the next sections of this chapter.

What leaders do

The most convincing analysis of what leaders do was produced by Adair (1973). He explained that the three essential roles of leaders are to:

1 *Define the task* – they make it quite clear what the group is expected to do.
2 *Achieve the task* – that is why the group exists. Leaders ensure that the group's purpose is fulfilled. If it is not, the result is frustration, disharmony, criticism and, eventually perhaps, disintegration of the group.

3 *Maintain effective relationships* – between themselves and the members of the group, and between the people within the group. These relationships are effective if they contribute to achieving the task. They can be divided into those concerned with the team and its morale and sense of common purpose, and those concerned with individuals and how they are motivated.

He suggested that demands on leaders are best expressed as three areas of need which they must satisfy. These are: 1) *task needs* – to get the job done, 2) *individual needs* – to harmonize the needs of the individual with the needs of the task and the group, and 3) *group maintenance needs* – to build and maintain team spirit. As shown in Figure 1.1, he modelled these demands as three interlocking circles.

Figure 1.1 John Adair's model of leadership

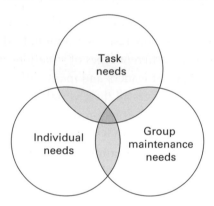

This model indicates that the task, individual and group needs are inter-dependent. Satisfying task needs will also satisfy group and individual needs. Task needs, however, cannot be met unless attention is paid to individual and group needs, and looking after individual needs will also contribute to satisfying group needs, and vice versa. There is a risk of becoming so task-orientated that leaders ignore individual and group or team needs. It is just as dangerous to be too people-orientated, focusing on meeting individual or group needs at the expense of the task. The best leaders are those who keep these three needs satisfied and in balance according to the demands of the situation.

To illustrate what leaders do, here are three examples of successful leaders: Herb Kelleber of Southwest Airlines, Bill George of Medtronic and Jack Welch of General Electric.

Herb Kelleber

Southwest Airlines is generally regarded as the world's most successful airline. It grew at a nearly constant annual rate of 10–15 per cent over its first 32 years of existence under the leadership of Herb Kelleber. He was described by *Fortune Magazine* as 'perhaps the best CEO in America'. His theme was that tasks are achieved through the goodwill and support of others. This goodwill and support originates in the leader seeing people as people, not as another resource for use in getting results. He elaborated on this as follows:

> *Take the organizational pyramid and turn it upside down. Turn it on its point. Down here, at the bottom, you've got the people at headquarters. Up there, at the top, you've got the people who are out there in the field, on the front lines. They're the ones that make things happen, not us. The people out there are the experts. You can compare our roles in the front offices to the military: We're the supply corps, we're not the heroes. We supply the heroes, period. The heroes are out there.*

The key ingredients of leadership effectiveness at Southwest were caring and respect. As a leader, Herb Kelleber focused on relationships based on shared goals, shared knowledge and mutual respect.

Bill George

Under the 12-year leadership of Bill George, chairman and CEO of Medtronic, the biomedical engineering company, the company's market capitalization increased from $1.1 billion to $60 billion, averaging 35 per cent per year. He defined his concept of the authentic leader as follows:

> *Authentic leaders genuinely desire to serve others through their leadership. They are more interested in empowering the people they lead to make a difference than they are in power, money or prestige for themselves. They lead with purpose, meaning and values. They build enduring relationships with them. Others follow them because they know where they stand. They are consistent and self-disciplined.*

Jack Welch

Jack Welch, former chief executive of General Electric, wrote that for a leader:

> *Success is all about growing others. It's about making the people who work for you smarter, bigger and bolder. Nothing you do as an individual matters, except how you nurture and support your team and increase their self-confidence. Your success as a leader will come not from what you do, but from the reflected glory of your team.*

Leadership style

Leadership style is the approach managers use in exercising leadership when they are relating to their team members. It is sometimes called management style. There are many styles of leadership and no one style is necessarily better than the other in any situation. To greater or lesser degrees, leaders can be autocratic or democratic, controlling or enabling, task-orientated or people-centred. The Hay/McBer research reported by Goleman (2000) identified the following six styles and indicated when they might be used:

1 *Coercive* – demands compliance (use in a crisis or with problem people).

2 *Authoritative* – mobilizes people (use when new vision and direction is needed).

3 *Affiliative* – creates harmony (use to heal wounds and to motivate people under stress).

4 *Democratic* – forges consensus (use to build agreement and get contributions).

5 *Pacesetting* – sets high standards (use to get fast results from a motivated team).

6 *Coaching* – develops people (to improve performance and develop strengths).

In line with contingency and situational theories, it should not be assumed that any one style is right in any circumstance. There is no such thing as an ideal leadership style. It all depends. The factors affecting the degree to which a style is appropriate will be the type of organization, the nature of the task, the characteristics of the individuals in the leader's team (the followers) and of the group as a whole and, importantly, the personality of the leader.

Effective leaders are capable of flexing their style to meet the demands of the situation. Normally democratic leaders may have to shift into more of a directive mode when faced with a crisis, but they make clear what they are doing and why. Poor leaders change their style arbitrarily so that their team members are confused and do not know what to expect next.

Good leaders may also flex their style when dealing with individual team members according to their characteristics. Some people need more positive directions than others. Others respond best if they are involved in decision making with their boss.

However, there is a limit to the degree of flexibility that should be used. It is unwise to differentiate too much between the ways in which individuals are treated or to be inconsistent in one's approach.

Types of leaders

To understand the process of leadership (and, incidentally, provide a basis for leadership development programmes) it is useful not only to analyse the styles that leaders can adopt but also to classify the different types of leaders that apply those styles. As described below, leaders can be charismatic, visionary, transformational, transactional or 'authentic'. However, typical leaders may exhibit any or even all of these characteristics either consistently or in response to the situation in which they find themselves.

Leadership may be exercised by a few selected authoritative individuals and many studies focus on top managers as 'charismatic' or 'visionary' leaders. But it may and indeed should take the form of distributed leadership that is spread through the organization among people working together by processes of influence and interdependencies. As Huczynski and Buchanan (2007: 720) commented: 'leadership is a widely distributed phenomenon. Leadership functions are best carried out by those who have the interest, knowledge, skills and motivation to perform them effectively'. The possibility that people who become managers may not have these qualities to a desirable extent creates a need for systematic leadership development programmes, as considered later.

Charismatic leaders

Charismatic leaders rely on their personality, their inspirational qualities and their 'aura' to get people to follow them. Burns (1978), who coined the term, suggested that charismatic leaders were set apart from ordinary people and treated as being endowed with exceptional powers or qualities that inspire followers.

Conger and Kanungo (1998) described charismatic leadership as a process of formulating an inspiring vision of the future and then demonstrating the importance of the articulated vision. This may involve unconventional behaviour that conveys important goals that are part of the vision and demonstrates means to achieve these goals. Charismatic leaders also take risks and motivate followers by setting a personal example. In this sense, charismatic leaders operate as visionary and transformational leaders, as described below.

However, Carey (1992: 232) argued that 'when the gifts of charisma, inspiration, consideration and intellectual strength are abused for the self-interest of the leader, the effect on followers ceases to be liberating and moral and becomes instead oppressive and ideological'. Bennis (2010: 4) commented that: 'the ability to inspire trust, not charisma, is what enables leaders to recruit others to a cause'.

Visionary leaders

Visionary leaders are inspired by a clear vision of an exciting future and inspire their followers by successfully conveying that vision to them. Bennis and Nanus (1985: 89) defined a vision as 'a target that beckons'. Their notion of visionary leadership was explained as follows:

> To choose a direction, a leader must first have developed a mental image of a possible and desirable future state of the organization. This image, which we call a vision, may be as vague as a dream or as precise as a goal or mission statement. The critical point is that a vision articulates a view of a realistic, credible and attractive future for the organization, a condition that is different in some important ways from one that now exists. (*ibid*: 89)

Kouzes and Posner (2003: 112) claimed that: 'One of *the* most important practices of leadership is giving life and work a sense of meaning and purpose by offering an exciting vision.'

Transformational leaders

Transformational leaders are able by their force of personality to make significant changes in the behaviour of their followers in order to achieve the leader's vision or goals. As described by Burns (1978), what he called transforming leadership involves motivating people to strive for higher level goals. He believed that good leadership implies a moral responsibility to respond to the values and needs of people in a way that is conducive to the highest form of human relations. As he put it: 'The ultimate test of moral leadership is its capacity to transcend the claims of the multiplicity of everyday needs, wants and expectations' (*ibid*: 46).

Another researcher, Bass (1985), extended the work of Burns (1978) by explaining the psychological mechanisms that underlie transforming leadership. He pointed out that the extent to which leaders are transformational is measured by their influence on the leader's followers in terms of the degree to which they feel trust, admiration, loyalty and respect for the leader and are willing to work harder than originally expected. As explained by Bass, this occurs because the leader transforms and motivates through an inspiring mission and vision and gives them an identity. Tichy and Devanna (1986) concluded that the transformational leader has three main roles: recognizing the need for revitalization, creating a new vision and institutionalizing change.

Yukl (1999) advised transformational leaders to:

- develop a challenging and attractive vision together with employees;
- tie the vision to a strategy for its achievement;
- develop the vision, specify and translate it to actions;
- express confidence, decisiveness and optimism about the vision and its implementation;
- realize the vision through small planned steps and small successes in the path for its full implementation.

Transactional leaders

Transactional leaders trade money, jobs and security for compliance. As Burns (1978: 19) noted: 'Such leadership occurs when a person takes the initiative in making contact with others for the purpose of an exchange of valued things.' Tavanti (2008: 169) stated that:

> Transactional leaders exhibit specific leadership skills usually associated with the ability to obtain results, to control through structures and processes, to solve problems, to plan and organize, and work within the structures and boundaries of the organization.

Put like this, a transactional leader conforms to the stereotype of the manager rather than the leader (the distinction between them is discussed in Chapter 2). Bass (1985) argued that leaders can display both transformational and transactional characteristics. Tavanti (2008) observed that transactional leadership behaviour is used to one degree or another by most leaders, but that:

> Particular instances of transactional leadership are motivated simply by people's wants and preferences. This form of leadership uncritically responds to our

preferences, that is, even when they are grounded in base motivations or an undeveloped moral sense. (*ibid*: 171)

Authentic leaders

Authenticity was defined by Harter (2002: 382) as 'owning one's personal experiences, be they thoughts, emotions, needs, preferences, or beliefs, processes captured by the injunction to know oneself and behaving in accordance with the true self'. A definition of what authentic leaders do was given by George (2003), quoted earlier in this chapter.

Authentic leadership is based on a positive moral perspective characterized by high ethical standards that guide decision making and behaviour (May *et al*, 2003). As Avolio *et al* (2004) explained, authentic leaders act in accordance with deep personal values and convictions to build credibility and win the respect and trust of followers. By encouraging diverse viewpoints and building networks of collaborative relationships with followers, they lead in a manner that followers perceive and describe as *authentic*.

George *et al* (2007: 129) described the basis of authentic leadership like this:

> We all have the capacity to inspire and empower others. But we must first be willing to devote ourselves to our personal growth and development as leaders... No one can be authentic by trying to imitate someone else. You can learn from others' experiences, but there is no way you can be successful when you are trying to be like them. People trust you when you are genuine and authentic, not a replica of someone else.

Authentic leadership is in essence ethical leadership. Walumbwa *et al* (2008) claimed that it can lead to enhanced trust, job satisfaction and performance.

Relational leadership

Relational leaders see leadership as a practice and process based on establishing good relationships with all stakeholders. They regard it as a service to the business rather than as an exercise of individual power and understand that people follow and trust leaders with whom they can relate.

As the CIPD (2014: 17) commented:

> Research shows that relational leaders emphasize the need to physically 'go and meet' their teams and employees rather than staying in their head office ivory towers. Employees want to see their leaders in action, in order to judge their benevolence and integrity. By meeting their employees, leaders are able to hear

and learn from them directly – an essential ingredient for creating a more collaborative and distributed style of leadership through which employees feel their opinions and voice are both heard and valued.

The reality of leadership

The reality of leadership is that many first line managers and supervisors are appointed or promoted to their posts with some idea, possibly, of what their managerial or supervisory duties are, but with no appreciation of the leadership skills they need. They see their role as being to tell people what to do and then see that they do it. They may tend to adopt a transactional approach, focusing on getting the job done and neglecting everything else. They may not be charismatic, visionary or transformational leaders because even if they have the latent qualities required, their situation does not seem to require or encourage any of these approaches.

However, the better ones will rely on their know-how (authority goes to the person who knows), their quiet confidence and their cool, analytical approach to dealing with problems. Any newly appointed leader or individual who is progressing to a higher level of leadership will benefit from a leadership development programme that will help them to understand and apply the skills they need.

CASE STUDY: John Lewis Partnership

The John Lewis Partnership approach to leadership emphasizes the need for their leaders to learn from their staff: As one senior manager said: 'I'm always very curious about what's on their minds so I think it's fascinating to see the diversity of thought patterns from our staff... I really enjoy the intellectual stimulus of that kind of debate.' Similarly, a John Lewis managing director described her job in the following terms: 'You're here on behalf of the people you lead... I feel really responsible for them.' This leadership style emphasizes humility as an aspect of leadership and enables such leaders to position transformation as in the best interests of people in the organization.

This is what John Lewis was able to do when announcing its first job redundancy programme, 'Branch of the Future', in its 80-year history. Since the John Lewis executives position their leadership role in terms of themselves as servants for the business, despite the job cuts the workforce were convinced of their benevolence and trust levels were actually increased.

Leadership development

It is sometimes said that leaders are born not made. This is a rather discouraging statement for those who are not leaders by birthright. It may be true to the extent that some exceptional people seem to be visionaries, have built-in charisma and a natural ability to impose their personality on others. However, even they probably have to develop and hone these qualities when confronted with a situation demanding leadership. Ordinary mortals need not despair: they too can build on their natural capacities and develop their leadership abilities.

This can be helped by leadership development programmes, which prepare people for leadership roles and situations beyond their current experience. As defined by Burgoyne (2010: 43): 'Leadership development in the widest sense involves the acquisition, development and utilization of leadership capability or the potential for it.' He identified the following leadership development activities:

- Job/work placements with leadership capability development as one of the purposes;
- Education, training and development of individuals including the 'context sensitive' methods of coaching, mentoring and action learning, and more formal education – training and development programmes;
- 'Soft' organization development processes including culture change, team-building and 'hearts and minds' collective mission/values-creating initiatives. (*ibid*: 44)

Yukl (2006) proposed the following conditions for successful leadership development:

- clear learning objectives;
- clear, meaningful content;
- appropriate sequencing of content;
- appropriate mix of training methods;
- opportunity for active practice;
- relevant, timely feedback;
- high trainee confidence;
- appropriate follow-up activities.

It is not all about subjecting leaders to development programmes, however. The organization has to ensure that leaders are provided with the support and the working conditions they need to carry out their role properly. As Fiedler (1967: 276) emphasized: 'If we wish to increase organizational and group effectiveness we must learn not only to train leaders more effectively but also to build an organizational environment in which the leaders can perform well.'

Interview

Leadership development – the views of Pierre Nanterme, CEO of Accenture, the global professional services firm with 330,000 employees

The following answer was given by Pierre Nanterme to the question: 'You served as Accenture's chief leadership officer at one point. What's your philosophy on the best way to train employees to be better leaders?'

I learnt a lot through that role, which frankly I had to figure out a bit, because it was quite new. My background is in economics and finance; yet of course, in professional services, talent is key. And for many of our clients, whatever the industry, they all are coming to me saying their number 1 challenge is getting the right talent. So first, I figured out that leadership and talent is the name of the game. Second, it's all about how you motivate people, how you're making sure they're going to stretch their own boundaries.

It's about selecting, hiring the best people, but that's not enough. Performance management is extraordinarily important to get people to their very best. Do you feel good in your role? If yes, that's the perfect time for you to experiment with something new, to get out of your comfort zone. This willingness to learn is probably the most important thing for leaders of today and tomorrow.

SOURCE https://www.washingtonpost.com/news/on-leadership/wp/2015/07/23/accenture-ceo-explains-the-reasons-why-hes-overhauling-performance-reviews/ [accessed 8 February 2016]

KEY LEARNING POINTS

Leadership defined
Leadership is the process of influencing the behaviour of others to achieve results.

Leadership theories

The main leadership theories are trait theory, leadership behaviour theory, contingent and situational theories, path-goal theory, leader–member exchange theory, emotional intelligence theory and the leadership brand.

What leaders do

Adair (1973) explained that the three essential roles of leaders are to define the task, achieve the task and maintain effective relationships. They have to satisfy interdependent task, individual and group needs.

Types of leaders

Leaders can be charismatic, visionary, transformational, transactional or 'authentic'.

The reality of leadership

The reality of leadership is that many first line managers and supervisors are appointed or promoted to their posts with some idea, possibly, of what their managerial or supervisory duties are, but with no appreciation of the leadership skills they need to get the results they want with the help of their team.

Leadership development

Leadership development programmes prepare people for leadership roles and situations beyond their current experience. 'Leadership development in the widest sense involves the acquisition, development and utilization of leadership capability or the potential for it' (Burgoyne, 2010: 43).

References

Adair, J (1973) *The Action-centred Leader*, London, McGraw-Hill

Avolio, B J, Gardner, W L, Walumbwa, F O, Luthans, F and May, D R (2004) Unlocking the mask: A look at the process by which authentic leaders impact follower attitudes and behaviours, *Leadership Quarterly*, **15**, pp 801–23

Bass, B M (1985) *Leadership and Performance*, New York, Free Press

Bennis, W (2010) We need leaders, *Leadership Excellence*, **27** (12), p 4

Bennis, W and Nanus, B (1985) *Leadership: The strategies for taking charge*, New York, Harper & Row

Buchanan, D and Huczynski, A (2007) *Organizational Behaviour*, Harlow, FT Prentice-Hall

Burgoyne J (2010) Crafting a leadership and management development strategy 1, in (eds) J Gold, R Thorpe and A Mumford, *Gower Handbook of Leadership and Management Development*, Aldershot, Gower, pp 42–55

Burns, J M (1978) *Leadership*, New York, Harper & Row

Carey, M R (1992) Transformational leadership and the fundamental option for self-transcendence, *Leadership Quarterly*, 3, pp 217–36

CIPD (2014) *Leading Transformational Change*, http://www.cipd.co.uk/hr-resources/research/transformational-change.aspx [accessed 2 January 2016]

Conger, J A, and Kanungo, R N (1998) *Charismatic Leadership in Organizations*, Thousand Oaks, CA, Sage

Dixon, N F (1994) *On the Psychology of Military Incompetence*, London, Pimlico

Fiedler, F E (1967) *A Theory of Leadership Effectiveness*, New York, McGraw-Hill

Gardner, H (2011) *Frames of Mind: The theory of multiple intelligence*, New York, Basic Books

George, B (2003) *Authentic Leadership*, San Francisco, CA, Jossey-Bass

George, B, Sims, P, McLean, A N and Mayer D (2007) Discovering your authentic leadership, *Harvard Business Review*, February, pp 129–38

Goleman, D (2001) *What Makes a Leader*, Boston, MA, Harvard Business School Press

Goleman, D (2000) Leadership that gets results, *Harvard Business Review*, March/April, pp 78–90

Graen, G (1976) Role-making processes within complex organizations, in (ed) M D Dunnette, *Handbook of Industrial and Organizational Psychology*, Chicago, IL, Rand-McNally

Grint, K (2005) *Leadership: Limits and possibilities*, Basingstoke, Palgrave Macmillan

Harter, S (2002) Authenticity, in (eds) C R Snyder and S J Lopez, *Handbook of Positive Psychology*, Oxford, Oxford University Press, pp 382–94

Hersey, P and Blanchard, K H (1974) So you want to know your leadership style? *Training and Development Journal*, 28, pp 22–37

Hersey, P, Blanchard, K H, and Johnson, D (2001) *Management of Organizational Behaviour: Leading human resources*, 8th edn, London, Prentice Hall

Hesketh, A and Hird, M (2010) Using relationships between leaders to leverage more value from people: building a golden triangle, in (eds) P Sparrow, A Hesketh, M Hird and C Cooper, *Leading HR*, Basingstoke, Palgrave Macmillan, pp 103–21

Higgs, M (2006) *Change and Its Leadership*, Rowland, Fisher, Lennox Consulting, www.rflc.co.uk accessed 5 March 2011

House, R J (1971) A path-goal theory of leader effectiveness, *Administrative Science Quarterly*, 16, pp 321–38

Huczynski, A A and Buchanan, D A (2007) *Organizational Behaviour*, 6th edn, Harlow, FT Prentice Hall

Katz, D, Maccoby, M and Morse, N C (1950) *Productivity, Supervision and Morale in an Office Situation*, Ann Arbor, MI, University of Michigan Institute for Social Research

Kelley, R (1988) In praise of followers, *Harvard Business Review*, November/December, pp 142–48

Kouzes, J and Posner, B (2003) *The Leadership Challenge*, San Francisco, CA, Jossey-Bass

Levine, K J (2008) Trait theory, in (eds) A Marturano and J Gosling, *Leadership: The key concepts*, London, Routledge, pp 163–66

May, D R, Chan, A, Hodges, T and Avolio, B J (2003) Developing the moral component of authentic leadership, *Organizational Dynamics*, 32 (3), pp 247–60

Meindl, J R, Ehrlich, S B and Dukerich, J M (1985) The romance of leadership, *Administrative Science Quarterly*, 30 (1), pp 78–102

Northouse, P G (2006) *Leadership: Theory and practice*, 4th edn, Thousand Oaks, CA, Sage

Perren, L and Burgoyne, J (2001) *Management and Leadership Abilities: An analysis of texts, testimony and practice*, London, Council for Excellence in Leadership and Management

Stogdill, R M (1950) Leaders, membership and organization, *Psychological Bulletin*, 25, pp 1–14

Stogdill, R M (1948) Personal factors associated with leadership: A survey of the literature, *The Journal of Psychology*, 25, pp 35–71

Tavanti, M (2008) Transactional leadership, in (eds) A Marturano and J Gosling, *Leadership: The key concepts*, London, Routledge, pp 166–70

Tichy, N M and Devanna, M A (1986) *The Transformational Leader*, New York, Wiley

Ulrich, D and Smallwood, N (2007) *Leadership Brand: Developing customer-focused leaders to drive performance and build lasting value*, Boston, MA, Harvard Business School Press

Walumbwa, F O, Avolio, B J, Gardner, W L, Wernsing, T S and Peterson, S J (2008) Authentic leadership: development and validation of a theory-based measure, *Journal of Management*, 34 (1), pp 89–126

Yukl, G (2006) *Leadership in Organizations*, 6th edn, Upper Saddle River, NJ, Prentice-Hall

Yukl, G (1999) An evaluation of conceptual weaknesses in transformational and charismatic leadership theories, *Leadership Quarterly*, 10, pp 285–305

QUESTIONS

1 What is leadership?

2 What is the trait theory of leadership?

3 What are the two dimensions of leadership behaviour?

4 What is the contingent theory of leadership?

5 What is situational leadership?

6 What is a transactional leader?

7 What is a transformational leader?

8 What is a charismatic leader?

9 What is an authentic leader?

10 What do leaders do – their essential roles?

11 What are the three needs that leaders must satisfy as defined by John Adair?

12 What are the main types of leadership styles?

13 What are the path-goal leadership styles?

14 What are the leadership styles identified by Hay/McBer?

15 What choice of style do leaders have?

16 What qualities do good leaders have?

17 What is emotional intelligence?

18 What is the significance of followers?

19 What are the characteristic activities in a leadership development programme?

20 What are the conditions required for successful leadership development?

Management 02

KEY CONCEPTS AND TERMS

Business model
Business model innovation
Competitive advantage
Core competencies
Horizontal integration
Management

Resource-based view
Strategic capability
Strategic fit
Strategic management
Strategy
Vertical integration

LEARNING OUTCOMES

On completing this chapter you should be able to define these key concepts. You should also understand:

- What managing means

- The purpose of managing

- The role of the manager

- Characteristics of an effective manager

- The process of strategic management

- The relationship between leadership and management

- Managing virtual teams

Introduction

Management has often been defined as 'getting things done through people' thus emphasizing its leadership component. But, as covered in this chapter, managers are also responsible for generally controlling the business or their part of it by managing their other resources – finance, work systems and technology. Additionally, they have to manage time and themselves. Managers may be in charge of virtual teams, as discussed in the last section of this chapter.

The word 'management' is derived from the Italian verb *maneggiare*, which means 'to handle a horse'. This definition at least states that to manage is to have charge of or responsibility for something, but there is clearly more to it than that and this is what this chapter is about.

Management defined

Management is the process of making things happen. Managers define goals, determine and obtain the resources required to achieve the goals, allocate those resources to opportunities and planned activities and ensure that those activities take place as planned in order to achieve predetermined objectives.

The role of the management of an organization

The role of the management of an organization is to satisfy a range of stakeholders. In the private sector, this means making a profit and creating value for shareholders, and producing and delivering valued products and services at a reasonable cost for customers. In the public sector, management is there to ensure that the services the nation or community requires are delivered effectively. In the voluntary sector, management sees that the purposes of the charity are achieved and also keeps the faith of the community and donors. In all sectors management is about exercising social responsibility and providing rewarding employment and development opportunities for employees.

The role of the manager

Drucker (1955: 1) stated that: 'The manager is the dynamic, life-giving element in every business.'

Managers are there to get results by ensuring that their function, unit or department operates effectively. They manage people and their other resources, which include time and themselves. They are accountable to a superior for attaining goals, having been given authority over those working in their unit or department.

The traditional model of what managers do is that it is a logical and systematic process of planning, organizing, motivating and controlling. However, this is misleading. Managers often carry out their work on a day-to-day basis in conditions of variety, turbulence and unpredictability. Managers may have to be specialists in ambiguity, with the ability to cope with conflicting and unclear requirements.

Managers are doers. They deal with events as they occur. But they must also be concerned with where they are going. This requires strategic thinking, especially at higher levels. As strategic thinkers, managers develop a sense of purpose and frameworks for defining intentions and future directions. They are engaged in the process of strategic management.

The characteristics that managers need

Research for The Commission on the Future of Management and Leadership (2014) produced the following list of the top 10 characteristics that managers need:

1 Clear sense of purpose.
2 Strong values and personal integrity.
3 Commitment to developing others through coaching and mentoring.
4 Champion of diversity.
5 Ability to engage and communicate across all levels.
6 Self-awareness and taking time to reflect.
7 Collaborative, networked and non-hierarchical.
8 Agile and innovative, technologically curious and savvy.
9 Personal resilience and grit.
10 Excellent track record of delivery.

Strategic management

Strategic management is an approach to management that involves taking a broad and longer-term view of where the business or part of the business is going and managing activities in ways that ensure this strategic thrust is maintained. Boxall and Purcell (2003: 44) explained that: 'Strategic management is best defined as a process. It is a process of strategy making, of forming and, if the firm survives, reforming its strategy over time.' The purpose of strategic management was expressed by Kanter (1984: 288) as being to: 'elicit the present actions for the future' and become 'action vehicles – integrating and institutionalizing mechanisms for change' (*ibid*: 301). The key strategic management activity at organizational level as identified by Thompson and Strickland (1996: 3) is:

> deciding what business the company will be in and forming a strategic vision of where the organization needs to be headed – in effect, infusing the organization with a sense of purpose, providing long-term direction, and establishing a clear mission to be accomplished.

The focus is on identifying the organization's mission and strategies, but attention is also given to the resource base required to make it succeed. Strategic management involves the development and implementation of strategy (business, HRM and L&D) as described below. It also includes the important activity of business model innovation that identifies opportunities to increase the competitiveness and prosperity of the business through a review of all the elements of its business model (a picture of an organization that explains how it achieves competitive advantage and makes money).

Strategic management involves the formulation and implementation of strategy. The process has to take account of the concepts of core competences or capabilities, the resource-based view, strategic fit and strategic capability.

Strategy

Strategy is a declaration of intent. It sets out the approach selected to achieve defined goals in the future. It was defined by Thompson and Strickland (1996: 20) as: 'The pattern of actions managers employ to achieve organizational objectives.' Strategy may be formulated at corporate level for the organization as a whole, where it is the responsibility of top management.

Strategy will also be formulated and implemented for specific activities such as product development, marketing and human resource management within the organization where it will be the concern of top management, but may also involve senior managers in charge of major units or functions and their staff.

Strategy is forward looking. It is about deciding where you want to go and how you mean to get there. It is concerned with both ends and means. It states: 'This is what we want to do and this is how we intend to do it.' Strategies define longer-term goals but they also cover how those goals will be attained (strategic planning). They guide purposeful action to deliver the required result.

Strategy formulation is, however, not such a deterministic, rational and continuous process as is often supposed. Sparrow *et al* (2010: 4) asserted succinctly that: 'Strategy is not rational and never has been.' It has been said (Bower, 1982: 631) that 'strategy is everything not well defined or understood'. This may be going too far, but in reality, strategy formulation can best be described as 'problem solving in unstructured situations' (Digman, 1990: 53) and strategies will always be formed under conditions of partial ignorance. Quinn (1980: 9) pointed out that a strategy may simply be 'a widely held understanding resulting from a stream of decisions'. He believed that strategy formulation takes place by means of 'logical incrementalism', ie it evolves in several steps rather than being conceived as a whole.

Mintzberg (1987) argued that in theory strategy is a systematic process: first we think, then we act; we formulate then we implement. But we also act in order to think. He said that in practice, 'a realized strategy can emerge in response to an evolving situation' and the strategic planner is often 'a pattern organizer, a learner if you like, who manages a process in which strategies and visions can emerge as well as be deliberately conceived' (*ibid*: 68). This concept of 'emergent strategy' conveys the essence of how in practice business and HR strategies are developed.

Core competencies and distinctive capabilities

Core competencies or distinctive capabilities describe what the organization is specially or uniquely capable of doing. The concept of core competencies was originated by Prahalad and Hamel (1990) who described them as a company's critical resource, which represented the collective learning in the organization. Distinctive capabilities can exist in such areas as technology, innovation, marketing, delivering quality and making good use of human and financial resources. Understanding distinctive capabilities – what they are and should become – is an essential task for those concerned with HRM and L&D in achieving their aim of enhancing the human resource capability of the organization.

The resource-based view

The resource-based view (RBV) of strategy is that the firm is a bundle of distinctive resources that are the keys to developing competitive advantage – the strategic capability of a firm depends on its resource capability. It is based on the ideas of Penrose (1959: 24–25) who wrote that the firm is 'an administrative organization and a collection of productive resources' and saw resources as 'a bundle of potential services'. It was expanded by Wernerfelt (1984: 172) who explained that strategy 'is a balance between the exploitation of existing resources and the development of new ones'. Resources were defined by Hunt (1991: 322) as 'anything that has an enabling capacity'. The concept was developed by Barney (1991: 102) who stated that:

> a firm is said to have a competitive advantage when it is implementing a value creating strategy which is not simultaneously being implemented by any current or potential competitors *and* when these other firms are unable to duplicate the benefits of this strategy.

This will happen if their resources are valuable, rare, inimitable and non-substitutable.

The resource-based view provides a practical justification for key aspects of a firm's HRM and L&D policies and practices such as human capital management, talent management, knowledge management, and learning and development. Kamoche (1996) stated that the RBV builds on and provides a unifying framework for the field of strategic HRM. Boxall (1996: 66) pointed out that: 'The resource-based view of the firm provides a conceptual basis, if we needed one, for asserting that key human resources are sources of competitive advantage.'

Strategic fit

Strategic fit is a way of achieving competitive advantage, which means attaining and sustaining better results than business rivals, thus placing the firm in a strong competitive position. The focus is upon the organization and the world around it. To maximize competitive advantage a firm must match its capabilities and resources to the opportunities available in the external environment. As Hofer and Schendel (1986: 4) concluded:

> A critical aspect of top management's work today involves matching organizational competences (internal resources and skills) with the opportunities and risks created by environmental change in ways that will be both effective and efficient over the time such resources will be deployed.

Strategic capability

Strategic capability refers to the ability of an organization to develop and implement strategies that will achieve sustained competitive advantage. It is therefore about the capacity to select the most appropriate vision, to define realistic intentions, to match resources to opportunities and to prepare and implement strategic plans.

The strategic capability of an organization depends on the strategic capabilities of its managers. People who display high levels of strategic capability know where they are going and know how they are going to get there. They recognize that although they must be successful now to succeed in the future, it is always necessary to create and sustain a sense of purpose and direction. Managers who think strategically will be aware that they are responsible, first, for planning how to allocate resources to opportunities that contribute to the implementation of strategy, and secondly, for managing these opportunities in ways that will add value to the results achieved by the firm.

Leadership and management compared

Are leadership and management the same or different? Some commentators regard leadership as synonymous with management, others see them as distinct but closely linked and equally necessary activities, others consider management a subset of leadership, and yet others praise leadership and demonize management.

Bennis (1989) viewed managers as those who promote efficiency, follow the rules and accept the status quo, while leaders focus on challenging the rules and promoting effectiveness. Kotter (1991) saw managers as being the ones who plan, budget, organize and control, while leaders set direction, manage change and motivate people. Hersey and Blanchard (1998) claimed that management merely consists of leadership applied to business situations; or in other words, management forms a sub-set of the broader process of leadership.

As Birkinshaw (2010: 23) commented: 'By dichotomizing the work of executives in this way, Kotter, Bennis and others squeezed out the essence of what managers do and basically left them with the boring work that "leaders" don't want.' His view on the leadership-versus management debate was that:

> Leadership is a process of social influence, concerned with the traits, styles and behaviours of individuals that causes others to follow them. Management is the act of getting people together to accomplish desired goals. To put it simply, we all need to be both leaders and managers. (*ibid*: 23)

Mintzberg (2004: 22) summed it all up (as he often did) when he wrote: 'Let's stop the dysfunctional separation of leadership from management. We all know that managers who don't lead are boring, dispiriting. Well, leaders who don't manage are distant, disconnected.'

The answer to the question posed at the beginning of this section is that management is different from leadership although they are closely associated. Management is the process of making effective use of *all* available resources in order to achieve goals while leadership focuses on the key resource that enables goals to be achieved, ie people. Management necessarily involves leadership and leadership necessarily involves management.

Managing virtual teams

Managers generally are responsible for a team of people to whom they provide leadership and guidance. It is usual for them to be in direct contact with their team but some managers are in charge of a virtual team. This is a work group whose members work in different locations, including at home, and are engaged in interdependent tasks; ie are truly teams and not just groups of independent workers. The virtual team manager has to exercise remote control through electronic means such as the internet and

Skype, and telephone or video conferencing will be used for team meetings. Team members may be spread out overseas and may seldom if ever get together in one place.

Management and leadership in these circumstances are much more difficult. Frequent face-to-face contacts are important ways of building team spirit and establishing rapport and trust. Without them it is hard for the team to function as a coherent whole. In a sense, a team whose members do not meet each other is a contradiction in terms. The best solution to this problem is to get the team together as often as possible. It is not enough for the manager to see members singly. Holding team meetings may be costly but it can be money well spent.

Watkins (2013) produced the following 10 basic principles on making virtual teams work:

1 Get the team together physically early on. Face-to-face communication is still better than virtual when it comes to building relationships and fostering trust, an essential foundation for effective teamwork. Reconnect regularly as much as possible.

2 Clarify tasks and processes. Simplify the work. Be clear about work processes, specifying who does what and when.

3 Be clear and disciplined about how the team will communicate.

4 Use the best collaborative technologies such as multi-point video conferencing.

5 Use communication technology to hold regular meetings.

6 If it is a multinational team, agree on a shared language.

7 Encourage informal interactions (a virtual water cooler). Start each meeting with a check-in, getting each member to take a couple of minutes to discuss what they are doing, what's going well and what's challenging. Use enterprise social networks (internal social networks that function in the same way as social networks such as Facebook) to extend contacts.

8 Clarify and track commitments.

9 Foster shared leadership. Find ways to involve others in leading the team, for example assigning responsibility for special projects.

10 One-to-one interactions are still important to provide feedback and ensure that individuals know how they are contributing to team effort.

Effective managers

Effective managers:

- are clear about what the organization as a whole and their part of it exist to do;
- fully understand the objectives they have to achieve;
- understand what good performance is and manage it accordingly;
- adopt a strategic approach that involves integrating their functional or unit strategies with corporate strategy, and planning ahead to achieve objectives, exploit opportunities and avoid problems;
- make things happen;
- are authentic leaders who, as Avolio *et al* (2004) explained, act in accordance with deep personal values and convictions to build credibility and win the respect and trust of followers;
- have high levels of social intelligence (getting on with people);
- exercise good judgement when making decisions and solving problems;
- are resilient in the face of pressure;
- are good communicators;
- are capable of 'thinking outside the box' – innovating and acting creatively.

KEY LEARNING POINTS

Management
Management is the process of making things happen. Managers define goals, determine and obtain the resources required to achieve the goals, allocate those resources to opportunities and planned activities and ensure that those activities take place as planned in order to achieve pre-determined objectives.

The purpose of management is to satisfy a range of stakeholders. The top 10 characteristics that managers need are:

Clear sense of purpose.
Strong values and personal integrity.

Commitment to developing others through coaching and mentoring.
Champion of diversity.

Ability to engage and communicate across all levels.

Agile and innovative, technologically curious and savvy.

Self-awareness and taking time to reflect.

Personal resilience and grit.

Collaborative, networked and non-hierarchical.

Excellent track record of delivery.

Strategic management

Strategic management is an approach to management that involves taking a broad and longer-term view of where the business or part of the business is going and managing activities in ways that ensure this strategic thrust is maintained.

Business model innovation

Business model innovation is an approach to strategy that focuses on how the firm creates value. The aim is to change the ways in which companies view their business operations and to provide guidance on mapping their future strategy.

Strategy

Strategies define longer-term goals; they also cover how those goals will be attained (strategic planning). They guide purposeful action to deliver the required result. Strategy formulation is not necessarily a deterministic, rational and continuous process.

Core competencies

Core competencies or distinctive capabilities describe what the organization is specially or uniquely capable of doing.

The resource-based view of strategy

A firm is a bundle of distinctive resources that are the keys to developing competitive advantage – the strategic capability of a firm depends on its resource capability. Boxall (1996) pointed out that: 'The resource-based view of the firm provides a conceptual basis, if we needed one, for asserting that key human resources are sources of competitive advantage.'

Strategic fit

To maximize competitive advantage a firm must match its capabilities and resources to the opportunities available in the external environment.

Strategic capability
The ability of an organization to develop and implement strategies that will achieve sustained competitive advantage.

Leadership and management
Leadership is a process of social influence, concerned with the traits, styles and behaviours of individuals that cause others to follow them. Management is the act of getting people together to accomplish desired goals.

Managing virtual teams
A virtual team is a work group whose members work in different locations including at home and are engaged in interdependent tasks. Lack of face-to-face contact makes them hard to manage. There are a number of ways of dealing with this problem but perhaps the best solutions are listed above. One of the solutions is to get the team together whenever possible.

References

Avolio, B J, Gardner, W L, Walumbwa, F O, Luthans, F and May, D R (2004) Unlocking the mask: A look at the process by which authentic leaders impact follower attitudes and behaviours, *Leadership Quarterly*, **15**, pp 801–23

Barney, J (1991) Firm resources and sustained competitive advantage, *Journal of Management Studies*, **17** (1), pp 99–120

Bennis, W (1989) *On Becoming a Leader*, New York, Addison Wesley

Birkinshaw, J (2010) An experiment in reinvention, *People Management*, 15 July, pp 22–24

Bower, J L (1982) Business policy in the 1980s, *Academy of Management Review*, **7** (4), pp 630–38

Boxall, P F (1996) The strategic HRM debate and the resource-based view of the firm, *Human Resource Management Journal*, **6** (3), pp 59–75

Boxall, P F and Purcell, J (2003) *Strategy and Human Resource Management*, Basingstoke, Palgrave Macmillan

The Commission on the Future of Management and Leadership (2014) *Management 2020: Leadership to unlock long-term growth*, www.managers.org.uk/management2020 [accessed 1 January 2016]

Digman, L A (1990) *Strategic Management: Concepts, decisions, cases*, Georgetown, Ontario, Irwin

Drucker, P (1955) *The Practice of Management*, London, Heinemann

Hersey, P and Blanchard, K H (1998) *Management of Organizational Behaviour*, Englewood Cliffs, NJ, Prentice Hall

Hofer, C W and Schendel, D (1986) *Strategy Formulation: Analytical concepts*, New York, West Publishing

Hunt, S (1991) The resource-advantage theory of competition, *Journal of Management Inquiry*, 4 (4), pp 317–22

Kamoche, K (1996) Strategic human resource management within a resource capability view of the firm, *Journal of Management Studies*, 33 (2), pp 213–33

Kanter, R M (1984) *The Change Masters*, London, Allen & Unwin

Kotter, J P (1991) Power, dependence and effective management, in (ed) J Gabarro, *Managing People and Organizations*, Boston, MA, Harvard Business School Publications

Mintzberg, H (2004) Enough leadership, *Harvard Business Review*, November, p 22

Mintzberg, H (1987) Crafting strategy, *Harvard Business Review*, July–August, pp 66–74

Penrose, E (1959) *The Theory of the Growth of the Firm*, Oxford, Blackwell

Prahalad, C K and Hamel, G (1990) The core competence of the organization, *Harvard Business Review*, May–June, pp 79–93

Quinn, J B (1980) *Strategies for Change: Logical incrementalism*, Georgetown, Ontario, Irwin

Sparrow, P, Hesketh, A, Hird, M and Cooper, C (2010) Introduction: Performance-led HR, in (eds) P Sparrow, A Hesketh, M Hird and C Cooper, *Leading HR*, Basingstoke, Palgrave Macmillan, pp 1–22

Thompson, A A and Strickland, A J (1996) *Strategic Management, Concepts and cases*, 9th edn, Chicago, IL, Irwin

Watkins, M (2013) *Making Virtual Teams Work*, https://hbr.org/2013/06/making-virtual-teams-work-ten [accessed 1 January 2016]

Wernerfelt, B (1984) A resource-based view of the firm, *Strategic Management Journal*, 5 (2), pp 171–80

QUESTIONS

1 How would you define management?

2 What is the purpose of management?

3 What is strategic management?

4 What is strategy?

5 How would you describe the process of strategy formulation?

6 What is a business model?

7   What is business model innovation?

8   What is a core competency?

9   What is the resource-based view?

10 What is the meaning and significance of strategic fit?

11 What is strategic capability?

12 What is the difference between management and leadership?

Developing people   03

Introduction

Developing people is the process of providing them with learning opportunities
that will enable them to acquire the knowledge and skills needed to carry out
their current jobs effectively and prepare them to exercise wider or increased

responsibilities. It involves growing and realizing a person's ability and potential by means of learning experiences and self-directed (self-managed) learning.

Bearing in mind that those responsible for helping people to learn – either specialists in an L&D function or line managers – will be much better at it if they understand *how* people learn, this chapter focuses on the learning process. The learning and development skills needed by line managers are described in Chapter 18.

How people learn

People learn by doing (experiential learning) and to a much lesser extent by instruction. They learn from other people – their managers and co-workers (social learning). The 70/20/10 model for learning and development based on research conducted by the Centre for Creative Leadership (Lombardo and Eichinger, 1996) explains that people's development will be about 70 per cent from work experience, about 20 per cent from social learning and 10 per cent from formal training courses. Most learning takes place in the workplace. Formal instruction plays a much less significant part. Discretionary, self-directed, learning takes place when individuals of their own volition actively seek to acquire the knowledge and skills they need to carry out their work.

The way in which individuals learn depends largely on how well they are motivated and is explained by learning theory and neuroscience.

The motivation to learn

People will learn more effectively if they are motivated to learn. As Reynolds *et al* (2002: 34) commented:

> The disposition and commitment of the learner – their motivation to learn – is one of the most critical factors affecting training effectiveness. Under the right conditions, a strong disposition to learn, enhanced by solid experience and a positive attitude, can lead to exceptional performance.

Two motivation theories are particularly relevant to learning. *Expectancy theory* states that goal-directed behaviour is driven by the expectation of achieving something that the individual regards as desirable. If individuals feel that the outcome of learning is likely to benefit them they will be more inclined to pursue it. When they find that their expectations have been fulfilled, their belief that learning is worthwhile will be reinforced.

Goal theory states that motivation is higher when individuals aim to achieve specific goals, when these goals are accepted and, although difficult, are achievable, and when there is feedback on performance. Learning goals may be set for individuals (but to be effective as motivators they must be agreed) or, better still, individuals may set their own goals (self-directed learning).

Learning theory

Learning theory describes how people learn. The main theories are:

- *Reinforcement theory* – based on the work of Skinner (1974) this expresses the belief that changes in behaviour take place as a result of an individual's response to events or stimuli and the ensuing consequences (rewards or punishments). Individuals can be 'conditioned' to repeat the behaviour by positive reinforcement in the form of feedback and knowledge of results. This is known as 'operant conditioning'.

- *Cognitive learning theory* – learning involves gaining knowledge and understanding by absorbing information in the form of principles, concepts and facts and then internalizing it. Learners can be regarded as powerful information-processing machines.

- *Experiential learning theory* – experiential learning takes place when people learn from their experience by absorbing and reflecting on it so that it can be understood and applied. Thus people become active agents of their own learning.

- *Social learning theory* – this states that effective learning requires social interaction. Wenger (1998) suggested that we all participate in 'communities of practice' (groups of people with shared expertise who work together) and that these are our primary sources of learning. Bandura (1977) viewed learning as a series of information-processing steps set in train by social interactions.

Learning styles

Learning theories describe in general terms how people learn, but individual learners will have different styles – a preference for a particular approach to learning. The most familiar classification of learning styles is that produced by Kolb *et al* (1974).

Figure 3.1 The Kolb learning cycle

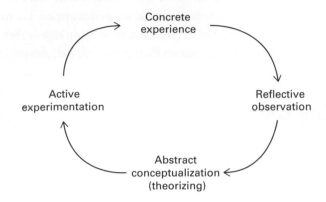

The Kolb learning cycle consists of four stages, as shown in Figure 3.1; these stages are:

- *Concrete experience* – this can be planned or accidental.
- *Reflective observation* – this involves actively thinking about the experience and its significance.
- *Abstract conceptualization (theorizing)* – generalizing from experience to develop various concepts and ideas that can be applied when similar situations are encountered.
- *Active experimentation* – testing the concepts or ideas in new situations. This gives rise to a new concrete experience and the cycle begins again.

The key to this model is that it is a simple description of how experience is translated into concepts that are then used to guide the choice of new experiences. To learn effectively, individuals must shift from being observers to participants, from direct involvement to a more objective analytical detachment. Every person has his or her own learning style, and one of the most important arts that trainers have to develop is adjusting their approaches to the learning styles of trainees. Trainers must acknowledge these learning styles rather than pursue their own preferred approach.

Lessons from neuroscience

Neuroscience is the study of the way in which the brain works. Over the last few years much has been discovered about how the brain functions and thus how we can learn most effectively. The CIPD (2014) commented that:

Although our development arises from an interaction of our genes with the environment, the brain's plasticity demonstrates very clearly that our genes only partly determine our progress. External environmental factors strongly influence how our brains are constructed and an important external factor, perhaps the most important for many of us, is our education. That includes opportunities for training that present themselves throughout our working lives.

The 2011 report by the Royal Society (2011: v) noted that: 'Biological factors play an important role in accounting for differences in learning ability between individuals.' The Royal Society listed five things that neuroscience has taught about what aids effective learning:

1 Emotional engagement with what is being learnt.

2 Keeping up physical exercise to prepare the brain for learning as well as maintaining learning energy.

3 We learn better in stimulating environments, both online and physically.

4 The aging brain needs attention but can maintain learning throughout life.

5 The brain needs time to reflect to embed the learning.

The Maritz Institute (Hendel-Giller, 2010: 6) produced the following learning design principles based on research linking the Kolb learning cycle to the structure of the brain:

- Engage the entire Kolb learning cycle. Make time for reflection, creating and active testing as well as absorbing new information.

- Make a connection with the learner's prior knowledge and experience.

- Create opportunities for social engagement and interaction as part of the learning process.

- Engage both feeling and thinking. Learning needs emotion as well as intellect.

- Actively attend to attention – gaining, holding and focusing the learner's attention.

- Engage a maximum number of senses – especially visual – when designing learning.

KEY LEARNING POINTS

The nature of people development

Developing people is the process of providing them with learning opportunities that will enable them to acquire the knowledge and skills needed to carry out their current jobs effectively and prepare them to exercise wider or increased responsibilities. It involves growing and realizing a person's ability and potential by means of learning experiences and self-directed (self-managed) learning.

How people learn

People learn by doing (experiential learning) and to a much lesser extent by instruction. They learn from other people – their managers and co-workers (social learning).

Discretionary, self-directed, learning takes place when individuals of their own volition actively seek to acquire the knowledge and skills they need to carry out their work. The way in which individuals learn depends largely on how well they are motivated and is explained by learning theory and neuroscience.

Motivation

People will learn more effectively if they are motivated to learn.

Learning theory

Learning theory describes how people learn. The main theories are reinforcement theory, cognitive learning theory, experiential learning theory and social learning theory.

Lessons from neuroscience

The five things that neuroscience has taught about what aids effective learning are emotional engagement with what is being learnt, keeping up physical exercise to prepare the brain for learning, we learn better in stimulating environments, the aging brain can maintain learning throughout life, and the brain needs time to reflect to embed the learning.

Learning styles

Learning theories describe in general terms how people learn, but individual learners will have different styles – a preference for a particular approach to learning. The most familiar classification of learning styles is that produced by Kolb who identified four styles: concrete experience, reflective observation, abstract conceptualization (theorizing) and active experimentation.

References

Bandura, A (1977) *Social Learning Theory*, Englewood Cliffs, NJ, Prentice Hall

CIPD (2014) Fresh thinking in learning and development Part 1: Neuroscience and learning, http://www.cipd.co.uk/binaries/fresh-thinking-in-learning-and-development_2014-part-1-neuroscience-learning.pdf [accessed 3 November 2015]

Hendel-Giller, R (2010) The neuroscience of learning: New paradigms for corporate education, http://www.themaritzinstitute.com/Perspectives/-media/Files/MaritzInstitute/White-Papers/The-Neuroscience-of-learning-The-Maritz-Institute.pdf [accessed 3 November 2015]

Kolb, D A, Rubin, I M and McIntyre, J M (1974) *Organizational Psychology: An experimental approach*, Englewood Cliffs, NJ, Prentice Hall

Lombardo, M M and Eichinger, R W (1996) *The Course Architect Development Planner*, Minneapolis, MN, Lominger

Reynolds, J, Caley, L and Mason, R (2002) *How Do People Learn?* London, CIPD

Royal Society (2011) Brain waves 2: Neuroscience: implications for education and lifelong learning, https://royalsociety.org/topics-policy/projects/brain-waves/education-lifelong-learning/ [accessed 3 November 2015]

Skinner, B F (1974) *About Behaviourism*, London, Random House

Skinner, B F (1953) *Science and Human Behavior*, New York, The Free Press

Wenger, E (1998) *Communities of Practice: Learning, meaning and identity*, Cambridge, Cambridge University Press

QUESTIONS

1 What is involved in the process of developing people?

2 What is learning and development?

3 What is learning?

4 What is development?

5 What is training?

6 What is experiential learning?

7 What is self-directed learning?

8 What is e-learning?

PART TWO
Human resource management and learning and development

The essence of human resource management 04

KEY CONCEPTS AND TERMS

Added value

Contextual model of human resource management (HRM)

European model of HRM

5-P model of HRM

Hard HRM

Harvard framework

HRM architecture

HR philosophy

Matching model of HRM

Resource-based theory

Soft HRM

Strategic alignment

Strategic human resource management

LEARNING OUTCOMES

On completing this chapter you should be able to define these key concepts. You should also know about:

- The fundamental concept of HRM
- The goals of HRM
- The philosophy of HRM
- Models of HRM
- Strategic HRM
- The HRM architecture
- The context of HRM

Introduction

Human resource management (HRM) is concerned with all aspects of how people are employed, managed and developed in organizations. Boxall (2013: 13) noted that: 'Human resources include the knowledge, skills, networks and energies of people and, underpinning them, their physical and emotional health, intellectual capabilities, personalities and motivations.' HRM is delivered through the HR architecture of systems and structures, the HR function and, importantly, line management.

HRM emerged in the 1980s as a philosophy of how people should be managed. As Hendry and Pettigrew (1990: 20) observed: 'What HRM did at this point was to wrap around some of the observable changes, while providing a focus for challenging deficiencies – in attitudes, scope, coherence and direction – of existing personnel management.' They also commented (*ibid*: 25) that HRM can be perceived as a 'perspective on personnel management and not personnel management itself'.

Some people criticize the notion of referring to people as resources as if they were any other factor of production. Osterby and Coster (1992: 31) argued that: 'The term "human resources" reduces people to the same category of value as materials, money and technology – all resources, and resources are only valuable to the extent they can be exploited or leveraged into economic value.' 'People management' is sometimes preferred as an alternative, but in spite of its connotations, HRM is the term that is most commonly used.

This chapter deals with the concept of HRM and its characteristics: its goals, philosophy and architecture within the context in which it operates. It also describes the concept of strategic HRM. The next chapter deals with the practice of HRM – how the concept is realized. The professional and ethical dimensions of HRM are covered in Chapter 8.

The concept of HRM

HRM as originally conceived had a conceptual framework consisting of a philosophy underpinned by a number of theories drawn from the behavioural sciences and from the fields of strategic management, human capital management and industrial relations. The HRM philosophy has been heavily criticized by some academics as being managerialist and manipulative but this criticism has subsided, perhaps because it became increasingly evident that the term 'HRM' had been adopted as a synonym for what used to be called 'personnel management' without paying much attention to the original philosophy. As noted by Storey (2007: 6): 'In its generic broad and popular sense it [HRM] simply refers to any system of people management.' HRM practice today is no longer governed by the original philosophy, if it ever was. It is just what HR people and line managers do.

HRM defined

Human resource management is defined as a strategic, integrated and co-herent approach to the employment, development and wellbeing of the people working in organizations. It was defined more pragmatically by Boxall and Purcell (2003: 1) as 'all those activities associated with the man-agement of employment relationships in the firm'. A more comprehensive definition was offered by Watson (2010: 919):

> HRM is the managerial utilization of the efforts, knowledge, capabilities and committed behaviours which people contribute to an authoritatively coordin-ated human enterprise as part of an employment exchange (or more temporary contractual arrangement) to carry out work tasks in a way which enables the enterprise to continue into the future.

The goals of HRM

The goals of HRM are to:

- support the organization in achieving its objectives by developing and implementing human resource (HR) strategies that are integrated with the business strategy (strategic HRM);
- contribute to the development of a high performance culture;
- ensure that the organization has the talented, skilled and engaged people it needs;
- create a positive employment relationship between management and employees and a climate of mutual trust;
- encourage the application of an ethical approach to people management.

The philosophy of HRM

The following explanation of HRM philosophy was made by Legge (1989: 25) whose analysis of a number of HRM models identified the following common themes:

> That human resource policies should be integrated with strategic business planning and used to reinforce an appropriate (or change an inappropriate) organizational culture, that human resources are valuable and a source of competitive advantage, that they may be tapped most effectively by mutually consistent policies that promote commitment and which, as a consequence, foster a willingness in employees to act flexibly in the interests of the 'adaptive organization's' pursuit of excellence.

Storey (2001: 7) noted that the beliefs of HRM included the assumptions that it is the human resource which gives competitive edge, that the aim should be to enhance employee commitment, that HR decisions are of strategic importance and that therefore HR policies should be integrated into the business strategy.

Underpinning theories of HRM

The original notion of HRM had a strong theoretical base. Guest (1987: 505) commented that: 'Human resource management appears to lean heavily on theories of commitment and motivation and other ideas derived from the field of organizational behaviour.' However, resource-based theory expressed as 'the resource-based view' has had the greatest influence on HRM. This theory states that competitive advantage is achieved if a firm's resources are valuable, rare and costly to imitate. It is claimed that HRM can play a major part in ensuring that the firm's human resources meet these criteria.

Models of HRM

Over the years a number of models, summarized below, have defined what HRM is and how it operates. Of these, the matching model and the Harvard framework have been the most influential.

The matching model

Fombrun *et al* (1984) proposed the 'matching model', which indicated that HR systems and the organization structure should be managed in a way that is congruent with organizational strategy. This point was made in their classic statement that: 'The critical management task is to align the formal structure and human resource systems so that they drive the strategic objectives of the organization' (*ibid*: 37). Thus they took the first steps towards the concept of strategic HRM.

The Harvard framework

Beer *et al* (1984) produced what has become known as the Harvard framework. They started with the proposition that: 'Human resource management (HRM) involves all management decisions and actions that affect the nature of the relationship between the organization and employees – its human resources' (*ibid*: 1). They believed that: 'Today... many pressures are demanding a broader, more comprehensive and more strategic perspective with regard to the organization's human resources' (*ibid*: 4). They also stressed that it was necessary to adopt 'a longer-term perspective in managing people and consideration of people as a potential asset rather than merely a variable cost' (*ibid*: 6).

Beer and his colleagues were the first to underline the HRM tenet that it belongs to line managers. They suggested that HRM had two characteristic features: 1) line managers accept more responsibility for ensuring the alignment of competitive strategy and HR policies; and 2) HR has the mission of setting policies that govern how HR activities are developed and implemented in ways that make them more mutually reinforcing.

Contextual model

The contextual model of HRM emphasizes the importance of environmental factors by including variables such as the influence of social, institutional and political forces that have been underestimated in other models. The model advocates integrating the HRM system in the environment in which it is developed. According to Martin-Alcázar *et al* (2005: 638): 'Context both conditions and is conditioned by the HRM strategy.' A broader set of stakeholders is involved in the formulation and implementation of human resource strategies. This is referred to by Schuler and Jackson (2000: 229) as a 'multiple stakeholder framework'. These stakeholders may be external as well as internal and both influence and are influenced by strategic decisions.

The 5-P model

The 5-P model of HRM, as formulated by Schuler (1992) describes the way HRM operates under the five headings of:

1 *HR philosophy* – a statement of how the organization regards its human resources, the role they play in the overall success of the business, and how they should be treated and managed.

2 *HR policies* – these provide guidelines for action on people-related business issues and for the development of HR programmes and practices based on strategic needs.

3 *HR programmes* – these are shaped by HR policies and consist of coordinated HR efforts intended to initiate and manage organizational change efforts prompted by strategic business needs.

4 *HR practices* – these are the activities carried out in implementing HR policies and programmes. They include resourcing, learning and development, performance and reward management, employee relations, and administration.

5 *HR processes* – these are the formal procedures and methods used to put HR strategic plans and policies into effect.

European model

Brewster (1993, 2004) described a European model of HRM as follows:

- Environment – established legal framework.
- Objectives – organizational objectives and social concern: people as a key resource.
- Focus – cost/benefits and environment analysis.
- Relationship with employees – union and non-union.
- Relationship with line managers – specialist/line liaison.
- Role of HR specialist – specialist managers: ambiguity, tolerance, flexibility.

The main distinction between this model and what Brewster referred to as 'the prescribed model' was that the latter involves deregulation (no legal framework), no trade unions and a focus on organizational objectives but not on social concern.

The hard and soft HRM models

Storey (1989: 8) distinguished between the 'hard' and 'soft' versions of HRM. He wrote that:

> The hard one emphasizes the quantitative, calculative and business-strategic aspects of managing human resources in as 'rational' a way as for any other economic factor. By contrast, the soft version traces its roots to the human-relations school; it emphasizes communication, motivation and leadership.

However, it was pointed out by Keenoy (1997: 838) that 'hard and soft HRM are complementary rather than mutually exclusive practices'. Research in eight UK organizations by Truss *et al* (1997) indicated that the distinction between hard and soft HRM was not as precise as some commentators have implied.

Strategic HRM

The matching and Harvard models of HRM both emphasized its strategic nature. This important aspect of HRM is known as strategic HRM (SHRM). It is concerned with how integration or 'fit' between HR and business strategies is achieved, the benefits of taking a longer-term view of where HR should be going and how to get there, and how coherent and mutually supporting HR strategies should be developed and implemented. Importantly, it is also about how members of the HR function should adopt a strategic approach on a day-to-day basis. This means that they operate as part of the management team, ensure that HR activities support the achievement of business strategies on a continuous basis, and add value.

The rationale for SHRM is the advantage of having an agreed and understood basis for developing and implementing approaches to people management that takes into account the firm's business plans and priorities and the changing context in which it operates. As Dyer and Holder (1988: 13) remarked, SHRM should provide 'unifying frameworks which are at once broad, contingency based and integrative'.

The HR architecture

HRM is delivered through the HR architecture of the HR system, the HR function and, importantly, line management. As explained by Becker *et al*

(2001: 12): 'We use the term HR architecture to broadly describe the continuum from the HR professionals within the HR function, to the system of HR related policies and practices, through the competencies, motivation and associated behaviours of the firm's employees.' It was noted by Hird *et al* (2010: 25) that: 'this architecture is seen as a unique combination of the HR function's structure and delivery model, the HR practices and system, and the strategic employee behaviours that these create'.

The HR system

The HR system consists of the interrelated and jointly supportive HR practices, which together enable HRM goals to be achieved. Boselie *et al* (2005: 73) pointed out that in its traditional form HRM can be viewed as 'a collection of multiple discrete practices with no explicit or discernible link between them. The more strategically minded system approach views HRM as an integrated and coherent bundle of mutually reinforcing practices'.

As illustrated in Figure 4.1, the HRM system brings together *HR philosophies* that describe the overarching values and guiding principles adopted in managing people and, taking account of the internal and external contexts in which the organization operates, develops *HR strategies* that define the direction in which HRM intends to go; *HR policies* that provide guidelines defining how these values, principles and strategies should be applied and implemented in specific areas of HRM; *HR processes* that comprise the formal procedures and methods used to put HR strategic plans and policies into effect; linked *HR practices* that consist of the approaches used in managing people; and *HR programmes* that enable HR strategies, policies and practices to be implemented according to plan.

The role and organization of the HR function

Members of the HR function provide insight, leadership, advice and services on matters affecting the management, employment, learning and development, reward and wellbeing of people, and the relationships between management and employees. Importantly, they contribute to the achievement of organizational effectiveness and success. The basic role of the HR function is to deliver HRM services; but it does or should do much more than that.

Increasingly, the role of HR is seen to be business-oriented – contributing to the achievement of sustained competitive advantage. Becker and Huselid (1998: 97) argued that HR should be 'a resource that solves real business

Figure 4.1 The HRM system

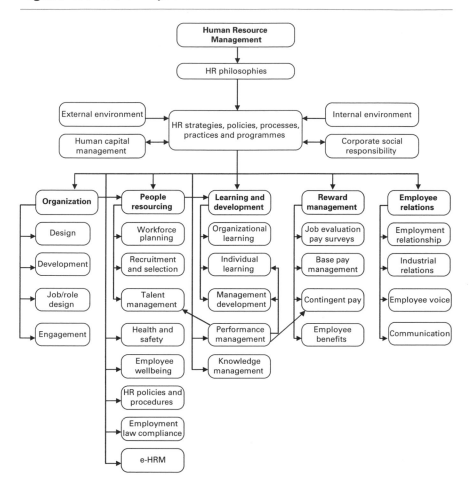

problems'. One of the issues explored by Francis and Keegan (2006) in their research was the tendency for a focus on business performance outcomes to obscure the importance of employee wellbeing in its own right. They quoted the view of Ulrich and Brockbank (2005: 201) that 'caring, listening to, and responding to employees remains a centrepiece of HR work'. The value of the HR function can be measured by the effectiveness with which it delivers HR services and the quality of advice and support it provides to management. But its value should also be assessed in terms of its contribution to the success of the business.

HR activities can be divided into two broad categories: 1) transformational (strategic) activities that are concerned with developing organizational effectiveness and the alignment and implementation of HR and business strategies; and 2) transactional activities, which cover the main areas of HR service delivery – resourcing, learning and development, reward and employee relations.

The ways in which HR operates vary immensely. As Sisson (1990) commented, HR management is not a single homogeneous occupation – it involves a variety of roles and activities that differ from one organization to another and from one level to another in the same organization. Tyson (1987) claimed that the HR function is often 'balkanized' – not only is there a variety of roles and activities but these tend to be relatively self-centred, with little passage between them. Hope-Hailey *et al* (1997: 17) believed that HR could be regarded as a 'chameleon function' in the sense that the diversity of practice established by their research suggests that 'contextual variables dictate different roles for the function and different practices of people management'.

The notion of delivering HRM through three major areas (sometimes called 'the three stool model') emerged from the HR model produced by Ulrich (1997, 1998), although Ulrich has stated that is not actually his idea at all but an interpretation of his writing. The areas are:

1 *Strategic business partners* – these work with line managers to help them reach their goals through strategy formulation and execution. They are often 'embedded' in business units or departments.

2 *Centres of expertise* – these specialize in the provision of high-level advice and services on key HR activities such as talent management, leadership development and reward.

3 *HR shared service centres* – these handle all the routine 'transactional' services across the business, which include such activities as recruitment, training, absence monitoring and advice on dealing with employee issues like discipline and absenteeism.

There are difficulties with the model. Gratton (2003: 18) commented that: 'this fragmentation of the HR function is causing all sorts of unintended problems. Senior managers look at the fragments and are not clear how the function as a whole adds value'. As Reilly (2007) observed, there are problems in introducing the new model. These included difficulties in defining roles and accountabilities, especially those of business partners, who, according to an HR director interviewed by Reilly, risk being 'hung, drawn and quartered by all sides'. At the same time, the segmented nature of the structure gives rise to 'boundary management' difficulties, for example when it comes to separating out transactional tasks from the work of centres of expertise. The model can also hamper communication between those engaged in different HR activities. Other impediments are technological failure, inadequate resources in HR and skills gaps.

The partnership role of HR

HR has to adopt a partnership approach with line managers and this applies to all HR professionals as well as those who are called 'business partners'. Partnership means working with line managers to deal jointly with issues, people problems and, importantly, implementing HR strategies containing new HR policies and practices. Traditionally, some HR specialists have tended to lay down the law to their line manager clients: 'This is the policy, this is what you have to do about it, this is how I am going to help you.' In a partnership mode, they will still explain what the policy is and what the responsibilities of the manager are in implementing it, and they will still provide guidance and advice. But in adopting a partnership approach, the HR professional will focus on understanding the particular preoccupations and concerns of individual managers and working alongside them to produce a joint agreement on how to proceed based on that understanding. It will be a matter of agreeing rather than prescribing.

When acting as partners HR specialists need to demonstrate to line managers that they understand the situation in which the latter operate and the pressures they face. HR people need to be appreciated as colleagues who understand the business and will listen to managers when they make suggestions or express doubts about a new policy. They will discuss possible approaches and even agree modifications to fit particular circumstances as long as these do not fundamentally affect the policy. They will work alongside line managers when a new policy is being introduced, not as a prescriptive trainer but as, in effect, a coach.

The following practical advice on carrying out the role was given by two strategic business partners in a London-based US investment bank interviewed by Pritchard (2010: 182, 184):

- I think the way you change their [the business clients'] behaviours in the longer term is by getting to be a trusted advisor, and the way to become a trusted advisor is to know your individual, to know your client and to know how to hook the individual.

- if you don't know the little things, they'll [the business leaders] never trust you with the bigger things... you survive by doing the little things and doing them right; and then building up that trust and that relationship with them.

CASE STUDY: HR organization at the National Australia Bank Group

HR at the National Australia Bank Group has a number of centres of expertise, business partners, solutions consultants, project managers, a shared services centre, and telephone advisory service for employees (the people advisory helpline).

Centres of expertise

Centres of expertise cover areas such as reward, employment policy, talent management, culture management, diversity and performance. The staff in the centres are specialists in their respective fields, while the other parts of HR can be found in the HR service centre, with the exception of recruitment, which is conducted by line managers.

Business partners

Business partners attend business unit leadership team meetings and set the company's people strategies and deliver the HR requirements emerging from various projects. They tend to work in the areas of talent, performance, leadership, diversity and culture and their job is to facilitate the implementation of corporate people initiatives with the relevant specialist HR partners. Unlike shared services staff, they only get involved in HR's daily operational matters if projects escalate and extra help is required.

Solutions consultants

Solutions consultants deal with operational queries referred to them from the people advisory helpline – mainly issues of case management and other more complex enquiries. They are a key point of contact for people leaders on matters of policy and procedure although they do participate in some transaction work as well.

Project staff

Project staff work on projects which emerge from strategic discussions.

(**SOURCE** IRS, 2010, *Employment Trends*, June, pp 15–16)

The HR role of line managers

HR can initiate new policies and practices but it is line managers who have the main responsibility for implementing them. In other words, HR proposes but the line disposes. Guest (1991: 159) observed that: 'HRM is too important to be left to personnel managers.'

If line managers are not inclined favourably towards what HR wants them to do they won't do it or, if compelled to against their will, they will be half-hearted about it. Following their research, Guest and King (2004: 421) commented that 'better HR depended not so much on better procedures but better implementation and ownership of implementation by line managers'.

As noted by Purcell *et al* (2003), high levels of organizational performance are not achieved simply by having a range of well-conceived HR policies and practices in place. What makes the difference is how these policies and practices are implemented. That is where the role of line managers in people management is crucial:

> Managers... play a vital role in making involvement happen, in communicating, in being open to allow employee concerns to be raised and discussed, in allowing people space to influence how they do their job, and in coaching, guiding and recognizing performance and providing help for the future.
> (*ibid*: 40)

Purcell and his colleagues emphasized that dealing with people is perhaps the aspect of their work in which line managers can exercise the greatest amount of discretion – and they can use that discretion by not putting HR's ideas into practice. As they pointed out, it is line managers who bring HR policies to life.

A further factor affecting the role of line managers is their ability to do the HR tasks assigned to them. People-centred activities such as defining roles (job design), interviewing, reviewing performance, providing feedback, coaching, identifying learning and development needs and deciding how their staff should be rewarded all require special skills. Some managers have them, many don't. Performance management systems and performance-related pay schemes can easily fail because of untrained line managers. The implementation of policies to enhance engagement levels depends largely on line managers.

The context of HRM

The design and operation of an HR system takes place within the context of the internal and external environments of the organization. These exert considerable influence on the HR architecture.

The external environment

The external environment consists of social, political, legal and economic developments and competitive pressures. Global competition in mature production and service sectors is increasing. This is assisted by easily transferable technology and reductions in international trade barriers. Customers are demanding more as new standards are reached through international competition. Organizations are reacting to this competition by becoming 'customer focused', speeding up response times, emphasizing quality and continuous improvement, accelerating the introduction of new technology, operating more flexibly and 'losing cost'. The pressure has been for businesses to become 'lean and mean', downsizing and cutting out layers of management and supervision. They reduce permanent staff to a core of essential workers, increase the use of peripheral workers (sub-contractors, temporary staff) and zero-hours contracts, and they 'outsource' work to external service providers. These pressures can be considerable in an economic downturn.

The internal environment

The following aspects of the internal environment will affect HR policy and practice:

- the type of business or organization – private, public or voluntary sector; manufacturing or service;
- the size of the organization – HR in small and medium sized enterprises (SMEs) will differ from that in larger and more complex businesses;
- the extent to which the organization operates internationally;
- the age or maturity of the organization;
- the technology or key activities of the business, which will determine how work is organized, managed and carried out;
- the type of people employed, eg professional staff, knowledge workers, technicians, administrators, production workers, sales and customer service staff;
- the financial circumstances of the organization, especially in economic downturns;
- the organization's culture – the established pattern of values, norms, beliefs, attitudes and assumptions that shape the ways in which people behave and things get done;
- the political and social climate within the organization.

CASE STUDY: Improving HR services at the Royal Bolton Hospital

The Royal Bolton Hospital became a foundation trust in October 2008, and serves around 263,000 people in the Bolton area. In 2011 it employed around 3,600 staff.

The newly appointed Head of HR found that the function was traditional and hierarchical and had a poor customer perspective. A significant cultural shift was needed to move to a 'can do' attitude and realize the potential within the function so that it added value to the business and to patients. HR services were therefore restructured, adopting a business partner model linked to the divisions within the trust.

Then the Strategic Health Authority (NHS North West) worked with the Institute for Employment Studies to develop a model of world-class HR and organizational development for health trusts in the region. World-class HR was defined in terms of six criteria: aligning and integrating with the business; proactively leading the people agenda; achieving the desired results for the business; having a compelling employee proposition; getting the basics right; and supporting people management.

An exercise was conducted with the executive board and staff to identify what HR should continue doing, what to improve, what to develop and what to stop doing. A peer review by another health trust and an HR customer survey identified the following issues: time to recruit, inconsistency in HR advice, and insufficient communication.

It was clear that the credibility of HR was based on getting the basics right, so that became a priority. The HR team was then set the challenge of changing customer perceptions. The realigned team structure was further embedded to provide more support for managers. The Employee Services Centre team streamlined its processes and particularly increased communication within the recruitment process.

The customer survey was repeated two years later and showed significant improvements in HR customer perceptions on the six world-class factors. Sixty per cent of management and clinician respondents rated their HR function as 'better' or 'much better' than before. People indicators across the trust, including attendance statistics, also showed improvement during the same period.

HRM today

As a description of people management activities in organizations, the term 'HRM' is here to stay even if it is applied diversely or only used as a label to describe traditional personnel management practices. Emphasis is now placed on the need for HR to be strategic and business-like and to add value, ie to generate extra value (benefit to the business) by the expenditure of effort, time and money on HRM activities. There have been plenty of new interests and developments including human capital management, engagement, talent management, competency-based HRM, e-HRM, high performance work systems, and performance and reward management, but these have not been introduced under the banner of the HRM concept as originally defined.

HRM has largely become something that organizations *do* rather than an aspiration or a philosophy and the term is generally in use as a way of describing the process of managing people. A convincing summary of what HRM means today, which focuses on what HRM *is* rather than on its philosophy, was provided by Peter Boxall, John Purcell and Patrick Wright.

The meaning of HRM – Boxall *et al* (2007: 1)

Human resource management (HRM), the management of work and people towards desired ends, is a fundamental activity in any organization in which human beings are employed. It is not something whose existence needs to be radically justified: HRM is an inevitable consequence of starting and growing an organization. While there are a myriad of variations in the ideologies, styles, and managerial resources engaged, HRM happens in some form or other. It is one thing to question the *relative* performance of particular models of HRM, it is quite another thing to question the necessity of the HRM process itself, as if organizations cannot survive or grow without making a reasonable attempt at organizing work and managing people.

KEY LEARNING POINTS

Human resource management (HRM) is concerned with all aspects of how people are employed, managed and developed in organizations. HRM is delivered through the HR architecture of systems and structures, the HR function and, importantly, line management.

Human resource management can be defined as a strategic, integrated and coherent approach to the employment, development and wellbeing of the people working in organizations.

The goals of HRM are to support the organization in achieving its objectives; contribute to the development of a high performance culture; ensure that the organization has the talented, skilled, and engaged people it needs; create a positive employment relationship between management and employees and a climate of mutual trust; and to encourage the application of an ethical approach to people management.

The main message of HRM philosophy is that human resource policies should be integrated with strategic business planning and used to reinforce an appropriate (or change an inappropriate) organizational culture.

Resource-based theory has had the greatest influence on the concept of HRM. The matching model and the Harvard framework have been the most influential models of HRM.

Strategic HRM is concerned with how integration or 'fit' between HR and business strategies is achieved, the benefits of taking a longer-term view of where HR should be going and how to get there, and how coherent and mutually supporting HR strategies should be developed and implemented.

HRM is delivered through the HR architecture of the HR system, the HR function and, importantly, line management.

The design and operation of an HR system takes place within the context of the internal and external environments of the organization. These exert considerable influence on the HR architecture.

References

Becker, B E and Huselid, M A (1998) High performance work systems and firm performance: a synthesis of research and managerial implications, *Research on Personnel and Human Resource Management*, **16**, Stamford, CT, JAI Press, pp 53–101

Becker, B E, Huselid, M A and Ulrich, D (2001) *The HR Scorecard: Linking people, strategy, and performance*, Boston, MA, Harvard Business School Press

Beer, M, Spector, B, Lawrence, P, Quinn Mills, D and Walton, R (1984) *Managing Human Assets*, New York, The Free Press

Boselie, P, Dietz, G and Boon, C (2005) Commonalities and contradictions in HRM and performance research, *Human Resource Management Journal*, **15** (3), pp 67–94

Boxall, P F (2013) Mutuality in the management of human resources: assessing the quality of alignment in employment relationships, *Human Resource Management Journal*, **23** (1), pp 8–17

Boxall, P F and Purcell, J (2003) *Strategy and Human Resource Management*, Basingstoke, Palgrave Macmillan

Boxall, P F, Purcell, J and Wright, P (2007) Human resource management: scope, analysis and significance, in (eds) P Boxall, J Purcell and P Wright, *Oxford Handbook of Human Resource Management*, Oxford, Oxford University Press, pp 1–16

Brewster, C (1993) Developing a 'European' model of human resource management, *The International Journal of Human Resource Management*, **4** (4), pp 765–84

Brewster, C (2004) European perspectives of human resource management, *Human Resource Management Review*, **14** (4), pp 365–82

Dyer, L and Holder, G W (1988) Strategic human resource management and planning, in (ed) L Dyer, *Human Resource Management: Evolving roles and responsibilities*, Washington, DC, Bureau of National Affairs

Fombrun, C J, Tichy, N M and Devanna, M A (1984) *Strategic Human Resource Management*, New York, Wiley

Francis, H and Keegan, A (2006) The changing face of HRM: in search of balance, *Human Resource Management Journal*, **16** (3), pp 231–49

Gratton, L A (2003) The humpty dumpty effect: a view of a fragmented HR function, *People Management*, 5 January, p 18

Guest, D E (1991) Personnel management: the end of orthodoxy, *British Journal of Industrial Relations*, **29** (2), pp 149–76

Guest, D E (1987) Human resource management and industrial relations, *Journal of Management Studies*, **24** (5), pp 503–21

Guest, D E and King, Z (2004) Power, innovation and problem-solving: the personnel managers' three steps to heaven? *Journal of Management Studies*, **41** (3), pp 401–23

Hendry, C and Pettigrew, A (1990) Human resource management: an agenda for the 1990s, *International Journal of Human Resource Management*, **1** (1), pp 17–44

Hird, M, Sparrow, P and Marsh, C (2010) HR structures: are they working? in (eds) P Sparrow, A Hesketh, M Hird and C Cooper, *Leading HR*, Basingstoke, Palgrave Macmillan, pp 23–45

Hope-Hailey, V, Gratton, L, McGovern, P, Stiles, P and Truss, C (1997) A chameleon function? HRM in the '90s, *Human Resource Management Journal*, **7** (3), pp 5–18

Keenoy, T (1997) HRMism and the images of re-presentation, *Journal of Management Studies*, **34** (5), pp 825–41

Legge, K (1989) Human resource management: a critical analysis, in (ed) J Storey, *New Perspectives in Human Resource Management*, London, Routledge, pp 19–40

Martin-Alcázar, F, Romero-Fernandez, P M and Sánchez-Gardey, G (2005) Strategic human resource management: integrating the universalistic, contingent, configurational and contextual perspectives, *Journal of International Human Resource Management*, **16** (5), pp 633–59

Osterby, B and Coster, C (1992) Human resource development – a sticky label, *Training and Development*, April, pp 31–32

Pritchard, K (2010) Becoming an HR strategic partner: tales of transition, *Human Resource Management Journal*, **20** (2), pp 175–88

Purcell, J, Kinnie, K, Hutchinson, S, Rayton, B and Swart, J (2003) *Understanding the People and Performance Link: Unlocking the black box*, London, CIPD

Reilly, P (2007) Facing up to the facts, *People Management*, 20 September, pp 43–45

Schuler, R S (1992) Strategic human resource management: linking people with the strategic needs of the business, *Organizational Dynamics*, **21** (1), pp 18–32

Schuler, R S and Jackson, S E (2000) *Strategic Human Resource Management*, Oxford, Blackwell

Sisson, K (1990) Introducing the Human Resource Management Journal, *Human Resource Management Journal*, **1** (1), pp 1–11

Storey, J (1989) From personnel management to human resource management, in (ed) J Storey, *New Perspectives on Human Resource Management*, London, Routledge, pp 1–18

Storey, J (2001) Human resource management today: an assessment, in (ed) J Storey, *Human Resource Management: A critical text*, 2nd edn, London, Thompson Learning, pp 3–20

Storey, J (2007) What is human resource management? in (ed) J Storey, *Human Resource Management: A critical text*, London, Thompson Learning, pp 3–19

Truss, C, Gratton, L, Hope-Hailey, V, McGovern, P and Stiles, P (1997) Soft and hard models of human resource management: a re-appraisal, *Journal of Management Studies*, **34** (1), pp 53–73

Tyson, S (1987) The management of the personnel function, *Journal of Management Studies*, **24** (5), pp 523–32

Ulrich, D (1998) A new mandate for human resources, *Harvard Business Review*, January–February, pp 124–34

Ulrich, D (1997) *Human Resource Champions*, Boston, MA, Harvard Business School Press

Ulrich, D and Brockbank, W (2005) *The HR Value Proposition*, Cambridge, MA, Harvard University Press

Watson, T J (2010) Critical social science, pragmatism and the realities of HRM, *The International Journal of Human Resource Management*, **21** (6), pp 915–31

QUESTIONS

1   What is human resource management (HRM)?

2   What are the fundamental characteristics of HRM?

3   What is the matching model of HRM?

3   What is the Harvard framework of HRM?

7   What characteristics did Storey attribute to HRM?

6   What is the difference between 'hard' and 'soft' HRM?

7   What are the goals of HRM as defined by Dyer and Holder?

8   What are the goals of HRM as defined by Guest?

9   What is strategic integration?

10 What is strategic human resource management (SHRM)?

The practice of HRM

LEARNING OUTCOMES

On completing this chapter you should be able to define these key concepts. You should also know about:

- Work, organization and job design
- People resourcing
- Performance management
- Reward management
- Managing the employment relationship

This chapter describes the HRM practices of successful organizations except learning and development, which, as a major activity, is covered separately in Chapter 6.

Work, organization and job design

Work, organization and job design are three distinct but closely associated processes that establish what work is carried out in organizations and how it is done. HR can and should make an important contribution to each of the processes, ensuring that they take account of human factors.

Work design deals with the ways in which things are done in the work system of a business by teams and individuals. Organization design is concerned with deciding how organizations should be structured. Job design is about establishing what people in individual jobs or roles are there to do. Although these three activities are dealt with separately below they share one purpose – to ensure that the organization's work systems and structure operate effectively, make the best use of people in their jobs and roles and take account of the needs of people at work.

Work design

Work design is the creation of systems of work and a working environment that enhance organizational effectiveness and productivity, ensure that the organization becomes 'a great place in which to work' and are conducive to the health, safety and wellbeing of employees. Work involves the exertion of effort and the application of knowledge and skills to achieve a purpose. Systems of work are the combined processes, methods and techniques used to get work done. The work environment comprises the design of jobs, working conditions and the ways in which people are treated at work by their managers and co-workers as well as the work system.

Work system design deals with how the various processes required to make a product or provide a service should operate. It covers the set of related activities that combine to give a result that customers want. The structure of the system describes the relations between different operations.

A work system may be centred on activities such as manufacturing, chemical or raw material processing, information processing, supply, distribution, transport, the provision of public services or customer service. There is usually a choice between different processes within the work system. As the design of the work system affects costs, quality and productivity it is important to provide the best match between the product or service and the process used to make or deliver it.

When designing a work system it is necessary to see that it will:

- fit work requirements for efficiency and flexibility;

- ensure the smooth flow of processes or activities, or of materials from supplier to customer;

- facilitate the effective use of resources and the control of waste;

- as far as possible enable employees to gain fulfilment from their work by providing scope for variety, challenge and autonomy;

- encourage cooperative effort through teamwork;

- provide a good work environment in terms of working conditions;

- take account of the need to provide a healthy and safe system of work ('build safety into the system') bearing in mind the need to minimize stress and pay attention to ergonomic considerations in the design of equipment and workstations to eliminate or at least significantly reduce the risk of conditions such as repetitive strain injury;

- take account of environmental considerations;

- operate generally in accordance with the principles of 'smart working', as described below.

Organization design

Organization design is the process of deciding how organizations should be structured in terms of the ways in which the responsibility for carrying out the overall task is allocated to individuals and groups of people and how the relationships between them function. The aim is to ensure that people work effectively together to achieve the overall purpose of the organization. The basic question of 'Who does what?' is answered by line managers but HR specialists are also involved in their capacity of helping the business to make the best use of its people. HR professionals can contribute to organization design or redesign activities by using their understanding of the factors affecting organizational behaviour and their knowledge of the business as a whole.

It is generally assumed that organization design is a logical and systematic affair, based on accepted principles and using analytical techniques that produce an inevitable 'best' result, but there is always organizational choice. There are certain guidelines to which consideration needs to be given, and organization reviews should be based on analysis. However, ultimately, the ways in which an organization functions and therefore its structure (or sometimes its lack of structure) are contingent on the context in terms of the business model, the people who work there and the systems and techniques the organization uses to achieve its purpose.

Research conducted by Whittington and Molloy (2005) indicated that to achieve success in organization design it is necessary to:

- obtain top management support, especially personal commitment and political support;
- avoid piecemeal, uncoordinated change initiatives by making a strategic business case that anticipates implications across the entire organization;
- achieve substantive, rather than tokenistic, employee involvement in the change process, moving beyond communication to active engagement;
- invest in communications with external stakeholders, including customers, suppliers and financial stakeholders;
- involve HR professionals closely, right from the start – involving HR has been proved to positively impact on a range of performance outcomes;
- maintain effective project management disciplines;
- build skilled change management teams – with the right mix of experience and abilities – that can work together.

Job design

Job design specifies the contents of jobs in order to satisfy work requirements and meet the personal needs of the job holder, thus increasing levels of employee engagement.

A distinction can be made between jobs and roles. A job is an organizational unit consisting of a group of defined tasks or activities to be carried out or duties to be performed. A role is the part played by individuals and the patterns of behaviour expected of them in fulfilling their work requirements. Jobs are about tasks, roles are about people. This distinction means that while jobs may be designed to fit work requirements, roles are developed as people work flexibly, demonstrate that they can do more and take on different responsibilities. Role development happens informally, in contrast to the more formal approaches to job design (considered below).

Factors affecting job design

Deciding on the content of a job starts from work requirements, because that is why the job exists. When the tasks to be done have been determined it is then necessary to consider how the jobs can be set up to provide the maximum degree of intrinsic motivation for those who have to carry them out with a view to improving performance and productivity. Consideration also has to be given to another important aim of job design: to fulfil the social responsibilities of the organization to the people who work in it by improving the quality of working life, an aim that depends upon both efficiency of performance and satisfaction of the worker.

Clearly, the content of a job depends on the work system in which it exists and the organization structure in which it is placed. Job design therefore happens within the context of work and organization design.

The most influential model for job design is the job characteristics model developed by Hackman and Oldham (1974). They identified five core job characteristics:

1 *Skill variety*: the degree to which a job requires an employee to perform activities that challenge his or her skills and abilities.

2 *Task identity*: the degree to which the job requires completion of an identifiable piece of work.

3 *Task significance*: the degree to which the job outcome has a substantial impact on others.

4 *Autonomy*: the degree to which the job gives an employee freedom and discretion in scheduling work and determining how it is performed.

5 *Feedback*: the degree to which an employee gets information about the effectiveness of his or her efforts – with particular emphasis on feedback directly related to the work itself rather than from a third party (for example, a manager).

Hackman and Oldham explained that if the design of a job satisfied the core job characteristics the employee would perceive that the work was worthwhile, would feel responsible for the work and would know if the work had been completed satisfactorily. The outcome of this would be high-quality work performance and high job satisfaction as a result of intrinsic motivation.

People resourcing

People resourcing, often called 'employee resourcing' or simply 'resourcing', is the term used to describe the employment activities of workforce planning and recruitment and selection that ensure the organization has the people it needs. It is also concerned with employee retention and absenteeism, flexible working and the management of diversity and inclusion (the last two activities are dealt with separately in Chapters 13 and 14). Resourcing is a vital organizational activity that recognizes that the strategic capability of a firm depends on its resource capability in the shape of people (the resource-based view).

Employee resourcing is not just about recruitment and selection. It is concerned with any means available to meet the firm's need for certain skills and behaviours. A strategy to ensure the organization has the talented people it needs (a talent management strategy) may start with recruitment and selection but would extend into learning and development to enhance abilities and skills and modify behaviours, and succession planning. Performance management processes can be used to identify development needs (skills and behaviours) and motivate people to make the most effective use of their abilities. Competency frameworks and profiles can be prepared to define the skills and behaviours required and can be used in selection, employee development and employee reward processes. The aim should be to develop a reinforcing bundle of strategies along these lines.

Workforce planning

The purpose of workforce planning is to establish an organization's people requirements so that plans can be made to satisfy them. It involves the following activities:

- *Scenario planning* – the assessment of changes in the business and its environment that are likely to affect the organization so that a prediction can be made of the possible situations that may have to be dealt with in the future.

- *Data collection* – workforce data on demographics, turnover, absence and availability of skills, and external data on the labour market demographics and skills availability that would include a PESTLE analysis covering political, economic, social, technological, legal and environmental factors.

- *Demand forecasting* – estimating the future numbers of people required and the likely skills they will need.

- *Supply forecasting* – measuring the number of people likely to be available from within and outside the organization. The internal supply analysis covers the forecast of future requirements – analysing the demand and supply forecasts to identify any deficits or surpluses, and action planning – preparing plans to meet future requirements through recruitment and retention, succession and talent management, the reduction of employee turnover and absenteeism, flexible working and outsourcing.

CASE STUDY: Workforce planning at Siemens (UK)

Workforce planning at Siemens (UK), the engineering and technology services company, involves obtaining answers to three fundamental questions: What do we have? What do we want? How do we fill the gap?

At the highest level, the corporate people strategy gives the context for workforce planning, the key objective of which is to ensure that Siemens has the right level of capability to execute its business strategy. In essence, the process of workforce planning is one in which the business strategy converges with the people strategy.

The workforce planning process starts with a review of the current workforce derived from SAP data (SAP is a business software system) and onto this is overlaid the likely attrition. Future requirements are identified by means of a dialogue between HR business partners and business unit managers. This enables the skills in each job family to be matched to business initiatives and provides the basis for the workforce forecast.

Recruitment and selection

Recruitment is the process of finding and engaging the people the organization needs. Selection is that part of the recruitment process concerned with deciding which applicants or candidates should be appointed to jobs. The stages of recruitment and selection are:

1 Defining requirements.

2 Attracting candidates.

3 Interviewing.

4 Selection testing.

5 Making the decision.

1. Defining requirements

The number and categories of people required may be set out in formal workforce plans from which are derived detailed recruitment plans. More typically, requirements are defined as ad hoc demands for people because of the creation of new posts, expansion into new activities or areas, or the need for a replacement. These short-term demands may put HR under pressure to deliver candidates quickly.

Requirements should be expressed in the form of role profiles and person specifications indicating what the role holder has to be able to do and the knowledge, skills and experience required. These provide the information needed to post vacancies on the company's website, the internet or a social network site such as LinkedIn, draft advertisements, brief agencies or recruitment consultants and assess candidates by means of interviews and selection tests.

2. Attracting candidates

The sources of candidates are online recruiting, social media, advertising, recruitment agencies, job centres, consultants, recruitment process outsourcing providers and direct approaches to educational establishments. There is usually a choice between different methods or combinations of them. The criteria to use when making the choice are: 1) the likelihood that it will produce good candidates; 2) the speed with which the choice enables recruitment to be completed; and 3) the costs involved, bearing in mind that there may be direct advertising costs or consultants' fees.

Online or e-recruitment is becoming increasingly popular. It uses the internet to advertise or 'post' vacancies, provides information about jobs and the organization and enables e-mail communications to take place between employers and candidates. The main types of online recruitment sites are corporate websites, commercial job boards and agency sites.

Social media are also used extensively. This means applying Web 2.0 technologies to search for recruits and find out more about them online. Social media are defined as any online platform for networking or sharing information or opinions, for example Facebook, LinkedIn, Twitter, or blogs, but not e-mail.

CASE STUDY: Use of social media for recruiting at CERN

At CERN, the world's largest particle physics laboratory, extensive use has been made of social media for recruiting purposes. All job vacancies are advertised on LinkedIn, Facebook and Twitter. These networks provide much more than simple job boards in that they are used as communication tools to interact with the audience, with candidates and with people who are not necessarily candidates but may know people who may want to apply. Appropriate use is made of each medium. For example, Facebook is used to host a weekly question and answer session between one of CERN's recruiters and anyone who wants to submit a question, whereas the professional network LinkedIn provides a forum for more specialized discussions.

3. Interviewing

The interview is the most familiar method of selection. The aim is to elicit information about candidates that will enable a prediction to be made about how well they will do the job and thus lead to a selection decision.

An interview involves face-to-face discussion. When it is an individual rather than a panel interview, it provides the best opportunity for the establishment of close contact – rapport – between the interviewer and the candidate, thus easing the acquisition of information about the candidate's suitability and how well he or she would fit into the organization.

The advantages of interviews are that they:

- provide opportunities for interviewers to ask probing questions about the candidate's experience and to explore the extent to which the candidate's competencies match those specified for the job;

- enable interviewers to describe the job (a 'realistic job preview') and the organization in more detail, providing some indication of the terms of the psychological contract;

- provide opportunities for candidates to ask questions about the job and to clarify issues concerning training, career prospects, the organization and terms and conditions of employment;

- enable a face-to-face encounter to take place so that the interviewer can make an assessment of how the candidate would fit into the organization and what he or she would be like to work with;

- give the candidate the same opportunity to assess the organization, the interviewer and the job.

The disadvantages of interviews are that they:

- can lack validity as a means of making sound predictions of performance, and lack reliability in the sense of measuring the same things for different candidates;
- rely on the skill of the interviewer – many people are poor at interviewing, although most think that they are good at it;
- do not necessarily assess competence in meeting the demands of the particular job;
- can lead to biased and subjective judgements by interviewers.

These disadvantages can be alleviated by using a structured approach. A structured interview is one based on a defined framework consisting of a set of predetermined questions that are derived from the person specification. All candidates are asked the same questions that will focus on the attributes and behaviours (competencies) required to succeed in the job. The answers may be scored through a rating system.

4. Selection testing

Selection tests are used to provide valid and reliable evidence of levels of abilities, intelligence, personality characteristics, aptitudes and attainments. Psychological tests are measuring instruments, which is why they are often referred to as psychometric tests ('psychometric' means mental measurement). Psychometric tests assess intelligence or personality. They use systematic and standardized procedures to measure differences in individual characteristics, thus enabling selectors to gain a greater understanding of candidates to help in predicting the extent to which they will be successful in a job. Research by Schmidt and Hunter (1998) showed that the best results were obtained by a combination of intelligence tests with structured interviews. The other types of tests described below are ability and aptitude tests.

A recent development in firms such as Deloitte is to use a recruitment app in the form of a mobile phone game to test mental agility, persistence and 'risk appetite'.

5. Making the decision

When making a selection decision the first step is to identify the candidates who have the abilities and personality that most closely match the specification for the job (person-job fit). Account may also be taken of the extent to which the candidates' personality and values will fit into the organization (person-organization fit).

The next step is to make a choice if there is more than one possible candidate. This choice should be evidence-based but judgement may still be required, which can be difficult. The decision may have to be a balanced one – the match may not be perfect but it may be felt that it will do. However, for the sake of the organization and the individual concerned, what has to be avoided at all cost is the selection in desperation of someone who is not properly qualified to do the job.

CASE STUDY: Recruitment assessment processes at Embarq

Embarq is the largest independent local telecoms provider in the United States. It suffered catastrophic rates of staff turnover in its call centres; then a new assessment process designed by PreVisor reduced turnover from 33.5 per cent in the first 90 days to 12.5 per cent.

The new process begins with an online screening tool that identifies characteristics and motivations that define long-term success in the roles, such as 'customer focus' and 'persistence'. There follows a behaviour-based structured interview and a sales-based role-play exercise. This exercise takes place over the phone, which tests candidates in the most realistic way possible and is more convenient and cost-effective.

Sales have since increased by 24 per cent, and customer service has also improved.

Talent management

Talent management is about ensuring that the organization has the talented people it needs to attain its goals. Talent is what people must have to perform well in their roles. They make a difference to organizational performance through their immediate efforts, they have the ability to learn and grow, and they have the potential to make an important contribution in the future. Talent management is based on the proposition that 'those with the best people win'. It emerged in the late 1990s when McKinsey and Company coined the phrase 'the war for talent'. It involves the systematic attraction, retention, identification and development of individuals who are of particular value to an organization.

As suggested by Younger *et al* (2007), approaches to talent management include emphasizing 'growth from within', regarding talent development as a key element of the business strategy, being clear about the competencies and qualities that matter, maintaining well-defined career paths, taking management development, coaching and mentoring seriously and demanding high performance.

There are many versions of talent management but in one way or another it can cover such traditional HRM activities as workforce planning, recruitment, managing employee retention, performance management, potential assessment, leadership and management development, succession planning and career planning. The difference is that talent management is a wider-reaching, holistic approach that 'joins up' these HR practices. A model of talent management produced by CEMEX Ltd is shown in Figure 5.1.

Figure 5.1 The CEMEX model of talent management

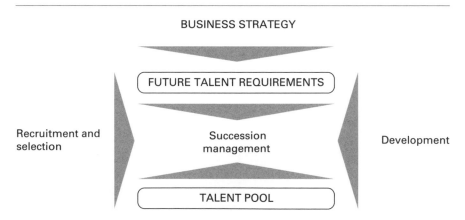

The process of talent management

The purpose of talent management is to establish a 'talent pool' (or pools) from which talented people can be obtained as required to fill key roles. This is achieved by operating a 'talent pipeline' that provides for the flow of talent needed to maintain the talent pool through the processes of resourcing, talent identification and talent development. These activities are initiated by the business strategy that informs workforce plans. Talent management policies and strategies determine the scope of the talent pool and influence workforce plans. The process is modelled in Figure 5.2.

Figure 5.2 The process of talent management

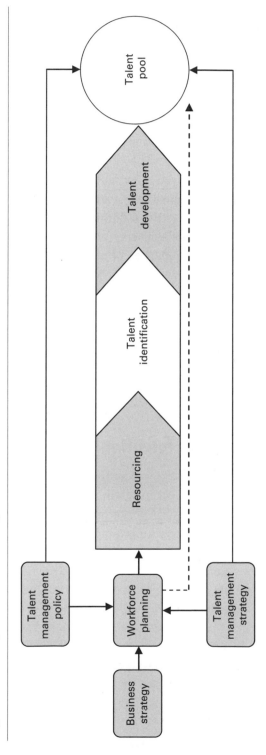

CASE STUDY: Talent management at BAE Systems

At BAE Systems there are five mandated core business management processes to support the delivery of corporate strategy and foster high performance. Talent management is seen within a business performance context. An annual Integrated Business Review Planning process is used by individual businesses to establish and plan for the delivery of objectives in line with corporate strategy, supported by quarterly business reviews, customer reviews and data from employee surveys. Project performance is assessed by Contract Reviews. Performance is reviewed throughout the year by the Performance Management System. A Performance Centred leadership framework is used to integrate management, resourcing and people development, focusing on the traditional outcomes of performance (financial, project and behavioural), reward and development. There is behavioural performance feedback and a performance potential rating (called Spectrum). Line leaders and functional directors ensure the framework is implemented. HR's role is one of assisting in development interventions and providing some oversight and governance of the processes.

(**SOURCE** Sparrow *et al*, 2015, reproduced with permission)

Managing employee retention

Losing key employees can have a disproportionate impact on the business. The people organizations wish to retain are often the ones most likely to leave. It has been said that every worker is 5 minutes away from handing in his or her notice, and 150 working hours away from walking out of the door to a better offer. There is no such thing as a job for life and today's workers have few qualms about leaving employers. Action is required to retain talented people, but there are limits to what any organization can do. Employees are more likely to stay willingly if they feel valued.

Employee turnover data

Actions to increase employee retention will be influenced by data on employee turnover or attrition. The employee turnover index (sometimes referred to as the employee or labour wastage index) shown below is the traditional formula for measuring turnover:

$$\frac{\text{Number of leavers in a specified period (usually 1 year)}}{\text{Average number of employees during the same period}} \times 100$$

This method is in common use because it is easy to calculate and to understand. It is a simple matter to work out that, if last year 30 out of an average force of 150 employees left (20 per cent turnover) and this trend continues, then the company will have to recruit 108 employees during the following year to increase and to hold the workforce at 200 in that year (50 extra employees, plus 40 to replace the 20 per cent wastage of the average 200 employees employed, plus 18 to replace wastage of the 90 recruits).

Retention strategies

Retention strategies should be based on an understanding of the factors that affect whether or not employees leave or stay. These include:

- company image (the employer brand);
- the employee value proposition – what the employer offers in the form of terms and conditions of employment and what has been called 'the quality of working life';
- the effectiveness of recruitment, selection and deployment (fitting people into jobs that suit them;
- leadership – 'employees join companies and leave managers';
- social factors (the extent to which individuals get on with their co-workers);
- learning and career opportunities;
- performance recognition and rewards.

Risk of leaving analysis

Risk analysis can be used to quantify the seriousness of losing key people. Risk analysis can be carried out by initially identifying potential risk areas (the key people who may leave) and, for each of them, as individuals or groups, estimate:

- the likelihood of this occurring;
- how serious the effects of a loss would be on the business;
- the ease with which a replacement could be made and the replacement costs.

Each of the estimates could be expressed on a scale, say: very high, high, medium, low, very low. An overview of the ratings under each heading could then indicate where action may need to be taken to retain key people or groups of people.

Areas for action

Depending on the outcome of the risk and reasons for leaving analyses the possible actions that can be taken are:

1 Take whatever steps are necessary to demonstrate that the organization values its employees, as long as this is expressed in deeds and not just words.

2 Ensure that selection and promotion procedures match the capacities of individuals to the demands of the work they have to do. Rapid turnover can result simply from poor selection or promotion decisions.

3 Reduce the losses of people who cannot adjust to their new job – the 'induction crisis' – by giving them proper training and support when they join the organization.

4 Design jobs to maximize skill variety, task significance, autonomy, control over work and feedback, and ensure that they provide opportunities for learning and growth. Some roles can be 'customized' to meet the needs of particular individuals.

5 Encourage the development of social ties within the company. In the words of Cappelli (2000: 108), 'Loyalty to companies may be disappearing but loyalty to colleagues is not.'

6 Deal with uncompetitive, inequitable or unfair pay systems. But as Cappelli (2000) pointed out, there is a limit to the extent to which people can be bribed to stay.

7 Take steps to improve work–life balance by developing policies, including flexible working, that recognize the needs of employees outside work.

8 Eliminate as far as possible unpleasant working conditions or the imposition of too much stress on employees.

9 Select, brief and train managers and team leaders so that they appreciate the positive contribution they can make to improving retention by the ways in which they lead their teams. Bear in mind that people often leave their managers rather than their organization.

10 Improve arrangements for giving employees a voice on matters that concern them.

11 Pay close attention to communications with employees to explain what is happening and underline improvements to their conditions of employment. Use all forms of media including social media.

12 Ensure that policies for controlling bullying and harassment are in place and are applied.

CASE STUDY: Staff retention at Paul UK

Paul UK operates a chain of 22 patisserie and bakery shops employing 400 people. Its staff turnover rate of 168 per cent was below the sector's average but still too high. The steps taken to overcome this problem were as follows:

- a robust recruitment process was introduced using branded application forms and centralized recruiting;
- role descriptions and skills specifications were created for posts;
- a competency-based approach to recruitment was introduced – the competencies are closely linked to the company's values and defined the behaviours and attitudes required;
- recruitment literature was professionally designed by an agency;
- an employer brand was built – the promotional leaflet highlights the benefits of working for the company;
- an employee referral scheme was introduced (helped by the employer brand);
- a resource centre for recruitment and training was established;
- a rolling induction training programme was introduced;
- a career progression framework was developed.

The outcome was that within two years staff turnover had dropped by 30 per cent and retention rates had doubled.

Absence management

Absence or attendance management is the development and application of policies and procedures designed to reduce levels of absenteeism. The CIPD (2015) survey of absence management revealed that the average length of employee absence was 6.9 days per employee per year.

Absence policies should cover:

- methods of measuring absence;
- setting targets for the level of absence;
- deciding on the level of short-term absence that would trigger action (the trigger period at the UK Department of Work and Pensions is eight days over 12 months);
- the circumstances in which disciplinary action might be taken;
- what employees must do if they are unable to attend work;
- sick-pay arrangements;
- provisions for the reduction and control of absence such as return-to-work interviews;
- other steps that can be taken to reduce absence, such as flexible working patterns.

CASE STUDY: Controlling sickness absence at Wincanton

Distribution company Wincanton had a problem controlling sickness absence because its large workforce is spread over 285 sites. The solution was to outsource absence management to Active Health Partners, which operates a call centre staffed by nurses – employees must report their absences and can receive medical advice. An online absence recording system is also provided, which gives line managers information on absences and access to absence statistics.

As soon as an employee calls Active Health Partners an e-mail or text is sent to the employee's line manager via an automated system, informing him or her of the absence and the reason for it and giving an approximate return-to-work date. The system also provides various triggers to line managers. For example, once an employee has been away for more than 15 days, the manager receives a message indicating that contact needs to be made. Managers are expected to conduct return-to-work interviews and have more formal discussions when an absence exceeds 15 days. They will explore why there has been this amount of time off, if there is an underlying health issue, if an employee should be referred to Occupational Health and if the disciplinary process should be started.

As a result, Wincanton reduced sickness absence by 10,000 days in six months.

Performance management

Performance management is the continuous process of improving performance by setting goals that are aligned to the strategic goals of the organization, planning performance to achieve the goals, reviewing progress, and developing the knowledge, skills and abilities of people. It is a means of getting better results by providing scope for individuals to perform well within an agreed framework of planned goals, standards and competency requirements. It involves developing a shared understanding about what is to be achieved and how. Its four elements are agreement, feedback, positive reinforcement and dialogue.

Principles of performance management

The principles governing effective performance management were defined well by Egan (1995):

> Most employees want direction, freedom to get their work done, and
> encouragement not control. The performance management system should be a
> control system only by exception. The solution is to make it a collaborative
> development system in two ways. First, the entire performance management
> process – coaching, counselling, feedback, tracking, recognition, and so forth –
> should encourage development. Ideally, team members grow and develop
> through these interactions. Second, when managers and team members ask
> what they need to be able to do to do bigger and better things, they move to
> strategic development.

The process of performance management

Performance management is a process that consists of a number of inter-related activities and processes. These are treated as an integrated and key component of an organization's approach to creating a high performance culture, managing performance through people and developing the skills and capabilities of its human capital, thus enhancing organizational capability and the achievement of sustained competitive advantage.

Performance management is a natural process of management: it is not an HRM technique or tool. As a natural process of management, performance management can be modelled as a cycle, as shown in Figure 5.3, which corresponds with Deming's (1986) plan-do-check-act model.

Figure 5.3 The performance management cycle

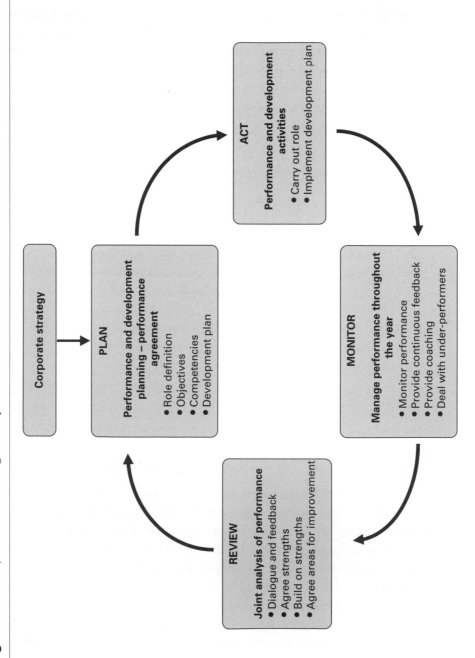

Performance planning

Performance planning is carried out within the context of the corporate strategy. It is based on performance agreements. These emerge from the analysis of role requirements and from performance reviews where assessments of performance lead to the definition of future requirements. Agreement is reached during the planning process on how performance will be measured. Changes to the role profile and objectives can be made as required by changing circumstances.

Expectations are defined generally in role profiles that specify key result areas; the knowledge, skills and abilities (KSAs) required and the behavioural competencies needed to perform well. What has to be accomplished in key result areas can be defined in the form of objectives or targets. The acronym 'SMART' is often used to define a good objective, although it has its limitations, especially that of rigidity. Traditionally, S stands for specific (sometimes 'stretching'), M for measurable, A for agreed, R for realistic and T for time-related or time-bound. An important aspect of performance planning is the process of aligning individual goals with the strategic goals of the organization.

The manager and the individual also agree on a development plan that specifies what the latter needs to do to achieve objectives and develop performance. The plan may incorporate a personal development plan that provides a learning action programme to be actioned by the individual with the support of the manager. This may include formal training but, more important, it will cover a wider set of learning and development activities such as self-managed learning, coaching, mentoring, project work and e-learning.

Managing performance throughout the year

Perhaps one of the most important features of performance management is that it is a continuous process, which reflects normal good management practices of setting direction, monitoring and measuring performance and taking action accordingly. Performance management should not be imposed on managers as something 'special' they have to do. It should instead be treated as a natural function that all good managers carry out.

The process of managing performance throughout the year needs to take into account that in these turbulent times it is probable that an annual goal-setting exercise will not be appropriate. Goals need to be reviewed as circumstances and demands change.

Performance reviews

Traditionally, formal performance reviews provided an annual (usually) focal point for the consideration of key performance and development issues. They led to the completion of the performance management process by informing performance agreements and often involved some form of assessment, as examined below.

The traditional formal appraisal review can be described as a dishonest annual ritual. Its primary purpose was often to inform performance pay decisions (or worse, in some systems, whether or not the individual should be retained). Reviews were backward-looking and judgmental rather than looking to the future to establish development needs.

Traditional formal reviews can be stressful for both parties. Managers often hate doing them and therefore do them badly, treating them as a ritual to be observed at the behest of HR and dishonestly fudging their judgements. Research by The Society for Human Resource Management (2012) found that as much as 90 per cent of employees (including managers) dislike formal reviews. Mueller-Hanson and Pulakos (2015) noted that: 'Study after study has shown that the performance review is dreaded – it is not only perceived to be of little value but it is highly demotivating to employees.'

The answer to this problem is to hold less formal conversations throughout the year as part of the normal process of management. These need not be stressful. They will provide an opportunity for feedback – people like to know how well they are doing – and can include a measure of self-assessment. They will be essentially an updating process and will be forward-looking, providing the means for participants to revise role profiles, objectives and development plans to meet changing circumstances.

Performance assessment

Performance management schemes usually but not inevitably include an assessment, which is done during or after a performance review meeting. This can be carried out by an overall assessment based on a general analysis of performance under the headings of the performance agreement. This should be provided on a 'what' and 'how' basis. The 'what' is the achievement of previously agreed objectives related to the headings on a role profile. The 'how' is behaviour described under competency framework headings. The results for each 'what' and 'how' analysis could be recorded following a discussion in a review meeting. The aim is to reach agreement about future action rather than to produce a summarized and potentially superficial judgement. Performance management is essentially about this sort of dialogue.

However, the most common form of assessment in traditional performance management schemes is rating. Rating summarizes on a scale (a, b, c, etc), the views of the rater on the level of performance achieved. A rating scale is supposed to assist in making judgements that inform performance pay decisions, or it simply produces an instant summary for the record of how well or not so well someone is doing.

The main problem with ratings is that they are largely subjective and it is difficult to achieve consistency between the ratings given by different managers. Because the notion of 'performance' is often unclear, subjectivity can increase. Even if objectivity is achieved, to sum up the total performance of a person with a single rating is a gross oversimplification of what may be a complex set of factors influencing that performance. To do this after a detailed discussion of strengths and weaknesses suggests that the rating will be a superficial and arbitrary judgement. To label people as 'average' or 'below average', or whatever equivalent terms are used, is both demeaning and demotivating. A study by Scullen and Mount (2000) in which 4,492 managers were rated on certain performance dimensions by two bosses, two peers and two subordinates, revealed that 62 per cent of the variance in the ratings could be accounted for by individual rater's peculiarities of perception. Actual performance accounted for only 21 per cent of the variance.

The biggest problem is that the whole performance review session may be dominated by the fact that it will end with a rating, thus severely limiting the forward-looking and developmental focus of the meeting, which is all important. This is particularly the case if the rating governs performance-pay increases. Another problem is that managers may inflate ratings to avoid confrontation with the individuals concerned.

Performance management issues

The many-faceted nature of performance was commented on as follows by Cascio (2010: 334): 'It is an exercise in observation and judgement, it is a feedback process, it is an organizational intervention. It is a measurement process as well as an intensely emotional process. Above all, it is an inexact, human process.'

As a human process, performance management can promise more than it achieves. Some years ago Grint (1993: 62), referring to performance appraisal, famously asserted that: 'Rarely in the history of business can such a system have promised so much and delivered so little.' More recently, Shields (2007: 6) argued that: 'Ill-chosen, badly designed or poorly implemented performance management schemes can communicate entirely the wrong messages as to what the organization expects from its employees.' Coens and Jenkins (2002: 1) delivered the following judgement:

> Throughout our work lives, most of us have struggled with performance appraisal. No matter how many times we redesign it, retrain the supervisors, or give it a new name, it never comes out right. Again and again, we see supervisors procrastinate or just go through the motions, with little taken to heart. And the supervisors who do take it to heart and give it their best mostly meet disappointment.

Performance management can be modelled convincingly as a system but the acts or failures to act of fallible human beings prejudice the effectiveness of the system in practice. Brown (2010) commented that:

> The problems [of performance management] are... not of ambition or intent, but rather practice and delivery. Low rates of coverage and even more frequently low quality conversations and non-existent follow-up are commonplace, in the wake of uncommitted directors, incompetent line managers, uncomprehending employees and hectoring HR with their still complex and bureaucratic HR processes.

On the basis of research conducted in 2011 by the Institute for Employment Studies, Brown also observed that:

> The main areas of concern [about performance management] were the skills and attitudes of reviewing managers, the consistency and quality of approach across large organizations, the complexity of the paperwork and the value of outputs... Performance management, it appears, isn't working. (2011: 16)

However well-designed a performance management system is, its effectiveness mainly depends on the commitment and skills of line managers. Postuma and Campion (2008: 47) remarked that:

One of the most dreaded tasks managers face is meeting with employees to discuss their job performance. These meetings present a dilemma for managers. On one hand, managers need to give constructive criticism so that employees can improve their performance. On the other hand, managers do not like to give negative feedback because of the bad feelings that often result. It is not surprising, then, that managers avoid giving accurate evaluations, give overly generous evaluations or avoid the process altogether.

They also noted that: 'Too much attention has been placed on the design of a [performance management] system and not enough on how it works when implemented' (*ibid*: 50).

The e-reward 2014 survey of performance management established that the top three issues concerning respondents about their performance management processes were:

1 The lack of line managers with the skills required to carry out performance management effectively.

2 Line managers who don't discriminate sufficiently when assessing performance.

3 Line managers who are reluctant to actually conduct performance management reviews.

Reinventing performance management

A number of companies have recently 'seen the light' and introduced radical changes to their performance management systems. They have belatedly come to realize that, in the words of one of them, 'traditional performance management is broken'. This applies to the reliance on the annual performance review, rating, especially forced distribution, and the direct link with performance-related pay. Commentators, including the writer, have been saying for years that these practices are dubious; the message has finally got through.

The focus is now on continuous coaching and development rather than one annual and stressful review, the abolition of ratings, and 'de-coupling' performance management from performance-related pay. Accenture has scrapped annual appraisals for its 300,000 plus workforce and instead instituted a 'continuous feedback' culture. Deloitte is joining the likes of Microsoft, Gap and Expedia in moving towards less formal, more frequent performance reviews. The latter has introduced a 'Passport to Performance' system of regular check-ins, which is more coaching-orientated. In other words, they are moving towards a 'managing performance throughout the year' approach.

CASE STUDY: Reinventing performance management at Adobe

Background

- 13,000 employees.
- Adobe estimated that managers spend 80,000 hours on PM.
- Had tried to realign and make incremental changes for five years and failed to satisfactorily align to needs for collaboration, creativity and innovation.
- 'Genuine, Exceptional, Innovative and Involved' – Adobe's founding values.
- Super-competitive industry.

The changes

- No annual review, no ratings, no prescribed format, no forms, no PM technology 'system'.
- Manager and employee 'check-ins' covering expectations, feedback, growth and development agenda.
- Frequency of check-ins – whenever sensible but at least quarterly.
- Employee support centre established.
- Extensive training support for managers – role plays, lectures and online.
- Managers manage pay outcomes and allocated budgets – entirely!
- Regular pulse survey provides insights on decisions and impact.
- Managers able to define their own processes and requirements for HR support.

Results

- Voluntary turnover down 30 per cent in two years.
- Employee engagement up.
- Fear of feedback gone.
- Frequent feedback is the new currency for employees and managers.

- Demand for training on coaching others, difficult conversations, mentoring, career development and managing reward up.
- Focus on process, chasing numbers and ratings wiped out.
- Regularity of check-ins: average of one a month per employee.
- Managers' knowledge of performance of individuals significantly greater than ever before.

Reward management

Reward management deals with the strategies, policies and processes required to ensure that the value of people and the contribution they make to achieving organizational, departmental and team goals is recognized and rewarded. It is concerned with the design, implementation and maintenance of reward systems (interrelated reward processes, practices and procedures covering how jobs and people should be valued, the design and management of grade and pay structures, rewarding and recognizing achievements and performance, providing employee benefits and managing the system). Reward systems aim to satisfy the needs of both the organization and its stakeholders and to operate fairly, equitably and consistently.

It should be emphasized that reward management is not just about pay and employee benefits. It is equally concerned with non-financial rewards such as recognition, learning and development opportunities, and increased job responsibility.

The reward system

A reward system as illustrated in Figure 5.4 consists of the interrelated processes and practices that combine to ensure that reward management is carried out effectively to the benefit of the organization and the people who work there. The system is driven by the business strategy, which in turn drives the reward strategy. As described below, its major components are financial and non-financial rewards, which are combined to form a total reward system. Performance management plays an important part in supporting non-financial rewards and may be used to inform performance or contribution pay decisions. All these components combine to influence levels of performance. The three key elements of a reward system – financial, non-financial and total rewards – are described below.

Figure 5.4 A reward system

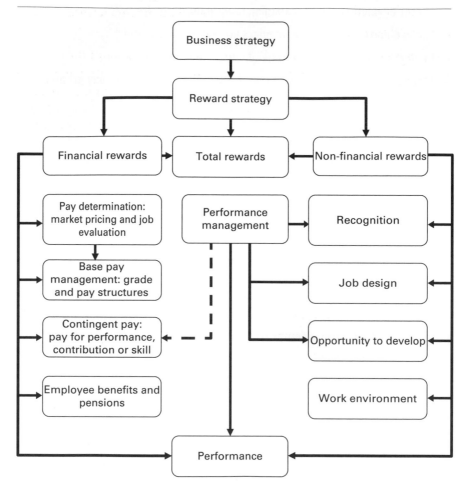

1. Financial rewards

Financial rewards consist of job-based pay, which provides pay related to the value of the job, and person-based pay, which provides rewards that recognize the individual's contribution. They also include employee benefits and pensions and financial recognition schemes. The management of job- and person-based pay involves:

- *Pay determination* – making decisions on the value of jobs by means of market pricing and job evaluation.

- *Base pay management* – developing and operating pay structures that group jobs into grades, bands or levels in accordance with internal and external relativities and usually provide for pay progression.

- *Contingent pay* – planning and managing schemes that provide for pay progression related to performance, contribution, competence, skill or length of service.

Labour economists distinguish between the incentive effect of financial rewards (generating more engagement and effort) and the sorting effect (attracting better quality employees). The fundamental issue is the extent to which financial rewards provide an incentive effect. The sorting effect is important but creates less controversy, perhaps because it is more difficult to pin down.

2. Non-financial rewards

Non-financial rewards focus on the needs people have to varying degrees for recognition, achievement, personal growth and acceptable working conditions. They include the non-financial recognition of achievements, the design of fulfilling jobs, giving people the scope to develop their skills and careers and offering a work environment that provides a high quality of working life and an appropriate relationship between work and private life (work–life balance). Non-financial rewards can be extrinsic, such as praise or recognition, or intrinsic, associated with job challenge and interest and feelings that the work is worthwhile.

3. Total rewards

Total rewards are the combination of financial and non-financial rewards made available to employees. The various aspects of reward, namely base pay, contingent pay, employee benefits and non-financial rewards, which include intrinsic rewards from the work itself, are linked together and treated as an integrated and cohesive whole.

The concept of total rewards describes an approach to reward management that emphasizes the need to consider all aspects of the work experience of value to employees, not just a few such as pay and employee benefits. A total rewards approach recognizes that it is necessary to get financial rewards (pay and benefits) right but it also appreciates the importance of providing people with rewarding experiences that arise from their work environment (the job they do and how they are managed) and the opportunity to develop their skills and careers. It contributes to the production of an employee value proposition that provides a clear, compelling reason why talented people should work for a company.

Managing the employment relationship

The employment relationship describes how employers and employees work together. A positive employment relationship is one in which management and employees are interdependent and both benefit from this interdependency, and where there is mutual trust. Such a relationship is based on the psychological contract and provides a foundation for the conduct of employee relations, as described later.

The psychological contract

The psychological contract is a set of unwritten expectations that exist between individual employees and their employers. It underpins the employment relationship. As Guest (2007: 133) explained, it is concerned with: 'The perceptions of both parties to the employment relationship, organization and individual, of the reciprocal promises and obligations implied in that relationship.'

The aspects of the employment relationship covered by the psychological contract will include, from the employees' point of view:

- how they are treated in terms of fairness, equity and consistency;
- security of employment;
- scope to demonstrate competence;
- career expectations and the opportunity to develop skills;
- involvement and influence;
- trust in the management of the organization to keep their promises.

The CIPD (2012: 16) suggested that to build trust leaders need to tell the truth and be willing to admit mistakes. They must share information openly, support transparency, and seek information from multiple sources, not merely relying on what they are told by their close advisers. Finally and importantly, they should be candid in their dealings with followers.

From the employer's point of view, the psychological contract covers such aspects of the employment relationship as competence, effort, compliance, commitment and loyalty.

Employee relations

Employee relations are concerned with managing and maintaining the employment relationship, taking into account the implications of the psychological contract. This means dealing with employees either collectively through their trade unions or individually; handling employment practices, terms and conditions of employment and issues arising from employment, providing employees with a voice and communicating with them.

Employee relations are basically about how managements and employees live together and what can be done to make that work. There are two views about the relationship. The *unitary* viewpoint is the belief that management and employees share the same concerns and it is therefore in both their interests to cooperate. This was expressed by Walton (1985: 64) as the principle of mutuality. A similar belief is expressed in the idea of social partnership, which states that as stakeholders, the parties involved in employee relations should aim to work together to the greater good of all. In contrast, the *pluralist* viewpoint is that the interests of employees will not necessarily coincide with their employers and that the unitary view is naive, unrealistic and against the interests of employees. People of this persuasion don't believe that partnership agreements can work.

There are four approaches to employee relations:

1 *Adversarial*: the organization decides what it wants to do, and employees are expected to fit in. Employees only exercise power by refusing to cooperate.

2 *Traditional*: a reasonably good day-to-day working relationship but management proposes and the workforce reacts through its elected representatives, if there are any; if not, employees just accept the situation or walk.

3 *Partnership*: the organization involves employees in the drawing up and execution of organization policies, but retains the right to manage.

4 *Power sharing*: employees are involved in both day-to-day and strategic decision making.

Adversarial approaches are less common now than in the 1960s and 1970s. The traditional approach is still the most typical but more interest is being expressed in partnership. Power sharing is rare.

Managing with unions

Managements and trade unions can learn to live together, often on a give-and-take basis, the presumption being that neither would benefit from a climate of hostility or by generating constant confrontation. It would be assumed in this situation that mutual advantage would come from acting in accordance with the spirit as well as the letter of collective agreements. However, both parties would probably adopt a realistic pluralist viewpoint. This means recognizing the inevitability of differences of opinion, even disputes, but believing that with goodwill on both sides they could be settled without resource to industrial action.

On the whole, pluralism prevails and management and unions will inevitably disagree from time to time on employment issues. The aim is to resolve these issues before they become disputes. This means adopting a more positive partnership approach. Where collective agreements are being made, a cooperative or integrative bargaining philosophy can be adopted, based on perceptions about the mutual interdependence of management and employees and the recognition by both parties that this is a means to achieve more for themselves.

Managing without unions

Some firms, especially larger ones, manage without trade unions by adopting a union substitution policy that offers employment policies and pay packages that employees will see as an attractive alternative to trade union membership. They may focus on communication and information sharing but they will basically deal with people individually rather than collectively. Others, especially smaller firms, simply deal with employees individually – sometimes well, sometimes not – and make no attempt to provide substitute arrangements.

Employee voice

The term 'employee voice' refers to the say that employees have in matters of concern to them in their organization. The purposes of employee voice are to:

- help organizations to understand what employees feel about their work;
- influence management decisions on matters affecting the workforce;
- tap into employees' ideas, knowledge and experience;
- promote a cooperative climate of employee relations.

Arrangements for employee voice enable dialogues to take place that allow employees to influence events at work. Opportunities are provided for employees to register discontent, express complaints or grievances, and modify the power of management. Employee voice can be expressed through:

- joint consultation;
- trade unions;
- employee surveys;
- social media, eg an enterprise social network (an internal social network that functions in the same way as social networks such as Facebook);
- suggestion schemes;
- quality circles.

Employee communications

Employee communication processes and systems provide for 'two-way communication'. In one direction they enable managements to inform employees on matters that concern them. In the other, they provide for upward communication by giving employees a voice.

Good communications are important for three reasons:

1 They are a vital part of any change management programme. If any change is proposed – in terms and conditions of employment, HR processes such as merit pay, working methods, technologies, products and services or organization (including mergers and acquisitions) – employees need to know what is proposed and how it will affect them. Resistance to change often arises simply because people do not know what the change is or what it implies for them.

2 Commitment to the organization will be enhanced if employees know what the organization has achieved or is trying to achieve and how this benefits them.

3 Effective communication generates trust as organizations take the trouble to explain what they are doing and why.

The main methods of communication are individual face-to-face communication, intranet, social media, team briefing, consultative committees, notice boards, speak-up programmes, magazines, newsletters and bulletins.

KEY LEARNING POINTS

Work, organization and job design

Work, organization and job design establish what work is done in organizations and how it is done.

Work design deals with the ways in which things are done in the work system of a business by teams and individuals. Organization design is concerned with deciding how organizations should be structured. Job design is about establishing what people in individual jobs or roles are there to do.

People resourcing

People resourcing, often called 'employee resourcing' or simply 'resourcing', is the term used to cover employment activities that ensure the organization has the people it needs. It is concerned with workforce planning, recruitment and selection, talent management, employment issues such as employee retention and absenteeism, flexible working, and the management of diversity and inclusion.

Performance management

Performance management is the continuous process of improving performance by setting goals that are aligned to the strategic goals of the organization, planning performance to achieve the goals, reviewing progress, and developing the knowledge, skills and abilities of people.

Reward management

Reward management deals with the strategies, policies and processes required to ensure that the value of people and the contribution they make to achieving organizational, departmental and team goals is recognized and rewarded.

It is concerned with the design, implementation and maintenance of reward systems, the design and management of grade and pay structures, rewarding and recognizing achievements and performance, providing employee benefits, and managing the system.

Managing the employment relationship

The employment relationship describes how employers and employees work together.

A positive employment relationship is one in which management and employees are interdependent and both benefit from this interdependency, and where there is mutual trust. Such a relationship is based on the psychological contract and provides a foundation for the conduct of employee relations.

References

Brown, D (2011) Performance management – can it ever work? *Manager*, Summer, p 16

Brown, D (2010) Practice what we preach? posted by Reward Blogger, 6 December, London, CIPD

Cappelli, P (2000) A market-driven approach to retaining talent, *Harvard Business Review*, January–February, pp 103–11

Cascio, W F (2010) *Managing Human Resources: Productivity, quality of work life, profits*, New York, McGraw-Hill Irwin

CIPD (2015) Survey of absence management, http://www.cipd.co.uk/hr-resources/survey-reports/absence-management-2015.aspx [accessed 2 January 2016]

CIPD (2012) Where has all the trust gone? http://www.cipd.co.uk/hr-resources/research/where-trust-gone.aspx [accessed 3 January 2016]

Coens, T and Jenkins, M (2002) *Abolishing Performance Appraisals: Why they backfire and what to do instead*, San Francisco, CA, Berrett-Koehler

Deming, W E (1986) *Out of the Crisis*, Cambridge, MA, Massachusetts Institute of Technology Centre for Advanced Engineering Studies

Egan, G (1995) A clear path to peak performance, *People Management*, 18 May, pp 34–37

e-reward (2014) *Survey of Performance Management Practice*, Stockport, e-reward

Grint, K (1993) What's wrong with performance appraisal? A critique and a suggestion, *Human Resource Management Journal*, 3 (3) pp 61–77

Guest, D (2007) HRM and the worker: towards a new psychological contract, in (eds) P Boxall, J Purcell and P Wright, *Oxford Handbook of Human Resource Management*, Oxford, Oxford University Press, pp 128–46

Hackman, J R and Oldham, G R (1974) Motivation through the design of work: test of a theory, *Organizational Behaviour and Human Performance*, 16 (2), pp 250–79

Mueller-Hanson, R A and Pulakos, E D (2015) *Putting the 'Performance' Back in Performance Management*, http://www.shrm.org/Research/Documents/SHRM-SIOP%20Performance%20Management.pdf [accessed 22 December 2015]

Postuma, R A and Campion, M A (2008) Twenty best practices for just performance reviews, *Compensation & Benefits Review*, January–February, pp 47–55

Schmidt, F L and Hunter, J E (1998) The validity and utility of selection methods in personnel psychology: practical and theoretical implications of 85 years of research findings, *Psychological Bulletin*, 124 (2), pp 262–74

Scullen, S E and Mount, M K (2000) Understanding the latent structure of job performance ratings, *Journal of Applied Psychology* 85 (6) pp 956–70

Shields, J (2007) *Managing Employee Performance and Reward*, Port Melbourne, Cambridge University Press

Society for Human Resource Management (2012) Performance Management Survey, http://www.shrm.org/HRStandards/PublishedStandards/Pages/

ANSISHRM090012012,%20Performance%20Management.aspx [accessed 22 December 2015]

Sparrow, P, Hird, M and Cooper C L (2015) *Do We Need HR?* Basingstoke, Palgrave Macmillan

Walton, R E (1985) From control to commitment in the workplace, *Harvard Business Review*, March–April, pp 77–84

Whittington, R and Molloy, E (2005) *HR's Role in Organizing: Shaping change*, London, CIPD

Younger, J, Smallwood, N and Ulrich, D (2007) Developing your organization's brand as a talent developer, *Human Resource Planning*, 30 (2), pp 21–29

The practice of learning and development 06

KEY CONCEPTS AND TERMS

Blended learning

Communities of practice

Development

E-learning

Education

Enterprise social networks

Learning

Learning analytics

Learning management system

Personal development planning

Self-directed learning

Self-managed learning

70/20/10 learning model

Social learning

LEARNING OUTCOMES

On completing this chapter you should be able to define these key concepts. You should also know about:

- Identifying learning needs
- The process of L&D
- The evaluation of learning
- The role of L&D
- The L&D role of line managers

Introduction

Learning and development (L&D) is defined as the process of ensuring that the organization has the knowledgeable, skilled and engaged workforce it needs and that individual employees have the opportunity to develop their abilities and maximize their potential. It means enabling the acquisition by individuals of knowledge and skills through experience, coaching provided by line managers and others, guidance and self-directed or self-managed learning activities carried out by individuals and learning events, programmes and facilities provided by the organization.

The components of L&D are:

- *Learning* – the process by which a person acquires and develops knowledge, skills, capabilities, behaviours and attitudes. It involves the modification of behaviour through experience as well as more formal methods of helping people to learn within or outside the workplace.

- *Development* – the growth or realization of a person's ability and potential through the provision of learning and educational experiences.

- *Training* – the systematic application of formal processes to impart knowledge and help people to acquire the skills necessary for them to perform their jobs satisfactorily.

- *Education* – the development of the knowledge, values and understanding required in all aspects of life rather than the knowledge and skills relating to particular areas of activity.

Learning should be distinguished from training. 'Learning is the process by which a person constructs new knowledge, skills and capabilities, whereas training is one of several responses an organization can undertake to promote learning' (Reynolds *et al*, 2002: 9). Learning is what individuals do; training is what organizations do to individuals. The components of learning and development are shown in Figure 6.1.

The term 'learning and development' (L&D) has largely replaced that of 'human resource development' (HRD), at least for practitioners. Harrison (2009: 5) observed that:

> The term human resource development retains its popularity among academics but it has never been attractive to practitioners. They tend to dislike it because they see its reference to people as a 'resource' to be demeaning. Putting people

on a par with money, materials and equipment creates the impression of 'development' as an unfeeling, manipulative activity, although the two terms are almost indistinguishable.

Figure 6.1 Components of learning and development

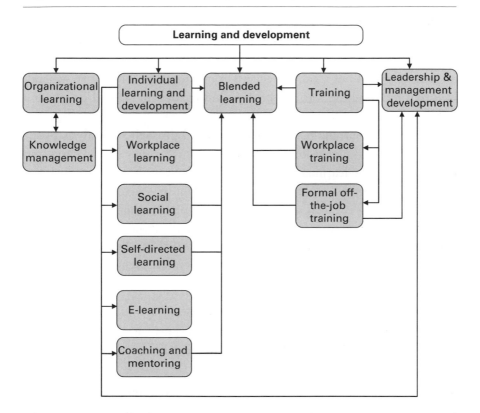

The terms are indeed often used interchangeably by commentators and practitioners although the introduction of 'learning' has emphasized the belief that what matters for individuals is that they are given the opportunity to learn, often for themselves, with guidance and support, rather than just being on the receiving end of what the organization provides.

This chapter extends the analysis of the learning and development responsibilities of line managers and the discussion of learning theory in Chapter 3 to examine how learning and development takes place in organizations. It traces the sequence of L&D activities starting with the identification of learning needs, followed by the various approaches to learning and development and completed by evaluation. The chapter ends with discussions of the role of L&D specialists and the L&D role of line managers.

Identifying learning needs

All learning activities need to be based on an understanding of what should be done and why. The purpose of the activities must be defined by identifying and analysing learning needs in the organization and for the people within it. Learning needs are often established on the basis of general assumptions about what people in particular occupations need to know and be able to do; for example managers need to learn about leadership. This is an easy approach but it can be facile. The assumptions could be so generalized that the resulting learning process will be all things to all people and nothing for anyone in particular.

Evidence on learning needs can be obtained through an analysis of the gap between what people know and can do and what they should know and be able to do. The learning needed to fill the gap can then be specified. But this 'deficiency model' – only putting things right that have gone wrong – is limited. Learning is much more positive than that. It should be concerned with identifying and satisfying development needs – fitting people to take on extra responsibilities, acquire new skills to deal with changing work demands, or develop a range of skills to facilitate multitasking. The following more positive methods can be used:

- *Analysis of business and workforce plans.* Business and workforce plans should indicate in general terms the types of skills and competencies that may be required in the future and the numbers of people with those skills and competencies who will be needed.

- *Surveys.* Special surveys or an interviewing programme can obtain the views of managers and other employees on what they need to learn. However, the material gathered from a survey may be unspecific and, when interviewed, people may find it difficult to articulate what they want. In the latter case it is best to lead with a discussion of the work they do and identify any areas where they believe that their performance and potential could be developed. This could lead to the identification of any additional things they feel they need to know or be able to do. Individual views can be amalgamated to provide a picture of common learning needs.

- *Role analysis.* This is the basis for preparing role profiles that provide a framework for analysing and identifying learning needs. Role profiles set out the key result areas of the role but, importantly, can also define the competencies required to perform it. Performance management should ensure that role profiles are updated regularly, and the review can be built on an analysis of the results achieved by reference to the key result areas and agreed objectives.

- *Skills analysis*. This determines the skills required to achieve an acceptable standard of performance. It is mainly used for technical, craft, manual and office jobs to provide the basis for devising learning and training programmes.

- *Performance management*. Performance management processes should be a prime source of information about individual learning and development needs. Performance management is based on an analysis of role requirements in the shape of knowledge, skills and abilities (KSAs) and the behavioural competencies needed to perform effectively, taking into account any new demands that will be made on the role holder. Performance reviews, which can be held whenever appropriate rather than simply being an annual event, will include discussions on the extent to which the individual would benefit, in career progression as well as performance terms, from some form of learning and development activity.

- *Learning evaluations*. Further information should be obtained from learning evaluations, as described later in this chapter.

The process of L&D

Learning and development can take place in a number of different forms and use a number of different processes. This means that there is always an element of choice in deciding what approach should be adopted to satisfy learning needs. L&D professionals have the demanding task of deciding which is most appropriate in particular circumstances.

Formal and informal learning

People learn both formally and informally. Formal learning is essentially classroom or training centre learning or prescribed e-learning. Informal learning is primarily experiential learning and may be self-directed and self-managed although support should be available from managers, coaches, mentors and social media. Formal learning presents difficulties. Hoyle (2015: 3) maintains that:

> For a formal programme to result in learning that actually enables people to do different things, training courses must require learners to take some tentative steps to try things out, to experience through trial and error, to reflect on lived experience, and to discuss and connect with others.

As described by Hoyle, informal learning is not entirely directed and controlled by the learner. He describes it as a continuum, illustrated in Figure 6.2.

Figure 6.2 Formal and informal learning

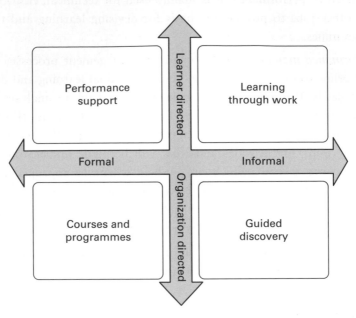

SOURCE Hoyle, 2015

In the south-west quadrant there are traditional courses and programmes. But these sessions only work if a degree of informal learning takes place to effect the traditional change in behaviour that improves performance. In the north-west quadrant there is performance support. This may be provided by the organization in the shape, for example, of e-learning programmes. Support may also be available from social networks. The south-east quadrant covers such activities as coaching and learning with colleagues – trying new things and reporting back on experiences. The north-east quadrant refers to work experiences from which people learn by reflecting, drawing conclusions and planning future actions. This model indicates that there are many varieties of informal training and that formal training does have a part to play but not in the old way of relying on classroom training and ignoring everything else. Further learning is required on the job.

Self-directed and self-managed learning

Self-directed learning takes place when individuals set their own learning goals and plan for themselves how they are to be attained. Self-managed learning is based on a process of recording achievement and action planning, which means that individuals review and reflect on what they have learnt, what they have achieved, what their goals are, how they are going to achieve those goals and what new learning they need to acquire. The learning programme can be 'self-paced' in the sense that learners can, up to a point, decide for themselves the rate at which they learn, and are encouraged to measure their own progress and adjust the programme accordingly.

Self-managed learning is based on the principle that people learn and retain more if they find things out for themselves. But they still need to be given guidance on what to look for and help in finding it. Learners have to be encouraged to define, with whatever help they need, the knowledge and skills required to do their work. They need information on where they can get the material or information that will enable them to learn. This can be done through personal development planning, as described below. They also need support from their manager and the organization with the provision of coaching, mentoring and learning facilities, including e-learning. The use of social media, as described later, can help.

Personal development planning

Personal development planning is carried out by individuals with guidance, encouragement and help from their managers, usually on the basis of performance and development reviews. A personal development plan sets out the actions people propose to take to learn and to develop themselves. They take responsibility for formulating and implementing the plan but they receive support from their managers in doing so.

Blended learning

Blended learning is the use of a combination of learning methods to increase the overall effectiveness of the learning process by providing for different parts of the learning mix to complement and support one another. A blended learning programme might be planned for an individual using a mix of planned experience, self-managed learning activities defined in a personal development plan, e-learning facilities, group action learning activities, coaching or mentoring, and instruction provided in an in-company or external course.

Use of social media

Social media can be used within the organization as a learning and development aid through enterprise social networks – Facebook-like platforms that sit within organizations. On the basis of its research the CIPD (2014: 4) concluded that:

> While there will always be a place for face-to-face learning interventions, social media can transform many aspects of learning and development, being used to curate knowledge, locate experts and facilitate peer-to-peer support, support self-directed learning and help employees prepare for and embed learning from training courses.

The CIPD also commented that: 'Social media blurs the traditional boundaries of learning and development. Sharing information and pointing to resources naturally leads to learner-led development, whereby people find out what they need to know when they need to know it' (*ibid*: 19).

Enterprise social networks are open communication tools that combine various functions, including being able to post announcements, comments, micro-blogs, questions and resources, join and set up special interest groups, follow colleagues and take part in forum discussions. As the CIPD (2014) pointed out, enterprise social networks can support learning and development in a number of ways. They can generate discussion and engage employees with learning events before and after they take place, thus boosting interest and focusing attention in the first instance and helping embed learning in day-to-day work afterwards. Social media itself provides a source for learning content. It helps to locate expertise within the organization and to catalogue insight and information for future reference. It can provide employees with access to bite-sized learning material so that they can learn in slots of five minutes or so. Forums can be created, as in Marks & Spencer, where employees can discuss training materials with the experts who created them, giving the employees greater clarity on how to use them.

CASE STUDY: Social networking in the Santa Fe Group

In the Santa Fe Group, a global organization with 1,700 employees involved in security risk management amongst other things, the learning and development team realized that the traditional model of residential workshops was not converting learning into practice. The solution was to develop The Academy Online, a learning management system fully integrated with a social networking platform. Based on the social media product Fuse, it enables employees to produce, share and comment on learning content. They can quickly post links to online learning content and The Academy Online is used to deliver blended learning and development. An intervention may start with a presentation or workshop and go on to self-directed e-learning through an online platform. As a social network, the platform facilitates conversations between colleagues.

Workplace learning

The 70/20/10 learning model suggests that 90 per cent of learning will take place through learning activities other than formal training courses or training programmes. Most of that will be gained from experience and social learning in the workplace. This recognizes that, in the words of Paine (2015: 46): 'Instead of putting learning *into* work (which is what a course essentially is) you extract learning *from* work and ensure it is accessible and shared' [italics in original].

Learning in the workplace is mainly informal although line managers have an important part to play in facilitating it through coaching and by arranging supporting activities, including formal training sessions. Much of it is experiential learning – learning by doing and by reflecting on experience so that it can be understood and applied. Workplace learning involves self-directed and self-managed learning and is enhanced by coaching, mentoring, e-learning and planned experience. But some more formal training activities can take place there. These include induction training – ensuring that new starters have the necessary knowledge and skills. Additional formal training may be provided later to develop new skills or enhance existing ones.

Social learning

As defined by Hart (2014):

> Social learning is about people connecting, conversing, collaborating and learning from, and with, one another on a daily basis at work... It's about helping teams learn as they work, rather than taking them out and forcing them to endure a learning 'experience'.

Social learning theory was formulated by Bandura (1977). It regards learning as a series of information-processing steps set in train by social interactions and emphasizes that effective learning requires such interaction. Wenger (1998) suggested that we all participate in 'communities of practice' (groups of people with shared expertise who work together) and that these are our primary sources of learning.

Some form of social learning happens continually in the workplace as individuals and groups work together. Groups solve problems jointly and learn in doing so. Project teams do the same. Individuals observe what their colleagues do and learn from their observations. But it should not be left to chance: social learning can be even more effective if supported by communities of practice, learning communities and online social learning, as described below.

Communities of practice

Communities of practice are groups of people bound together by shared expertise who meet together to share knowledge. They may be set up by individuals or groups, but L&D may support them as an approach to learning that offers more than traditional training.

Learning communities

Learning communities are groups of people who get together to learn from one another. They are usually set up by L&D professionals to support a training course or an online programme. Learning communities might be established before a course to prepare participants and give them some preliminary material to absorb. After the course community members can get together to discuss what they have learnt and how they are applying it. Problems can be raised and solutions considered. The emphasis is on interaction, sharing and conversations between the participants. In effect, learning communities may become communities of practice in which further learning possibilities can be explored and agreement reached on how they should be pursued by the community itself or with help from L&D.

Online social learning

Online social learning tools enable people to share with others what they know and what they have learnt. The learning is not structured but it is real – based on the actual experiences of colleagues – and therefore more effective than a formal presentation by a trainer on a course.

Social learning can be encouraged by the use of an enterprise social network (ESN) such as Yammer. ESN technology is similar to public social networking tools like Facebook in that it supports a constant flow of real-time, threaded conversations through user updates and replies. Within an organization people can share their experiences and thoughts and learn from one another. In using an ESN, individuals' personal activity streams will consist of all their activity streams – from all their learning initiatives as well as from their work teams and communities. Learning is no longer seen as a separate activity from working and it can become a continuous, social experience.

E-learning

E-learning is learning that is delivered through electronic Web 2.0 technology. The content of e-learning can consist of a whole programme covering, for example health and safety compliance, or it can usefully contain small and easily assimilated segments or 'bites' of material dealing with a specific topic such as handling difficult conversations. A Web 2.0 site allows users to interact and collaborate with each other by reference to user-generated content in a virtual community. It can be used to promote organizational learning and knowledge management through intranets and enterprise social networks within organizations. The aim is to enhance learning. It extends and supplements face-to-face learning rather than replaces it. E-learning can provide reinforcement through post-event reading, help with self-assessment and lead to chatroom support. The emphasis is on self-paced learning – learners control the rate at which they learn although they may be given targets for completion and guidance from tutors on how they should learn. However, the impact of e-learning is strongly influenced by the quality of the support provided to learners. It is the effectiveness of this support rather than the sophistication of the technology that counts.

E-learning material may be managed by means of a learning management system (LMS), a software application for e-learning administration, curriculum management, documentation, tracking the progress of learners, reporting and delivery. E-learning modules, especially those designed for compliance training, often test participants on what they have learnt by getting them to tick boxes in such formats as multiple-choice questions.

E-learning is most commonly used for compliance training (for example, health and safety, hygiene and data protection). It is also often used for induction training. E-learning can be used to support informal learning in the workplace. It may be blended with other types of learning. For example, the majority of learning content may be delivered through face-to-face lectures or coaching or through textual material, but the dialogue with other learners, the conduct of collaborative activities and the searching for supporting material are all conducted online.

Training

Training is the use of systematic and planned instruction activities to promote learning. The approach can be summarized in the phrase 'learner-based training.' It is one of several responses an organization can undertake to promote learning.

As Reynolds (2004: 45) pointed out, training has a complementary role to play in accelerating learning: 'It should be reserved for situations that justify a more directed, expert-led approach rather than viewing it as a comprehensive and all-pervasive people development solution.' He also commented that the conventional training model has a tendency to 'emphasize subject-specific knowledge, rather than trying to build core learning abilities'.

Justification of training

Formal training is indeed only one of the ways of ensuring that learning takes place, but it can be justified in the following circumstances:

- The knowledge or skills cannot be acquired satisfactorily by experiential learning in the workplace or by self-managed learning.
- Different skills are required by a number of people, which have to be developed quickly to meet new demands and cannot be gained by relying on experience.
- The tasks to be carried out are so specialized or complex that people are unlikely to master them on their own initiative at a reasonable speed.
- When a learning need common to a number of people has to be met that can readily be dealt with in a training event or programme; for example: induction, essential IT skills, communication skills.

Systematic training

Training should be systematic in that it is specifically designed, planned, implemented and evaluated to meet defined needs. It is provided by people who know how to train and the impact of training is carefully evaluated. The concept was originally developed for the industrial training boards in the 1960s and, as illustrated in Figure 6.3, consists of a four-stage model:

1 Identify training needs.

2 Decide what sort of training is required to satisfy these needs.

3 Use experienced and trained trainers to implement training.

4 Follow up and evaluate training to ensure that it is effective.

Figure 6.3 Systematic training model

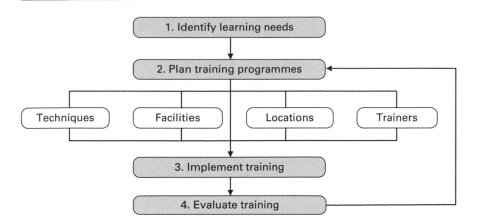

Effective training practices

Effective training uses the systematic approach with an emphasis on skills analysis. The purpose of the training should be clearly defined in terms of the behaviour required as a result of training. The focus of the training should be to develop transferable skills and it will only be successful if those skills are put to good use in the place of work. The training should be evaluated on the basis of the extent to which it has achieved its purpose.

Planning and delivering training events and programmes

This process of planning and delivering training or learning events and programmes is described by the ADDIE model, which has five phases: analysis, design, development, implementation and evaluation:

1 In the analysis phase the learning goals and objectives are established and the learning environment and learners' existing knowledge and skills are identified.

2 The design phase deals with subject matter analysis and the methods to be used. This should be a 'blended learning' approach making appropriate use of presentations, discussions, case studies, role plays and simulations and games. The maximum amount of learner involvement rather than spoon-feeding through lectures should be planned.

3 In the development phase the detailed programme is constructed as conceived in the design phase. This covers the session plan, the outline content and learning outcomes of each session, nomination and briefing

of the people who will be involved in delivering the programme, methods of delivery, preparation of visual aids, handouts, supporting material, games and exercises and the arrangements for administering the programme.

4 The programme is implemented as planned.

5 Each session is evaluated by the programme director and, at the end, by participants. The impact of the programme on performance is measured and the degree to which it met expectations assessed.

CASE STUDY: Training overhaul for Scottish police

A radical overhaul of training for the Scottish police has created more opportunities for promotion and culminated in a prestigious National Training Award. The improved training scheme uses facilitated learning delivery, where trainees pre-read all information before attending sessions and then discuss issues and learn from each other. Responsibility for learning is now firmly placed on the shoulders of the individual – you have got to want to be a police officer and you have got to want to learn. After 15 weeks of initial training, a two-week 'reconvention' period helps staff with the areas they particularly need to address. This training is tailored to individual requirements: syndicates of recruits with similar needs are put together to receive it. This 'partnership approach' had helped the participants to focus on communication and problem-solving skills. A Certificate of Higher Education in policing, accredited by the University of Stirling, is awarded on completion of the programme. There are also opportunities to take a diploma in management skills.

CASE STUDY: Training and learning at a customer support centre

The customer support centre employs 300 people. Customer service agents work in a group of five, known as a 'pod'. One of the pod members will be a team coach who provides support and advice to his or her agent colleagues.

A working knowledge of each customer support system is essential to do the job and one of the central tasks of the training department is to bring new entrants up to competence as quickly as possible. The following pattern is adopted.

New entrants join in cohorts of 8 to 10 and spend their first week in the training room. As the week progresses they spend periods in a pod sitting next to a 'buddy', listening to calls. At the end of that week they are allocated to a pod team and receive close ongoing support from the pod team coach.

Given the emphasis on learning in the workplace, the role of the team coach is critical and there are a number of steps in place to support and enhance their role. A set of skills and needs have been defined and these are delivered to the 30 centre team coaches in 90-minute modules in the training room.

Leadership and management development

Leadership and management development programmes provide for managers to have the leadership and managerial qualities required to achieve success. They form a vital ingredient in talent management, in association with career planning and career management activities. A blended learning approach is used, which combines a number of learning activities such as planned experience, self-managed learning, coaching, mentoring, action learning, outdoor learning and formal education and training in programmes based on an analysis of learning needs.

Leadership and management development compared

In some quarters the term 'leadership development' has replaced 'management development', perhaps because the importance of ensuring that people have leadership qualities has been recognized, while it is believed that they can be safely left to acquire management skills in other ways, eg experience. However, they are not the same although they are closely associated.

The difference between them is that leadership development tends to be concerned with nurturing the softer skills of leadership through various educational processes, including formal learning events and programmes and coaching. This is illustrated in the case studies set out below. In contrast, management development relies more on ensuring that managers have the right sequence of experience, which may be supplemented by self-directed learning and courses on management techniques. Further guidance may be provided by coaching and from mentors. But management development programmes traditionally also cover leadership skills.

CASE STUDY: Leadership development at Cargill

Cargill is an international provider of food, agricultural and risk management products and services. Those in Cargill's different talent pools, such as the 'Next Generation Leaders' and 'Emerging Leaders' undertake both formal and informal development. In Cargill's high-performance Leadership Academy, entrants learn about the fundamentals of leadership and management in the company and work through a number of accelerated leadership modules, gaining the knowledge to enable them to lead Cargill businesses. All of these courses are interspersed with more challenging projects and work assignments. Cargill corporate leaders also take part in the Leadership Academy, where they learn transformational leadership skills and the essentials of coaching and mentoring in formal programmes and informal learning activities, all of which form an important part of their leadership development.

CASE STUDY: Leadership development at Diageo

At Diageo, the international beverages company, a series of development strategies, particularly for leadership, have been based on Diageo's five values, which were created as the common heartbeat of all the component businesses. The values – 'Be the best', 'Passionate about consumers', 'Proud of what we do', 'Freedom to succeed' and 'Valuing each other' – have become central to Diageo's success, alongside a comprehensive performance management framework. Conversations about performance are now on a 'partnership' basis, where managers, with their employees, are expected to discuss the latter's aspirations and how their growth needs can be satisfied by the business.

The company's first leadership development programme, 1998's 'Building Diageo talent', was designed to help link strategy and organizational performance with individual performance. This had many components, including coaching and benchmarking for leadership development for 4,000 managers. Since then the company's leadership training has evolved to focus more on building 'a core Diageo mindset'. The senior team has prioritized developing a 'total talent strategy' and HR processes have been thoroughly embedded in management thinking worldwide.

Leadership development

As defined by Burgoyne (2010: 43): 'Leadership development in the widest sense involves the acquisition, development and utilization of leadership capability or the potential for it.' Leadership development programmes prepare people for leadership roles and situations beyond their current experience. The essential elements of leadership development, as suggested by Bolden (2010: 129), are reflection, practice, self-awareness, personal support, opportunities to apply learning and relevance to work. He identified the following leadership development activities:

- job/work placements with leadership capability development as one of the purposes;
- education, training and development of individuals including the 'context sensitive' methods of coaching, mentoring and more formal education, training and development programmes;
- 'soft' organization development processes including culture change, team-building and 'hearts and minds' collective mission/values-creating initiatives.

Management development

Management development is concerned with improving the performance of managers in their present roles, preparing them to take on greater responsibilities in the future and also developing their leadership skills. The aim is to find ways in which the organization can produce, mainly from within, a supply of managers better equipped for their jobs at all levels. The principal method of doing this is to ensure that managers gain the right sequence and variety of experience, in good time, that will equip them for whatever level of responsibility they have the ability to reach in the course of their career. This experience can be supplemented – but never replaced – by courses carefully timed and designed to meet particular needs.

Evaluation of learning

It is important to evaluate learning to assess its effectiveness in producing the outcomes specified when the activity was planned. Evaluation can indicate where improvements or changes are required to make the training even more effective. As noted by Tamkin *et al* (2002), learning can be modelled as a chain of impact from the planning of learning to meet organizational or individual learning needs to the learning that takes place in a learning event, from learning to changed behaviour, and from changed behaviour to impact on others and the organization as a whole.

Evaluation is an integral feature of learning activities. In essence, it is the comparison of objectives with outcomes to answer the question of how far the event has achieved its purpose. The setting of objectives and the establishment of methods of measuring results are, or should be, an essential part of the planning stage of any L&D programme. Evaluation provides guidance on what needs to be done to ensure that learning activities are effective. The methods used for evaluation are:

- The Kirkpatrick (1994) system, which has four levels: 1) reaction to the training event; 2) learning from the training event; 3) behaviour on return to work; and 4) evaluate results in terms of impact on organizational performance.

- Return on expectations measures – the extent to which the objectives and anticipated benefits of any learning investment have been realized.

- Return on investment (RoI) calculated as:

$$\frac{\text{Benefits from training}(£) - \text{Costs of training}(£)}{\text{Costs of training}(£)} \times 100$$

- Learning analytics, which uses 'big data', defined as data that is too complex to be analysed by normal statistical techniques to provide insights into the effectiveness and impact of learning and development interventions.

The need for evaluation is generally recognized by L&D specialists and the Kirkpatrick model is well known, but Grove and Ostroff (1990) noted that there were five barriers that appeared to explain why training evaluations were not carried out very effectively in organizations:

1 Senior management often not insisting on or requesting information on the impact of the training that was provided.

2 The lack of expertise among L&D professionals on how to carry out training evaluations.

3 A lack of clear objectives attached to training programmes so that actually knowing what to evaluate against is difficult if not impossible.

4 The limited budgets available to training departments means that resources are devoted to training provision rather than training evaluation.

5 The risks associated with evaluation may be too great, given that the evaluation data might reveal that the training had little impact.

The role of L&D

What might be called a 'learning and development revolution' has taken place over the last few years. The emphasis is now on informal, workplace, social and self-managed learning rather than spoon-feeding people with formal training courses where the learning was seldom transferred satisfactorily on return to work. This has had a huge effect on the roles of the L&D function and its members and on the L&D role of line managers.

The role of the L&D function

The role of the L&D function is to provide advice, guidance and services in order to develop the capability of employees and thus improve individual and organizational performance. As Harrison (2009: 8) observed, the primary purpose of the L&D function is 'to aid collective progress through the collaborative, expert and ethical stimulation and facilitation of learning and knowledge that support business goals, develop individual potential, and respect and build on diversity'.

The L&D function needs to adopt a strategic approach. This means supporting the achievement of business goals by aligning L&D strategies to business strategies. These L&D strategies are designed to provide a comprehensive framework for developing people through the establishment of a learning culture and the encouragement of organizational learning. Strategies are also formulated for ensuring that L&D activities support talent management and knowledge management processes.

The L&D function operates as a centre of expertise, providing advice and support to line managers on how they should fulfil their responsibilities for promoting learning in their departments, overseeing the implementation of social learning, developing e-learning, and planning, delivering and supervising learning events and programmes. Research by Hird and Sparrow (2012: 7) led to the conclusion that:

> Traditionally L&D departments have been transactional support functions that
> supply a range of courses that satisfy requests for support from the business.
> However, the business is increasingly looking for learning support that fits the
> requirements of knowledge workers – embedded in day-to-day activity, supporting

development of professional networks and ultimately ensuring that the business has the knowledge and skills to deliver the business plan.

They also noted (*ibid*: 8) that:

> The influence of L&D in the organization was expanding, their learning offerings would grow, online learning was set to take centre stage, the majority of learning would become collaborative, and would be delivered in short timescales using micro-modules to provide more focused learning. This would require significant change in course design and presentation, a move beyond current primary offerings of mainly foundational skills, and the need to embrace more blended learning (ie combining different learning methods).

The role of the L&D specialist

The old-style training managers were mainly engaged in providing formal courses or supervising formal training programmes. The new-style learning and development specialists have a very different role. They no longer spend most if not all of their time delivering training events or supervising training. Instead their role is much more that of an internal consultant advising on and promoting workplace and social learning, acting as a coach but not an old-fashioned trainer. This was confirmed through research conducted by the CIPD (2015: 3) which noted:

> A key shift is a move away from learning delivery to performance consultancy, underpinned by the need for L&D to be aligned to the business and deliver tangible organizational and individual impact. There is also increasingly a need for L&D to support social learning.

The CIPD also commented that:

> L&D roles are becoming more diverse in response to a complex external environment. This represents a challenge for how to best focus roles. Do you build 'performance consultants' able to diagnose, develop and curate? Or do you need experts who are focused entirely on data analytics, coaching or online learning? (*ibid*: 15)

L&D specialists analyse learning needs and make proposals on how these can best be satisfied. They advise line managers on the achievement of workplace learning and coach them on the learning and development skills they need. They promote social learning, develop e-learning and the use of social media to aid learning, provide individual coaching, and plan, implement and evaluate training events and programmes, often outsourcing training to external providers.

The skills required

To do all the above L&D specialists need to understand the business and the critical factors that determine success, possess insight into the people issues relating to capability and skill in order to establish learning and development needs, have the ability to facilitate workplace and social learning, and possess technological capability, especially related to the use of e-learning. Skill is also required in the diagnosis of problems, the development of the right solutions and the use of learning analytics to evaluate learning. They may also need coaching and instructing skills.

The role of line managers

Most learning happens in the workplace. This means that line managers have a key part to play in ensuring that this learning is accomplished. They use performance management to identify learning needs and provide the basis for development plans, and are there to see that new or promoted employees acquire the skills they need, they provide coaching whenever required. Every time they delegate work or give someone an instruction provides a learning opportunity for the individual concerned. The L&D skills managers need are examined in Chapter 18.

KEY LEARNING POINTS

Learning and development defined
Learning and development (L&D) is defined as the process of ensuring that the organization has the knowledgeable, skilled and engaged workforce it needs and that individual employees have the opportunity to develop their abilities and maximize their potential.

Identifying learning needs
Learning activities need to be based on an understanding of what should be done and why it should be done. The purpose of the activities must be defined by identifying and analysing learning needs in the organization and for the people within it.

Evidence on learning needs can be obtained through an analysis of the gap between what people know and can do and what they should know and be able to do. The learning needed to fill the gap can then be specified. The other methods are: analysis of business and workforce plans; surveys; role analysis; skills analysis; performance management; and learning evaluations.

Formal and informal learning

People learn both formally and informally. Formal learning is essentially classroom or training centre learning or prescribed e-learning. Informal learning is primarily experiential learning and may be self-directed and self-managed although support may be available from managers, coaches, mentors and social media.

Workplace learning

The 70/20/10 learning model suggests that 90 per cent of learning will take place through learning activities other than formal training courses or training programmes. Most of that will be gained from experience and social learning in the workplace.

Social learning

As defined by Hart (2014): 'Social learning is about people connecting, conversing, collaborating and learning from, and with, one another on a daily basis at work... It's about helping teams learn as they work, rather than taking them out and forcing them to endure a learning "experience".'

E-learning

E-learning is learning that is delivered through electronic Web 2.0 technology. The content of e-learning can consist of a whole programme covering, for example health and safety compliance, or it can contain small and easily assimilated segments or 'bites' of material dealing with a specific topic such as handling difficult conversations.

Training

Training is the use of systematic and planned instruction activities to promote learning. Formal training is indeed only one of the ways of ensuring that learning takes place, but it can be justified when the knowledge or skills cannot be acquired satisfactorily by experiential learning in the workplace or by self-managed learning; different skills are required by a number of people; the tasks to be carried out are so specialized or complex that people are unlikely to master them on their own initiative at a reasonable speed; or when a learning need common to a number of people has to be met that can readily be dealt with in a training event or programme.

Systematic training
Training should be systematic in that it is specifically designed, planned, implemented and evaluated to meet defined needs.

Effective training practices
Effective training uses the systematic approach with an emphasis on skills analysis. The purpose of the training should be clearly defined in terms of the behaviour required as a result of training. The focus of the training should be to develop transferable skills and it will only be successful if those skills are put to good use in the place of work.

Planning and delivering training events and programmes
The process of planning and delivering training or learning events and programmes is described by the ADDIE model, which has five phases: analysis, design, development, implementation and evaluation.

Leadership and management development
Leadership and management development programmes provide for managers to have the leadership and managerial qualities required to achieve success.

A blended learning approach is used, which combines a number of learning activities such as planned experience, self-managed learning, coaching, mentoring, action learning, outdoor learning and formal education and training in programmes based on an analysis of learning needs.

Evaluation of learning
It is important to evaluate learning to assess its effectiveness in producing the outcomes specified when the activity was planned. Evaluation can indicate where improvements or changes are required in order to make the training even more effective.

The methods used for evaluation are the Kirkpatrick (1994) system, which has four levels, return on expectations measures, return on investment (RoI), and learning analytics.

The role of the L&D function
The role of the L&D function is to provide advice, guidance and services in order to develop the capability of employees and thus improve individual and organizational performance.

The role of the L&D specialist
L&D specialists no longer spend most if not all of their time delivering training events or supervising training programmes although they may still be involved

in the development of e-learning programmes. Instead their role is much more that of an internal consultant advising on and promoting workplace and social learning who may act as a coach but not an old-fashioned trainer.

L&D specialists analyse learning needs and make proposals on how these can best be satisfied; advise line managers on the achievement of workplace learning and coach them on the learning and development skills they need; promote social learning; develop e-learning and the use of social media to aid learning; provide individual coaching; and plan, implement and evaluate training events and programmes, often outsourcing training to external providers.

The role of L&D in workplace learning
L&D has in effect a consultancy and coaching role – much harder and more demanding than laying on a course but more rewarding. What L&D has to do is to focus on line managers and their team leaders who need to be briefed on their responsibilities for learning and coached in how to fulfil them.

The role of L&D in social learning
The role of L&D in social learning is basically to liaise with work teams to build or enhance existing sharing practices as an integral part of their daily work, not as an extra initiative.

The skills required
L&D specialists need to understand the business, possess insight into the people issues relating to capability and skill in order to establish learning and development needs, have the ability to facilitate workplace and social learning, possess technological capability, especially related to the use of e-learning and have diagnostic and analytical skills.

The role of line managers
Most learning happens in the workplace. This means that line managers have a key part to play in ensuring that this learning is accomplished.

References

Bandura, A (1977) *Social Learning Theory*, Englewood Cliffs, NJ, Prentice-Hall

Bolden, R (2010) Leadership, management and organizational development, in (eds) J Gold, R Thorpe and A Mumford, *Gower Handbook of Leadership and Management Development*, Aldershot, Gower, pp 118–32

Burgoyne, J (2010) Crafting a leadership and management development strategy, in (eds) J Gold, R Thorpe and A Mumford, *Gower Handbook of Leadership and Management Development*, Aldershot, Gower, pp 42–55

CIPD (2015) *Learning and Development: Evolving roles, enhancing skills*, http://www.cipd.co.uk/binaries/l-d-evolving-roles-enhancing-skills_2015.pdf [accessed 4 January 2016]

CIPD (2014) *Putting Social Media to Work: Lessons for employers*, http://www.cipd.co.uk/binaries/6545%20Social%20media%20research%20report%20(WEB).pdf [accessed 3 January 2016]

Grove, D A and Ostroff, C (1990) Training programme evaluation, in (eds) K N Wexley and J R Hinrichs, *Developing Human Resources*, Washington, DC, Bureau of National Affairs

Harrison, R (2009) *Learning and Development*, 5th edn, London, CIPD

Hart, J (2014) *The Social Learning Handbook*, http://www.c4lpt.co.uk/blog/2014/01/27/social-learning-handbook-pdf-now-available/ [accessed 4 January 2016]

Hird, M and Sparrow, P (2012) *Learning and Development: Seeking a renewed focus?* White Paper 12/01, October 2012, Centre for Performance-Led HR, Lancaster University, http://www.lancaster.ac.uk/media/lancaster-university/content-assets/documents/lums/cphr/LDWP.pdf, [accessed 4 January 2016]

Hoyle, R (2015) *Informal Learning in Organizations*, London, Kogan Page

Kirkpatrick, D L (1994) *Evaluating Training Programmes*, San Francisco, CA, Berret-Koehler

Paine, M (2015) *The Learning Challenge*, London, Kogan Page

Reynolds, J (2004) *Helping People Learn*, London, CIPD

Reynolds, J, Caley, L and Mason, R (2002) *How Do People Learn?* London, CIPD

Tamkin, P, Pearson, G, Hirsh, W and Constable, S (2010) *Exceeding Expectation: The principles of outstanding leadership*, London, The Work Foundation

Tamkin, P, Yarnall, J and Kerrin, M (2002) *Kirkpatrick and Beyond: A review of training evaluation*, Report 392, Brighton, Institute for Employment Studies

Wenger, E (1998) *Communities of Practice: Learning, meaning and identity*, Cambridge, Cambridge University Press

The contribution 07 of HRM and L&D in different types of organizations

KEY CONCEPTS AND TERMS

Big idea

The black box

Causal ambiguity

Contingency variables

Employee champion

Employee value proposition

Organizational effectiveness

Reversed causality

LEARNING OUTCOMES

On completing this chapter you should be able to define these key concepts. You should also understand:

- The overall contribution the HRM and L&G functions can make to organizational capability and effectiveness
- How HR makes an impact on organizational performance
- The contribution HR can make in the public and voluntary sectors, in small to medium sized enterprises and international organizations

Introduction

This chapter starts with a study of the overall contribution of the human resources (HR) and learning and development (L&D) functions to organizational effectiveness and an analysis of how this contribution is made. The rest of the chapter is devoted to the contribution of HR in organizations in the public and voluntary sectors, in SMEs (small to medium-sized enterprises) and in international organizations.

The overall contribution of HR

The overall contribution that HR can make is to:

- *Provide insight* – seek understanding of the issues affecting the organization and its employees, explore the implications of these issues for business and people management and convey these messages to management. The aim is to help organizations 'to find new ways of meeting current and future challenges' (CIPD, 2010a: 5).

- *Contribute to the formulation and implementation of business strategy* – as Lawler and Mohrman (2003: 16) commented: 'HR can play an important role in the formulation of strategy by making explicit the human capital resources required to support various strategies and strategic initiatives, by playing a leadership role in helping the organization develop the necessary capabilities to enact the strategy, and by playing a strong role in implementation and change management.'

- *Improve organizational effectiveness* (the ability of an organization to achieve its goals by making effective use of the resources available) – plan and implement organization development programmes. As emphasized by the CIPD (2010a: 7): 'HR has a unique role to play in helping an organization succeed today in a way that lays the foundations for future, sustainable success.'

- *Facilitate change* – fulfil the role of change agent, leading and advise senior and line managers how best to manage organizational change. Ulrich (1998: 125) suggested that HR should become 'an agent of continuous transformation'.

- *Deliver HR services* – provide effective and efficient services in such fields as recruitment, learning and development, reward management and employee relations that meet the needs of the organization, its management and its employees.

- *Provide expertise* – in contributing to the achievement of the organization's strategy, developing HR strategies and delivering advice and services in accordance with good practice in each aspect of HRM.

- *Provide advice* – improve the quality of employment relationships by advising managers on the implementation of HR policies and procedures, on employment issues and on handling people problems.

- *Develop the employee value proposition* – take action to improve the value of what the organization offers to prospective or existing employees in order to persuade them to join or remain with the business.

- *Promote the wellbeing of employees* – help to improve the quality of the work environment covering how people are treated at work in such areas as health and safety, reduction of stress and work–life balance issues.

- *Promote social responsibility* – formulate socially responsible HR policies on such issues as equal opportunity, the management of diversity, flexible working, harassment and bullying, and ensure they are implemented. Act as the guardian of the organization's values and ethical standards concerning people. The value of the HR function is measured by the extent to which it meets these requirements. Ulrich (1998) called this the 'employee champion' role.

- *Ensure compliance with employment law* – develop and implement policies and procedures that ensure the provisions of employment law are fully taken into account.

The contribution of learning and development

The CIPD research on the value of learning (Anderson, 2007) found that senior managers and L&D specialists believed generally that learning was expected to ensure the strategic readiness of employees; deliver performance improvement; deliver cost-effective labour, and enable effective career/talent management processes. In more detail, the contribution that L&D can make is to:

- *Provide insight* – seek understanding of the issues affecting the organization and its employees, explore the implications of these issues for learning and development strategy and practice.

- *Improve organizational effectiveness* – plan and implement learning and development policies designed to improve performance and help the organization achieve its goals.

- *Facilitate change* – support change management programmes by developing the knowledge, skill and understanding required to implement change.

- *Help to ensure that the organization has the skilled, knowledgeable and engaged people it needs* – contribute to talent management programmes and organize learning and development events and programmes to meet identified needs.

- *Deliver L&D services* – provide effective and efficient services in the provision of learning and development events and programmes that meet the needs of the organization, its management and its employees.

- *Promote individual development* – encourage and support the development of individuals to their own benefit and that of the organization.

- *Provide expertise* – to contribute to the achievement of the organization's strategy, develop L&D strategies and deliver advice and services in line with good practice in each aspect of L&D.

- *Provide advice* – help managers to improve the quality of workplace learning.

The impact of HR

As Guest (1997: 269) argued: 'The distinctive feature of HRM is its assumption that improved performance is achieved through the people in the organization.' If, therefore, appropriate HR policies and processes are introduced, it can also be assumed that HRM will impact on firm performance. Much research has been carried out showing that good HRM practice and firm performance are correlated; notable examples in the UK are Patterson *et al* (1997), Guest *et al* (2000a), Thompson (2002), West *et al* (2002) and Purcell *et al* (2003) as summarized in Table 7.1.

The problem of establishing how HRM makes an impact

Storey *et al* (2009: 4) observed that:

> The premise is that, in some shape or form, HR policies have an effect on HR practices and these in turn influence staff attitudes and behaviours which will, in turn again, impact on service offerings and customer perceptions of value.

Table 7.1 Research on the link between HRM and firm performance

Researcher(s)	Methodology	Outcomes
Patterson et al (1997)	The research examined the link between business performance and organization culture and the use of a number of HR practices.	HR practices explained significant variations in profitability and productivity (19 per cent and 18 per cent respectively). Two HR practices were particularly significant: 1) the acquisition and development of employee skills; and 2) job design including flexibility, responsibility and variety.
Guest et al (2000a)	An analysis of the 1998 WERS survey, which sampled some 2,000 workplaces and obtained the views of about 28,000 employees.	A strong association exists between HRM and both employee attitudes and workplace performance.
Thompson (2002)	A study of the impact of high performance work practices such as teamworking, appraisal, job rotation, broad-banded grade structures and sharing of business information in UK aerospace establishments.	The number of HR practices and the proportion of the workforce covered appeared to be the key differentiating factor between more and less successful firms.
West et al (2002)	Research conducted in 61 UK hospitals obtaining information on HR strategy, policy and procedures from chief executives and HR directors and on mortality rates.	An association between certain HR practices and lower mortality rates was identified. As noted by Professor West: 'If you have HR practices that focus on effort and skill; develop people's skills; encourage cooperation, collaboration, innovation and synergy in teams for most, if not all employees, the whole system functions and performs better.'

(*Continued*)

Table 7.1 Continued

Researcher(s)	Methodology	Outcomes
Purcell et al (2003)	A University of Bath longitudinal study of 12 companies to establish how people management impacts on organizational performance.	The most successful companies had 'the big idea'. They had a clear vision and a set of integrated values. They were concerned with sustaining performance and flexibility. Clear evidence existed between positive attitudes towards HR policies and practices, levels of satisfaction, motivation and commitment, and operational performance. Policy and practice implementation (not the number of HR practices adopted) is the vital ingredient in linking people management to business performance and this is primarily the task of line managers.

However, Guest *et al* (2000b) commented that much of the research has demonstrated an association between HRM and performance but left uncertainties about cause and effect. Ulrich (1997: 304) pointed out that:

> HR practices seem to matter; logic says it is so; survey findings confirm it. Direct relationships between performance and attention to HR practices are often fuzzy, however, and vary according to the population sampled and the measures used.

There are two issues that affect the determination of a link between HRM and firm performance: causal ambiguity and contingency factors. These contribute to what is known as 'the black box' phenomenon.

Causal ambiguity

The term 'causal ambiguity' refers to the numerous, subtle and often hidden interconnections between the factors influencing cause and effect. Boselie *et al* (2005: 75) referred to the causal distance between an HRM input and an output such as financial performance: 'Put simply, so many variables and events, both internal and external, affect organizations that this direct linkage strains credibility.'

A basic reason for ambiguity is multiple causation; ie there is more than one possible cause for an effect. HRM may have caused an improvement in performance but there may be many other economic or business factors that did so, and it could be difficult to unravel them. Another factor is the possibility of reversed causality (a situation where A might have caused B but B might well have caused A). As Purcell *et al* (2003: 2) expressed it: 'Although it is nice to believe that more HR practices leads to higher economic return, it is just as possible that it is successful firms that can afford more extensive (and expensive) HRM practices.'

Contingency factors

Causation will additionally be affected by the organization's context, ie the internal and external environmental factors that influence what happens within the organization.

The black box phenomenon

Causal ambiguity also stems from the black box phenomenon, as illustrated in Figure 7.1. This is the situation in which while it may be possible to observe HRM inputs in the form of HR practices and measure firm performance outputs, it may be difficult or hard to be certain through research about what happened in between – what the HRM outcomes were that converted

Figure **7.1** The black box phenomenon

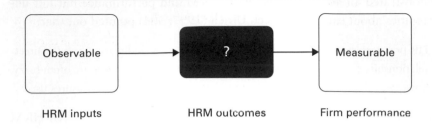

the input of HR practices into firm performance outputs. As Alvesson (2009: 56) commented: 'Research does not proceed beyond attempts to find an empirical association between HR practices and organizational performance. The phenomena are in a black box, only input and output are registered and what is happening remains clouded in the dark.'

Explanations of how HRM makes an impact

Guest (1997: 268) stated that: 'The assumption is that "appropriate" HRM practices tap the motivation and commitment of employees.' He explained how expectancy theory might help to explain the HR/performance link as follows:

> The expectancy theory of motivation provides one possible basis for developing a more coherent rationale about the link between HRM practices and performance. Although expectancy theory is concerned primarily with motivation, it is also a theory about the link between motivation and performance. Specifically, it proposes that high performance, at the individual level, depends on high motivation plus possession of the necessary skills and abilities and an appropriate role and understanding of that role. It is a short step to specify the HRM practices that encourage high skills and abilities, for example careful selection and high investment in training; high motivation, for example employee involvement and possibly performance-related pay; and an appropriate role structure and role perception, for example job design and extensive communication and feedback.

Following this contribution from Guest, any explanation of the impact of HRM on organizational performance is likely to be based on three propositions: 1) that HR practices can make a direct impact on employee characteristics such as engagement, commitment, motivation and skill; 2) if employees have these characteristics it is probable that organizational performance in terms of productivity, quality and the delivery of high levels of customer service will improve; and 3) if such aspects of organizational performance improve the financial results achieved by the organization will improve. These propositions highlight the existence of an intermediate factor between HRM and financial performance. This factor consists of the HRM outcomes in the shape of employee characteristics affected by HR practices. Therefore, HRM does not make a direct impact. A model of the impact of HRM taking into account the considerations of reverse causation and contingency effects is shown in Figure 7.2.

However, high performance is not just about HR practices. The case-based research by Purcell *et al* (2003) showed that the key to activating what they called the 'People–Performance' link lies not only in well-crafted 'bundles' of HR practices, but in their conjunction with a powerful and co-hering organizational vision (or 'big idea') and corporate leadership, together with front-line leadership's action and use of its discretionary power.

HRM in different contexts

The discussion so far in this chapter on the contribution and impact of HRM and the description of HR practices in Chapter 5 applies generally to any large private sector firm and, in a number of respects, to organizations in the public and voluntary sectors. The HR activities of organization design and development, resourcing, learning and development, reward, and employee relations may appear on the surface to be basically similar in any organization in which they take place. In practice, however, the way in which they are applied and to what extent will, in accordance with contingency theory, be dependent on the organization's environment and circumstances, ie the context in which HRM takes place. Two of the most important contextual factors are the organization's sector and its size.

With regard to the sector, the major distinctions are between private sector, public sector and voluntary organizations. Most of the discourse on HRM over the years has been focused on the private sector. But there are significant differences in the HRM context between the private sector and the other two sectors and in the next two parts of this chapter these differences are analysed.

The other major contextual factor is the size of the organization. Again, descriptions of HRM often seem to assume that all organizations are alike, irrespective of sector *and* size. But small to medium-sized organizations (SMEs) are different in many ways and this affects how HRM takes place; these differences are therefore explored in this chapter after the public and voluntary sectors have

Figure 7.2 Impact of HRM on organizational performance

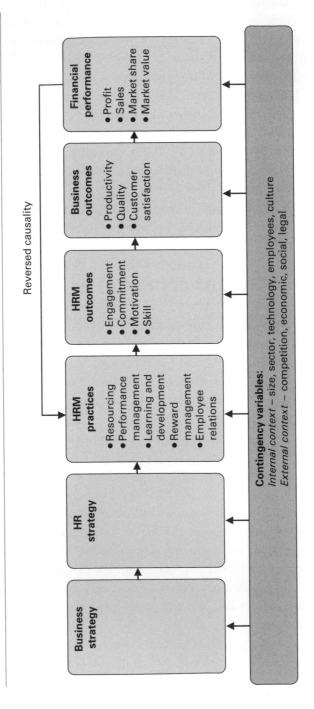

Business strategy

HR strategy

HRM practices
- Resourcing
- Performance management
- Learning and development
- Reward management
- Employee relations

HRM outcomes
- Engagement
- Commitment
- Motivation
- Skill

Business outcomes
- Productivity
- Quality
- Customer satisfaction

Financial performance
- Profit
- Sales
- Market share
- Market value

Reversed causality

Contingency variables:
Internal context – size, sector, technology, employees, culture
External context – competition, economic, social, legal

SOURCE Based on Paauwe, 2004

been dealt with. Finally, there is the significant effect of international activities on HRM, which is considered in the last section of the chapter.

The contribution of HRM in the public sector

An analysis of the contribution of HRM in the public sector has to be made against the background of a definition of the public sector and descriptions of the considerations affecting the sector and its main characteristics. These are dealt with in the first three parts of this section. The role and the contribution of HRM in the sector are examined in the next two parts of the section.

Definition of the public sector

The public sector was first defined by Smith (1776: 1220) as:

> those public institutions and those public works, which though they may be in the highest degree advantageous to a great society, are, however, of such a nature that the profit could never repay the expense to any individual, or small number of individuals, and, therefore, it cannot be expected that any individual, or small number of individuals, should erect or maintain.

Today, the public sector can be defined as containing those organizations and activities that exist to provide services for the state, the community and individual citizens. Public sector organizations at national or local level execute political policy decisions but senior or specialized members of such institutions will provide advice to politicians on the factors affecting political policies and on their implementation. Public sector organizations are concerned with revenues and expenditures but do not exist to create profits. They are, in effect, owned by the public and not, as is the case in private sector businesses, by shareholders.

Considerations affecting the public sector

The considerations affecting public sector organizations, as noted by Vere (2005: 5–6) are:

- the pressure for smaller government;
- better delivery;
- improved efficiency;
- cost reduction; and
- release resources to the front line.

Characteristics of the public sector

The main characteristics of the public sector are:

- *Public scrutiny.* As Bach and Kessler (2007: 470–71) noted: 'The degree of public scrutiny and the amount of direct and indirect intervention has no direct equivalent in the private sector.'

- *Range of stakeholders.* Truss (2008: 1073) commented that: 'public organizations have a much broader range of stakeholders than their private sector counterparts. Compared with the more limited number of stable goals that exist for private sector firms, these bring a multiplicity of objectives and priorities. This creates a complex and qualitatively different working environment for public managers'.

- *Governance.* Top managers in the public sector are very much subject to the will and sometimes the foibles of their masters – the politicians. As Parry *et al* (2005: 590) noted: 'Management of human resources in the public sector is subject to direct and indirect political intervention brought about by the tripartite nature of the relationship among employer, employee and government. Historically, public sector employment has been influenced by the desire of the government to be a "model employer".'

- *Funding uncertainties.* Funding uncertainties and funding constraints are endemic to public services as exemplified by government imposed cuts.

The HR function in the public sector

Vere and Butler (2007: *viii*) stated that: 'Public sector organizations are under continual pressure to provide better services with fewer resources at a time of increasing expectations from stakeholders, customers and tax payers.' Truss (2008: 1071–72) observed that there has been 'increasing pressure from government on organizations to emulate private sector managerial practices, including performance management, customer orientation, and a heightened strategic focus'. She pointed out that: 'Since, in the public sector, salaries can amount to up to 80 per cent of organizational costs, the domain of human resource management (HRM) has received renewed attention under these reforms.' She also argued that: 'Historically, compared with other more powerful groups vying for resources, the HR function in the public sector has lacked credibility and been regarded as peripheral and relatively powerless' (*ibid*: 1072–73).

Challenges to the HR function in the public sector

HR in the public sector is involved in the same transactional activities such as recruitment, training and pay administration as in other sectors. But it is much more concerned with industrial relations than in the majority of private sector firms and it is particularly involved in ensuring that the organization sets an example in people management in such areas as equal opportunity, diversity and employee wellbeing. The CIPD (2010b: 7) highlighted particular areas of performance management in the public sector that need to be improved to support more effective service delivery, namely: managing absence, managing stress, managing conflict.

What HR can contribute in the public sector

Apart from providing efficient and effective transactional HR services, HR in the public sector can make the following key contributions:

- Enable an integrated strategic approach to HRM to be adopted that responds to the challenges presented by multiple stakeholders, governance issues and funding uncertainties and ensures that the organization has the skilled and engaged workforce it needs and that a cooperative climate of employee relations is maintained.

- Meet the exacting demands of good practice in the fields of equal opportunity, equal pay, diversity management and employee wellbeing.

- Contribute to the management of constant and often unpredictable change.

The contribution of HRM in the voluntary sector

The voluntary sector, sometimes called the third sector, consists of organizations such as charities whose purpose is to help people, provide services or promote causes. The larger charities, especially international ones, are often referred to as 'non-government organizations' (NGOs). Voluntary organizations function on a 'not-for-profit' basis and their income is obtained from voluntary contributions, gifts, earnings from the services they provide to the public or to government and local government organizations on a contractual basis, and funding from the state or local government. They are typically governed by unelected boards of trustees.

The sector is large, complex and fragmented. According to Sargeant (2005: 7): 'One of the oldest surviving charities in England is Weeks' charity, an organization originally set up in the fifteen century to provide faggots (bundles of sticks) for burning heretics.' Cunningham (2010: 344) recorded that 608,000 people are employed in the voluntary sector and 21.4 million people in the UK volunteer at least once a year. The voluntary sector contributes £21 billion to the economy.

Voluntary sector issues

On the basis of their research, Birdi *et al* (2007) noted that the performance of voluntary organizations is closely related to the knowledge and skills of their employees. The human factor is indeed an important issue, as discussed below.

Managing people with particular values and beliefs

In many charities a large proportion of employees are professionally quali-fied and 'knowledge workers' – individuals who may be averse to bureau-cratic HR policies. The writer observed on the basis of his extensive experience in the voluntary sector that employees, especially those con-cerned with service delivery, were often highly committed but that the high commitment had its downside:

> The very high levels of commitment mean that individuals are reluctant to change or recognize any priorities other than their own. The organization is perceived as an unnecessary distraction, and this can make the life of a personnel director who is trying to establish a consistent approach to personnel manage-ment practices very difficult. (Armstrong, 1992: 30)

Hudson (1999: 16) observed that:

> Managing third-sector (ie voluntary) organizations is subtly different from managing in the private or public sectors. Managers who have transferred from either the public or the private sector quickly discover that there is something intrinsically different in making things happen in a not-for-profit context. It is difficult to spot the relevant differences and distinguish them from the superfi-cial ones. The symbols of informal dress, cramped offices and seemingly endless meetings hide more deep-seated differences in people's values and beliefs. Yet it is these values and beliefs that are at the root of the differences.

Kendall (2003: 215) wrote of voluntary sector organizations: 'These organiza-tions are awkward customers. They cannot be steered by fiat or finance to the extent that state entities or for-profit organizations can.'

Governance issues

As noted by Brewster and Lee (2006a: 135):

> Governance problems in the NGOs vary considerably and depend on the type of organization that is being considered. However, a crucial distinctive element in the nature of governance in NGOs is that it remains the ultimate responsibil-ity of part-time volunteers, usually meeting no more than four or six times a year in the form of a trustee board or committee of management.

Funding and regulatory pressures

Cunningham (2008: 1034–35) pointed out that:

> HR practitioners will operate across a spectrum of 'high' and 'low' road employment strategies in an effort to coordinate organizational responses to diverse and contradictory external funding and regulatory constraints while at the same time attempting to exercise degrees of strategic freedom from the funding bodies.

The role of HR in the voluntary sector

Parry *et al* (2005: 591) commented that in the voluntary sector 'people management had traditionally taken a back seat to the management of fundraising activities and service delivery'. Sargeant (2005) observed that HRM specialist skills at board level in non-profit organizations are often under-represented or non-existent, dwarfed by the more urgent priorities associated strategically with the demands of resource attraction (fundraising and marketing) and resource allocation (service provision, campaigning and education).

Research conducted by Brewster and Lee (2006a) in NGOs found that HR issues were frequently overlooked in favour of campaigning programmes, with HR specialists – where they existed – rarely represented at senior levels. As Brewster and Lee (2006b: 44) commented, 'The success of NGOs hinges on their people – but HR is neglected in the sector.' They also found that HR usually had no place on trustee boards and pointed out that the HRM function is often characterized as:

- a supporting rather than a leading function when viewed in terms of its contribution towards mission achievement;
- an administrative function that is predominately reactive to the decisions of others, not proactive in its own right;
- being emasculated by comparison with staff and budget resource allocated to other functions (ie service delivery, income generation, etc);
- lacking in participation in the identification and selection process associated with the appointment of the most senior staff and trustees;
- uninvolved in corporate strategy.

However, research by Birdi *et al* (2007) established that non-profit organizations did appear to be better than private or public sector organizations in the range of individual learning opportunities offered to, and taken up by, their employees.

What HR can contribute in the voluntary sector

The four core needs for charities that can be addressed by HR and L&D are effective management, enhancing performance, staff development, and governance, with board-level leadership development being an urgent priority. As in the public sector, the function can provide efficient and effective transactional HR services but beyond this the role of HR in the voluntary sector is not easy. Ideally, it should be there to ensure that a strategic approach to managing and developing people is adopted that will meet the needs of both the charity and those it employs. But this can be difficult if the function is not represented at the highest level (which is often the case) and if in practice HR strategies for a large part of the workforce and for volunteers are evolved elsewhere, if they exist at all.

The contribution of HRM in SMEs

SMEs are defined as companies with up to 250 employees. In the private sector they are usually founded by entrepreneurs and often remain family owned as they grow. They may be more proactive and innovative than larger firms and more prepared to take risks.

Clearly they vary widely, as does the approach to HR they adopt. However, people management activities tend to be informal, at least in the early stages of development. SMEs are generally regarded as providing a friendlier and less formal working environment than larger firms. As Stavrou-Costea and Manson (2006: 111) pointed out: 'The major strength of SMEs is flexibility in the way they manage human resources.'

Research conducted by Miller (2015) established that there were four stages of SME growth:

Stage 1 Start-up. In this initial stage business people matters tend to be dealt with by the owner, with no formal HR role. Overall the business is characterized by informality, with an emergent strategy, fluid structures and flexible job roles. The owner takes responsibility for hiring, looking for someone who 'fits' with what the company is all about. The people-related requirements tend to be minimal, centred on pay and contracts, with the rate for the job set by the owner.

Stage 2 Emerging enterprise. In a growing business the owner will have to delegate more and people issues become more important. Someone may be appointed to look after HR matters, possibly on a part-time basis for any of the following reasons:

- The business has reached a size where policies and procedures are needed to guide work and create a sense of fairness.
- The owner feels that people issues are taking up too much of their time.
- People management is seen as vital for growth and to achieve the company's vision.
- There is a specific people issue that needs to be addressed; for example tribunal cases, skills shortages, high turnover.

But the owner may decide simply to outsource HR work such as recruitment and seek advice from consultants on any serious people problem.

Stage 3 Consolidation. As the business develops and expands it may appoint a full-time HR specialist who will introduce more sophisticated practices in areas such as recruitment, talent management, or reward or performance management to meet the needs of the business for talented high performing employees.

Stage 4 Established business. Fully established businesses will set up an HR department under a generalist manager with specialized assistants, for example one focusing on recruitment and talent management and another dealing with learning and development.

As a company moves through each change different HR requirements emerge that may lead to the appointment of full- or part-time HR professionals or the extended use of external agencies and consultants.

The research by Miller found that attaching workforce numbers to the stages did not reveal any particular pattern. SMEs tended to develop more formal HR practices and a dedicated HR manager or function at different workforce sizes, depending on the people requirements of the business, the leader's view on people management and the industry the business operates in.

However, Marlow *et al* (2010) established through their research in six growing SMEs that although there was some formalization of HR, many owners still retained informal control over employment matters. They commented that SMEs did not necessarily move from informality to formality and that it could be argued that in a small firm there may be advantages in maintaining an informal approach to people management.

International HRM

International human resource management is the process of managing people across international boundaries by multinational companies. It involves the worldwide management of people, not just the management of expatriates.

Michael Dickman of the Cranfield School of Management, as reported by Welfare (2006), believes that the main contrast between national and global HR practice is the need to see the bigger picture. Sensitivity is necessary in dealing with different cultures and there are complex challenges involved when operating in different business environments. Understanding the local context is key and an international HR person needs to be asking questions such as: What is the business environment here? What is the role of the trade unions? What is the local labour law? Are these people different? Are their motivation patterns different?

Issues in international HRM

There are a number of issues that specifically affect the practice of international as distinct from domestic HRM. These comprise the impact of globalization, the influence of environmental and cultural differences, the extent to which HRM policy and practice should vary in different countries (convergence or divergence), and the approaches used to employ and manage expatriates.

Globalization

Globalization is the process of international economic integration in worldwide markets. It involves the development of single international markets for goods or services accompanied by an accelerated growth in world trade. As Ulrich (1998: 126) put it, globalization requires organizations to:

> move people, ideas, products, and information around the world to meet local needs. They must add new and important ingredients to the mix when making strategy: volatile political situations, contentious global trade issues, fluctuating exchange rates, and unfamiliar cultures. They must be more literate in the ways of international customers, commerce, and competition than ever before. In short, globalization requires that organizations increase their ability to learn and collaborate and to manage diversity, complexity, and ambiguity.

Research conducted over a number of years by Brewster and Sparrow (2007: 48) demonstrated the growth of what they called 'globalized HRM'. They noted that:

whereas international human resource management has tended to operate in the same way as local HRM but on a wider scale, globalized HRM exploits the new technologies available in order to manage all the company's staff around the world in the same way that it has traditionally managed staff in the home country.

Cultural differences

Cultural differences must also be taken into account. Hiltrop (1995) noted the following HR areas that may be affected by national culture:

- decisions of what makes an effective manager;
- giving face-to-face feedback;
- readiness to accept international assignments;
- pay systems and different concepts of social justice;
- approaches to organizational structuring and strategic dynamics.

Convergence and divergence

According to Brewster *et al* (2002) the dilemma facing all multinational corporations is that of achieving a balance between international consistency and local autonomy. They have to decide on the extent to which their HR policies should either 'converge' worldwide to be basically the same in each location, or 'diverge' to be differentiated in response to local requirements.

Global HR policies and practices

The research conducted by Brewster *et al* (2005) identified three processes that constitute global HRM: talent management/employee branding, international assignments management, and managing an international workforce. It was established by the Global HR Research Alliance research (Stiles, 2007) that global HR policies and practices were widespread in the areas of maintaining global performance standards, the use of common evaluation processes, common approaches to rewards, the development of senior managers, the application of competency frameworks and the use of common performance management criteria.

Generally the research has indicated that while global HR policies in such areas as talent management, performance management and reward may be developed, communicated and supported by centres of excellence, often through global networking, a fair degree of freedom has frequently been allowed to local management to adopt their own practices in accordance with the local context as long as in principle these are consistent with global policies.

Managing expatriates

Expatriates are people working overseas on long- or short-term contracts who can be nationals of the parent company or 'third country nationals' (TCNs) – nationals of countries other than the parent company who work abroad in subsidiaries of that company.

The management of expatriates is a major factor determining success or failure in an international business. Expatriates are expensive; they can cost three or four times as much as the employment of the same individual at home. They can be difficult to manage because of the problems associated with adapting to and working in unfamiliar environments, concerns about their development and careers, difficulties encountered when they re-enter their parent company after an overseas assignment, and how they should be remunerated. Policies to address all these issues are required.

Contribution of HR to international management

The contribution HR can make to international management is to:

- formulate strategies for the development and deployment of talented people to meet worldwide needs;
- advise on the cultural factors involved in managing overseas businesses;
- create HR systems based on successful policies and practices in the parent company that can be adapted to fit local contexts and conditions;
- facilitate the transfer of good practice from wherever it may be found in the international organization;
- ensure that expatriates are managed effectively with regard to assignments, terms and conditions, career development and return to the parent company.

KEY LEARNING POINTS

HR contribution
The contribution that HR can make in carrying out these activities is to:

- provide insight;
- contribute to the formulation and implementation of business strategy;
- improve organizational effectiveness;

- facilitate change;
- provide expertise;
- promote social responsibility;
- deliver HR services;
- provide advice;
- develop an employee value proposition;
- promote the wellbeing of employees.

The contribution of L&D

- provide insight;
- improve organizational effectiveness;
- help to ensure that the organization has the skilled, knowledgeable and engaged people it needs;
- promote individual development;
- provide expertise;
- deliver L&D services;
- provide advice;
- facilitate change.

Issues in the public sector

- Public scrutiny.
- Range of stakeholders.
- Governance.
- Funding uncertainties and constraints.
- The bureaucratic role.

What HR can contribute in the public sector

- Enable an integrated strategic approach to HRM.
- Meet the exacting demands of good practice in the fields of equal opportunity, equal pay, diversity management and employee wellbeing.
- Contribute to the management of constant and often unpredictable change.

HR in the voluntary sector

The HRM function in charities is often characterized as:

- a supporting rather than a leading function when viewed in terms of its contribution to mission achievement;

- an administrative function that is predominately reactive to the decisions of others, not proactive in its own right;

- being emasculated by comparison with staff and budget resource allocated to other functions (ie service delivery, income generation, etc);

- lacking in participation in the appointment of the most senior staff and trustees;

- uninvolved in corporate strategy.

HR international issues

International human resource management is the process of managing people across international boundaries by multinational companies. It involves the worldwide management of people not just the management of expatriates.

There are a number of issues that specifically affect the practice of international HRM: the impact of globalization, the influence of environmental and cultural differences, the extent to which HRM policy and practice should vary in different countries (convergence or divergence), and the approaches used to employ and manage expatriates.

The contribution HR can make to international management is to:

- develop strategies for the development and deployment of talented people to meet worldwide needs;

- advise on the cultural factors involved in managing overseas businesses;

- create HR systems based on successful policies and practices in the parent company that can be adapted to fit local contexts and conditions;

- facilitate the transfer of good practice from wherever it may be found in the international organization;

- ensure that expatriates are managed effectively with regard to assignments, terms and conditions, career development and return to the parent company.

References

Alvesson, M (2009) Critical perspectives on strategic HRM, in (eds) J Storey, P M Wright and D Ulrich, *The Routledge Companion to Strategic Human Resource Management*, Abingdon, Routledge, pp 53–68

Anderson, V (2007) *The Value of Learning: From return on investment to return on expectation*, London, CIPD

Armstrong, M (1992) A charitable approach to personnel, *Personnel Management*, December, pp 28–32

Bach, S and Kessler, I (2007) HRM and the new public management, in (eds) P Boxall, J Purcell and P Wright, *Oxford Handbook of Human Resource Management*, Oxford, Oxford University Press, pp 469–88

Birdi, K S, Patterson, M G and Wood, S J (2007) Learning to perform? A comparison of learning practices and organizational performance in profit- and non-profit-making sectors in the UK, *International Journal of Training and Development*, 11 (4), pp 265–81

Boselie, P, Dietz, G and Boon, C (2005) Commonalities and contradictions in HRM and performance research, *Human Resource Management Journal*, 15 (3), pp 67–94

Brewster, C and Lee, S (2006a) HRM in not-for-profit international organizations: different but also alike, in (eds) H H Larsen and W Mayrhofer, *Managing Human Resources in Europe*, London, Routledge, pp 131–48

Brewster, C and Lee, S (2006b) The success of NGOs hinges on their people – but HR is neglected in the sector, *People Management*, 23 March, p 44

Brewster, C, Harris, H and Sparrow, P (2002) *Globalizing HR*, London, CIPD

Brewster, C and Sparrow, P (2007) Advances in technology inspire a fresh approach to international HRM, *People Management*, 8 February, p 48

Brewster, C, Sparrow, P and Harris, H (2005) Towards a new model of globalizing HRM, *The International Journal of Human Resource Management*, 16 (6), pp 949–70

CIPD (2010a) *Next Generation HR*, London, CIPD

CIPD (2010b) *Building Productive Public Sector Workplaces*, London, CIPD

Cunningham, I (2008) A race to the bottom? Exploring variations in employment conditions in the voluntary sector, *Public Administration*, 86 (4), pp 1033–53

Cunningham, I (2010) HRM in the not-for-profit sector, in (eds) I Roper, R Prouska and U Ayudhya, *Critical Issues in Human Resource Management*, London, CIPD, pp 341–55

Guest, D E (1997) Human resource management and performance; a review of the research agenda, *The International Journal of Human Resource Management*, 8 (3), 263–76

Guest, D E, Michie, J, Sheehan, M and Conway, N (2000a) *Employee Relations, HRM and Business Performance: An Analysis of the 1998 Workplace Employee Relations Survey*, London, CIPD

Guest, D E, Michie, J, Sheehan, M, Conway, N and Metochi, M (2000b) *Effective People Management: Initial findings of future of work survey*, London, CIPD

Hiltrop, J M (1995) The changing psychological contract: the human resource challenge of the 1990s, *European Management Journal*, **13** (3), pp 286–94

Hudson, M (1999) *Managing Without Profit*, Harmondsworth, Penguin Books

Kendall, J (2003) *The Voluntary Sector: Comparative prospects in the UK*, London, Routledge

Lawler, E E and Mohrman, S A (2003) What does it take to make it happen? *Human Resource Planning*, **26** (3), pp 15–29

Marlow, S, Taylor, S and Thompson, A (2010) Informality and formality in medium sized companies: contestation and synchronization, *British Journal of Management*, **21**, pp 954–66

Miller, J (2015) *What does the future of HR in an SME look like?* http://www.cipd.co.uk/research/changing-hr-operating-models/hr-models-smes.aspx [accessed 7 January 2016]

Paauwe, J (2004) *HRM and Performance: Achieving long term viability*, Oxford, Oxford University Press

Parry, E, Kelliher, C, Mills, T and Tyson, S (2005) Comparing HRM in the voluntary and public sectors, *Personnel Review*, **34** (5), pp 599–602

Patterson, M G, West, M A, Lawthom, R and Nickell, S (1997) *Impact of People Management Practices on Performance*, London, CIPD

Purcell, J, Kinnie, N, Hutchinson, S, Rayton, B and Swart, J (2003) *Understanding the People and Performance Link: Unlocking the black box*, London, CIPD

Sargeant, A (2005) *Marketing Management for Non-profit Organizations*, 2nd edn, Oxford, Oxford University Press

Smith, A (1776) *The Wealth of Nations*, Letchworth, Dent

Stavrou-Costea, E and Manson, B (2006) HRM in small and medium enterprises: typical but typically ignored, in (eds) H H Larsen and W Mayrhofer, *Managing Human Resources in Europe*, London, Routledge, pp 107–30

Stiles, P (2007) A world of difference? *People Management*, 15 November, pp 36–41

Storey, J, Wright P M and Ulrich D (2009) Introduction, in (eds) J Storey, P M Wright and D Ulrich, *The Routledge Companion to Strategic Human Resource Management*, Abingdon, Routledge, pp 3–13

Thompson, M (2002) *High Performance Work Organization in UK Aerospace*, London, The Society of British Aerospace Companies

Truss, C (2008) Continuity and change: the role of the HR function in the modern public sector, *Public Administration*, **86** (4), pp 1071–88)

Ulrich, D (1998) A new mandate for human resources, *Harvard Business Review*, January–February, pp 124–34

Ulrich, D (1997) *Human Resource Champions*, Boston, MA, Harvard Business School Press

Vere, D (2005) *Fit for Business: Building a strategic HR function in the public sector*, London, CIPD

Vere, D and Butler, L (2007) *Fit for Business: Transforming HR in the public service*, London, CIPD

Welfare, S (2006) A whole world out there: managing global HR, *IRS Employment Review* 862, 29 December, pp 8–12

West, M A, Borrill, C S, Dawson, C, Scully, J, Carter, M, Anclay, S, Patterson, M and Waring, J (2002) The link between the management of employees and patient mortality in acute hospitals, *International Journal of Human Resource Management*, 13 (8), pp 1299–310

QUESTIONS

1 What is the overall contribution the HRM function can make to organizational effectiveness?

2 Research by the CIPD published in *Next Generation HR* (2010) stressed that HR practitioners needed 'insight' to ensure that their function maximized its contribution. What did the CIPD mean by this and how is insight developed?

3 What is the overall contribution the L&D function can make to organizational effectiveness?

4 How does HR make an impact on organizational effectiveness?

5 What are the most significant outcomes of research into the impact of HRM conducted within the last 10 years in the UK? Refer to at least two projects.

6 What is the 'black box'?

7 What is meant when reference is made to 'contingency variables' in research on the link between HR and performance?

8 What is meant by reverse causality?

9 What are the characteristics of the public sector that might affect HRM?

10 What are the challenges to HRM in the public sector?

11 What contribution can HRM make in the public sector?

12 What are the issues in the voluntary sector that are likely to affect HRM?

13   What is the role of HRM in the voluntary sector?

14   What contribution can HRM make in the voluntary sector?

15   What are the characteristics of SMEs (small to medium enterprises)?

16   What are the HR issues in SMEs?

17   What contribution can HRM make in an SME?

18   What is international human resource management?

19   What are the key issues in international organizations that affect HRM?

20   What contribution can HR make to international management?

The professional 08 and ethical approach to HRM and L&D

KEY CONCEPTS AND TERMS

Bounded rationality
Core values
Deontological ethics theory
Discourse ethics theory
Distributive justice
Ethics
Fair-dealing

Morality
Morals
Natural justice
Procedural justice
Social justice
Stakeholder theory
Utilitarianism

LEARNING OUTCOMES

On completing this chapter you should be able to define these key concepts. You should also understand:

- The nature of professionalism in HR
- The role of professional codes of conduct
- The nature of professional ethical standards
- The role and nature of organizational codes of conduct
- The meaning of ethics
- The nature of ethical decisions and judgements
- The ethical concepts of deontology, utilitarianism, stakeholder theory and discourse theory

- The significance of the concepts of equity, justice and fair-dealing
- The ethical dimension of HRM
- HRM ethical guidelines
- Ethical dilemmas and how to deal with them
- What is involved in managing within the expectations of the law

Introduction

The theme of this chapter is that there is an ethical dimension to human re-source management which requires HR specialists to act professionally. To do this they need initially to appreciate what professionalism means in terms of ethical standards, and the role of professional and organizational codes of conduct. To grasp the ethical dimension in their work they need to understand the nature and principles of ethics, the ethical role of HR and the ethical guidelines they can use. They should also know about approaches to resolving ethical dilemmas and the issues relating to managing within the law.

Professionalism in HR

Professionalism in HR as in other fields can be defined generally as the con-duct exhibited by people who are providing advice and services that require expertise and who meet defined or generally accepted standards of behav-iour. Work done by a professional is usually distinguished by its reference to a framework of fundamental concepts that reflect the skilful application of specialized education, training and experience. It is accompanied by a sense of responsibility and an acceptance of recognized standards. HR profes-sionals who are members of the Chartered Institute of Personnel and Development (the CIPD) are required to uphold the standards laid down by that body. More loosely, people can be described as acting 'professionally' when they do their work well and act with integrity.

The CIPD (2015: 12) advocates the following approach to professionalism:

> Rather than focusing on the activities it delivers, the (HR) profession should build
> its credibility and trust by showing its capability and courage to challenge
> accepted practice and offer business leaders a range of critical perspectives on

how to create sustainable organisational value through people, underpinned by a body of fundamental and internationally relevant knowledge rather than anecdotal 'best practice'. We propose that a principles-based approach to HR practice can elevate the definition of 'good' from practice to the systems level, while giving freedom to individual people management professionals to apply their professional judgement in designing bespoke 'good' practices in real-life scenarios.

However, it was argued by Farndale and Brewster (2005: 35, 46) following a worldwide study of professional HR associations including the CIPD, that there was:

> a paradox at the heart of HR professionalism: one of the hallmarks of HRM is the attempt to align it with business strategy and to follow the interest of the owners of the business; one of the hallmarks of a profession is having its own standards that override those of the business. Most of the time, of course, these will be complementary, but the professional associations have no mechanisms in place to deal with the situations where they are not… There is no mandatory requirement for specialists to be certified, and national associations do not apply common standards of entry and performance monitoring to members. Indeed, practitioners are not legally required to be members of these professional bodies.

Codes of professional conduct

Codes of professional conduct define the ethical standards that members of a profession should adhere to. The CIPD Code of Professional Conduct (2008) states, inter alia, that:

> CIPD members are expected to exercise relevant competence in accordance with the Institute's professional standards and qualifications. In the public interest and in the pursuit of its objects, the Chartered Institute of Personnel and Development is committed to the highest possible standards of professional conduct and competency. To this end members are required to exercise integrity, honesty, diligence and appropriate behaviour in all their business, professional and related personal activities.

The principles set out in the Recruitment and Employment Confederation code of practice (2016) are:

1 Respect for laws.
2 Respect for honesty and transparency.
3 Respect for work relationships.

4 Respect for diversity.

5 Respect for safety.

6 Respect for professional knowledge.

7 Respect for certainty of engagement.

8 Respect for prompt and accurate payment.

9 Respect for ethical international recruitment.

10 Respect for confidentiality and privacy.

The National School of Government (2010) has produced a code of ethics and practice for L&D specialists that includes the following 'issues of responsibility':

1 You should demonstrate a commitment to professional and ethical practice.

2 You should ensure that your relationships with learners are not exploitative or a misuse of your role or power.

3 You should behave with sensitivity and professionalism, being an ambassador for your organization and your profession.

4 You should at all times make every effort to avoid bringing the profession into disrepute.

5 You should demonstrate a respect for individuals and their needs.

6 You should deal with trainees fairly, consistently and with impartiality.

7 You should avoid language that could be regarded as offensive, suggestive or discriminatory.

8 You should avoid behaviour that could be regarded as harassment, bullying, exploitation or intimidation.

Professional ethical standards

Professional ethics are the moral principles and values governing professional behaviour, which may or may not be enshrined in codes of practice. The ethical principles of the HR profession require HR professionals to take account of the dignity and rights of employees when making employment decisions.

The ethical frameworks for judging HR practices are the basic rights of people, the principles of social, natural, procedural and distributive justice (these are defined later), the need to achieve fairness, equity and consistency in managing people and the obligation to treat them with respect and consideration. These principles can conflict with organizational objectives to maximize performance, increase shareholder value and achieve more with less. They are also affected by issues such as pressure for more flexibility, work intensification, the use of HR techniques like performance-related pay and performance management, and management practices such as expecting people to meet demanding performance targets and closely monitoring employee performance.

HR specialists are part of management, but there will be occasions when in their professional capacity they should speak out against plans or actions that are not in accord with the ethical standards or values professed by the organization in its code of conduct, if it has one. If not, HR professionals should speak out in accordance with the standards and values they believe in. They should also do their best to develop more exacting ethical standards and influence changes in core values where they feel they are necessary. They must not tolerate injustice or inequality of opportunity. Speaking out is probably the most demanding task that HR people have to do. It is never easy to challenge a course of action proposed or taken by management, which may well be supported by a compelling business case. It takes courage and determination and it is, of course, advisable to be sure that there are good grounds for doing so.

HR professionals may often find themselves in a hard-nosed, entrepreneurial environment, but this does not mean that they can remain unconcerned about developing and helping to uphold organizational core values in line with their own values on the ethical principles, which govern how people should be managed. These may not always be reconcilable, and if this is strongly the case, the HR professional may have to make a choice on whether he or she can remain with the organization.

Professionalism in human resource management means acting in accordance with ethical standards. It means recognizing that there is an important ethical dimension to the work of HR professionals.

Organizational codes of practice (ethics policies)

Organizational codes of practice provide rules, policies and guidelines on what is considered to be appropriate ethical behaviour. The Institute of Business Ethics (2011) has stated that the proportion of larger UK companies with explicit ethics policies has risen over the last 10 years from a third to more than a half. Having an ethics policy is now considered a hallmark of a well-managed company. The ethics policy is normally expressed in a code of business ethics, sometimes called a code of business conduct or principles. As described by the Institute of Business Ethics, an ethics policy:

- details an organization's ethical values, standards and commitments to stakeholders that will underpin the way that it does business;
- confirms leadership commitment to the above;
- describes how this will be achieved and monitored through an ethics programme;
- identifies the main ethical issues faced by the organization/sector;
- identifies other policies and documents that support and detail aspects of the ethics policy – such as a code of ethics, a speak-up policy, a bullying and harassment policy, a gifts and hospitality policy, an environment policy, etc.

Aims

The main aims of an ethics policy, code and programme can be set out under the following headings:

- *Values* – to embed a set of ethical values into the organization's goals and strategies and the way it seeks to do what it does.
- *Ethical behaviour* – to provide guidance and support to staff for making decisions and carrying out their work in a way that is compatible with the organization's ethical values and standards.
- *Corporate culture* – to consolidate and strengthen a culture of integrity and openness so as to facilitate a sustainable business.
- *Risk* – to minimize operational and integrity risks.
- *Reputation* – to enhance trust among stakeholders so as to facilitate business success.
- *Sustainability* – to minimize the organization's negative impacts on and maximize its positive contribution to the social, economic and environmental wellbeing of wider society.

Here are some extracts from company codes to provide a flavour of what they can contain.

CASE STUDY: Santander – respect for people

- Harassment, abuse, intimidation, lack of respect and consideration are unacceptable and will not be permitted or tolerated in the workplace.
- Those employees with personnel reporting to them in the Group's organizational units should ensure, with the resources available to them, that such situations do not occur.
- All employees, especially those with managerial responsibilities, shall uphold at all times and at all professional levels, relations based on respect for the dignity of others, participation, equality and reciprocal cooperation, fostering a respectful and positive working environment.

CASE STUDY: Shell Code of Conduct

- You should base hiring, evaluation, promotion, training, development, discipline, compensation and termination decisions on qualifications, merit, performance and business considerations only.
- Do not discriminate according to race, colour, religion, age, gender, sexual orientation, marital status, disability, ethnic origin or nationality.
- Be aware of local legislation and cultural factors that may impact decisions.

CASE STUDY: Unilever Code of Business Principles – employees

Unilever is committed to diversity in a working environment where there is mutual trust and respect and where everyone feels responsible for the performance and reputation of our company. We will recruit, employ and promote employees on the sole basis of the qualifications and abilities needed for the work to be performed. We are committed to safe and healthy working conditions for all employees. We will not use any form of forced, compulsory or child labour. We are committed to working with employees to develop and enhance each individual's skills and capabilities. We respect the dignity of the individual and the right of employees to freedom of association. We will maintain good communications with employees through company based information and consultation procedures.

Reservations about codes of ethics

Codes of ethics are desirable but they are not the whole answer. As Bagley (2003: 19) commented:

> It would be naive to think that devising a corporate ethics policy is easy or that simply having a policy will solve the ethical dilemmas companies face. Directors, managers, and employees need to exercise their own fundamental sense of right and wrong when making decisions on behalf of the corporation and its shareholders. There is a lesson in the story of the pension fund manager who was asked whether she would invest in a company doing business in a country that permits slavery. 'Do you mean me, personally, or as a fund manager?' she responded. When people feel entitled or compelled to compromise their own ethics to advance the interests of a business or its shareholders, it is an invitation to mischief.

Reservations have also been expressed by Webley and Werner (2008: 405–06). They observed that: 'Though necessary, having an ethics policy based solely on a code of ethics is not sufficient to affect employee attitudes and behaviour.' This conclusion was similar to that reached by Schwartz (2004) whose research established that the mere existence of a code is unlikely to influence employee behaviour and that companies simply possessing a code could be subject to allegations of window-dressing.

Webley and Werner (2008: 406) commented that many of the businesses being singled out by the media as less than ethical have had an explicit ethics policy: 'Enron is but one dramatic example... This is what Kenneth Lay wrote in 2000: "We want to be proud of Enron and know that it enjoys a reputation for fairness and honesty and that it is respected."' They also reported on research by the UK Institute of Business Ethics, conducted in 2005, covering 759 full-time employees. In the survey, one in two respondents said that they had noticed unethical behaviour but had failed to report it. Further analysis revealed that two out of three of the employees who had noticed unethical behaviour worked for organizations that had a code of ethics. Webley and Werner argued that formal ethics programmes can be deficient for any or all of the following reasons:

- they only encompass a narrow set of issues without addressing wider obligations;
- they might be compliance-based, simply consisting of a set of rules that the employees are expected to follow ('do it or else');

- the code is not company-specific reflecting real issues and involving employees in their identification;
- management commitment is absent;
- the code is not sufficiently communicated and embedded in the organization;
- the code is inconsistent with embedded corporate culture, for example pressure on managers to meet targets.

The point about embedding is especially pertinent. As Collier and Estaban (2007: 30) concluded: 'It is not enough to have mission statements and codes of ethics. It is necessary for ethics to be embedded in the cultural fabric of the business as well as in the hearts and minds of its members.' This is where HR professionals come in, as explained later in this chapter. But to play a part in embedding ethics and resolving ethical dilemmas it is necessary to understand the nature of ethics and the ethics dimension, as described below.

The meaning and nature of ethics

Ethics is concerned with making judgements and decisions about what is the right course of action to take. It is defined by the *Compact Oxford Dictionary* (1971) as being 'related to morals, treating of moral questions', and ethical is defined as 'relating to morality'. Morals define what is right rather than wrong. Morality is behaving in a moral or ethical way; possessing moral qualities.

Petrick and Quinn (1997: 42) wrote that ethics 'is the study of individual and collective moral awareness, judgement, character and conduct'. Hamlin *et al* (2001: 98) noted that ethics is concerned with rules or principles that help us to distinguish right and wrong.

Ethics and morality are sometimes treated as being synonymous although Beauchamp and Bowie (1983: 1–2) wrote that they are different: 'Whereas morality is a social institution with a history and code of learnable rules, ethical theory refers to the philosophical study of the nature of ethical principles, decisions and problems.' Clearly, ethics is concerned with matters of right and wrong and therefore involves moral judgements. Even if they are not the same, the two are closely linked. Clegg *et al* (2007: 111) wrote: 'We understand ethics as the social organizing of morality.'

The nature of ethical decisions and judgements

As defined by Jones (1991: 367) an ethical decision is one that is morally acceptable to the larger community. He also noted that:

> A moral issue is present where a person's actions, when freely performed, may harm or benefit others. In other words, the action or decision must have consequences for others and must involve choice, or *volition*, on the part of the actor or decision maker. (*ibid*: 367)

Winstanley and Woodall (2000b: 8–9) pointed out that:

> Ethics is not about taking statements of morality at face value; it is a critical and challenging tool. There are no universally agreed ethical frameworks... Different situations require ethical insight and flexibility to enable us to encapsulate the grounds upon which competing claims can be made. Decisions are judgements usually involving choices between alternatives, but rarely is the choice between right and wrong... Moral disagreement and judgements are concerned with attitudes and feelings, not facts.

Clegg *et al* (2007: 112) emphasized that: 'Ethical decisions emerge out of dilemmas that cannot be managed in advance through rules.' People have to make choices. Foucault (1997: 284) asked: 'What is ethics, if not the practise of freedom?'

Ethics can be described in terms of a framework that is based on ethical theory and makes use of particular concepts such as equity, justice and fair-dealing that guide ethical behaviour. Such frameworks can be used to develop, apply and evaluate HRM policies and practices.

Ethical theories

There are a number of theories explaining the nature of ethics. The main ones are. deontology, utilitarianism, stakeholder theory and discourse theory, described below.

Deontological theory

Deontological (from the Greek for 'what is right') theory maintains that some actions are right or wrong irrespective of their consequences. It is

associated with Kant's notion of the categorical imperative, which contains two main propositions: 1) that one should follow the principle that what is right for one person is right for everyone, and thus you must do to others as you would be done by; and 2) that you should respect all people and treat them as ends in themselves, not as the means to an end.

Utilitarianism

Utilitarianism is the belief that actions are justified when they result in the greatest good to the greatest number. Actions should be judged in terms of their consequences. This is sometimes interpreted as supporting the dubious principle that the end justifies the means.

Stakeholder theory

In accordance with the ideas of Freeman (1984), stakeholder theory states that the organization should be managed on behalf of its stakeholders: its owners, employees, customers, suppliers and local communities. As Legge (1998: 22) described it, management must act in the interests of the stakeholders as their agent, and also act in the interests of the organization to ensure the survival of the firm, safeguarding the long-term stakes of each group.

Discourse ethics

Foucault (1972) defined discourse as the taken for granted ways that people are collectively able to make sense of experience. Discourse ethics as explained by Winstanley and Woodall (2000b: 14) suggests that 'the role of ethicists is not to provide solutions to ethical problems, but rather to provide a practical process and procedure which is both rational and consensus enhancing, through which issues can be debated and discourse can take place'.

Ethical concepts

The ethical concepts of equity, justice and fair-dealing complement the theories described above by providing more specific guidance on ethical behaviour.

Equity

Equity theory, as formulated by Adams (1965), is concerned with the perceptions people have about how they are being treated as compared with others. To be dealt with equitably is to be treated fairly in comparison with another group of people (a reference group) or a relevant other person. Equity involves feelings and perceptions and is always a comparative process. It is not synonymous with equality, which means treating everyone the same, since this would be inequitable if they deserve to be treated differently.

Justice

Justice is the process of treating people in a way that is inherently fair, right and proper. An egalitarian theory of justice was proposed by Rawls (2005), which contained two principles: 1) every person has the right to basic liberty compatible with similar liberty for others; and 2) inequalities should be arranged so that they are expected to be to everyone's advantage and attached to positions open to all.

There are four types of justice: social justice, natural justice, procedural justice and distributive justice, discussed below.

1. Social justice

Social justice means treating people in accordance with the principles of human rights, human dignity and equality. In society, as argued by Rawls (2005: 3): 'Each person possesses an inviolability founded on justice that even the welfare of society as a whole cannot override. For this reason justice denies that the loss of freedom for some is made right by a greater good shared by others.' Rawls thus rejected the principle of utilitarianism and the pernicious belief that the end justifies the means.

In organizations, it means relating to employees generally in ways that recognize their natural rights to be treated justly, equitably and with respect.

Natural justice

According to the principles of natural justice employees should know the standards they are expected to achieve and the rules to which they are expected to conform. They should be given a clear indication of where they are failing or what rules have been broken, and, except in cases of gross misconduct, they should be given a chance to improve before disciplinary action is taken.

3. Procedural justice

Procedural justice (Adams, 1965; Leventhal, 1980) involves treating people in ways that are fair, consistent, transparent and properly consider their views and needs. It is concerned with fair process and the perceptions employees have about the fairness with which company procedures in such areas as performance appraisal, promotion and discipline are being operated. The five factors that affect perceptions of procedural justice as identified by Tyler and Bies (1990) are:

1 Adequate consideration of an employee's viewpoint.

2 Suppression of personal bias towards an employee.

3 Applying criteria consistently across employees.

4 Providing early feedback to employees about the outcome of decisions.

5 Providing employees with an adequate explanation of decisions made.

4. Distributive justice

Distributive justice (Adams, 1965; Leventhal, 1980) means ensuring that people are rewarded equitably in comparison with others in the organization and in accordance with their contribution, and that they receive what was promised to them.

Fair-dealing

Fair-dealing occurs when people are treated according to the principles of social, natural, procedural and distributive justice, and when the decisions or policies that affect them are transparent in the sense that they are known, understood, clear and applied consistently.

The ethical dimension of HRM

Legge (1998: 20–21) commented that: 'In very general terms I would suggest that the experience of HRM is more likely (but not necessarily) to be viewed positively if its underlying principles are ethical.' HR professionals have a special responsibility for guarding and promoting core values in the organization on how people should be managed and treated generally. They are particularly concerned with values relating to just and fair treatment. They need to take a deontological stance that emphasizes that some actions are right or wrong irrespective of their consequences and that all people should be respected and treated as ends in themselves, not as the means to an end. This is not easy. Ethical decisions may not be clear-cut. Interests conflict. But it is a necessary part of professionalism in HRM.

An important role for HR professionals is to do whatever they can to embed the consistent application of ethical values in the organization so that they can become values in use rather than simply professed values in a code of practice or values statement. As Winstanley and Woodall (2000a: 7) observed:

> HR professionals have to raise awareness of ethical issues, promote ethical behaviour, disseminate ethical practices widely among line managers, communicate codes of ethical conduct, ensure people learn about what constitutes ethical behaviours, manage compliance and monitor arrangements.

To do all this HR professionals may sometimes have to nag away without appearing to nag. They need the courage to stand up and be counted. They need determination, persuasive skills and the ability to deal with the ethical dilemmas that they and line managers face in as rational a manner as possible. In the field of organizational ethics, HR people can lead by example. They can handle ethical issues in ways that become part of the organization's culture – 'the way we do things around here'.

The difficulties that HR professionals face in doing all this have been described by Guest and King (2004: 421) as follows:

> Much management activity is typically messy and ambiguous. This appears to apply more strongly to people management than to most other activities. By implication, the challenge lies not in removing or resolving the ambiguities in the role but in learning to live with them. To succeed in this requires skills in influencing, negotiating and learning when to compromise. For those with a high tolerance of ambiguity, the role of HR specialist, with its distinctive opportunity to contribute to the management of people in organizations, offers unique challenges; for those only comfortable if they can resolve the ambiguities, the role may become a form of purgatory.

HRM ethical guidelines

The guidelines set out below relate to how employees are treated in general and to the major HRM activities of organization development, recruitment and selection, learning and development, performance management, reward management, employee relations, and employment practices concerning the work environment, employee wellbeing, equal opportunities, managing diversity, handling disciplinary matters and grievances, job security and redundancy.

General guidelines

- Recognize that the strategic goals of the organization should embrace the rights and needs of employees as well as those of the business. This is in line with the comment made by Boxall *et al* (2007: 5) that: 'While HRM does need to support commercial outcomes (often called "the business case"), it also exists to serve organizational needs for social legitimacy.'

- Recognize that employees are entitled to be treated as full human beings with personal needs, hopes and anxieties.

- Do not treat employees simply as means to an end or mere factors of production. This accords with the comment made by Osterby and Coster (1992: 31) that: 'The term "human resources" reduces people to the same category of value as materials, money and technology – all resources, and resources are only valuable to the extent they can be exploited or leveraged into economic value.'

- Relate to employees generally in ways that recognize their natural rights to be treated justly, equitably and with respect.

Organization development

- Agree in advance with clients and individuals the goals, content and risks of an OD programme.

- Make explicit any values or assumptions used in the programme.

- Obtain the maximum involvement of all concerned in the programme so that they understand the processes involved and how they can benefit from them.

- Work with clients to plan and implement change to the benefit of all stakeholders.

- Enable individuals to continue with their development on completing the programme.

- Protect confidentiality.

Recruitment and selection

- Treat candidates with consideration – applications should be acknowledged, candidates should be kept informed without undue delay of decisions made about their application and they should not be kept waiting for the interview.

- Avoid intrusive questioning in interviews.

- Do not put candidates under undue stress in interviews.

- Do not criticize any aspect of the candidate's personality or experience.

- Use relevant selection criteria based on a proper analysis of job requirements.

- Give candidates reasonable opportunity to present their case and to ask questions.

- Avoid jumping to conclusions about candidates on inadequate evidence or as a result of prejudice.

- Give accurate and complete information to candidates about the job, prospects, security and terms and conditions of employment.

- Only use properly validated tests administered by trained testers.

- Do not use discriminating or biased tests.

- Monitor tests for impact and unintended bias.

- Ensure that candidates are not unfairly disadvantaged by testing processes.

- Give candidates feedback on test results unless there are compelling reasons why feedback should not be given.

- Ensure that selection decisions are free of discrimination or bias on the grounds of sex, sexual orientation, race, age or disability.

- Give unsuccessful candidates the reason for the decision if they request it.

Learning and development

- Respect individual rights for dignity, self-esteem, privacy and autonomy.

- Recognize that it is necessary and legitimate to provide individuals with learning opportunities that enable them to gain the knowledge and skills required to perform well in their jobs and develop their potential. But note that individuals should still be allowed autonomy to choose the extent to which they pursue learning and development programmes beyond this basic requirement.

- Accept that while the organization has the right to conduct learning and development activities that enhance performance, individuals also have the right to be provided with opportunities to develop their own knowledge, skills and employability.

- Ensure that people taking part in learning events feel 'psychologically safe' in accordance with the view expressed by Schein (1993: 91) that: 'To make people feel safe in learning, they must have a motive, a sense of direction, and the opportunity to try out new things without the fear of punishment.'

- Avoid manipulating people to accept imposed organizational values.

Performance management

Performance management ethical principles have been defined by Winstanley and Stuart-Smith (1996) as follows:

- *Respect for the individual* – people should be treated as 'ends in themselves' and not merely as 'means to other ends'.

- *Mutual respect* – the parties involved in performance management should respect each other's needs and preoccupations.

- *Procedural fairness* – the procedures incorporated in performance management should be operated fairly in accordance with the principles of procedural justice.

- *Transparency* – people affected by decisions emerging from performance management processes should have the opportunity to scrutinize the basis upon which decisions were made.

Reward management

- Generally apply the principles of procedural and distributive justice.

- Ensure that reward policies and practices are fair, equitable and transparent and that they are applied consistently.

- Reward people according to their contribution.

- Ensure that people know in general the basis upon which rewards are provided and in particular how their own reward package is determined.

- Maintain reasonable and defensible pay differentials.

- Ensure that equal pay is provided for work of equal value.

- Base decisions on performance pay or bonuses on fair and equitable criteria.
- Avoid bonus schemes that encourage undesirable behaviour.

Employee relations

- Deliver the deal.
- Be open to employees' input and responsive to justifiable questions and concerns about employment policies and practices.
- Provide genuine opportunities and channels for employees to express their views and influence decisions on matters that affect them.
- Negotiate in good faith.
- Recognize that the interests of management and employees do not necessarily coincide and develop and implement employee relations policies accordingly.

Employment practices

- Create a healthy, safe and fulfilling work environment.
- Promote the wellbeing of employees by improving the quality of working life provided for them, exercising concern for work–life balance and developing family-friendly policies.
- Provide equal opportunities for all with regard to recruitment and selection, learning and development, talent management, career progression and promotion.
- Manage diversity and inclusion by recognizing the differences between people and ensuring that everyone feels valued and that the talents of all employees will be properly utilized.
- Handle disciplinary matters according to the principles of natural justice.
- Recognize that people may have legitimate grievances and respond to them promptly, fully and sympathetically.
- Preserve job security as far as possible and take alternative action to avoid compulsory redundancies.
- If compulsory redundancy is unavoidable do whatever is possible to alleviate the distress by, for example, helping people to find work.

Ethical dilemmas

'Ethics will be enacted in situations of ambiguity where dilemmas and problems will be dealt with without the comfort of consensus or certitude' (Clegg *et al*, 2007: 109). As Baumann, quoted in Bauman and Tester (2001: 44), remarked: 'Morality concerns choice first of all – it is the predicament human beings encounter when they must make a selection amongst various possibilities.' Derrida (1992) commented that ethical responsibility can exceed rational calculation.

Typical ethical dilemmas, with examples and approaches to dealing with them are examined below.

Ethical dilemma situations

The following is a sample of the sort of HRM situations that may create ethical dilemmas:

- There is tension between the needs of the organization and the needs of individuals, for example when an organization changes working arrangements and prejudices the work–life balance of some but not all employees.
- There is conflicting evidence in a disciplinary case and it is difficult to decide who to believe.
- The pressure to achieve targets creates corner-cutting in achieving results involving contraventions of company rules.
- There are apparently mitigating circumstances in a disciplinary case and the question is whether these justify not taking action.
- An accusation of bullying has been made but it is difficult to ascertain whether this is a clear case of bullying or overreaction on the part of the complainant to the normal pressures of day-to-day work.

Resolving ethical dilemmas

As Adam Smith (1759) wrote in *The Theory of Modern Sentiments* (quoted by Harrison, 2009: 246): 'When ethically perplexed, the question we should always ask is: would a disinterested observer, in full possession of the relevant facts, approve or disapprove of our actions?' This guidance is just as compelling and relevant today.

Woodall and Winstanley (2000: 285) pointed out that 'being ethical is not so much about finding one universal principle to govern all action, but more about knowing how to recognize and mediate between often un-acknowledged differences of view'. By definition, an ethical dilemma is one that will be difficult to resolve. There may be all sorts of issues surrounding the situation, some of which will be unclear or contentious. The extent to which people react or behave rationally may by limited by their capacity to understand the complexities of the situation they are in and affected by their emotional reactions to it (the concept of bounded rationality). Faced with factors such as these resolving an ethical dilemma can be hard going.

There is no 'one right way' to deal with an ethical dilemma, but an approach based on systematic questioning, analysis and diagnosis to get at the facts and establish the issues involved is more likely to produce a reasonably satisfactory outcome than one relying purely on 'gut feeling'. The following checklist – used judiciously and selectively according to the circumstances – can provide a basis for such questioning and analysis:

1 What are the known facts about the situation and is it possible that there are facts or circumstances that have not come to light, and if so what can be done to uncover them?

2 In disciplinary or conduct cases, to what extent does the conduct contravene the organization's code of ethical conduct (if one exists) or any other relevant organizational policy guidelines and rules?

3 Have different versions or interpretations of the facts and circumstances been offered and if so, what steps can be taken to obtain the true and full picture?

4 Is the proposed action in line with both the letter and the spirit of the law?

5 Is the proposed action and any investigations leading to it consistent with the principles of natural, procedural or distributive justice?

6 Will the proposed action benefit the organization and if so how?

7 Is there any risk of the proposed action doing harm to the organization's reputation for fair-dealing?

8 Will the proposed action be harmful to the individual affected or to employees generally in any way and if so how?

9 Do the facts as established and confirmed justify the proposed action?

10 Are there any mitigating circumstances (in disciplinary cases)?

Managing within the expectations of the law

HR professionals must clearly comply with the requirements of employment and health and safety law but they also have the important responsibility of ensuring the compliance of managers and individual employees.

Providing for compliance means that HR should educate and inform managers and team leaders of their legal obligations and how they can best fulfil them. This can be done formally through guidance notes and training but there is a continuing need to provide advice and guidance on specific issues and to help deal with problems that require a deeper knowledge of the law than it would be reasonable to expect managers to possess.

This is an area of management where HR is expected to take the lead. The HR function will be judged on the extent to which it minimizes references to employment tribunals and ensures that legal (and moral) health and safety regulations are applied. However, HR professionals should go beyond simple compliance and also be concerned with seeing that the spirit of the law in such areas as discrimination, equal pay and providing a healthy and safe working environment is upheld.

KEY LEARNING POINTS

Professionalism
Professionalism can be defined as the conduct exhibited by people who are providing advice and services that require expertise and that meet defined or at least generally accepted standards of behaviour.

HR professionals
HR professionals are required to uphold the standards laid down by their professional body but they must also adhere to their own ethical values.

Codes of professional conduct
Codes of professional conduct define the ethical standards that members of the profession should adhere to. Professional ethics are the moral principles and values governing professional behaviour which may or may not be enshrined in codes of practice.

Organizational codes of practice

Organizational codes of practice provide rules and guidelines on what is considered to be appropriate ethical behaviour. Professionalism in HRM means acting in accordance with ethical standards. It means recognizing that there is an important ethical dimension to the work of HR professionals. Codes of ethics are desirable but they are not the whole answer.

Ethics and morality defined

Ethics is defined by the *Compact Oxford Dictionary* (1971) as being 'related to morals, treating of moral questions', and ethical is defined as 'relating to morality'. Morality is defined as 'having moral qualities or endowments' and moral is defined as 'of or pertaining to the distinction between right and wrong' Simplistically, ethics could be described as being about behaviour while morality is about beliefs.

Ethics is concerned with making ethical decisions and judgements. It can be described in terms of an ethical framework that sets out different approaches and can be extended to embrace particular concepts that affect and guide ethical behaviour, namely: equity, justice and fair-dealing). An ethical decision is one that is morally acceptable to the larger community.

Ethical concepts

The ethical concepts of deontology, utilitarianism, stakeholder theory and discourse theory provide frameworks that can be used to evaluate HRM policies and practices.

Fair-dealing

Fair-dealing occurs when people are treated according to the principles of natural, procedural and distributive justice, and when the decisions or policies that affect them are transparent in that they are known, understood, clear and applied consistently.

The role of HR

HR professionals have a special responsibility for guarding and promoting core values in the organization on how people should be managed and treated generally. They are particularly concerned with values relating to just and fair treatment.

An important role for HR professionals is to do whatever they can to embed the consistent application of ethical values in the organization so that they can become values in use rather than simply professed values in a code of practice or values statement.

Ethical guidelines

Ethical guidelines set out how employees are treated in general and cover the major HRM activities of organization development, recruitment and selection, learning and development, performance management, reward management, employee relations, and employment practices concerning the work environment, employee wellbeing, equal opportunities, managing diversity, handling disciplinary matters and grievances, job security and redundancy.

Handling ethical dilemmas

There is no 'one right way' to deal with an ethical dilemma but an approach based on systematic questioning, analysis and diagnosis to get at the facts and establish the issues involved is more likely to produce a reasonably satisfactory outcome than one relying purely on 'gut feeling'. An ethical dilemma is one that will be difficult to resolve. There may be all sorts of issues surrounding the situation, some of which will be unclear or contentious.

Managing within the expectations of the law

HR professionals must clearly comply with the requirements of employment law but they also have the important responsibility of ensuring the compliance of managers and individual employees.

References

Adams, J S (1965) Injustice in social exchange, in (ed) L Berkowitz, *Advances in Experimental Psychology*, New York, Academic Press

Bagley, C E (2003) The ethical leader's decision tree, *Harvard Business Review*, February, pp 18–19

Bauman, Z and Tester, K (2001) *Conversations with Zygmunt Bauman*, Cambridge, Polity Press

Beauchamp, T L and Bowie, N E (1983) *Ethical Theory and Business*, 2nd edn, New Jersey, Prentice Hall

Boxall, P F, Purcell, J and Wright, P (2007) Human resource management; scope, analysis and significance, in (eds) P Boxall, J Purcell and P Wright, *The Oxford Handbook of Human Resource Management*, Oxford, Oxford University Press, pp 1–18

CIPD (2015) *From best to good practice HR: developing principles for the profession*, http://www.cipd.co.uk/hr-resources/research/best-good-practice-hr-developing-principles-profession.aspx [accessed 28 December 2015]

CIPD (2008) *Code of Professional Conduct*, London, CIPD

Clegg, S, Kornberger, M and Rhodes, C (2007) Business ethics as practice, *British Journal of Management*, **18** (2), pp 107–22

Collier, J and Esteban, R (2007) Corporate social responsibility and employee commitment, *Business Ethics: A European Review*, **16** (1), pp 28–52

Derrida, J (1992) Forces of law: the mystical foundation of authority, in (eds) D Cornell, M Rosenfeld and D G Carlson, *Deconstruction and the Possibility of Justice*, London, Routledge, pp 3–68

Farndale, E and Brewster, C (2005) In search of legitimacy: personnel management associations worldwide, *Human Resource Management Journal*, **15** (3), pp 33–48

Foucault, M (1972) *The Archaeology of Knowledge and the Discourse on Language*, New York, Pantheon Books

Foucault, M (1997) *Ethics, Subjectivity and Truth. Essential works of Foucault, 1954–1984*, Rabinow, P (ed) New York, The New Press

Freeman, R E (1984) *Strategic Management: A stakeholder perspective*, Englewood Cliffs, NJ, Prentice Hall

Guest, D E and King, Z (2004) Power, innovation and problem-solving: the personnel managers' three steps to heaven? *Journal of Management Studies*, **41** (3), pp 401–23

Hamlin, B, Keep, J and Ash, K (2001) *Organizational Change and Development: A reflective guide for managers*, London, Financial Times/Pitman

Harrison, R (2009) *Learning and Development*, 5th edn ed, London, CIPD

Institute of Business Ethics (2011) http://www.ibe.org.uk/index.asp?upid=57&msid=11 [accessed 29 January 2011]

Jones, T M (1991) Ethical decision making by individuals in organizations: an issue-contingent model, *Academy of Management Review*, **16** (2), pp 366–95

Legge, K (1998) The morality of HRM, in (eds) C Mabey, D Skinner and T Clark, *Experiencing Human Resource Management*, London, Sage, pp 14–32

Leventhal, G S (1980) What should be done with equity theory? in (eds) G K Gergen, M S Greenberg and R H Willis, *Social Exchange Advances in Theory and Research*, New York, Plenum

National School of Government (2010) *Code of Ethics for Learning and Development Specialists*, NationalSchool.gov.uk/about_us/jobs/associate_working/CodeOEthics.pdf [accessed February 2011]

Osterby, B and Coster, C (1992) Human resource development – a sticky label, *Training and Development*, April, pp 31–32

Petrick, J A and Quinn, J F (1997) *Management Ethics: Integrity at work*, London, Sage

Rawls, J (2005) *A Theory of Justice*, Cambridge, MA, Harvard University Press

Recruitment and Employment Confederation (2016) https://www.rec.uk.com/membership/compliance/code-of-practice [accessed 15 March 2016]

Schein, E (1993) How can organizations learn faster? The challenge of entering the green room, *Sloan Management Review*, 34 (2), pp 85–92

Schwartz, M (2004) Effective corporate codes of practice: perception of code users, *Journal of Business Ethics*, 55 (4), pp 323–43

Tyler, T R and Bies, R J (1990) Beyond formal procedures: the interpersonal context of procedural justice, in (ed) J S Carrol, *Applied Social Psychology and Organizational Settings*, Hillsdale, NJ, Lawrence Erlbaum

Webley, S and Werner, A (2008) Corporate codes of ethics: necessary but not sufficient, *Business Ethics: A European Review*, 17 (4), pp 405–15

Winstanley, D and Stuart-Smith, K (1996) Policing performance: the ethics of performance management, *Personnel Review*, 25 (6), pp 66–84

Winstanley, D and Woodall, J (2000a) Introduction, in (eds) D Winstanley and J Woodall, *Ethical Issues in Contemporary Human Resource Management*, Basingstoke, Macmillan, pp 3–22

Winstanley, D and Woodall, J (2000b) The ethical dimension of human resource management, *Human Resource Management Journal*, 10 (2), pp 5–20

Woodall, J and Winstanley, D (2000) Concluding comments: ethical frameworks for action, in (eds) D Winstanley and J Woodall, *Ethical Issues in Contemporary Human Resource Management*, Basingstoke, Macmillan, pp 3–22

QUESTIONS

1 What is a profession?

2 What is professionalism?

3 What are the main elements of a professional ethos? Name at least three.

4 What is a code of professional conduct?

5 What are the key points made in the CIPD code of professional conduct?

6 What are professional ethics?

7 What is the ethical framework for judging HR practices?

8 What is the purpose of organizational codes of ethics?

9 What reservations can be made about the effectiveness of organizational codes of ethics?

10 What are ethics?

11 What is the nature of ethical judgements?

12 What is the deontological theory of ethics

13 What is the utilitarian theory of ethics?

14 What did Rawls have to say about social justice?

15 What is stakeholder theory?

16 What is procedural justice?

17 What is distributive justice?

18 What is the ethical dimension of HRM?

19 What are commonly accepted general guidelines on HR ethical behaviour? Name at least three.

20 How should ethical dilemmas be dealt with? List at least three approaches.

PART THREE
People management processes

Motivation 09

Introduction

Motivation is the force that energizes, directs and sustains behaviour. High performance is achieved by well-motivated people who are prepared to exercise discretionary effort, ie independently do more than is expected of them. The aims of this chapter are to explore the meaning of motivation, define the two main types of motivation (intrinsic and extrinsic), describe and critically evaluate the main theories of motivation, discuss two related aspects of motivation – its relationship to job satisfaction and money – and outline approaches to motivation strategy.

The meaning of motivation

The term 'motivation' derives from the Latin word for movement (*movere*). A motive is a reason for doing something. Motivation is the strength and direction of behaviour and the factors that influence people to behave in certain ways. People are motivated when they expect that a course of action is likely to lead to the attainment of a goal and a valued reward – one that satisfies their needs and wants. The term 'motivation' can refer variously to the goals that individuals have, the ways in which individuals chose their goals and the ways in which others try to change their behaviour.

Well-motivated people engage in positive discretionary behaviour – they decide to make an effort. Such people may be self-motivated, and as long as this means they are going in the right direction to attain what they are there to achieve, this is the best form of motivation. But additional motivation provided by the work itself, the quality of leadership, and various forms of recognition and reward, builds on self-motivation and helps people to make the best use of their abilities and to perform well.

Types of motivation

There are two types of motivation and a number of theories explaining how it works, as discussed below.

Intrinsic motivation

Intrinsic motivation takes place when individuals feel that their work is important, interesting and challenging and that it provides them with a reasonable degree of autonomy (freedom to act), opportunities to achieve and advance, and scope to use and develop their skills and abilities. It can be described as motivation by the work itself. It is not created by external incentives. Deci and Ryan (1985) suggested that intrinsic motivation is based on the need to be competent and self-determining (that is, to have a choice). Sandel (2012: 122) remarked that: 'When people are engaged in an activity they consider intrinsically worthwhile, offering money may weaken their motivation by "crowding out" their intrinsic interest or commitment.'

Intrinsic motivation can be enhanced by job design. Hackman and Oldham (1974) in their job characteristics model identified the five core characteristics of jobs that result in intrinsic motivation: skill variety, task identity, task significance, autonomy and feedback. Pink (2009) stated that there are three steps that managers can take to improve motivation:

1 *Autonomy* – encourage people to set their own schedule and focus on getting work done, not how it is done.

2 *Mastery* – help people to identify the steps they can take to improve and ask them to identify how they will know they are making progress.

3 *Purpose* – when giving instructions explain the *why* as well as the *how*.

Intrinsic motivation is associated with the concept of employee engagement, as explained in Chapter 11.

Extrinsic motivation

Extrinsic motivation occurs when things are done to or for people in order to motivate them. These include rewards such as incentives, increased pay, praise, or promotion; and punishments such as disciplinary action, withholding pay, or criticism.

Extrinsic motivators can have an immediate and powerful effect, but it will not necessarily last long. The intrinsic motivators, which are concerned with the 'quality of working life' (a phrase and movement that emerged from this concept), are likely to have a deeper and longer-term effect because they are inherent in individuals and the work – and are not imposed from outside in such forms as incentive pay.

Motivation theory, discussed next, explains the ways in which intrinsic and extrinsic motivation take place.

Motivation theory

The three main areas of motivation theory – instrumentality, content and process – are examined below.

Instrumentality theory

Instrumentality theory states in effect that rewards and punishments are the best instruments with which to shape behaviour. It assumes that people will be motivated to work if rewards and penalties are tied directly to their performance; thus the awards are contingent upon effective performance.

This theory provides a rationale for financial incentives such as performance-related pay, albeit a dubious one. Motivation using this approach has been and still is widely adopted.

Content theory

The aim of the content or needs theories produced by Maslow and Herzberg was to identify the factors associated with motivation. The theory focuses on the content of motivation in the shape of needs. Its basis is the belief that an unsatisfied need creates tension and a state of disequilibrium. To restore the balance a goal is identified that will satisfy the need, and a behaviour pathway is selected that will lead to the achievement of the goal and the satisfaction of the need. Behaviour is therefore motivated by unsatisfied needs. A content theory model is shown in Figure 9.1. Content theory, as the term implies, indicates the components of motivation but it does not explain how motivation affects performance – a necessary requirement if the concept is to provide guidance on HR policy and practice. This was the role of expectancy theory, discussed later.

Figure 9.1 The process of motivation according to content theory

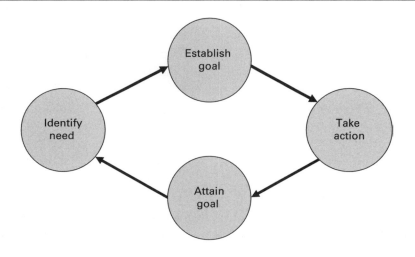

Maslow's hierarchy of needs

The most famous classification of needs is the one formulated by Maslow (1954). He suggested that there are five major need categories that apply to people in general, starting from the fundamental physiological needs and leading through a hierarchy of safety, social and esteem needs to the need for self-fulfilment, the highest need of all. When a lower need is satisfied the next highest becomes dominant and the individual's attention is turned to satisfying this higher need. The need for self-fulfilment, however, can never be satisfied. 'Man is a wanting animal'; only an unsatisfied need can motivate behaviour and the dominant need is the prime motivator of behaviour. Psychological development takes place as people move up the hierarchy of needs, but this is not necessarily a straightforward progression. The lower needs still exist, even if temporarily dormant as motivators, and individuals constantly return to previously satisfied needs.

Maslow's needs hierarchy has an intuitive appeal and has been very popular. But it has not been verified by empirical research such as that conducted by Wahba and Bridwell (1979), and it has been criticized for its apparent rigidity – different people may have different priorities and the underpinning assumption that everyone has the same needs is invalid. It is difficult to accept that needs progress steadily up the hierarchy and Maslow himself expressed doubts about the validity of a strictly ordered hierarchy. However, he did emphasize that the higher-order needs are more significant.

Herzberg's two-factor model

The two-factor model of motivation was developed by Herzberg (1966) on the basis of his research. He claimed that there were two factors that affected feelings of satisfaction or dissatisfaction.

Motivating factors or 'satisfiers' relate to the job content and consist of the need for achievement, the interest of the work, responsibility and opportunities for advancement. These needs are the intrinsic motivators. He summed this up in the phrase 'motivation by the work itself'.

Hygiene factors relate to the job context, including such things as pay and working conditions. 'Hygiene' is used in the medical use of the term, meaning preventative and environmental. In themselves hygiene factors neither satisfy nor motivate; they serve primarily to prevent job dissatisfaction while having little effect on positive job attitudes. Pay is not a satisfier but if it is inadequate or inequitable it can cause dissatisfaction. However, its provision does not provide lasting satisfaction.

Herzberg's two-factor theory in effect identifies needs but the research method he used has been attacked on the grounds that the two-factor nature of the theory was an inevitable result of the questioning method used during the research, that wide and unwarranted inferences have been drawn from small and specialized samples, and that there is no evidence to suggest that the satisfiers do improve productivity.

In spite of these objections the Herzberg two-factor theory continues to thrive, partly because it is easy to understand and seems to be based on real-life rather than academic abstractions, and partly because it convincingly emphasizes the positive value of the intrinsic motivating factors and highlights the need to consider both financial and non-financial factors when developing reward systems.

Process theory

In process theory, the emphasis is on the psychological or mental processes and forces that affect motivation, as well as on basic needs. It is also known as cognitive theory because it refers to people's perceptions of their working environment and the ways in which they interpret and understand it. The main process theories are concerned with reinforcement, expectancy, goals, equity, social learning and cognitive evaluation.

Reinforcement theory

This theory states that if people believe that something has worked well for them previously, they will do it again. The assumption is that positive reinforcement of desired behaviour elicits more of the same; punishment of undesired behaviour (negative reinforcement) elicits less of the same.

Reinforcement theory can be criticized for taking an unduly mechanistic view of human nature. It implies that people can be motivated by treating them as machines – by pulling levers. In assuming that the present choices of individuals are based on an understanding of the outcomes of their past choices, reinforcement theory ignores the existing context in which choices are made.

Expectancy theory

Expectancy theory states that motivation is only likely when a clearly perceived and usable relationship exists between performance and outcome, and the outcome is seen as a means of satisfying needs. This explains why extrinsic financial motivation – for example, an incentive or bonus scheme – works only if the link (line of sight) between effort and reward is clear and the value of the reward is worth the effort. It also explains why intrinsic motivation arising from the work itself can be more powerful than extrinsic motivation. Intrinsic motivation outcomes are more under the control of individuals, who can place greater reliance on their past experiences to indicate the extent to which positive and advantageous results are likely to be obtained by their behaviour.

Alongside goal theory (see below), expectancy theory has become the most influential motivation theory, particularly as it affects performance and reward management.

Goal theory

Goal theory as developed by Latham and Locke (1979) following their research states that motivation and performance are higher when individuals are set specific goals, when goals are demanding but accepted, and when there is feedback on performance. Goals must be clearly defined. Participation in goal setting is important as a means of getting agreement to demanding goals. Feedback is vital in maintaining motivation, particularly towards the achievement of even higher goals.

Equity theory

Equity theory, as defined by Adams (1965), is concerned with the perceptions people have about how they are being treated as compared with others. He proposed that employees assess the fairness or otherwise of their rewards (outcomes) in relation to their effort or qualifications (inputs) and that they do this by comparing their own input/output ratio against that of other individuals. If the input/output ratio is perceived to be unfavourable, they will feel that there is reward inequity.

Social learning theory

Social learning theory as formulated by Bandura (1977) combines aspects of both reinforcement and expectancy theory. It recognizes the significance of the basic behavioural concept of reinforcement as a determinant of future behaviour but also emphasizes the importance of internal psychological factors, especially expectancies about the value of goals and the individual's ability to reach them.

Cognitive evaluation theory

Cognitive evaluation theory contends that the use of extrinsic rewards may destroy the intrinsic motivation that flows from inherent job interest. It was formulated by Deci and Ryan (1985) who, referring to their research, stated that:

> Rewards, like feedback, when used to convey to people a sense of appreciation for work well done, will tend to be experienced informationally and will

maintain or enhance intrinsic motivation. But when they are used to motivate people, they will be experienced controllingly and will undermine intrinsic motivation.

However, as noted by Gerhart and Rynes (2003: 52): 'The vast majority of research on this theory has been performed in school rather than work settings, often with elementary school-aged children.' That did not stop other commentators assuming that the results were equally significant for working adults.

Flow

The concept of flow was originated by Csíkszentmihályi, who described it as the mental state of someone who is fully focused and immersed in an activity and enjoys doing it. It can be described as fully-focused motivation. According to Csíkszentmihályi, the flow experience is characterized by immediate feedback, feeling that you have the potential to succeed and feeling so engrossed in the experience that other needs become negligible.

Schaffer (2013) proposed seven flow conditions:

1 Knowing what to do.

2 Knowing how to do it.

3 Knowing how well you are doing.

4 Knowing where to go.

5 High perceived challenges.

6 High perceived skills.

7 Freedom from distractions.

The notion of flow usefully encapsulates a number of familiar concepts from the fields of motivation, engagement and job design theory.

Comment on process theories

Process theories are not based on suspect assumptions about the universality of needs, as are content theories. Process theories emphasize the importance of individual decision making on work behaviour. As pointed out by Shields (2007: 85) they 'acknowledge the importance of social and job context as co-determinants of motivational strength while those other than reinforcement theory also highlight the importance of self-efficacy, task or goal clarity and motivational learning'.

A summary of motivation theories is set out in Table 9.1.

Table 9.1 Summary of motivation theories

Category	Theory	Summary of theory	Implications
1. Instrumentality	*Taylorism* Taylor (1911)	If we do one thing it leads to another. People will be motivated to work if rewards and punishments are directly related to their performance.	Basis of crude attempts to motivate people by incentives. Often used as the implied rationale for performance-related pay although this is seldom an effective motivator.
2. Content or needs	*Hierarchy of needs* Maslow (1954)	A hierarchy of needs exists: physiological, safety, social, esteem, self-fulfilment. Needs at a higher level only emerge when a lower need is satisfied.	Focuses attention on the various needs that motivate people and the notion that a satisfied need is no longer a motivator. The concept of a hierarchy has no practical significance.
	Two-factor model Herzberg *et al* (1957), (1966)	Two groups of factors affect job satisfaction: 1) those intrinsic to the work itself; 2) those extrinsic to the job such as pay and working conditions. The factors that affect positive feelings (the motivating factors) are quite different from those that affect negative feelings (the hygiene factors).	The research methodology has been strongly criticized (it does not support the existence of two factors) and the underpinning assumption that everyone has the same needs is invalid. But it has influenced approaches to job design (job enrichment) and it supports the proposition that reward systems should provide for both financial and non-financial rewards.

(Continued)

Table 9.1 Continued

Category	Theory	Summary of theory	Implications
3. Process	*Reinforcement*	As experience is gained in satisfying needs, people perceive that certain actions help to achieve goals while others are unsuccessful. The successful actions are repeated when a similar need arises.	Provides feedback that positively reinforces effective behaviour.
	Expectancy Vroom (1964) Porter and Lawler (1968)	Effort (motivation) depends on the likelihood that rewards will follow effort and that the reward is worthwhile.	The key theory informing approaches to rewards, ie that they must be a link between effort and reward (line of sight), the reward should be achievable and it should be worthwhile.
	Goal Latham and Locke (1979)	Motivation will improve if people have demanding but agreed goals and receive feedback.	Influences performance management and learning and development practices.
	Equity Adams (1965)	People are better motivated if treated equitably, ie treated fairly in comparison with another group of people (a reference group) or a relevant other person.	Need to have equitable reward and employment practices.

Table 9.1 Continued

Category	Theory	Summary of theory	Implications
	Social learning Bandura (1977)	Recognizes the significance of reinforcement as a determinant of future behaviour but also emphasizes the importance of expectancies about the value of goals and the individual's ability to reach them.	The emphasis is on expectancies, individual goals and values and the influence of both person and situational factors as well as reinforcement.
	Cognitive evaluation Deci and Ryan (1985)	The use of extrinsic rewards may destroy the intrinsic motivation that flows from inherent job interest.	Emphasizes the importance of non-financial rewards. The conclusions reached from Deci and Ryan's research have been questioned.
	Flow Csíkszentmihályi (1990)	The mental state of someone who is fully focused and immersed in an activity and enjoys doing it. It can be described as fully-focused motivation.	Encapsulates approaches to motivation such as an emphasis on feedback and setting goals. Also refers to principles of job design and the factors that contribute to high levels of engagement.

Conclusions

All the theories referred to above make some contribution to an under-standing of the processes that affect motivation. Instrumentality theory provides only a simplistic explanation of how motivation works, while needs and content theories are more sophisticated but have their limitations.

However, needs theory still offers an indication of the factors that motivate people and content theory provides useful explanations of how motivation takes place. And while instrumentality and reinforcement theories may be simplistic they still explain some aspects of how rewards affect motivation and performance and they continue to exert influence on the beliefs of some people about the power of incentives to motivate people. Herzberg's research may be flawed but he still contributed to the recognition of the importance of job design.

KEY LEARNING POINTS

The process of motivation
Motivation is goal-directed behaviour. People are motivated when they expect that a course of action is likely to lead to the attainment of a goal and a valued reward – one that satisfies their needs and wants.

Types of motivation
The two basic types are intrinsic and extrinsic motivation.

Motivation theories
There are a number of motivation theories that, in the main, are complementary to one another. The most significant theories are those concerned with expectancy, goal setting, equity and cognitive evaluation, which are classified as process or cognitive theories.

References

Adams, J S (1965) Injustice in social exchange, in (ed) L Berkowitz, *Advances in Experimental Psychology*, New York, Academic Press

Bandura, A (1977) *Social Learning Theory*, Englewood Cliffs, NJ, Prentice-Hall

Csíkszentmihályi, M (1990) *Flow: The psychology of optimal experience*, New York, Harper & Row

Deci, E L and Ryan, R M (1985) *Intrinsic Motivation and Self-determination in Human Behaviour*, New York, Plenum

Gerhart, B and Rynes, S L (2003) *Compensation: Theory, evidence and strategic implications*, Thousand Oaks, CA, Sage

Hackman, J R and Oldham, G R (1974) Motivation through the design of work: test of a theory, *Organizational Behaviour and Human Performance*, **16** (2), pp 250–79

Herzberg, F (1966) *Work and the Nature of Man*, New York, Staple Press

Herzberg, F W, Mausner, B and Snyderman, B (1957) *The Motivation to Work*, New York, Wiley

Latham, G and Locke, E A (1979) Goal setting – a motivational technique that works, *Organizational Dynamics*, Autumn, pp 68–80

Maslow, A (1954) *Motivation and Personality*, New York, Harper & Row

Pink, D H (2009) *Drive: The surprising truth about workplace motivation*, New York, Riverhead Books

Porter, L W and Lawler, E E (1968) *Managerial Attitudes and Performance*, Homewood, IL, Irwin-Dorsey

Sandel, M (2012) *The Moral Limits of Markets: What money cannot buy*, London, Allen Lane

Schaffer, O (2013) *Crafting Fun User Experiences: A method to facilitate flow*, London, Human Factors International

Shields, J (2007) *Managing Employee Performance and Reward*, Port Melbourne, Cambridge University Press

Taylor, F W (1911) *Principles of Scientific Management*, New York, Harper

Vroom, V (1964) *Work and Motivation*, New York, Wiley

Wahba, M A and Bridwell, L G (1979) Maslow reconsidered: a review of research on the need hierarchy theory, in (eds) R M Sters and L W Porter, *Motivation and Work Behaviour*, New York, McGraw-Hill

Commitment 10

KEY CONCEPTS AND TERMS

Commitment   Pluralist
High-commitment model   Psychological contract
Mutuality   Unitarist
Organizational engagement

LEARNING OUTCOMES

On completing this chapter you should be able to define these key concepts. You should also understand:

- The meaning of organizational commitment
- The importance of commitment
- Commitment and engagement
- Problems with the concept of commitment
- The impact of high commitment
- Factors affecting commitment
- Developing a commitment strategy

Introduction

Commitment represents the strength of an individual's identification with, and involvement in, an organization. It refers to attachment and loyalty and is associated with the feelings of individuals about their organization. The three characteristics of commitment identified by Mowday *et al* (1982) are:

1 A strong desire to remain a member of the organization.
2 A strong belief in and acceptance of the values and goals of the organization.
3 A readiness to exert considerable effort on behalf of the organization.

It is a concept that has played an important part in HRM philosophy. As Guest (1987: 503) suggested, HRM policies are designed to 'maximize organizational integration, employee commitment, flexibility and quality of work'. Beer *et al* (1984: 20) identified commitment in their concept of HRM as a key dimension because it 'can result not only in more loyalty and better performance for the organization, but also in self-worth, dignity, psychological involvement, and identity for the individual'.

The importance of commitment

The importance of commitment was highlighted by Walton (1985a). His theme was that improved performance would result if the organization moved away from the traditional control-oriented approach to workforce management, which relies upon establishing order, exercising control and achieving efficiency. He proposed that this approach should be replaced by a commitment strategy that would enable workers:

> to respond best – and most creatively – not when they are tightly controlled by management, placed in narrowly defined jobs, and treated like an unwelcome necessity, but, instead, when they are given broader responsibilities, encouraged to contribute and helped to achieve satisfaction in their work. (*ibid*: 77)

He described the commitment-based approach as follows:

> Jobs are designed to be broader than before, to combine planning and implementation, and to include efforts to upgrade operations, not just to maintain them. Individual responsibilities are expected to change as conditions change, and teams, not individuals, often are the organizational units accountable for

performance. With management hierarchies relatively flat and differences in status minimized, control and lateral coordination depend on shared goals. And expertise rather than formal position determines influence. (*ibid*: 79)

Expressed like this, a commitment strategy sounds idealistic ('the American dream' as Guest, 1990, put it) but it does not appear to be a crude attempt to manipulate people to accept management's values and goals, as some have suggested. In fact, Walton did not describe it as being instrumental in this manner. His prescription was for a broad HRM approach to the ways in which people are treated, jobs are designed and organizations are managed. He believed that the aim should be to develop 'mutuality', a state that exists when management and employees are interdependent and both benefit from this interdependency. The importance of mutuality and its relationship to commitment was spelt out by Walton (1985b: 64) as follows:

> The new HRM model is composed of policies that promote mutuality – mutual goals, mutual influence, mutual respect, mutual rewards, mutual responsibility. The theory is that policies of mutuality will elicit commitment which in turn will yield both better economic performance and greater human development.

It is probably unwise to expect too much from commitment as a means of making a direct and immediate impact on performance. It is not the same as motivation. It is possible to be dissatisfied with a particular feature of a job while retaining a fairly high level of commitment to the organization as a whole. But it is reasonable to believe that strong commitment to work may result in conscientious and self-directed application to do the job, regular attendance, the need for less supervision and a high level of discretionary effort. Commitment to the organization will certainly be related to the intention to stay there.

Commitment and engagement

The notion of commitment as described above appears to be very similar if not identical to that of organizational engagement, which focuses on attachment to, or identification with, the organization as a whole. Are there any differences? It can be argued that commitment is a distinct although closely linked entity. Macey and Schneider (2008: 8–9) observed that:

> Organizational commitment is an important facet of the state of engagement when it is conceptualized as positive attachment to the larger organizational entity and measured as a willingness to exert energy in support of the

organization, to feel pride as an organizational member, and to have personal identification with the organization.

Critical evaluation of the concept of commitment

A number of commentators have raised questions about the concept of commitment. These relate to three main problem areas: the imprecise nature of the term, its unitary frame of reference, and commitment as an inhibitor of flexibility.

1. The imprecise nature of the term

Guest (1987: 513) raised the question of what commitment really means:

> The case for seeking high commitment among employees seems plausible but the burgeoning research on the topic has identified a number of problems. One of these concerns the definition of the concept. The first issue is – commitment to what? Most writers are interested in commitment to the organization, but others have examined career commitment and job commitment. Once the general concept of commitment is utilized, then union commitment, workgroup commitment and family commitment should also be considered. The possibility of multiple and perhaps competing commitments creates a more complex set of issues.

2. Unitary frame of reference

The concept of commitment, especially as put forward by Walton (1985a), can be criticized as being simplistic, even misguided, in adopting a unitary frame of reference that assumes that organizations consist of people with shared interests. It can be argued that an organization is really a coalition of interest groups where political processes are an inevitable part of everyday life.

Legge (1989: 38) also raised this question in her discussion of strong culture as a key requirement of HRM, which she criticized because it implies 'a shared set of managerially sanctioned values... that assumes an identification of employee and employer interests'. As Coopey and Hartley (1991: 21) put it: 'Commitment is not an all-or-nothing affair (though many managers might like it to be) but a question of multiple or competing commitments for the individual.' A pluralist perspective recognizes the legitimacy of different interests and is more realistic.

3. Commitment and flexibility

It was pointed out by Coopey and Hartley (1991: 22) that: 'The problem for a unitarist notion of organizational commitment is that it fosters a conformist approach which not only fails to reflect organizational reality, but can be narrowing and limiting for the organization.' They argued that if employees are expected and encouraged to commit themselves tightly to a single set of values and goals they will not be able to cope with the ambiguities and uncertainties that are endemic in organizational life in times of change. Conformity to 'imposed' values will inhibit creative problem solving, and high commitment to present courses of action will increase both resistance to change and the stress that invariably occurs when change takes place.

Factors affecting commitment

Kochan and Dyer (1993) indicated that the factors affecting the level of commitment in what they called 'mutual commitment firms' were as follows:

1 *Strategic level*: supportive business strategies, top management value commitment and effective voice for HR in strategy making and governance.

2 *Functional (human resource policy) level*: staffing based on employment stabilization, investment in training and development and contingent compensation that reinforces cooperation, participation and contribution.

3 *Workplace level*: selection based on high standards, broad task design and teamwork, employee involvement in problem solving and a climate of cooperation and trust.

The research conducted by Purcell *et al* (2003) identified the following key policy and practice factors that influence levels of commitment:

- received training last year;
- satisfied with career opportunities;
- satisfied with the performance appraisal system;

- think managers are good in people management (leadership);
- find their work challenging;
- think their firm helps them achieve a work–life balance;
- satisfied with communication or company performance.

Developing a commitment strategy

A commitment strategy can be based on the high-commitment model in-corporating policies and practices in areas of HR such as job design, learning and development, career planning, performance management, reward management, participation, communication and employee wellbeing. HR should play a major part in developing a high-commitment organization. The 10 steps that can be taken are:

1 Advise on methods of communicating the values and aims of management and the achievements of the organization so that employees are more likely to identify the organization as one they are proud to work for.

2 Emphasize to management that commitment is a two-way process; employees cannot be expected to be committed to the organization unless management demonstrates that it is committed to them and recognizes their contribution as stakeholders.

3 Impress on management the need to develop a climate of trust by being honest with people, treating them fairly, justly and consistently, keeping its word, and showing willingness to listen to the comments and suggestions made by employees during processes of consultation and participation.

4 Develop a positive psychological contract (the set of reciprocal but unwritten expectations that exist between individual employees and their employers) by treating people as stakeholders, relying on consensus and cooperation rather than control and coercion, and focusing on the provision of opportunities for learning, development and career progression.

5 Advise on the establishment of partnership agreements with trade unions that emphasize unity of purpose, common approaches to working together and the importance of giving employees a voice in matters that concern them.

6 Recommend and take part in the achievement of single status for all employees (often included in a partnership agreement) so that there is no longer an 'us and them' culture.

7 Encourage management to declare a policy of employment security and ensure that steps are taken to avoid involuntary redundancies.

8 Develop performance management processes that provide for the alignment of organizational and individual objectives.

9 Advise on means of increasing employee identification with the company through rewards related to organizational performance (profit sharing or gainsharing) or employee share ownership schemes.

10 Enhance employee job engagement, ie identification of employees with the job they are doing, through job design processes that aim to create higher levels of job satisfaction (job enrichment).

KEY LEARNING POINTS

The meaning of commitment
Commitment refers to attachment and loyalty. It is associated with the feelings of individuals about their organization. The three characteristics of commitment identified by Mowday *et al* (1982) are: a strong desire to remain a member of the organization; a strong belief in and acceptance of the values and goals of the organization; and a readiness to exert considerable effort on behalf of the organization.

The impact of high commitment
Walton (1985a) stated that 'eliciting employee commitment will lead to enhanced performance [and] the evidence shows this belief to be well founded.' The importance of commitment was highlighted by Walton. His theme was that improved performance would result if the organization moved away from the traditional control-oriented approach to workforce management, which relies upon establishing order, exercising control and achieving efficiency. He proposed that this approach should be replaced by a commitment strategy.

Problems with the concept of commitment
There are four main problem areas: 1) the imprecise nature of the term, 2) its unitary frame of reference, 3) commitment as an inhibitor of flexibility, and 4) the extent to which high commitment does in practice result in improved organizational performance.

Engagement and commitment
Organizational engagement and commitment are closely associated. Commitment was included by the Institute for Employment Studies (IES) in

its model as an element of engagement. But commitment is a somewhat wider concept in that it is concerned with both job engagement and organizational engagement.

The factors affecting the level of commitment were identified by Kochan and Dyer (1993) at the strategic, functional (human resource policy) and workplace levels.

HR's role in enhancing commitment

HR should play a major part in developing a high-commitment organization. The steps it can take are:

- Advise on methods of communicating the values and aims of management.

- Emphasize to management that commitment is a two-way process.

- Impress on management the need to develop a climate of trust.

- Develop a positive psychological contract.

- Advise on the establishment of partnership agreements with trade unions.

- Recommend and take part in the achievement of single status for all employees.

- Encourage management to declare a policy of employment security.

- Develop performance management processes.

- Advise on means of increasing employee identification with the company.

- Enhance employee job engagement through job design processes.

References

Beer, M, Spector, B, Lawrence, P, Quinn Mills, D and Walton, R (1984) *Managing Human Assets*, New York, The Free Press

Coopey, J and Hartley, J (1991) Reconsidering the case for organizational commitment, *Human Resource Management Journal*, 1 (3), pp 18–31

Guest, D E (1990) HRM and the American dream, *Journal of Management Studies*, 27 (4), pp 377–97

Guest, D E (1987) Human resource management and industrial relations, *Journal of Management Studies*, 24 (5), pp 503–21

Kochan, T A and Dyer, L (1993) Managing transformational change: the role of human resource professionals, *International Journal of Human Resource Management*, 4 (3), pp 569–90

Legge, K (1989) Human resource management: a critical analysis, in (ed) J Storey, *New Perspectives in Human Resource Management*, London, Routledge, pp 19–40

Macey, W H and Schneider, B (2008) The meaning of employee engagement, *Industrial and Organizational Psychology*, 1, pp 3–30

Mowday, R, Porter, L and Steers, R (1982) *Employee-Organization Linkages: The psychology of commitment, absenteeism and turnover*, London, Academic Press

Purcell, J, Kinnie, K, Hutchinson, R, Rayton, B and Swart, J (2003) *Understanding the People and Performance Link: Unlocking the black box*, London, CIPD

Walton, R E (1985a) From control to commitment in the workplace, *Harvard Business Review*, March–April, pp 77–84

Walton, R E (1985b) Towards a strategy of eliciting employee commitment based on principles of mutuality, in (eds) R E Walton and P R Lawrence, *HRM Trends and Challenges*, Boston, MA, Harvard Business School Press, pp 35–65

Employee engagement

Introduction

Engagement takes place when people are committed to their work and the organization and are motivated to achieve high levels of performance. According to the CIPD (2012: 13):

> Engagement has become for practitioners an umbrella concept for capturing the various means by which employers can elicit additional or discretionary effort from employees – a willingness on the part of staff to work beyond contract. It has become a new management mantra.

The notion that individuals can be 'personally' engaged in their work was first proposed by Kahn (1990) in his seminal article in the *Academy of Management Journal*. He defined employee engagement as 'the harnessing of organization members' selves to their work roles; in engagement, people employ and express themselves physically, cognitively, and emotionally during role performances'.

The meaning of employee engagement

There have been dozens of definitions of employee engagement since the explosion of interest in the concept during the 2000s. Harter *et al* (2002: 269) stated that engagement was 'the individual's involvement and satisfaction with as well as enthusiasm for work'. A later definition was produced by Macey *et al* (2009: 7) who defined engagement as 'an individual's purpose and focused energy, evident to others in the display of personal initiative, adaptability, effort and persistence directed towards organizational goals.'

Job or organizational engagement or both

The term 'engagement' can be used in a specific job-related way to describe what takes place when people are interested in and positive – even excited – about their jobs, exercise discretionary behaviour and are motivated to achieve high levels of performance. Truss *et al* (2006: *ix*) stated that: 'Put simply, engagement means feeling positive about your job.' They went on to explain that: 'The engaged employee is the passionate employee, the employee who is totally immersed in his or her work, energetic, committed and completely dedicated' (*ibid*: 1).

Organizational engagement focuses on attachment to or identification with the organization as a whole. The Conference Board (2006) defined employee engagement as the heightened connection that employees feel for their organization. Robinson *et al* (2004: 9) emphasized the organizational aspect of engagement when they referred to it as 'a positive attitude held by the employee towards the organization and its values'. This definition of organizational engagement resembles the traditional notion of commitment. Perhaps the most illuminating and helpful approach to the definition of engagement is to recognize that it involves both job and organizational engagement, as suggested by Saks (2006) and Balain and Sparrow (2009).

The components of employee engagement

Engagement can be regarded as having three overlapping components: motivation, commitment and organizational citizenship behaviour (OCB). A model of engagement containing these components produced by the Institute for Employment Studies (Armstrong *et al*, 2010) is shown in Figure 11.1. Work or job engagement is also associated with job satisfaction. These components of engagement are considered below.

Figure 11.1 IES model of employee engagement

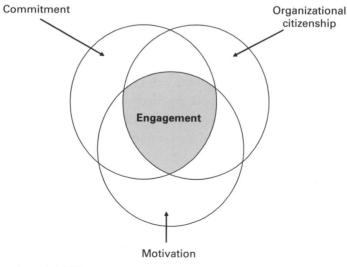

SOURCE Armstrong *et al*, 2010

Engagement and commitment

The concepts of commitment and organizational engagement are closely related, although Robinson *et al* (2004) stated that while engagement contains many of the elements of commitment it is not a perfect match. They suggested that the term 'commitment' does not reflect sufficiently two aspects of engagement – its two-way nature, and the extent to which engaged employees are expected to have positive attitudes about their job. However, Storey (2007: 8) referred to the concept of employee engagement as 'a term that broadly equates with the notion of high commitment'.

Engagement and motivation

The motivation element in engagement is intrinsic. Macey *et al* (2009: 67) commented that: 'When the work itself is meaningful it is also said to have intrinsic motivation. This means that it is not the pay or recognition that yields positive feelings of engagement but the work itself.' They also pointed out that engaged employees 'feel that their jobs are an important part of what they are' (*ibid*: 127).

Engagement and organizational citizenship behaviour

Organizational citizenship behaviour (OCB), as originally defined by Organ (1988), is employee behaviour that goes above and beyond the call of duty and contributes to organizational effectiveness. It is discretionary and not explicitly recognized by the employing organization's formal reward system.

As Little and Little (2006) observed, OCB is an outcome of the attitudes of job satisfaction and organizational commitment. It is similar to the definitions in the engagement literature of being respectful of and helpful to colleagues, and the willingness to go the extra mile or work longer hours, try harder, accomplish more and speak positively about the organization. They noted that this desirable behaviour has been shown to be related more to the work situation than to individual dispositions.

Engagement and job satisfaction

Job satisfaction was defined by Locke (1976: 1304) as 'a pleasurable or positive emotional state resulting from the appraisal of one's job and job experiences'. Engaged employees are likely to be satisfied with their jobs.

Job satisfaction, like commitment, is regarded by Yalabik *et al* (2013: 2805) as an antecedent of work engagement. It has been shown to be related to other attitudes and behaviours. Positively, it is related to organizational commitment, job involvement, organizational citizenship behaviours and mental health. Negatively, it is related to turnover and stress.

Drivers of employee engagement

To be able to do anything about engagement it is necessary to understand the factors that affect it. Crawford *et al* (2014: 59–62) listed the following drivers:

- *Job challenge* – this takes place when the scope of jobs is broad, job responsibility is high and there is a high workload. It enhances engagement because it creates potential for accomplishment and personal growth.

- *Autonomy* – the freedom, independence and discretion allowed to employees in scheduling their work and determining the procedures for carrying it out. It provides a sense of ownership and control over work outcomes.

- *Variety* – jobs which allow individuals to perform many different activities or use many different skills.

- *Feedback* – providing employees with direct and clear information about the effectiveness of their performance.

- *Fit* – the existence of compatibility between an individual and a work environment (eg job, organization, manager, co-workers) which allows individuals to behave in a manner consistent with how they see or want to see themselves.

- *Opportunities for development* – these make work meaningful because they provide pathways for employee growth and fulfilment.

- *Rewards and recognition* – these represent both direct and indirect returns on the personal investment of one's time in acting out a work role.

In addition, the quality of leadership exercised by line managers is an important driver. Research by MacLeod and Clarke (2009) confirmed that line managers played a key part in promoting engagement by providing clarity of purpose, appreciating employees' effort and contribution, treating their people as individuals and ensuring that work is organized efficiently and effectively so that employees feel they are valued, and equipped and supported to do their job.

Macey *et al* (2009: 11) emphasized the work environment and the jobs people do. They noted that:

> Engagement requires a work environment that does not just demand more but promotes information sharing, provides learning opportunities and fosters a balance in people's lives, thereby creating the bases for sustained energy and personal initiative.

Outcomes of engagement

Stairs and Galpin (2010) claimed that high levels of engagement result in the following, although they did not produce convincing evidence to support those claims:

- lower absenteeism and higher employee retention;
- increased employee effort and productivity;
- improved quality and reduced error rates;
- increased sales;
- higher profitability, earnings per share and shareholder returns;
- enhanced customer satisfaction and loyalty;
- faster business growth; and
- higher likelihood of business success.

Alfes *et al* (2010: 2) asserted that engaged employees perform better, are more innovative than others, are more likely to want to stay with their employers, enjoy greater levels of personal wellbeing and perceive their workload to be more sustainable than others. However, Sparrow (2014: 102) warned against over-confident claims that high engagement results in high performance. He suggested that it is possible that being in a well-performing unit makes employees engaged and not the other way round, ie reverse causation.

Enhancing employee engagement

To enhance employee engagement employers have to address issues concerning both aspects of engagement – job and organizational engagement. These are interrelated, and any actions taken to enhance either aspect will be mutually supporting. However, it is useful to consider what can be done specifically in each area, bearing in mind the particular circumstances and needs of the organization.

Enhancing job engagement

Line managers play a key role in enhancing job engagement with the support of organizational initiatives in the areas of job design, learning programmes, including leadership development for line managers, and performance and reward management systems.

Line managers

Research by Lewis *et al* (2012) for the Chartered Institute of Personnel and Development resulted in the production of the competency framework for employee engagement management set out in Table 11.1.

Table 11.1 Employee engagement management competency framework

Competency	Description
Autonomy and empowerment	Trusts and involves employees
Development	Helps to develop employees' careers
Feedback, praise and recognition	Gives positive feedback and praise and rewards good work
Individual interest	Shows concern for employees
Availability	There when needed
Personal manner	Positive approach, leads by example
Ethics	Treats employees fairly
Reviewing and guiding	Helps and advises employees
Clarifying expectations	Sets clear goals and defines what is expected
Managing time and resources	Ensures resources are available to meet workload
Following processes and procedures	Understands and explains processes and procedures

SOURCE Adapted from Lewis *et al*, 2012: 9

Job design

Job design is an important factor in enhancing engagement. Macey *et al* (2009: 69) commented that: 'People come to work for pay but get engaged at work because the work they do is meaningful.' Intrinsic motivation and therefore increased engagement can be generated by the work itself if it provides interest and opportunities for achievement and self-fulfilment. Robertson and Smith (1985) suggested that the aim should be to influence skill variety, task identity, task significance, autonomy and feedback.

Learning and development programmes

Learning and development programmes can ensure that people have the opportunity and are given the encouragement to learn and grow in their roles. This includes the use of policies that focus on role flexibility – giving people the chance to develop their roles by making better and extended use of their talents. It also means going beyond talent management for the favoured few and developing the abilities of the core people on whom the organization depends.

The strategy should also cover career development opportunities and how individuals can be given the guidance, support and encouragement they need if they are to fulfil their potential and achieve a successful career with the organization in tune with their talents and aspirations. Included in the strategy should be the actions required to provide men and women of promise with a sequence of learning activities and experiences that will equip them for whatever level of responsibility they have the ability to reach.

Developing engagement through performance management

Performance management processes can be used to define individual goals and responsibilities, offer feedback on performance and provide the basis for developing skills and planning career development. Although the organization can create a performance management system, its effectiveness will depend on the interest and competence of line managers.

Developing engagement through reward

Reilly and Brown (2008) asserted that appropriate reward practices and processes, both financial and non-financial, and managed in combination (ie a total rewards approach) can help to build and improve employee engagement, and that badly designed or executed rewards can hinder it. Their model, based on research into how reward policies influence performance through engagement, is shown in Figure 11.2.

Figure 11.2 How reward policies influence performance through engagement

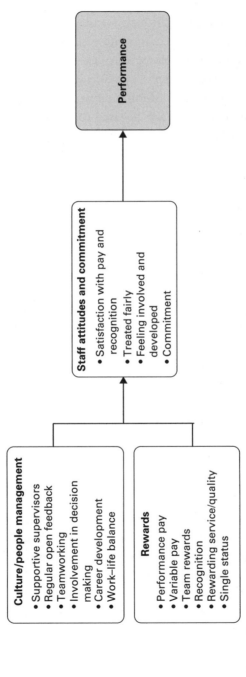

Culture/people management
- Supportive supervisors
- Regular open feedback
- Teamworking
- Involvement in decision making
- Career development
- Work–life balance

Rewards
- Performance pay
- Variable pay
- Team rewards
- Recognition
- Rewarding service/quality
- Single status

Staff attitudes and commitment
- Satisfaction with pay and recognition
- Treated fairly
- Feeling involved and developed
- Commitment

Performance

SOURCE Reilly and Brown, 2008

Organizational engagement

It was suggested by Guest (2009) that engagement can be achieved through effective leadership of a strong, positive culture that ensures the enactment of organizational values; through strong management that supports employees' work and wellbeing; through careful design of systems and jobs to enable employees to contribute through full use of their knowledge and skills; through effective employee voice; and through provision of appropriate resources, tools and information to perform effectively.

Other approaches that can be used to enhance organizational engagement consist of high-involvement management, providing more scope for employee voice, developing 'the big idea' and tackling the work environment.

1. High-involvement management

Organizational engagement can be developed through high-involvement management – a term first used by Lawler (1986) to describe management systems based on commitment and involvement, as opposed to the old bureaucratic model based on control. The underlying hypothesis is that employees will increase their involvement with the company if they are given the opportunity to manage and understand their work. Lawler claimed that high-involvement practices worked well because they acted as a synergy and had a multiplicative effect.

High-involvement management means treating employees as partners in the enterprise, whose interests are respected. It also means providing employees with a voice, as discussed below.

2. Employee voice

Employee voice policies enable employees to communicate their concerns to management effectively. Rees *et al* (2013: 2781) suggested that there is a direct relationship between the effectiveness of such policies and levels of employee engagement. They invoked social exchange theory, which states that employees engage in reciprocal relationships that can develop into trusting, loyal and mutual commitments when certain 'rules of exchange' are observed. Employees will demonstrate positive attitudes and behaviours when they perceive that their employer values them and their contribution. They will demonstrate higher levels of performance if the work environment is one in which employees have a voice in the sense that they can share their concerns, opinions and ideas with their employers.

3. The 'big idea'

A basis for building organizational engagement was established by the longitudinal research in 12 companies conducted by Professor Purcell and his colleagues (Purcell *et al*, 2003: 13). They found that the most successful companies had 'the big idea', ie 'a clear sense of mission underpinned by values and a culture expressing what a firm is and its relationship with its customers and employees'.

4. The work environment

Increasing organizational engagement through the work environment means developing a culture that encourages positive attitudes to work, promoting interest and excitement in the jobs people do, reducing stress and recognizing the importance of social interaction. For example, Lands' End, the clothing company, believes that staff who are enjoying themselves, who are being supported and developed and who feel fulfilled and respected at work, will provide the best service to customers.

CASE STUDY: Land Registry – modernizing the public sector

The Land Registry is a government executive agency employing 300 people. Engaging and enthusing its staff has been a challenge. The Swansea site was an underperforming office within an otherwise successful organization. Today it is one of the most productive Land Registry offices as a result of a planned high-engagement working change process.

The change process focused on the engagement of individuals at all levels. An internal project board masterminded a series of staff surveys and conferences. Senior management team away-days and line management training and coaching to improve performance management and the development of soft skills were all resourced in-house. Training initially focused on senior management team development, so they could understand and lead the changes, building middle management skills so that they could lead change and create an atmosphere in which employees could have confidence in an open appraisal process, and team-building and development. Service to customers was always at the centre of the process. Personal development plans, based on Land Registry's national core competency framework, provided the opportunity to discuss knowledge, skills and 'most importantly' attitudes. The framework bands nine competencies in five main performance areas:

1 *Delivering results*: planning and organizing the workload; and dealing effectively with/managing change.

2 *Effective teamwork*: contributing to the team's performance; and building and leading a team.

3 *Knowledge and experience*: acquiring and applying technical/specialist knowledge.

4 *Providing a quality service*: meeting customers' needs; and anticipating problems and achieving solutions.

5 *Personal effectiveness*: communicating effectively; and showing initiative and determination.

Each of these competencies can be demonstrated at four levels, from entry to senior management level.

Measuring engagement

Engagement surveys provide the basis for the development and implementation of engagement strategies. A review by Vance (2006) of a number of such surveys identified the following common themes:

- pride in employer;
- satisfaction with employer;
- job satisfaction;
- opportunity to perform well at challenging work;
- recognition and positive feedback for one's contributions;
- personal support from one's supervisor;
- effort above and beyond the minimum;
- understanding the link between one's job and the organization's mission;
- prospects for future growth with one's employer;
- intention to stay with one's employer.

The most commonly used measure within the research community has been the one associated with the definition of engagement as 'a positive, fulfilling, work-related state of mind'. This is known as the Utrecht Work Engagement Scale (UWES), which captures feelings of vigour, eg 'At my work, I feel that I am bursting with energy', dedication, eg 'I am enthusiastic about my job', and absorption, eg 'I am immersed in my work.'

The important thing with an engagement survey, as with any form of employee survey, is to ensure that proper use is made of it through the 'triple-A' approach: Analysis, Assessment and Action. It is also important to inform employees of the results of the survey in full and involve them in assessing those results and agreeing actions.

Critical evaluation of the concept of employee engagement

As Guest (2014: 231) remarked: 'One of the attractions of engagement is that it is clearly a good thing. Managers are attracted to the concept because they like the idea of having engaged employees and dislike the prospect of having disengaged employees', but he warned that:

> The risk must be that it [employee engagement] will soon join the pantheon of laudable aspirations with which we can all agree, including happiness, quality, growth and sustainability; goals that most of us would like to pursue, concepts that some people think we can measure, but goals that will remain ultimately elusive in many if not most cases. (*ibid*: 233)

These problems may mean that engagement programmes can be matters of faith. They could involve doing a number of seemingly useful and necessary things but the hoped for results are not guaranteed. However, that does not mean that the attempt should not be made. Guest (2009) defined the benefits of engagement as follows:

> Employee engagement will be manifested in positive attitudes (for example job satisfaction, organizational commitment and identification with the organization) and behaviour (low labour turnover and absence and high citizenship behaviour) on the part of employees; and evidence of perceptions of trust, fairness and a positive exchange within a psychological contract where two-way promises and commitments are fulfilled.

KEY LEARNING POINTS

The meaning of employee engagement

Engagement happens when people are committed to their work and the organization and are motivated to achieve high levels of performance. It has two interrelated aspects: 1) job engagement, which takes place when employees exercise discretionary effort because they find their jobs interesting, challenging and rewarding; and 2) organizational engagement, when they identify with the values and purpose of their organization and believe that it is a great place in which to work and to continue to work.

Components of engagement

The components of engagement are commitment, organizational citizenship behaviour, motivation and job satisfaction.

Theory of engagement

Engagement will have behavioural outcomes leading to what can be described as an 'engaged employee'. A strong theoretical rationale for engagement is provided by social exchange theory.

Drivers of engagement

Macey *et al* (2009) emphasize the importance of the work environment and the jobs people do. Alfes *et al* (2010) established that the main drivers of engagement are meaningful work (the most important), senior management vision and communication, positive perceptions of one's line manager and employee voice – employees having a say in matters that concern them.

Enhancing engagement

Line managers play a key role in enhancing job engagement with the support of organizational initiatives in job design; learning programmes, including leadership development for line managers; and performance and reward management systems.

The approaches that can be used to enhance organizational engagement include high-involvement management, developing 'the big idea' and tackling the work environment.

Measuring engagement

Engagement surveys provide the basis for the development and implementation of engagement strategies.

References

Alfes, K, Truss, C, Soane, E C, Rees, C and Gatenby, M (2010) *Creating an Engaged Workforce*, London, CIPD

Armstrong, M, Brown, D and Reilly, P (2010) *Evidence-based Reward Management*, London, Kogan Page

Balain, S and Sparrow, P (2009) *Engaged to Perform: A new perspective on employee engagement*, Lancaster, Lancaster University Management School

CIPD (2012) *Where has all the trust gone?* http://www.cipd.co.uk/hr-resources/research/where-trust-gone.aspx [accessed 16 March 2016]

Conference Board (2006) *Employee Engagement: A review of current research and its implications*, New York, Conference Board

Crawford, E R, Rich, B L, Buckman, B and Bergeron, J (2014) The antecedents and drivers of employee engagement, in (eds) C Truss, R Delbridge, K Alfes, A Shantz and E Soane, *Employee Engagement in Theory and Practice*, London, Routledge, pp 57–81

Guest, D E (2014) Employee engagement: fashionable fad or long-term fixture? in (eds) C Truss, R Delbridge, K Alfes, A Shantz and E Soane, *Employee Engagement in Theory and Practice*, London, Routledge, pp 221–35

Guest, D E (2009) *Review of Employee Engagement: Notes for a discussion* (unpublished), prepared specifically for the MacLeod and Clarke 2009 review of employee engagement

Harter, J K, Schmidt, F L and Hayes, T L (2002) Business-unit level relationship between employee satisfaction, employee engagement, and business outcomes: a meta-analysis, *Journal of Applied Psychology*, 87, pp 268–79

Kahn, W A (1990) Psychological conditions of personal engagement and disengagement at work, *Academy of Management Journal*, 33 (4), pp 692–724

Lawler, E E (1986) *High Involvement Management*, San Francisco, CA, Jossey-Bass

Lewis, R, Donaldson-Feilder, E and Tharani, T (2012) *Management Competencies for Enhancing Employee Engagement*, London, CIPD

Little, B and Little, P (2006) Employee engagement: conceptual issues, *Journal of Organizational Culture, Communications and Conflict*, 10 (1), pp 111–20

Locke, E A (1976) The nature and causes of job satisfaction, in (ed) M D Dunnette, *Handbook of Industrial and Organizational Psychology*, Chicago, IL, Rand McNally, pp 1297–343

Macey, W H, Schneider, B, Barbera, K M and Young, S A (2009) *Employee Engagement*, Malden, MA, Wiley-Blackwell

MacLeod, D and Clarke, N (2009) *Engaging for Success: Enhancing performance through employee engagement*, London, Department for Business Innovation and Skills

Organ, D W (1988) *Organizational Citizenship Behaviour: The good soldier syndrome*, Lexington, MA, Lexington Books

Purcell, J, Kinnie, K, Hutchinson, N, Rayton, B and Swart, J (2003) *People and Performance: How people management impacts on organizational performance*, London, CIPD

Rees, C, Alfes, K and Gatenby, M (2013) Employee voice and engagement: connections and consequences, *International Journal of Human Resource Management*, **24** (14), pp 2780–98

Reilly, P and Brown, D (2008) Employee engagement: future focus or fashionable fad for reward management? *WorldatWork Journal*, **17** (4), pp 37–49

Robertson, I T and Smith, M (1985) *Motivation and Job Design*, London, IPM

Robinson, D, Perryman, S and Hayday, S (2004) *The Drivers of Employee Engagement*, Brighton, Institute for Employment Studies

Saks, A M (2006) Antecedents and consequences of employee engagement, *Journal of Managerial Psychology*, **21** (6), pp 600–19

Sparrow, P (2014) Strategic HRM and employee engagement, in (eds) C Truss, R Delbridge, K Alfes, A Shantz and E Soane, *Employee Engagement in Theory and Practice*, London, Routledge, pp 99–115

Stairs, M and Galpin, M (2010) Positive engagement: from employee engagement to workplace happiness, in (eds) P A Linley, S Harrington and N Garcea, *The Oxford Handbook of Positive Psychology and Work*, New York, Oxford University Press

Storey, J (2007) What is human resource management? in (ed) J Storey, *Human Resource Management: A critical text,* London, Thompson Learning, pp 3–19

Truss, C, Soane, E, Edwards, C, Wisdom, K, Croll, A and Burnett, J (2006) *Working Life: Employee attitudes and engagement*, London, CIPD

Vance, R J (2006) *Employee Engagement and Commitment: A guide to understanding, measuring and increasing engagement in your organization*, Alexandria, VA, SHRM Foundation

Yalabik, Z Y, Popaitoon, P, Chowne, J A and Rayton, B A (2013) Work engagement as mediator between employee attitudes and outcomes, *International Journal of Human Resource Management*, **24** (14), pp 2799–823

Change management

12

KEY CONCEPTS AND TERMS

Change agent
Change management
Field force analysis
Gamma change
Incremental change

Operational change
Organizational
   transformation
Second order change
Strategic change

LEARNING OUTCOMES

On completing this chapter you should be able to define these key concepts. You should also know about:

- Types of change
- The change process
- Change models
- Reasons for resistance to change
- Overcoming resistance to change
- Implementing change
- Strategies for organizational transformation
- The role of HR in managing change

Introduction

Change management is defined as the process of achieving the smooth implementation of change by planning and introducing it systematically, taking into account the possibility of it being resisted or at least misunderstood. However, Kotter (1996) emphasized the importance of leading change rather than simply managing it.

As described in this chapter, to manage change it is first necessary to understand the types of change and how the process works. It is important to bear in mind that while those wanting change need to be constant about ends, they have to be flexible about means. This requires them to come to an understanding of the various models of change that have been developed and of the factors that create resistance to change and how to minimize such resistance. In the light of an understanding of these models and the phenomenon of resistance to change they will be better equipped to make use of the guidelines for change set out here. The role of HR in leading and managing change is examined in the last section of the chapter.

Types of change

There are three types of change: transformational, strategic and operational.

1. *Transformational change*

Transformational change takes place when there are fundamental and comprehensive changes in structures, processes and behaviours that have a dramatic effect on the ways in which the organization functions.

2. *Strategic change*

Strategic change is concerned with broad, long-term and organization-wide issues involving change. It is about moving to a future state that has been defined generally in terms of strategic vision and scope. It will cover the purpose and mission of the organization, its corporate philosophy on such matters as growth, quality, innovation and values concerning employees and customers, competitive positioning and strategic goals for achieving and maintaining competitive advantage and for product-market development. These goals are supported by policies concerning marketing, sales, manufacturing, product and process development, finance and human resource management.

Strategic change takes place within the context of the external competitive, economic and social environment, and the organization's internal resources, capabilities, culture, structure and systems. Its successful implementation requires thorough analysis and understanding of these factors in the formulation and planning stages.

Strategic change should not be treated simplistically as a linear process of getting from A to B that can be planned and executed as a logical sequence of events. Pettigrew and Whipp (1991: 31) issued the following warning based on their research into competitiveness and managing change in the motor, financial services, insurance and publishing industries.

> The processes by which strategic changes are made seldom move directly through neat, successive stages of analysis, choice and implementation. Given the powerful internal characteristics of the firm it would be unusual if they did not affect the process: more often they transform it. Changes in the firm's environment persistently threaten the course and logic of strategic changes: dilemma abounds... We conclude that one of the defining features of the process, in so far as management action is concerned, is ambiguity; seldom is there an easily isolated logic to strategic change. Instead, that process may derive its motive force from an amalgam of economic, personal and political imperatives. Their interaction through time requires that those responsible for managing that process make continual assessments, repeated choices and multiple adjustments.

3. Operational change

Operational change relates to new systems, procedures, structures or technology which will have an immediate effect on working arrangements within a part of the organization. But their impact on people can be more significant than broader strategic change and they have to be handled just as carefully.

The change process

Conceptually, the change process starts with an awareness of the need for change. An analysis of this situation and the factors that have created it leads to a diagnosis of their distinctive characteristics and an indication of the direction in which action needs to be taken. Possible courses of action can then be identified and evaluated and a choice made of the preferred action. It is then necessary to decide how to get from here to there. Managing change during this transition state is a critical phase in the change process.

It is here that the problems of introducing change emerge and have to be managed. These problems can include resistance to change, low stability, high levels of stress, misdirected energy, conflict and loss of momentum; hence the need to do everything possible to anticipate reactions and likely impediments to the introduction of change.

The installation stage can also be demanding, indeed painful. As described by Pettigrew and Whipp (1991: 27), the implementation of change is an 'iterative, cumulative and reformulation-in-use process'. The issue is how to hold on to the gains. The change process has been described in the various change models set out below.

Change models

The best known change models are those developed by Lewin (1951) and Beckhard (1969). Other important contributions to an understanding of the mechanisms for change have been made by Thurley (1979), Bandura (1986) and Beer *et al* (1990).

Lewin

The basic mechanisms for managing change as set out by Lewin (1951) are:

- *Unfreezing* – altering the present stable equilibrium that supports existing behaviours and attitudes. This process must take account of the inherent threats change presents to people and the need to motivate those affected to attain the natural state of equilibrium by accepting change.

- *Changing* – developing new responses based on new information.

- *Refreezing* – stabilizing the change by introducing the new responses into the personalities of those concerned.

Lewin also suggested the following methodology for analysing change, which he called 'field force analysis':

- Analyse the restraining or driving forces that will affect the transition to the future state – these restraining forces will include the reactions of those who see change as unnecessary or as constituting a threat.

- Assess which of the driving or restraining forces are critical.

- Take steps both to increase the critical driving forces and to decrease the critical restraining forces.

Beckhard

Beckhard (1969) proposed that a change programme should incorporate the following processes:

- Set goals and define the future state or organizational conditions desired after the change.
- Diagnose the present condition in relation to these goals.
- Define the transition state activities and commitments required to meet the future state.
- Develop strategies and action plans for managing this transition in the light of an analysis of the factors likely to affect the introduction of change.

Thurley

Thurley (1979) described the following five approaches to managing change.

1 *Directive* – the imposition of change in crisis situations or when other methods have failed. This is done by the exercise of managerial power without consultation.

2 *Bargained* – this approach recognizes that power is shared between the employer and the employed and change requires negotiation, compromise and agreement before being implemented.

3 *'Hearts and minds'* – an all-embracing thrust to change the attitudes, values and beliefs of the whole workforce. This 'normative' approach (ie one that starts from a definition of what management thinks is right or 'normal') seeks 'commitment' and 'shared vision' but does not necessarily include involvement or participation.

4 *Analytical* – a theoretical approach to the change process using models of change such as those described above. It proceeds sequentially from the analysis and diagnosis of the situation, through the setting of objectives, the design of the change process, the evaluation of the results and, finally, the determination of the objectives for the next stage in the change process. This is the rational and logical approach much favoured by consultants – external and internal. But change seldom proceeds as smoothly as this model would suggest. Emotions, power politics and external pressures mean that the rational approach, although it might be the right way to start, is difficult to sustain.

5 *Action-based* – this recognizes that the way managers behave in practice bears little resemblance to the analytical, theoretical model. The distinction between managerial thought and managerial action blurs in practice to the point of invisibility. What managers think is what they do. Real life therefore often results in a 'ready, aim, fire' approach to change management. This typical approach to change starts with a broad belief that some sort of problem exists, although it may not be well defined. The identification of possible solutions, often on a trial or error basis, leads to a clarification of the nature of the problem and a shared understanding of a possible optimal solution, or at least a framework within which solutions can be discovered.

Bandura

The ways in which people change was described by Bandura (1986). He suggested that people make conscious choices about their behaviours. The information people use to make their choices comes from their environment and their choices are based upon the things that are important to them, the views they have about their own abilities to behave in certain ways and the consequences they think will accrue to whatever behaviour they decide to engage in.

For those concerned in change management, the implications of Bandura's concept of change (which is associated with expectancy theory) are that:

- the tighter the link between a particular behaviour and a particular outcome, the more likely it is that we will engage in that behaviour;
- the more desirable the outcome, the more likely it is that we will engage in behaviour that we believe will lead to it;
- the more confident we are that we can actually assume a new behaviour, the more likely we are to try it.

To change people's behaviour, therefore, we have first to change the environment within which they work; secondly, convince them that the new behaviour is something they can accomplish (training is important); and thirdly, persuade them that it will lead to an outcome that they will value. None of these steps is easy.

Beer, Eisenstat and Spector

Beer (1990: 159) and his colleagues suggested in a seminal *Harvard Business Review* article 'Why change programs don't produce change', that most such programmes are guided by a theory of change that is fundamentally flawed. This theory states that changes in attitudes lead to changes in behaviour. 'According to this model, change is like a conversion experience. Once people get religion, changes in their behaviour will surely follow.' They thought that this theory gets the change process exactly backwards and made the following comment on it.

> In fact, individual behaviour is powerfully shaped by the organizational roles people play. The most effective way to change behaviour, therefore, is to put people into a new organizational context, which imposes new roles, responsibilities and relationships on them. This creates a situation that in a sense 'forces' new attitudes and behaviour on people.

They prescribe six steps to effective change that concentrate on what they call 'task alignment' – reorganizing employee's roles, responsibilities and relationships to solve specific business problems in small units where goals and tasks can be clearly defined. The aim of following the overlapping steps is to build a self-reinforcing cycle of commitment, coordination and competence:

1 Mobilize commitment to change through the joint analysis of problems.

2 Develop a shared vision of how to organize and manage to achieve goals such as competitiveness.

3 Foster consensus for the new vision, competence to enact it, and cohesion to move it along.

4 Spread revitalization to all departments without pushing it from the top – don't force the issue; let each department find its own way to the new organization.

5 Institutionalize revitalization through formal policies, systems and structures.

6 Monitor and adjust strategies in response to problems in the revitalization process.

Resistance to change

People resist change because it is seen as a threat to familiar patterns of behaviour as well as to status and financial rewards. Woodward (1968: 80) made this point clearly:

> When we talk about resistance to change we tend to imply that management is always rational in changing its direction, and that employees are stupid, emotional or irrational in not responding in the way they should. But if an individual is going to be worse off, explicitly or implicitly, when the proposed changes have been made, any resistance is entirely rational in terms of his (*sic*) own best interest. The interests of the organization and the individual do not always coincide.

Hamlin and Davies (2001: 58) commented that 'Any change creates stress and anxiety; this is because as human beings we deal individually with uncertainty in different ways.' However, some people will welcome change as an opportunity. These need to be identified and where feasible they can be used to help in the introduction of change as change agents.

Reasons for resisting change

Specifically, the reasons for resisting change are:

- *The shock of the new* – people are suspicious of anything that they perceive will upset their established routines, methods of working or conditions of employment. They do not want to lose the security of what is familiar to them. They may not believe statements by management that the change is for their benefit as well as that of the organization; sometimes with good reason. They may feel that management has ulterior motives and, sometimes, the louder the protestations of management the less they will be believed.
- *Economic fears* – loss of money, threats to job security.
- *Inconvenience* – the change will make life more difficult.
- *Uncertainty* – change can be worrying because of uncertainty about its likely impact.
- *Symbolic fears* – a small change that may affect some treasured symbol, such as a separate office or a reserved parking space, may symbolize big ones, especially when employees are uncertain about how extensive the programme of change will be.

- *Threat to interpersonal relationships* – anything that disrupts the customary social relationships and standards of the group will be resisted.
- *Threat to status or skill* – the change is perceived as reducing the status of individuals or as de-skilling them.
- *Competence fears* – concern about the ability to cope with new demands or to acquire new skills.

Overcoming resistance to change

Resistance to change can be difficult to overcome even when it is not detrimental to those concerned. But the attempt must be made. The first step is to analyse the potential impact of change by considering how it will affect people in their jobs. The reasons for resisting change set out above can be used as a checklist to establish where there might be problems, generally, with groups or with individuals.

The analysis should indicate what aspects of the proposed change may be supported overall or by specified individuals and which aspects may be resisted. As far as possible, the potentially hostile or negative reactions of people and the reasons for them should be identified. It is necessary to try to understand the likely feelings and fears of those affected so that unnecessary worries can be relieved and ambiguities can be resolved. In making this analysis, the individual introducing the change – the change agent – should recognize that new ideas are likely to be suspect and should make ample provision for the discussion of reactions to proposals to ensure complete understanding of them.

Involvement in the change process gives people the chance to raise and resolve their concerns and make suggestions about the form of the change and how it should be introduced. The aim is to get 'ownership' – a feeling amongst people that the change is something that they are happy to live with because they have been involved in its planning and introduction: it has become *their* change.

A communication strategy to explain the proposed change should be prepared and implemented so that unnecessary fears are allayed. All the available channels should be used but face-to-face communication direct from managers to individuals or through a team briefing system are best.

Implementing change

The problems of implementing change were summed up by Lawler and Mohrman (2003: 24) as follows:

> Most strategies, like most mergers, fail not because of poor thinking, but because of poor implementation. Implementation failures usually involve the failure to acknowledge and build the needed skills and organizational capabilities, to gain support of the workforce, and to support the organizational changes and learning required to behave in new ways. In short, execution failures are often the result of poor human capital management. This opens the door for HR to add important value if it can deliver change strategies, plans, and thinking that aid in the development and execution of business strategy.

Implementing change can indeed be difficult. Research by Carnall (1991) in 93 organizations identified the following explanations for failures to implement change effectively:

- implementation took more time than originally allowed;
- major problems emerged during implementation that had not been identified beforehand;
- coordination of implementation activities was not effective enough;
- competing activities and other crises distracted management from implementing the change decision;
- the capabilities of the employees involved were not sufficient;
- training and instruction to lower level employees were inadequate;
- uncontrollable factors in the external environment had an adverse effect on implementation.

The following suggestions on how to minimize such problems were produced by Nadler and Tushman (1980):

- *Motivate* in order to achieve changes in behaviour by individuals.
- *Manage the transition* by making organizational arrangements designed to assure that control is maintained during and after the transition and by developing and communicating a clear image of the future.
- *Shape the political dynamics of change* so that power centres develop that support the change rather than block it.

- *Build in stability* of structures and processes to serve as anchors for people to hold on to – organizations and individuals can only stand so much uncertainty and turbulence, hence the emphasis by Quinn (1980) on the need for an incremental approach.

The role of change agents

The change process will take place more smoothly with the help of credible internal or external change agents –– people who help to manage change by providing advice and support on its introduction and management. A change agent was defined by Caldwell (2003: 139–40) as 'an internal or external individual or team responsible for initiating, sponsoring, managing and implementing a specific change initiative or complete change programme'. As described by Balogun and Hope-Hailey (2004) the role of the change agent is to lead change. Alfes *et al* (2010) noted that change agents establish what is required, involve people in planning and managing change, advise on how change should be implemented and communicate to people the implications of change.

It is often assumed that only people from outside the organization can take on the change agent role because they are independent and do not 'carry any baggage'. They can be useful but people from within the firm who are respected and credible will do the job well. This is often the role of HR specialists, but the use of line managers adds extra value.

Guidelines for change management

- The achievement of sustainable change requires strong commitment and visionary leadership from the top.
- Understanding is necessary of the culture of the organization and the levers for change that are most likely to be effective in that culture.
- Those concerned with managing change at all levels should have the temperament and leadership skills appropriate to the circumstances of the organization and its change strategies.
- Change is more likely to be successful if there is a 'burning platform' to justify it, ie a powerful and convincing reason for change.
- It is important to build a working environment that is conducive to change. Learning and development programmes can help to do this.
- People support what they help to create. Commitment to change is improved if those affected by change are allowed to participate as fully as

possible in planning and implementing it. The aim should be to get them to 'own' the change as something they want and will be glad to live with.

- The reward system should encourage innovation and recognize success in achieving change.

- Change will always involve failure as well as success. The failures must be expected and learnt from.

- Hard evidence and data on the need for change are the most powerful tools for its achievement, but establishing the need for change is easier than deciding how to satisfy it.

- It is easier to change behaviour by changing processes, structure and systems than to change attitudes or the organizational culture.

- There are always people in organizations who can act as champions of change. They will welcome the challenges and opportunities that change can provide. They are the ones to be chosen as change agents.

- Resistance to change is inevitable if the individuals concerned feel that they are going to be worse off – implicitly or explicitly. The inept management of change will produce that reaction.

- In an age of global competition, technological innovation, turbulence, discontinuity, even chaos, change is inevitable and necessary. The organization must do all it can to explain why change is essential and how it will affect everyone. Moreover, every effort must be made to protect the interests of those affected by change.

Organizational transformation

Organizational transformation was defined by Cummins and Worley (2009: 752) as 'A process of radically altering the organization's strategic direction, including fundamental changes in structures, processes and behaviours.' Transformation involves what is called 'second order' or 'gamma' change involving discontinuous shifts in strategy, structure, processes or culture. Transformation is required when:

- significant changes occur in the competitive, technological, social or legal environment;

- a demanding programme of business model innovation is planned;

- major changes take place to the product lifecycle requiring different product development and marketing strategies;

- major changes take place in top management;
- a financial crisis or large downturn occurs;
- an acquisition or merger takes place.

Transformation strategies

Transformation strategies are usually driven by senior management and line managers with the support of HR rather than OD specialists. The key roles of management as defined by Tushman *et al* (1988) are envisioning, energizing and enabling.

Organizational transformation strategic plans may involve radical changes to the structure, culture and processes of the organization – the way it looks at the world. They may include planning and implementing significant and far-reaching developments in corporate structures and organization-wide processes. The change is neither incremental (bit by bit) nor transactional (concerned solely with systems and procedures). Transactional change, according to Pascale (1990) is merely concerned with the alteration of ways in which the organization does business and people interact with one another on a day-to-day basis, and is only effective when what you want is more of what you've already got. He advocates a discontinuous improvement in capability and this he describes as transformation.

Managing the transition

Strategies need to be developed for managing the transition from where the organization is to where the organization wants to be. This is the critical part of a transformation programme. It is during the transition period of getting from here to there that change takes place. Transition management starts from a definition of the future state and a diagnosis of the present state. It is then necessary to define what has to be done to achieve the transformation. This means deciding on the new processes, systems, procedures, structures, products and markets to be developed. Having defined these, the work can be programmed and the resources required (people, money, equipment and time) can be defined. The strategic plan for managing the transition should include provisions for involving people in the process and for communicating to them about what is happening, why it is happening and how it will affect them. Clearly the aim is to get as many people as possible committed to the change. The eight steps required to transform an organization recommended by Kotter (1995) are:

1 Establish a sense of urgency.

2 Form a powerful guiding coalition.

3 Create a vision.

4 Communicate the vision.

5 Empower others to act on the vision.

6 Plan for and create short-term wins.

7 Consolidate improvements and produce still more.

8 Institutionalize new approaches.

Kotter's prescription has been criticized by Hughes (2010) on the grounds that there is no supporting evidence from research or from successful organizational change arising from the eight steps.

The role of HR in managing change

If HR is concerned – as it should be – in playing a major role in the achievement of continuous improvement in organizational capability and individual performance and in the HR processes that support that improvement, then it will need to be involved in facilitating change. Ulrich (1997) believes that one of the key roles of HR professionals is to lead change by acting as change agents, delivering organizational transformation and facilitating culture change.

HR professionals as change agents

Caldwell (2001) stated that the change agent roles that can be carried out by HR professionals are those of change champions, change adapters, change consultants and change synergists. As such they can be involved in transformational or incremental change. Transformational change is a major change that has a dramatic effect on HR policy and practice across the whole organization, while incremental change consists of gradual adjustments of HR policy and practices.

Keep (2001: 89) listed the following change practitioner competencies:

- Project management – planning and resource allocation.
- Contracting with clients – defining the task, establishing relationships.
- Team-building – defining roles, maintaining good working relationships.
- Analysis and diagnosis – data collection, problem solving, systems thinking.
- Data utilization – qualitative or quantitative data, paper-based review, survey techniques.
- Interpersonal skills – dealing with people, leadership.
- Communication skills – speaking, written presentations/reports, listening.
- Political awareness – sensitivity, influencing.
- Intervention implementation – participation, involvement.
- Monitoring and evaluation – criteria setting and reviewing, measuring effectiveness.
- Technical skills – financial interpretation, psychometrics.
- Process skills – facilitation.
- Insight – reflection, awareness of key issues, critical thinking, intuition.

HR's and L&D's role in supporting and delivering change

HR and L&D can support change by actively influencing values, beliefs and behaviour through HR initiatives, by ensuring that employees have the skills, capabilities and knowledge to manage the stress of transition effectively and function well after the change process. HR also contributes by maintaining good relations with employees generally and with their unions, adopting a consultative approach and paying attention to good communication.

Case study research by Balogun *et al* (2015) found that the HR and OD professionals involved in transformational change programmes tended to focus more than previously on dialogue that recognized the importance of hearing employee voice during the change process. Instead of simply 'selling' a senior management view of change, they showed an appreciation of hearing different views on the experience of change and working with those differences to secure more sustainable change within the workplace. Where the earlier tendency had been for practitioners to focus on structures and processes or workforce planning, knowledge-sharing and design, there was a notable increase in the attention paid to softer techniques involving communication and dialogue and other approaches used to enhance engagement. These softer techniques had augmented rather than superseded the harder elements of structure and design. A second development was HR's contribution to maintaining the momentum of change across the organization, using their energy to keep managers motivated to make the transformation happen.

Leading and facilitating change

Potentially, leading and facilitating change are two of the key roles of HR professionals. In practice, they are probably the most demanding of all HR roles. The processes involved are discussed below.

Leading change

Leading change involves initiating and managing culture change (the process of changing the organization's culture in the shape of its values, norms and beliefs) and the introduction of new structures, systems, working practices and people management processes. The aim is to increase organizational capability (the ability of the organization to perform well) and organizational effectiveness (how well the organization performs).

Ulrich (1997: 7) observed that HR professionals should be 'as explicit about culture change as they are today about the requirements for a successful training program or hiring strategy'. He later emphasized that 'HR should become an agent of continuous transformation, shaping processes and a culture that together improve an organization's capacity for change' Ulrich (1998: 125). Change leadership means:

- identifying where change is required;
- specifying what changes should take place;
- assessing the benefits of the change and what it will cost;
- establishing the consequences of the change;
- assessing any problems the change may create, eg resistance to the change, and any risks involved;
- persuading management and anyone else affected by the change that it is necessary, spelling out the benefits and indicating what will be done to deal with potential problems;
- planning how the change should be implemented, which includes nominating and briefing change agents (people responsible for achieving change), minimizing potential resistance through communication and involvement, and managing risks;

- facilitating the introduction and management of the change;

- ensuring that the change is embedded successfully – 'holding the gains'.

Facilitating change

Facilitating change is the process of making change happen. As Hamlin (2001: 13) commented, one of the major challenges facing HR 'is how to help people through the transitions of change, and how to survive in working conditions that are in a constant state of flux'. Brown and Eisenhardt (1997: 21) noted that managers who were successful in the art of continuous change 'carefully managed the transition between the past and the future. Much like the pit stop in a car race or the baton pass in track, this transition appeared critical'.

The role of HR in facilitating change was described by Vere and Butler (2007: 34) as follows:

- The issue needs to be on the strategic business agenda and managers must see how action will improve business results: that is, there needs to be a sound business case for the initiative. HR managers need to be able to demonstrate the return on the planned investment.

- The change needs to have the active backing of those at the top of the organization, so it is for the HR Director to gain the commitment of the top team and engage them in a practical way in taking the work forward.

- HR needs to engage managers in the design of change from the outset (or, if this is a business-driven change, HR needs to be involved at the outset.

- The programme needs to be framed in the language of the business to have real meaning and achieve 'buy in' for all parties; if there is too much HR jargon, this will be a turn off.

- Project and people management skills are crucial to ensure the programme is well planned and resourced and risks are assessed and managed.

- As in all change programmes the importance of communication is paramount to explain, engage and commit people to the programme.

- In this respect the crucial role that HR can play is to ensure that employees are fully engaged in the design and implementation of the change.

- HR needs to draw on others' experience and learning.

To do all this, Ulrich (1997: 8) pointed out that 'HR professionals need a model of change and the ability to apply the model to a specific situation'. The models as described in this chapter need to be understood and applied as appropriate. The other qualities required are insight – to understand the need for change, courage – to pursue change, and determination – to achieve change.

Leading and facilitating change is hard work. As Alfes *et al* (2010: 111) observed on the basis of their research: 'The role [of HR] is generally constrained and reactive.' They also noted that: 'HR professionals may find their roles circumscribed by expectations of their role, the nature of the change process, capability and capacity' (*ibid*: 125). Ulrich (1997) may emphasize that one of the key roles of HR professionals is to act as change agents, but it is a difficult role to play. Perhaps, as Thornhill *et al* (2000) pointed out, the main contribution HR can make is to generate and support change where a core feature is the development and alignment of HRM practices such as culture management, performance management, learning and development, reward management and employee relations.

CASE STUDY: All change at Zurich

Zurich UK Life has 7,000 employees in the UK. The insurance industry was experiencing significant change. Zurich UK Life had become risk-averse, bureaucratic and slow-moving, struggling to adapt to changing market conditions and customer behaviours. A new CEO was recruited to change the organization. He worked with the HR director and communications director to agree a new set of behaviours they felt were required to deliver the change and create the desired culture. This produced ACE:

Agility – flexibility and adapting appropriately to the circumstances.
Collaboration – addresses the need for the three streams of business, teams and individuals to work together.
Externally focused – focusing on what others need (both customers and staff).

The change programme
Before launching ACE, the CEO got members of the executive to work on their behaviours so that when ACE was launched, their behaviours would be consistent with it. He then did the same through one-to-one interviews with each of the top 80 managers. The aim was to cascade management behaviours that promoted empowerment.

HR recruited champions to develop initiatives to improve employee engagement and to promote ACE. Two initiatives organized by the champions chaired by

HR were a learning week in which people were encouraged to take some responsibility for their own learning, and a 'Changing the habits of a lifetime' week.

Managers were provided with a Navigator Pack to work through the strategy and translation of ACE to individual behaviours with their teams.

Outcomes

The following comments were made by staff about the changes:

'[The biggest change] is red tape going… it's about having a go, and it's that support that you then get when you've had a go.'

'Gathering the information from the customer and actually taking it on board has improved a great deal over the last two or three years.'

'People are much more flexible in their working day… to meet with people and make the decisions that need to me made.'

'The results this year were great… So definitely, you can see that we're doing the right things and that we are getting the right financial results.'

(**SOURCE** Balogun *et al*, 2015)

KEY LEARNING POINTS

Types of change

The main types are: strategic change, operational change and transformational change.

The change process

The change process starts with an awareness of the need for change. An analysis of this situation and the factors that have created it leads to a diagnosis of their distinctive characteristics and an indication of the direction in which action needs to be taken. Possible courses of action can then be identified and evaluated and a choice made of the preferred action.

Change models

The main change models are those produced by Lewin, Beckhard, Thurley, Bandura and Beer *et al*.

Reasons for resistance to change

The shock of the new, economic fears, inconvenience, uncertainty, symbolic fears, threat to interpersonal relationships, threat to status or skills, competence fears.

Overcoming resistance to change

1 Analyse the potential impact of change by considering how it will affect people in their jobs.

2 Identify the potentially hostile or negative reactions of people.

3 Make ample provision for the discussion of reactions to proposals to ensure complete understanding of them.

4 Get 'ownership' – a feeling amongst people that the change is something that they are happy to live with because they have been involved in its planning and introduction.

5 Prepare and implement a communication strategy to explain the proposed change.

Implementing change

Implementation failures usually involve the failure to acknowledge and build the needed skills and organizational capabilities, to gain support of the workforce, and to support the organizational changes and learning required to behave in new ways (Lawler and Mohrman, 2003: 24).

Organizational transformation

Organizational transformation was defined by Cummins and Worley (2009: 752) as 'A process of radically altering the organization's strategic direction, including fundamental changes in structures, processes and behaviours.' Transformation involves 'second order' or 'gamma' change involving discontinuous shifts in strategy, structure, processes or culture.

Transformation is required when: significant changes occur in the external environment; major changes take place to the product lifecycle; there are major changes in top management; a financial crisis or large downturn occurs; or an acquisition or merger takes place.

The role of HR in managing change

HR specialists in their role of change agents will be continuously involved in developing processes for involving people in planning and managing change and communicating information on proposed changes – what they are, why they are taking place and how they will affect employees. Change often requires adopting new behaviours and acquiring different skills, and HR can organize the learning and development programmes required to do this. But it is not an easy role to play.

References

Alfes, K, Truss, C and Gill, J (2010) The HR manager as change agent: evidence from the public sector, *Journal of Change Management*, **10** (1), pp 109–27

Balogun, K and Hope-Hailey, V (2004) *Exploring Strategic Change*, 2nd edn, London, Prentice Hall

Balogun, K, Hope Hailey, V and Cleaver, I (2015) *Landing transformational change: closing the gap between theory and practice*, London, CIPD, http://www.cipd.co.uk/binaries/landing-transformation-change_2015-gap-theory-practice.pdf [accessed 28 January 2016]

Bandura, A (1986) *Social Boundaries of Thought and Action*, Englewood Cliffs, NJ, Prentice Hall

Beckhard, R (1969) *Organization Development: Strategy and models*, Reading, MA, Addison-Wesley

Beer, M, Eisenstat, R and Spector, B (1990) Why change programs don't produce change, *Harvard Business Review*, November–December, pp 158–66

Brown, S L and Eisenhardt, K M (1997) The art of continuous change: linking complexity theory and time-paced evolution in relentlessly shifting organizations, *Administrative Science Quarterly*, **42** (1), pp 1–24

Caldwell, R (2003) Models of change agency: a fourfold classification, *British Journal of Management*, **14** (2), pp 131–42

Caldwell, R (2001) Champions, adapters, consultants and synergists: the new change agents in HRM, *Human Resource Management Journal*, **11** (3), pp 39–52

Carnall, C (1991) *Managing Change*, London, Routledge

Cummins, T G and Worley, C G (2009) *Organization Development and Change*, 9th edn, Mason, OH, South Western

Hamlin, B (2001) A review and synthesis of context and practice, in (eds) B Hamlin, J Keep and K Ash, *Organizational Change and Development: A reflective guide for managers, trainers and developers*, Harlow, Pearson Education, pp 13–38

Hamlin, B and Davies, G (2001) Managers, trainers and developers as change agents, in (eds) B Hamlin, J Keep and K Ash, *Organizational Change and Development: A reflective guide for managers, trainers and developers*, Harlow, Pearson Education, pp 39–60

Hughes, M (2010) *Managing Change*, London, CIPD

Keep, J (2001) The change practitioner: perspectives on role, effectiveness, dilemmas and challenges, in (eds) B Hamlin, J Keep and K Ash, *Organizational Change and Development: A reflective guide for managers, trainers and developers,* Harlow, Pearson Education, pp 13–38

Kotter, J J (1996) *Leading Change*, Boston, MA, Harvard University Press

Kotter, J J (1995) Leading change, *Harvard Business Review*, March–April, pp 59–67

Lawler, E E and Mohrman S A (2003) HR as a strategic partner: what does it take to make it happen? *Human Resource Planning*, **26** (3), pp 15–29

Lewin, K (1951) *Field Theory in Social Science*, New York, Harper & Row

Nadler, D A and Tushman, M L (1980) A congruence model for diagnosing organizational behaviour, in (ed) R H Miles, *Resource Book in Macro-organizational Behaviour*, Santa Monica, CA, Goodyear Publishing

Pascale, R (1990) *Managing on the Edge*, London, Viking

Pettigrew, A and Whipp, R (1991) *Managing Change for Competitive Success*, Oxford, Blackwell

Quinn, J B (1980) Managing strategic change, *Sloane Management Review*, **11** (4/5), pp 3–30

Thornhill, A, Lewis, P, Saunders, M and Millmore, M (2000) *Managing Change: A human resource strategy approach*, Harlow, Financial Times/Prentice Hall

Thurley, K (1979) *Supervision: A reappraisal*, London, Heinemann

Tushman, M, Newman, W and Nadler, D (1988) Executive leadership and organizational evolution: managing incremental and discontinuous change, in (eds) R Kilmann and T Covin, *Corporate Transformation: Revitalizing organizations for a competitive world*, San Francisco, CA, Jossey-Bass

Ulrich, D (1998) A new mandate for human resources, *Harvard Business Review*, January–February, pp 124–34

Ulrich, D (1997) *Human Resource Champions*, Boston, MA, Harvard Business School Press

Vere, D and Butler, L (2007) *Fit for Business: Transforming HR in the public service*, London, CIPD

Woodward, J (1968) Resistance to change, *Management International Review*, **8**, pp 78–93

QUESTIONS

1 What is change management?

2 What is transformational change?

3 What is strategic change?

4 What is operational change?

5 What is the change process?

6 What are the main problems in implementing change?

7 What is Lewin's change model?

8 What is field force analysis?

9   Why do people resist change?

10 How can resistance to change be overcome?

11 What is the role of a change agent?

12 What are the key guidelines for change management? List at least four.

13 What is organizational transformation?

14 How can the 'transition' be managed?

15 What is the role of HR professionals as change agents?

Flexible working 13

KEY CONCEPTS AND TERMS

Core-periphery organization   Numerical flexibility

Flexible firm   Operational flexibility

Functional flexibility   Structural flexibility

Multiskilling   Zero-hours contracts

Multitasking

LEARNING OUTCOMES

On completing this chapter you should be able to define these key concepts. You should also know about:

- Why flexibility is important
- The nature of the flexible firm
- The different types of flexibility
- Zero-hours contracts

Introduction

Organizations have to be able to adjust quickly and smoothly to rapidly changing circumstances. They have to be flexible. This was the case in 1984 when John Atkinson wrote his seminal article 'Manpower strategies for flexible organizations'. He stated that firms:

> have put a premium on achieving a workforce which can respond quickly, easily and cheaply to workforce changes, which may need to contract as smoothly as they expand, in which worked time precisely matches job requirements, in which unit labour costs can be held down.

This applies as much today as it did then.

The aim of flexible working is to satisfy the operational requirements spelt out above and in so doing improve the use of employees' skills and capacities, increase productivity and reduce employment costs. This means reconsidering traditional employment patterns. It could include operational flexibility, multiskilling, flexible hours, or adopting different working arrangements such as job sharing, homeworking and 'hot desking'. All of these can be facilitated by HR by developing policies and practices that support flexibility and by L&D through the provision of learning programmes.

The flexible firm

The flexible firm model was developed by Atkinson (1984) following research by the Institute of Manpower Studies. It makes a distinction between the core and the peripheral workforce and is sometimes called the 'core-peripheral model'. As illustrated in Figure 13.1, the model consists of:

- *The core* which consists of workers who have the security of permanent (ie not fixed-term) contracts, and have skills which are very important to the employer. These employees are to apply their skills across a wide range of tasks. The firm will want to retain these employees even in hard times.

- *The first peripheral group* comprises workers who are employed on contracts which have some degree of permanence (some part-timers could be included in this category), but due to their lower levels of skills they will not have the same level of security as their colleagues in the core. Typically, their work will be characterized by little responsibility and lower pay. These employees can be laid off relatively easily since people with similar skills can be hired quickly if necessary.

- *The second peripheral group* consists of workers who are part-timers or are on temporary contracts. They have little employment security and can be taken on or discharged easily.

- *The external workforce* consists of people who work for another employer or are self-employed. This includes workers in firms to which work has been sub-contracted or outsourced and agency workers.

The flexible firm model is a convenient method of summing-up the ways in which firms can achieve flexibility by using various types of peripheral workers while retaining a core of essential employees. But it cannot fully represent the reality of how firms manage flexibility. This is more likely to be on an ad hoc basis, selecting whatever method of dealing with employment problems is readily available rather than consciously and systematically applying the model to their organization. Hunter and MacInnes (1991) found little evidence of a drive towards the flexible firm in the companies they studied, which were selected on the basis of likely fit with the model. However, the model is a help in understanding how the various forms of operational flexibility as described below can take place.

Figure 13.1 The core-periphery model

External workforce

Second peripheral
workforce

First peripheral
workforce

Core workers

Permanent contracts
Long-term careers

Permanent contracts
Insecure employment

Part-timers
Temporary contracts

Agency and outsourced workers
Self-employed workers

SOURCE Adapted from Atkinson, 1984

Operational flexibility

Operational flexibility refers to flexibility in the ways in which work is carried out. The term is sometimes extended to include financial flexibility. The three main forms of operational flexibility are:

1 *Functional flexibility* so that employees can be redeployed quickly and smoothly between activities and tasks. It may require multiskilling – workers who possess and can apply a number of skills, for example both mechanical and electrical engineering; or multitasking – workers who carry out a number of different tasks in a work team.

2 *Structural flexibility* in a 'flexible firm' where the core of permanent employees is supplemented by a peripheral group of part-time employees, employees on short- or fixed-term contracts or sub-contracted workers.

3 *Numerical flexibility*, which is associated with structural flexibility and means that the number of employees can be quickly and easily increased or decreased in line with even short-term changes in the level of demand for labour.

In addition, there is financial flexibility, which provides for pay levels to reflect the state of supply and demand in the external labour market and also means the use of flexible pay systems that facilitate either functional or numerical flexibility.

Flexible working arrangements

Flexible working arrangements as described below consist of multiskilling, flexible hours and other approaches such as job sharing, hot-desking and homeworking.

Multiskilling

Multiskilling takes place when workers acquire through experience and training a range of different skills they can apply when carrying out different tasks (multitasking). This means that they can be used flexibly, transferring from one task to another as the occasion demands.

A multiskilling strategy will mean providing people with a variety of experience through, for example, moving them between different jobs or tasks (job rotation) and secondments, and by making arrangements for them to acquire new skills through training. It typically includes setting up flexible work teams, the members of which can be deployed on all or many of the team's tasks. A flexible employee resourcing policy can then be established that enables the organization to redeploy people rapidly to meet new demands. This implies abandoning the traditional job description that prescribes the tasks to be carried and replacing it with a role profile that specifies the range of knowledge and skills the role holder needs to possess to achieve the role's objectives.

Flexible hour arrangements

Flexible hour arrangements can be included in a flexibility plan in one or more of the following ways:

- *Flexible daily hours* – these may follow an agreed pattern day by day according to typical or expected workloads.

- *Flexitime systems* – these provide a core period when employees are expected to be at work (for example, between 11 am and 3 pm), while the rest of the working day is 'flexible time', in which employees can choose when they work, subject to achieving total daily, weekly or monthly hours in the region of what the employer expects, and subject to the necessary work being done.

- *Flexible weekly hours* – providing for longer weekly hours to be worked at certain peak periods during the year.

- *Flexible daily and weekly hours* – varying daily or weekly hours or a combination of both to match the input of hours to the required output. Such working times, unlike daily or weekly arrangements, may fluctuate between a minimum and a maximum.

- *Compressed working weeks* – employees work fewer than the five standard days.

- *Annual hours* – scheduling employee hours on the basis of the number of hours to be worked, with provisions for the increase or reduction of hours in any given period, according to the demand for goods or services.

- *Zero-hours contracts* – these have recently become prominent and controversial and are dealt with separately below.

Zero-hours contracts

The CIPD (2015a) defines a zero-hours contract as:

> an agreement between two parties that one may be asked to perform work for another but there is no minimum set contracted hours. The contract will provide what pay the individual will get if he or she does work and will deal with circumstances in which work may be offered and possibly turned down.

The exact nature of zero-hours contracts may differ from organization to organization; for example:

- Individuals on zero-hours contracts may be engaged as employees or workers.
- In some zero-hours contracts the individual will be obliged to accept work if offered, but in others he or she will not.
- The pay arrangements and benefits provided may differ.

They are most suited to situations where work fluctuates unexpectedly so that the employer cannot always guarantee work. They are most common in retail, hospitality and restaurants.

Zero-hours contracts have received a very bad press but the CIPD 2013 survey of 479 zero-hours contract workers found they were as satisfied with their job as the average UK employee, were more likely to be happy with their work–life balance than other workers and were less likely to think they are treated unfairly by their employer. However, the research showed that poor practice does exist. For example, 40 per cent of zero-hours workers report they have had work cancelled at the last minute with no notice from their employer. The CIPD (2015a) believes that, used responsibly, zero-hours contracts can provide flexibility that works for both employers and individuals.

In a later report, the CIPD (2015b: 2) summarized its views on zero-hours contracts as follows:

> Zero-hours contracts have sometimes, it seems, been singled out as an especially unfair form of employment. In our view, this is unjustified. Our research shows that zero-hours contracts appear to work well for many of those on them. But they are not for everybody and that's why zero-hours contract workers need to understand their employment rights as well as how these contracts are likely to work in practice. Zero-hours contracts work best when there's an element of give and take: recognition that flexibility works both ways. A small minority of employers using them don't seem to recognize this, but there are many 'permanent'

jobs where the actions of employers can make them anything but secure. There may be too much emphasis at times on the precise terms of the employment contract with not enough attention given to the spirit in which the employment relationship is conducted.

Other approaches

Job-sharing is an arrangement in which two employees share the work of one full-time position, dividing pay and benefits between them according to the time each works. Job-sharing can mean splitting days or weeks or, less frequently, working alternate weeks. Because it may suit the needs of individuals, job-sharing can reduce employee turnover and absenteeism. There can be greater operational continuity because if one half of the job-sharing team is ill or leaves, the sharer will continue working for at least half the time. Job-sharing also means that a wider employment pool can be tapped for those who cannot work full time but want permanent employment. The disadvantages are the administrative costs involved and the risk of responsibility being divided.

Hot-desking means that individual desks are shared between several people who use them at different times. Those involved do not therefore have a permanent workstation. This is convenient for the organization but not everyone likes it.

Homeworking involves home-based employees who carry out such roles as consultants, analysts, designers or programmers, or they can undertake administrative work. The advantages are flexibility to respond rapidly to fluctuations in demand, reduced overheads and lower employment costs if the homeworkers are self-employed (care, however, has to be taken to ensure that they are regarded as self-employed for Income Tax and National Insurance purposes).

KEY LEARNING POINTS

Flexibility
Organizations have to be able to adjust quickly and smoothly to rapidly changing circumstances. The aim of managing flexibility is to satisfy this requirement and in so doing improve the use of employees' skills and capacities, increase productivity and reduce employment costs.

The flexible firm

The flexible firm model was developed by Atkinson (1984) following research by the Institute of Manpower Studies. It makes a distinction between the core and the peripheral workforce.

Operational flexibility

Operational flexibility refers to flexibility in the ways in which work is carried out. The three main forms of operational flexibility are: functional, structural and numerical flexibility.

Multiskilling

Multiskilling takes place when workers acquire through experience and training a range of different skills they can apply when carrying out different tasks (multitasking).

Flexible hour arrangements

Flexible hour arrangements can be included in a flexibility plan in one or more of the following ways: flexible daily hours, flexitime systems, flexible weekly hours, flexible daily and weekly hours, compressed working weeks, annual hours and zero-hours contracts.

Zero-hours contracts

The CIPD (2015) defines a zero-hours contract as 'an agreement between two parties that one may be asked to perform work for another but there is no minimum set contracted hours.' It believes that, used responsibly, zero-hours contracts can provide flexibility that works for both employers and individuals.

Hot-desking

Hot-desking means that individual desks are shared between several people who use them at different times

Homeworking

Home-based employees can carry out such roles as consultants, analysts, designers or programmers, or they can undertake administrative work.

References

Atkinson, J (1984) Manpower strategies for the flexible organization, *Personnel Management*, August, pp 28–31

CIPD (2015a) Fact sheet: zero-hours contracts, http://www.cipd.co.uk/hr-resources/factsheets/zero-hours-contracts.aspx [accessed 29 October 2015]

CIPD (2015b) Zero-hours and short-hours contracts in the UK, http://www.cipd.co.uk/binaries/zero-hours-and-short-hours-contracts-in-the-uk_2015-employer-employee-perspectives.pdf [accessed 26 December 2015]

CIPD (2013) Zero-hours contracts: myth and reality, http://www.cipd.co.uk/binaries/zero-hours-contracts_2013-myth-reality.pdf [accessed 29 October 2015]

Hunter, L and MacInnes J (1991) *Employers' Labour Use Strategies*, Research Paper No 87, London, Employment Department

Managing diversity and inclusion

14

Introduction

The management of diversity and inclusion is based on the proposition that everyone should be valued as an individual and treated fairly irrespective of their race, gender, level of disability, religion, sexual orientation or age. A number of personal characteristics are covered by discrimination law to give people protection to ensure that this happens. These 'protected characteristics' are race, disability, gender reassignment, sex, marriage and civil partnership, pregnancy and maternity, religion and belief, sexual orientation and age. But it is not enough to rely on the law. More needs to be done to create and maintain a culture that recognizes that although people are different, they all need to be treated in ways that are fair and tailored to their individual needs and that ensure they feel they belong and that they are important to the organization.

This chapter examines the meaning and significance of managing diversity and inclusion and the ways in which they can be managed.

The meaning and significance of managing diversity and inclusion

Managing diversity in the workplace means bringing together people of different ethnic backgrounds, religions, gender and age groups into cohesive and productive organizational units. It involves formulating and implementing policies and processes that maximize the potential advantages of diversity while minimizing the potential disadvantages. It means developing a culture that spells out that 'this is the way we do things around here about diversity'. It is a concept that recognizes the benefits to be gained from differences. It is not the same as equal opportunity, which aims to legislate against discrimination, assumes that people should be assimilated into the organization and, often, relies on affirmative action.

Managing inclusion is about forming and maintaining a culture in which individuals of all backgrounds – not just members of historically favoured groups – are fairly treated and valued for who they are. Inclusive cultures are characterized by a collective commitment to integrating diverse identities as a source of insight and skill. It is the process of ensuring that people feel they belong and are connected.

The management of diversity and the management of inclusion are closely connected. In fact they overlap and much of what can be done to improve one will affect the other. But both diversity issues concerning distinct groups of people and more general inclusion issues need to be considered when developing policy and practice and ensuring that everyone knows what they need to do through means such as communications, workshops and training interventions. Stephen Frost, who headed the highly successful diversity and inclusion programme for the London 2012 Olympics was quoted by the CIPD (2012a: 5) as saying: 'It is important to recognize the easy potential trap of achieving diversity without inclusion, and inclusion without diversity. Only both in unison really add value to the organization.'

As Nishii (2013: 1754–55) pointed out:

> To the extent that diversity management practices that focus specifically on improving the outcomes of historically disadvantaged groups cause resentment or backlash on the part of individuals who do not directly benefit from these practices, they can have the unintended effect of exacerbating negative stereotypes and perceived intergroup competition… To really manage both the problems and the potential benefits associated with diversity, organizations need to create environments that are inclusive of all employees.

The rationale for managing diversity and inclusion

The case for managing diversity was made by Kandola and Fullerton (1994) as follows:

> The basic concept of managing diversity accepts that the workforce consists of a diverse population of people. The diversity consists of visible and non-visible differences which include factors such as sex, age, background, race, disability, personality and workstyle. It is founded on the premise that harnessing these differences will create a productive environment in which everybody feels valued, where their talents are being fully utilized and in which organizational goals are met.

There is a social justice argument for pursuing diversity and inclusion policies: everyone has the right to be treated fairly in a workplace that values the differences between people and promotes an environment of fairness, dignity and respect. They will have career development and promotion opportunities based on merit and will be given the opportunity for work–life balance, for example through working flexible hours.

There is also a business case. The effective management of diversity and inclusion can help to increase levels of engagement, promote cooperation and reduce conflict. It can provide for the best candidates from the widest possible pool of applicants to be selected for jobs.

How to manage diversity and inclusion

The overall aim of a diversity and inclusion programme should be to achieve culture change so that the approach to dealing with diversity and inclusion issues becomes a way of life for all concerned. To manage diversity and inclusion by achieving culture change it is necessary to:

- develop a diversity and inclusion strategy;
- define the values of the organization concerning diversity and inclusion;
- set out the diversity and inclusion policies of the organization;
- implement programmes for communicating the values and policies;
- pay particular attention to potential problem areas – recruitment, appointments and promotions, learning and career development opportunities, and pay;
- devise and run training programmes designed to increase awareness and influence behaviour;
- create diversity networks, as described later;
- monitor progress and evaluate training.

Diversity and inclusion strategy

When developing a diversity and inclusion strategy it is first necessary to ensure that initiatives will have the support of the board and senior management. This will mean preparing a business case but equal emphasis should be placed on the moral imperative. In preparing the business case consideration should be given to the areas of diversity and inclusion that should be covered. A survey by the CIPD (2012b) found that the most typical areas included in the programmes of the respondents were gender, ethnicity, age, disability, sexual orientation and religion. These would be appropriate in most organizations.

The strategy should make it plain that the focus will be on fairness and inclusion, ensuring that merit, competence and potential are the basis for all decisions about recruitment and development, and being alert to the influence of conscious and unconscious biases. However, it should emphasize that the aim will be to support business goals as well as responding to moral imperatives.

The strategy should cover the need to define the values of the organization concerning diversity and inclusion and it should stress the importance of involving employees both in agreeing those values and, importantly, discussing how they should be put into effect as 'values in use'.

A broad indication of the methods that will be used in a programme for managing diversity and inclusion such as communications, the creation of diversity networks and training, should be given, bearing in mind that managing diversity and inclusion is a continuous process of improvement, not a one-off initiative. Additionally, the strategy should set out the employment areas that will be covered. These are typically recruitment and selection, performance management, rewards, opportunities for learning and development, career development and talent management, and work–life balance.

Consideration should be given to what needs to be done to deal specifically with diversity and with inclusion. Actions should be planned that will support the management of diversity and other actions proposed that will support the management of inclusion. There will be some planned actions that support both. For example, Northern Rail introduced diversity ambassadors, an inclusion charter, and e-learning on unconscious bias. It reached out to local schools and colleges, and targeted advertising on Asian TV networks to encourage candidates from previously untapped audiences.

Defining the values

The values could be defined under such headings as:

- fairness;
- equality;
- inclusion;
- respect for the individual;
- care for the individual;
- valuing individuals;
- developing staff and their careers.

It is important to involve employees in discussing these values

Diversity and inclusion policy

A policy on managing diversity should be produced to provide guidelines to managers on their role in managing diversity and information to employees in general on the part they are expected to play. It could:

- acknowledge cultural and individual differences in the workplace;
- state that the organization values the different qualities that people bring to their jobs;
- emphasize the need to eliminate bias in such areas as selection, promotion, performance assessment, pay and learning opportunities;
- indicate the need to promote inclusion, the process of ensuring that people from all backgrounds feel they belong and are connected;
- focus attention on individual differences rather than group differences.

Critical areas

The critical areas where there can be diversity and inclusion issues are recruitment, appointments and promotions, learning and career development opportunities, pay, bullying and harassment. In each case policies and definitions of good practice need to be developed to avoid biased and prejudiced decisions. These policies and practices should be communicated extensively and form the base of training programmes.

Communicating

It is essential to let everyone know about the diversity and inclusion values and policies of the organization and what is being done about them. This is a continuous process, not a one-off campaign. All available media should be used including newsletters, the intranet, enterprise social networks, consultative committees, briefing groups, in-house magazines and notice boards.

Training

The aims of diversity and inclusion training should be to alert people to the importance of dealing with the issues involved, communicate the values and policies of the organization and indicate the sort of behaviours required. This should be part of the induction training programmes for new employees. It should be provided for all existing managers and those who are about to be promoted and should emphasize the vital part they have to play in creating an inclusive culture and how they should set about doing it. Specifically the training for managers should cover how to create an inclusive culture, leadership behaviours, interviewing and assessing people, performance management and dealing with bullying and harassment. Briefing programmes for other members of staff should also be held.

The methods used should be participative – the minimum amount of lecturing and the maximum amount of participation in discussions, the analysis of case studies and role plays illustrating situations where bias might creep in and what can be done about it.

Diversity networks

Diversity networks can be set up that act as support groups for minority staff to share problems and swap tips. They can additionally help organizations to understand the people who work for them and help the business to perform better. For example:

- At Cisco, the women's network helps business development by hosting events for prospective and existing customers.

- At PwC there are four main networks: for women, ethnic minorities, disabled people and GLEE (an inclusive business network for gays, lesbians and everyone else).

- At BT a disability network focuses on awareness-raising about different disabilities to help managers understand them and get the best from people living with a disability. 'Knowledge calls' are provided, consisting of presentations via conference calls and desktop technology with expert speakers on particular subjects such as Parkinson's and migraines. They typically include someone who has experienced the condition, a Q&A session and inputs from HR relating to the condition or disability. There are online forums and sub-groups offering support.

Evaluation

It is essential to monitor and evaluate progress. The key performance indicators that can be used for evaluating progress are representation/demographic data by group of employee, employee survey results, trend data on demographics by recruitment and by promotions. Actions should be tracked to see if they have had the intended results so that changes can be made if necessary.

CASE STUDY: London 2012 Olympics

Stephen Frost made the following comments about the London 2012 Olympics diversity and inclusion programme in the CIPD 2012 publication *Game on! How to keep diversity progress on track*:

- We were able to achieve significant, and in some cases unprecedented, diversity in our workforce of 200,000, increasing a 30 per cent ethnic minority to 49 per cent. This happened because of strong and thoughtful leadership and the achievement of effective delivery with limited resources (in terms of people and money).

- We had to work hard, be bold and, to a certain extent, experiment in order to integrate diversity and inclusion as core to our way of doing business.

- To help everyone to understand diversity and inclusion and its organizational relevance, it is important to provide practical examples of what it means to people.

- Leadership is critical in terms of executing diversity and inclusion, but many people (especially 'management') fail to realize that everyone at all levels can be empowered to lead, and lead on diversity and inclusion issues.

- It is definitely the case that without strong top team leadership backing for diversity and inclusion, progress and traction suffers hugely. Nevertheless, leadership is not only the preserve of the top team. Everyone can be, and should be encouraged to be, a leader. We set in place several frameworks to help everyone act as a leader to drive the diversity and inclusion agenda. The most important frameworks we put in place were our Leadership Pledge and our Diversity Board.

- The Leadership Pledge was launched by Paul Deighton, CEO, Sebastian Coe, Chair, and Archbishop Desmond Tutu. It was a voluntary process that people signed up to which was designed to get them to think about and integrate diversity and inclusion into everything they did and every decision they made. Over 90 per cent of our workforce signed up to the pledge as part of their induction – and it was something which we constantly and consistently reinforced.

- The second important leadership framework we had was our Diversity Board, chaired by Paul Deighton. Membership of this board included directors across the business and each was accountable for leading a stream of diversity and inclusion. The board also included a number of well-known external people recognized for their personal interest and influence in diversity and inclusion.

- The Diversity Board had a crucial role in making sure the Diversity and Inclusion Team and functional management were held to account for progressing diversity and inclusion and maintaining momentum. This leadership mechanism helped to keep people on their toes and to maintain traction.

- To be successful in making diversity and inclusion responses systemic, it is vital that each functional area of an organization takes responsibility for it and is held accountable for driving the agenda and that everyone involved in the diversity and inclusion team feels empowered to lead.

Delivering well meant tracking our achievement of results. We did this by carrying out granular, detailed work on diversity and inclusion metrics and indicators across departments and across our total workforce on a monthly basis. We found that the use of different league tables based on this comparative data provided an internal competitive stimulus for the progress of diversity and inclusion.

KEY LEARNING POINTS

The management of diversity and inclusion is based on the proposition that everyone should be valued as an individual and treated fairly.

The meaning and significance of managing diversity and inclusion

Managing diversity in the workplace means bringing together people of different ethnic backgrounds, religions, gender and age groups into cohesive and productive organizational units.

Managing inclusion is about forming and maintaining a culture in which individuals of all backgrounds – not just members of historically favoured groups – are fairly treated and valued for who they are.

The rationale for managing diversity and inclusion

There is a social justice argument for pursuing diversity and inclusion policies: everyone has the right to be treated fairly in a workplace that values the differences between people and promotes an environment of fairness, dignity and respect.

There is also a business case. The effective management of diversity and inclusion can help to increase levels of engagement, promote cooperation and reduce conflict.

How to manage diversity and inclusion

To manage diversity and inclusion it is necessary to:

- develop a diversity and inclusion strategy;
- define the values of the organization concerning diversity and inclusion;
- set out the diversity and inclusion policies of the organization;
- implement programmes for communicating the values and policies;
- pay particular attention to potential problem areas – recruitment, appointments and promotions, learning and career development opportunities and pay;
- devise and run training programmes designed to increase awareness and influence behaviour;
- create diversity networks;
- monitor progress and evaluate training.

References

CIPD (2012a) *Game On! How to keep diversity progress on track*, http://www.cipd.co.uk/binaries/game-on-how-to-keep-diversity-progress-on-track_2012.pdf [accessed 30 October 2015]

CIPD (2012b) Diversity and inclusion – fringe or fundamental? http://www.cipd.co.uk/binaries/diversity-and-inclusion_2012-fringe-or-fundamental.pdf [accessed 30 October 2015]

Kandola, R and Fullerton, J (1994) *Managing the Mosaic: Diversity in action*, London, CIPD

Nishii, L H (2013) The benefits of climate for inclusion for gender-diverse groups *Academy of Management Journal*, 56 (6), pp 1754–74

PART FOUR
Leadership, management and learning and development skills

Leadership skills 15

LEARNING OUTCOMES

On completing this chapter you should be able to define these key concepts. You should also know about:

- Qualities of a good leader
- Effective leadership
- Motivating people

Introduction

The concept of leadership as described in Chapter 1 indicates that to lead people is to inspire, influence and guide. In doing so, leaders have to display certain qualities and motivate people, as explained in this chapter.

The skills required by effective leaders

Effective leaders need the ability to:

- understand the best way to motivate the team and its individual members;
- communicate clearly and positively what it is they expect people to do;
- use powers of persuasion to get people into action;
- analyse and read situations and establish order and clarity in conditions of ambiguity;
- understand what sort of leadership style works best for them and flex it to deal with different situations and people;
- promote good teamwork;
- handle people problems;
- develop the skills of team members.

The qualities of a good leader

Research conducted by the Work Foundation (Tamkin *et al*, 2010) involving 260 in-depth interviews conducted with 77 business leaders from six high-profile organizations found that outstanding leaders:

- view things as a whole rather than compartmentalizing them;
- connect the parts through a guiding sense of purpose;
- are highly motivated to achieve excellence and are focused on organizational outcomes, vision and purpose;
- understand they cannot create performance themselves but are conduits for performance through their influence on others;
- watch themselves carefully and act consistently to achieve excellence through their interactions and their embodiment of the leadership role.

Gold *et al* (2010: 6) stated that: 'Leadership demands a sense of purpose, and an ability to influence others, interpret situations, negotiate and express their views, often in the face of opposition.' Leaders are confident and know where they want to go and what they want to do. They have the ability to take charge, convey their vision to their team, get their team members into action and ensure that they achieve their agreed goals. They are trustworthy and earn the respect of their team. They are aware of their own strengths and weaknesses and are skilled at understanding what will motivate their team members. They appreciate the advantages of consulting and involving people in decision making. They can switch flexibly from one leadership style to another to meet the demands of different situations and people.

Effective leaders ask the following questions about the individuals in the team and the team itself. The answers provide a guide to action for the leader and the basis for team-building.

Individuals in the team

- What are their strengths and weaknesses?
- What are their needs, attitudes, perspectives and preferences?
- What are likely to be the best ways of motivating them?
- What tasks are they best at doing?
- Is there scope to increase flexibility by developing new skills?
- How well do they perform in achieving targets and performance standards?
- To what extent can they manage their own performance and development?
- Are there any areas where there is a need to develop skill or competence?
- How can I provide them with the sort of support and guidance that will improve their performance?
- What can be done to improve the performance of any individuals in the group by coaching or mentoring?

The team

- How well is the team organized?
- Is the team clear about what is expected of it?
- Do the members of the team work well together?
- If there is any conflict between team members, how can I resolve it?
- How can the commitment and motivation of the team be achieved?

- Are team members flexible – capable of carrying out different tasks?
- To what extent can the team manage its own performance?
- Is there scope to empower the team so that it can take on greater responsibility for setting standards, monitoring performance and taking corrective action?
- Can the team be encouraged to work together to produce ideas for improving performance?
- What is the team good and not so good at doing?
- What can I do to improve the performance of the team through coaching and mentoring?

How to motivate people

There are 10 steps leaders can take to achieve higher levels of motivation:

1 Exercise authentic leadership, as described in Chapter 1.

2 Get to know individual team members to understand what is likely to motivate them.

3 Set and agree demanding but achievable goals.

4 Provide feedback on performance.

5 Create expectations that certain behaviours and outputs will produce worthwhile rewards when people succeed.

6 Design jobs that enable people to feel a sense of accomplishment, to express and use their abilities and to exercise their own decision-making powers.

7 Provide appropriate financial incentives and rewards for achievement (pay-for-performance).

8 Provide appropriate non-financial rewards such as recognition and praise for work well done.

9 Select and train team leaders who will exercise effective leadership and have the required motivating skills.

10 Give people guidance and training that will develop the knowledge, skills and competencies they need to improve their performance.

KEY LEARNING POINTS

Leaders need the ability to analyse and read situations and to establish order and clarity in situations of ambiguity.

Leadership demands a sense of purpose, and an ability to influence others, interpret situations, negotiate and express their views, often in the face of opposition.

There are 10 steps that can be taken to motivate people, set out in the text.

References

Gold, J, Thorpe, R and Mumford, A (2010) *Gower Handbook of Leadership and Management Development*, Aldershot, Gower

Tamkin, P, Pearson, G, Hirsh, W and Constable, S (2010) *Exceeding Expectation: The principles of outstanding leadership*, London, The Work Foundation

Management skills

16

Introduction

HR and L&D specialists have to understand the qualities and skills that line managers need so as to provide them with advice and to plan management and leadership development programmes. In their capacity as line managers they have to practise such skills as those involved in delegating work and motivating. They also have to exercise a wide range of management skills such as influencing people, chairing meetings, facilitating discussions and project management.

This chapter complements the previous one on leadership by concentrating on the management skills required to get things done through people. Managing interpersonal relationships at work, including handling teams, is dealt with in Chapter 19.

Effective supervision: providing direction

Effective supervision is the process of directing people to ensure that they get the work done. Supervisors or team leaders are concerned with meeting the needs of the task. They define the task, provide direction – making it clear what the group and its individual members are expected to do and what results are to be achieved – and supervise the work to ensure that it is done as required. To do this the team leader has to answer the following questions:

- What results have to be achieved, why and by when?
- What needs to be done to achieve those results?
- What are the priorities?
- What resources (people, money and equipment) are needed and where can they be obtained?
- What problems do we face?
- To what extent are these problems straightforward?
- How are we going to overcome the difficult problems?
- Is there a crisis situation?
- What has to be done now to deal with the crisis?
- What pressures are likely to be exerted to get results?

Effective supervisors will provide clear answers to those questions, which will guide their actions and the behaviour of the group.

Delegating

You can't do everything yourself, so you have to delegate. It is one of the most important things you do. At first sight delegation looks simple: just tell people what you want them to do and then let them get on with it. But there is more to it than that. It is not easy. It requires courage, patience and skill.

And it is an aspect of your work in which you have more freedom of choice than in any other of your activities. What you choose to delegate, to whom and how, is almost entirely at your discretion.

What is delegation?

Delegation is not the same as handing out work. There are some things that your team members do that go with the territory. They are part of their normal duties and all you have to do is to define what those duties are and allocate work accordingly.

Delegation is different. It takes place when you deliberately give someone the authority to carry out a piece of work that you could have decided to keep and carry out yourself. Bear in mind that what you are doing is delegating authority to carry out a task and make the decisions this involves. You are still accountable for the results achieved. It is sometimes said that you cannot delegate responsibility but this is misleading if responsibility is defined, as it usually is, as what people are expected to do – their work, their tasks and their duties. What you cannot do is delegate accountability. In the last analysis you as the manager or team leader always carry the can. What managers have to do is to ensure that people have the authority to carry out their responsibilities. A traffic warden without the power to issue tickets would have to be exceedingly persuasive to have any chance of dealing with parking offences.

What are the advantages of delegation?

The advantages of delegation are that it:

- enables you to focus on the things that really matter in your job – those aspects that require your personal experience, skill and knowledge;
- relieves you of less critical and routine tasks;
- frees you from being immersed in detail;
- extends your capacity to manage;
- reduces delay in decision making, as long as authority is delegated close to the scene of action;
- allows decisions to be taken at the level where the details are known;
- empowers and motivates your staff by extending their responsibilities and authority and providing them with greater autonomy;
- develops the knowledge and skills of your staff and increases their capacity to exercise judgement and make decisions.

What are the difficulties of delegation?

The advantages of delegation are compelling but there are difficulties. The main problem is that delegation often involves risk. You cannot be absolutely sure that the person to whom you have delegated something will carry out the work as you would wish. The temptation therefore is to over-supervise, breathe down people's necks and interfere. This inhibits their authority, makes them nervous and resentful and destroys their confidence, thus dissipating any advantages the original act of delegation might have had. Another difficulty is that many managers are reluctant to delegate because they want to keep on top of everything. They really think they know best and cannot trust anyone else to do it as well, never mind better. Finally, some managers are reluctant to delegate simply because they enjoy what they are doing and cannot bear the possibility of giving it away to anyone else.

Approaches to delegation

To a degree, overcoming these difficulties is a matter of simply being aware of them and appreciating that if there are any disadvantages, they are outweighed by the advantages. Approaches to delegation such as those discussed below help. You need to understand the process of delegation, when to delegate, what to delegate, how to choose people to whom you want to delegate, how to give out the work and how to monitor performance.

The process of delegation

Delegation is a process that goes from the point when total control is exercised (no freedom of action for the individual to whom work has been allocated) to full devolution (the individual is completely empowered to carry out the work). This sequence is illustrated in Figure 16.1.

When to delegate

You should delegate when you:

- have more work than you can carry out yourself;
- cannot allow sufficient time for your priority tasks;
- want to develop a member of your team;
- believe that it will increase someone's engagement with their job;
- think that the job can be done adequately by the individual or the team to whom you delegate.

Figure 16.1 The sequence of delegation

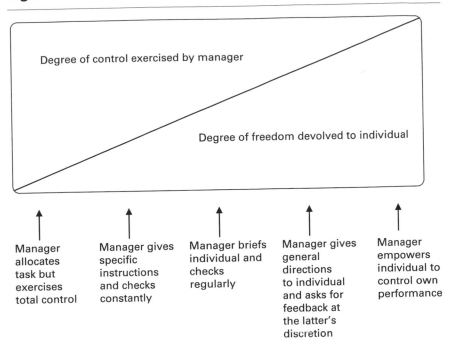

What to delegate

The tasks you delegate are ones that you don't need to do yourself. You are not just ridding yourself of the difficult, tedious or unrewarding tasks, nor are you trying simply to win for yourself an easier life. In some ways delegation will make your life more difficult, but also more rewarding.

You delegate routine and repetitive tasks that you cannot reasonably be expected to do yourself – as long as you use the time you have won productively. You can delegate specialist tasks to those who have the skills and know-how to do them. You cannot be expected to do it all yourself nor can you be expected to know it all yourself.

Giving out the work

When you delegate you should ensure that the individuals or team concerned understand:

- why the work needs to be done;
- what they are expected to do;
- the date by which they are expected to do it;
- the end-results they are expected to achieve;

- the authority they have to make decisions;
- the problems they must refer back;
- the progress or completion reports they should submit;
- any guidance and support that will be available to them.

You have to consider how much guidance will be required on how the work should be done. You don't want to give directions in such laborious detail that you run the risk of stifling initiative nor do you want to infuriate people by explaining everything needlessly. As long as you are reasonably certain that they will do the job to your satisfaction without embarrassing you or seriously upsetting people, exceeding the budget or breaking the law, let them get on with it.

Influencing people

HR professionals are very much in the business of influencing thinking and decision making on the part of others. They must know about persuading people, making a business case and case presentation.

Persuading people

A manager's job is 60 per cent getting it right and 40 per cent putting it across. Managers spend a lot of time persuading other people to accept their ideas and suggestions. Persuasion is just another word for selling. It may be felt that good ideas should sell themselves, but life is not like that. People resist change and anything new is usually treated with suspicion. Here are 10 rules for effective persuasion:

1 *Define the objective and get the facts.* When persuading someone to agree to a proposal first decide what is to be achieved and why. Assemble all the facts needed to support the case. Eliminate emotional arguments so that the proposition is based on the facts alone.

2 *Define the problem.* If there is a problem to resolve, when trying to persuade someone to accept a view on what should be done about it first decide whether the problem is a misunderstanding (a failure to understand each other accurately) or a true disagreement (a failure to agree even when both parties understand one another). It is not necessarily possible to resolve a true disagreement by understanding each other better. People generally believe that an argument is a battle to understand who is correct. More often, it is a battle to decide who is more stubborn.

3 *Find out what the other party wants.* The key to all persuasion is to see the proposition from the other person's point of view. Find out how they look at things. Establish what they need and want.

4 *Accentuate the benefits.* Present the case in a way that highlights the benefits to the other party or at least reduces any objections or fears.

5 *Predict the other person's response.* Everything we say should be focused on that likely response. Anticipate objections by considering how the other party might react negatively to their proposition and thinking up ways of responding to them.

6 *Create the person's next move.* It is not a question of deciding what we want to do but what we want the other person to do.

7 *Convince people by reference to their own perceptions.* People decide on what to do on the basis of their own perceptions, not anyone else's.

8 *Prepare a simple and attractive proposition.* Make it as straightforward as possible. Present the case 'sunny side up', emphasizing its benefits. Break the problem into manageable pieces and deal with them one step at a time.

9 *Make them a party to the ideas.* Get them to contribute. Find some common ground so that the discussion starts with agreement. Don't try to defeat them in an argument – this will only antagonize them.

10 *Clinch and take action.* Choose the right moment to clinch the proposal – don't prolong the discussion and risk losing it. Follow up promptly.

Case presentation

Persuasion frequently means presenting a case, which means persuading people to believe in the proposition and accept the recommendation. To do this, it is necessary to have a clear idea of what is wanted and to demonstrate belief in it. Above all, the effectiveness of the presentation will depend upon the care with which it has been prepared.

Thorough preparation is vital. You must think through not only what should be done and why, but also how people will react. Only then can you decide how to make your case: stressing the benefits without underestimating the costs, and anticipating objections. The steps you should take are:

1 Show that your proposal is based on a thorough analysis of the facts and that the alternatives were properly evaluated before the conclusion was reached. If you have made assumptions, you must demonstrate that these are reasonable on the basis of relevant experience and justifiable projections that allow for the unexpected. Bear in mind that a proposal is only as strong as its weakest assumption.

2 Spell out the benefits – to the company and the individuals to whom the case is being made. Wherever possible, express benefits in financial terms. Abstract benefits, such as customer satisfaction or workers' morale, are difficult to sell. But don't produce 'funny numbers' – financial justification that will not stand up to examination.

3 Reveal costs. Don't try to disguise them in any way. And be realistic. Your proposition will be destroyed if anyone can show that you have underestimated the costs.

4 Remember, senior management decision makers want to know in precise terms what they will get for their money. Most are likely to be cautious, being unwilling and often unable to take much risk. For this reason, it can be difficult to make a case for experiments or pilot schemes unless the decision maker can see what the benefits and the ultimate bill will be.

Making a business case

You may be asked specifically to produce a business case. This will set out the reasons why a proposed course of action will benefit the business, how it will provide that benefit and how much it will cost. A business case is a particular form of persuasion and all the points made above apply to its preparation and presentation; there are also some special features about business cases, as described below.

A business case is typically made either in added value terms (ie the income generated by the proposal will significantly exceed the cost of implementing it), or on the basis of the return on investment (ie the cost of the investment, say in training, is justified by the financial returns in such areas as increased productivity). Clearly, a business case is more convincing when it is accompanied by realistic projections of added value or return on investment. The case for capital expenditure can be made by an analysis of the cash flows associated with the investment and appraisals of the benefits that are likely to arise from them. The objective is to demonstrate that in return for paying out a given amount of cash today, a larger amount will be received over a period of time. There are a number of investment appraisal techniques available such as payback, the accounting rate of return, discounted cash flow and net present value.

A business case will be enhanced if:

- Information is available on the impact the proposal is likely to make on key areas of the organization's operations, eg customer service levels, quality, shareholder value, productivity, income generation, innovation, skills development, talent management.

- It can be shown that the proposal will increase the business's competitive edge, for example enlarging the skill base or multiskilling to ensure that it can achieve competitive advantage through innovation and/or reducing time-to-market.

- There is proof that the innovation has already worked well within the organization (perhaps as a pilot scheme) or represents 'good practice' that is likely to be transferable to the organization.

- It can be implemented without too much trouble, for example not taking up a lot of managers' time, or not meeting with strong opposition from line managers, employees or trade unions (it is as well to check the likely reaction before launching a proposal).

- It will add to the reputation of the company by showing that it is a 'world class' organization, ie what it does is as good as, if not better than, the world leaders in the sector in which the business operates (a promise that publicity will be achieved through articles in professional journals, press releases and conference presentations will help).

- It will enhance the 'employer brand' of the company by making it a 'best place to work'.

- The proposal is brief, to the point and well argued – it should take no more than five minutes to present orally and should be summarized in writing on the proverbial one side of one sheet of paper (supplementary details can be included in appendices).

Making the business case is obviously easier where management is pre-conditioned to agree to the proposition. For example, it is not hard to convince top managers that performance-related pay is a good thing – they may well be receiving bonus payments themselves and believe, rightly or wrongly, that because it motivates them it will motivate everyone else. Talent management is another process where top management needs little persuasion that things need to be done to enhance and preserve the talent flow, although they will have to be convinced that, in practice, innovations will achieve that aim. Performance management may be slightly more difficult because it is hard to demonstrate that it can produce measurable improvements in performance, but senior managers are predisposed towards an approach that at least promises to improve the level of performance.

The toughest area for justification in added value terms can be expenditure on learning and development programmes. This is where a return on investment (RoI) approach is desirable. The business case for learning and development should demonstrate how learning, training and development programmes will meet business needs. Kearns and Miller (1997) go as far as to claim that: 'If a business objective cannot be cited as a basis for designing training and development, then no training and development should be offered.'

How to make an effective presentation

The three keys to delivering an effective presentation are thorough preparation, good delivery and overcoming nervousness.

1. Thorough preparation

Allow yourself ample time for preparation. You will probably need at least 10 times as much as the duration of your talk. The main stages are:

1 *Get informed.* Collect and assemble all the facts and arguments you can get hold of.

2 *Decide what to say.* Define the main messages you want to get across. Limit the number to three or four – few people can absorb more than this number of new ideas at any one time. Select the facts, arguments and examples that support your message.

3 *Structure your talk* into the classic beginning, middle and end.

- Start thinking about the middle first, with your main messages and the supporting facts, arguments and illustrations.

- Arrange your points so that a cumulative impact and a logical flow of ideas are achieved.

- Then turn to the opening of your talk. Your objectives should be to create attention, arouse interest and inspire confidence. Give your audience a trailer to what you are going to say. Underline the objective of your presentation – what *they* will get out of it.

- Finally, think about how you are going to close your talk. First and last impressions are very important. End on a high note.

4 *Think carefully about length*. Never talk for more than 40 minutes at a time – 20 or 30 minutes is better.

5 *Keep the audience's attention throughout*. Give interim summaries that reinforce what you are saying and, above all, hammer home your key points at intervals throughout your talk.

6 *Ensure continuity*. You should build your argument progressively until you come to a positive and convincing conclusion. Provide signposts, interim summaries and bridging sections that lead your audience naturally from one point to the next.

7 *Prepare your notes*. In the first place write out your introductory and concluding remarks in full and set out in some detail the main text of your talk. It is not usually necessary to write everything down. You should then boil down your text to the key headings to which you will refer in your talk. Your aim should be to avoid reading your speech if you possibly can as this can remove any life from what you have to say. So as not to be pinned down behind a lectern it is better to write your summarized points on lined index cards to which you can refer easily as you go along.

8 *Prepare and use visual aids*. As your audience will only absorb one-third of what you say, if that, reinforce your message with visual aids. Appeal to more than one sense at a time. PowerPoint slides provide good back-up, but don't overdo them and keep them simple. Too many visuals can be distracting (use no more than 15 or so in a half-hour presentation) and too many words, or an over-elaborate presentation, will divert, bore and confuse your audience. As a rule of thumb, try not to put more than five or six bullet points on a slide. Each point should contain fewer than six or seven words. Audiences dislike having to read a lot of small print on an over-busy slide. Use diagrams and charts wherever possible to break up the flow of words and to illustrate points. If you want the members of your audience to read something fairly elaborate, distribute the material as a handout and take them through it.

9 *Rehearse*. Rehearsal is vital. It instils confidence, helps you to get your timing right, and enables you to polish your opening and closing remarks and coordinate your talk and visual aids. Rehearse the talk to yourself several times and note how long each section takes. Get used to expanding on your notes without waffling. Practise giving your talk out loud – standing up, if that is the way you are going to present it. Get someone to hear you and provide constructive criticism. It may be hard to take but

it could do you a world of good. But remember the Zen saying: 'Practice the performance, then forget the practice when you perform.'

10. *Check arrangements in the room.* Ensure that your projector works and you know how to operate it. Check also on focus and visibility. Before you begin your talk, check that your notes and visual aids are in the right order and to hand.

2. *Good delivery*

To deliver a presentation effectively the following approaches should be used.

- Talk audibly and check that you can be heard at the back. Your task is to *project* your voice. It's easier when there is a microphone, but even then you have to think about getting your words across.

- Vary the pace (not too fast, not too slow), pitch and emphasis of your delivery. Use pauses to make a point.

- Try to be conversational and as informal as the occasion requires (but not too casual).

- Convey that you truly believe in what you are saying: audiences respond well to enthusiasm.

- Avoid a stilted delivery. That is why you must not read your talk. If you are your natural self, people are more likely to be on your side. They will forgive the occasional pause to find the right word.

- Light relief is a good thing but don't drag in irrelevant jokes or, indeed, make jokes at all if you are no good at telling them. You do not *have* to tell jokes.

- Use short words and sentences.

- Keep your eyes on the audience, moving from person to person to demonstrate that you are addressing them all, and also to gauge their reactions to what you are saying. Worry a little if they look at their watches. Worry even more if they shake their watches to find out if they have stopped.

- If you can manage without elaborate notes (your slides or a few cards may be sufficient) come out from behind the desk or lectern and get close to your audience. It is best to stand up so that you can project what you say more effectively unless it is a smallish meeting round a table.

- Use hands for gesture and emphasis in moderation (don't put them in your pocket – if you have one).
- Don't fidget.
- Stand naturally and upright.
- You can move around the platform a little to add variety – you don't want to look as if you are clutching the lectern for much needed support – but avoid pacing up and down like a caged tiger.

3. Overcoming nervousness

Some nervousness is a good thing. It makes you prepare, makes you think and makes the adrenaline flow, thus raising performance. But excessive nervousness ruins your effectiveness and must be controlled.

The common reasons for excessive nervousness are: fear of failure, fear of looking foolish, fear of breakdown, a sense of inferiority and dread of the isolation of the speaker. To overcome nervousness you should:

- *Practise.* Take every opportunity you can get to speak in public. The more you do it, the more confident you will become. Solicit constructive criticism and act on it.
- *Know your subject.* Get the facts, examples and illustrations you need to put across.
- *Know your audience.* Who is going to be there? What are they expecting to hear? What will they want to get out of listening to you?
- *Know your objective.* Make sure that you know what you want to achieve. Visualize, if you can, each member of your audience going away having learnt something new that he or she is going to put into practical use.
- *Prepare.* If you know that you have prepared carefully as suggested above you will be much more confident on the day.
- *Rehearse.* This is an essential method of overcoming nervousness.

Chairing meetings

Most managers, including those in HR, will find themselves required to chair a meeting. The success or failure of a meeting largely depends on the effectiveness with which it is chaired. If you are chairing a meeting, this is what you must do.

Prior to the meeting

Before the meeting starts ensure that it has proper terms of reference and that the members are briefed on what to expect and what they should be prepared to contribute. Plan the agenda to provide for a structured meeting, covering all the issues in a logical order. Prepare and issue briefing papers that will structure the meeting and spell out the background, thus saving time going into detail or reviewing purely factual information during the meeting.

During the meeting

1   Start by clearly defining the objective of the meeting, setting a timescale, which you intend to keep.

2   Go through each item of the agenda in turn, ensuring that a firm conclusion is reached and recorded.

3   Initiate the discussion on each item by setting the scene very briefly and asking for contributions – ask for answers to specific questions (which you should have prepared in advance) or you may refer the matter first to a member of the meeting who can make the best initial contribution (ideally, you should have briefed that individual in advance).

4   Invite contributions from other members of the meeting, taking care not to allow anyone to dominate the discussions.

5   Bring people back to order if they drift from the point.

6   If there is too much talk, remind members that they are there to make progress.

7   Encourage the expression of different points of view and avoid crushing anyone too obviously if they have not made a sensible comment.

8   Allow disagreement between members of the meeting but step in smartly if the atmosphere becomes too contentious.

9   Chip in with questions or brief comments from time to time, but do not dominate the discussion.

10 At appropriate moments during the meeting summarize the discussion, express views on where the committee has got to and outline your perception of the interim or final decision that has been made. Then check that the meeting agrees, amending the conclusion as necessary, and ensuring that the decision is recorded exactly as made.

11 Summarize what has been achieved at the end of the meeting, indicating who has to do what by when.

12 If a further meeting is needed, agree the purpose of the meeting and what has to be done by those present before it takes place.

Facilitating and coordinating discussions

More frequently than chairing meetings HR specialists will be involved in facilitating and coordinating discussions.

Facilitating

Facilitating meetings is the process of helping a group reach conclusions in the shape of ideas and solutions. Facilitators do not exist to 'chair' the meeting in the sense of controlling the discussion and pressurizing the group to agree to a course of action. The group is there to make up its own mind and the facilitator helps it to do so. The help is provided by asking questions that encourage the group members to think for themselves. These can be challenging and probing questions but the facilitator does not provide the answers – that is the role of the group. Neither do facilitators allow their own opinions to intrude – they are there to help the group marshal its opinions, not to enforce their own ideas. However, by using questioning techniques carefully, facilitators can ensure that the group does thoroughly discuss and analyse the issues and reaches conclusions by consensus rather than allowing anyone to dominate the process.

Facilitators ensure that everyone has their say and that they are listened to. They step in quickly to defuse unproductive arguments. They see that the group defines and understands its objectives and any methodology they might use. They summarize from time to time the progress made in achieving the objectives without bringing their own views to bear. Facilitators are there to ensure that the group makes progress and does not get stuck in fruitless or disruptive argument, but they encourage the group rather than drive it forward.

The aim of the facilitator is to guide the group's thinking. He or she may, therefore, be more concerned with shaping attitudes than convincing people about what to do or imparting new knowledge. The facilitator has to unobtrusively stimulate people to talk, guide the discussion along predetermined lines (there must be a plan and an ultimate objective), and provide interim summaries and a final summary.

Coordinating discussions

Coordinating discussions is a matter of getting active participation and then ensuring that the discussion informs people of the issues related to the subject and leads to a conclusion that satisfies the participants. The following techniques can be used to get active participation and to coordinate the process:

- Ask for contributions by direct questions.
- Use open-ended questions, which will stimulate thought.
- Check understanding; make sure that everyone is following the argument.
- Encourage participation by providing support rather than criticism.
- Prevent domination by individual members of the group by bringing in other people and asking cross-reference questions.
- Avoid dominating the group yourself. The leader's job is to guide the discussion, maintain control and summarize from time to time. If necessary, 'reflect' opinions expressed by individuals back to the group to make sure they find the answer for themselves. The leader's job is to help them reach a conclusion, not to do it for them.
- Maintain control – ensure that the discussion is progressing along the right lines towards a firm conclusion.

Project management

HR professionals are involved in project management when they lead or take part in the introduction of a new HR system or process such as job evaluation, performance management or performance-related pay or, on a wider scale, when they are involved in an organization development programme. Project management is the planning, supervision and control of any activity or set of activities that leads to a defined outcome at a predetermined time and in accordance with specified performance or quality standards at a budgeted cost. Project management is concerned with *deliverables* – getting things done as required or promised. While delivering results on time is important, it is equally important to deliver them to meet the specification and within the projected cost.

Project management involves action planning – deciding *what* work is to be done, *why* the work needs to be done, *who* will do the work, *how* much will it cost, *when* the work has to be completed (totally or stage by stage) and *where* the work will be carried out. The three main project management activities are project planning, setting up the project and project control.

Project planning

Project planning starts with a definition of the objectives of the project. A business case has to be made. This means answering three basic questions: why is this project needed; what benefits are expected from the project, and how much will it cost? The answers to these questions should be quantified. The requirement could be spelt out in such terms as new systems or facilities to meet defined business needs, new plant required for new products or to improve productivity or quality. The benefits are expressed as revenues generated, productivity, quality or performance improvements, added value, costs saved and return on investment.

Projects involve investing resources – money and people. Investment appraisal techniques are used to ensure that the company's criteria on return on investment are satisfied. Cost-benefit analysis may be used to assess the degree to which the benefits justify the costs, time and number of people required by the project. This may mean identifying opportunity costs, which establish if a greater benefit would be obtained by investing the money or deploying the people on other projects or activities.

A performance specification is required that indicates the expected outcome of the project – how it should perform – and describes how it will operate. This leads to a project plan that sets out:

- the major operations in sequence – the main stages of the project;

- a breakdown, where appropriate, of each major operation into a sequence of subsidiary tasks;

- an analysis of the interrelationships and interdependencies of major and subsidiary tasks;

- an estimate of the time required to complete each major operation or stage;

- a procurement plan to obtain the necessary materials, systems and equipment;

- a workforce resource plan that defines how many people will be allocated to the project with different skills at each stage and who is to be responsible for controlling the project as a whole and each of the major stages or operations.

Setting up the project

Setting up the project involves:

- obtaining and allocating resources;
- selecting and briefing the project management teams;
- finalizing the project programme – defining each stage;
- defining and establishing control systems and reporting procedures (format and timing of progress reports);
- identifying key dates, stage by stage, for the project (milestones) and providing for milestone meetings to review progress and decide on any actions required.

Controlling the project

The three most important things to control are:

1 *Time* – achievement of project plan as programme.
2 *Quality* – achievement of project specifications.
3 *Cost* – containment of costs within budget.

Project control is based on progress reports showing what is being achieved against the plan. The planned completion date, actual achievement and forecast completion date for each stage or operation are provided. The likelihood of delays, over-runs or bottlenecks is thus established so that corrective action can be taken in good time. Control can be achieved by the use of Gantt or bar charts and by reference to network plans or critical path analyses.

KEY LEARNING POINTS

Effective supervision

Effective supervision is the process of directing people to ensure that they get the work done. Supervisors define the task and provide direction, making it clear what the group and its individual members are expected to do and what results are to be achieved, and ensure that the work is done as required.

Effective leadership
Effective leaders are confident and know where they want to go and what they want to do. They have the ability to take charge, convey their vision to their team, get their team members into action and ensure that they achieve their agreed goals.

Delegation
Delegation takes place when you deliberately give someone the authority to carry out a piece of work that you could have decided to keep and carry out yourself.

Influencing people
HR professionals are often involved in influencing thinking and decision making on the part of others. They must know about persuading people and case presentation.

Making a presentation
The three keys to delivering an effective presentation are thorough preparation, good delivery and overcoming nervousness.

Chairing meetings
Most managers, including those in HR, will find themselves required to chair a meeting. The success or failure of a meeting largely depends on the effectiveness with which it is chaired.

Facilitating
Facilitating is the process of helping a group reach conclusions in the shape of ideas and solutions.

Coordinating discussions
Coordinating discussions is a matter of getting active participation and then ensuring that the discussion informs people of the issues related to the subject and leads to a conclusion that satisfies the participants.

Presentations
The three keys to delivering an effective presentation are thorough preparation, good delivery and overcoming nervousness.

Project management
Project management is the planning, supervision and control of any activity or set of activities that leads to a defined outcome at a predetermined time and in accordance with specified performance or quality standards at a budgeted cost.

Reference

Kearns, P and Miller, T (1997) Measuring the impact of training and development on the bottom line, *FT Management Briefings*, London, Pitman

QUESTIONS

1   What is effective supervision?

2   What are the main steps you should take to motivate people?

3   What is delegation?

4   What are the advantages of delegation?

5   When should you delegate?

6   How should you delegate?

7   What are the most important rules for effective persuasion?

8   What are the key steps required for effective case presentation?

9   How should a business case be made?

10   What steps should you take before chairing a meeting?

11   What are the most important actions required to chair a meeting successfully?

12   What is facilitating?

13   How should facilitation be carried out?

14   How should discussions be coordinated?

People management skills

Introduction

This chapter covers a number of the key people management skills used by managers and HR specialists.

How to conduct a selection interview

One of the most important people management tasks carried out by managers and HR specialists is to conduct a selection interview. The aim of such interviews is to provide answers to three fundamental questions:

1 *Can* the individual do the job? Is the person capable of doing the work to the standard required?

2 *Will* the individual do the job? Is the person well motivated?

3 *How* is the individual likely to fit into the team? Will I and other team members be able to work well with this person?

Form of the selection interview

A selection interview should take the form of a conversation with a purpose. It is a conversation because candidates should be given the opportunity to talk freely about themselves and their careers, but the conversation has to be planned, directed and controlled to achieve your aims in the time available.

Your task as an interviewer is to draw candidates out to ensure that you get the information you want. Candidates should be encouraged to do most of the talking – one of the besetting sins of poor interviewers is that they talk too much. You have to plan the structure of the interview to achieve its purpose and decide in advance the questions you need to ask – questions that will give you what you need to make an accurate assessment.

A selection interview has three sections:

1 *Beginning.* At the start of the interview candidates are put at their ease. They need to be encouraged to talk freely in response to questions.

2 *Middle.* This is where interviewers find out what they need to know about candidates to establish the extent to which they meet the requirements of the job as set out in a person or job specification. This indicates what experience, qualifications and competencies (characteristics of a person that results in effective job performance) are required. This part should take at least 80 per cent of the time, leaving, say, 5 per cent at the beginning and 15 per cent at the end.

3 *End.* At the end of the interview candidates are given the opportunity to ask about the job and the company. More details about the job can be given to promising candidates who are told what the next step will be.

Preparing for the interview

Your first step in preparing for an interview is to familiarize or re-familiarize yourself with the person specification and candidate's CV, application form or letter. General questions should be prepared that will be put to all candidates, also specific questions for individuals about their career or qualifications.

Structuring the interview

The best approach is one that is criteria- or target-based, using competencies as the criteria (this is often called a 'competency-based interview'). A competency is a measurable aspect of a person's behaviour that results in effective or superior performance.

The competencies required should be set out in the person specification and the interviewer 'targets' these key criteria, having decided on what the questions should be asked to draw out from candidates information about their competencies (knowledge, skills capabilities and personal qualities) that can be compared with the criteria to assess the extent to which candidates meet the specification. Each candidate is asked the same questions to facilitate comparisons (this is known as a structured interview).

Planning the interview

A biographical approach is probably the most popular because it is simple to use and logical. The interview can be sequenced chronologically, starting with the first job or even before that at school and, if appropriate, college or university. The succeeding jobs, if any, are then dealt with in turn, ending with the present job on which most time is spent if the candidate has been in it for a reasonable time. Using the chronological method for someone who has had a number of jobs can mean spending too much time on the earlier jobs, leaving insufficient time for the most important recent experiences. To overcome this problem, an alternative biographical approach is to start with the present job, which is discussed in some depth. The interviewer then works backwards, job by job, but only concentrating on particularly interesting or relevant experience in earlier jobs.

Interviewing techniques – asking questions

The interviewer's job is to draw the candidate out, at the same time ensuring that the information required is obtained. To this end it is desirable to ask a number of open-ended questions, ie questions that cannot be answered by yes or no and which prompt a full response. A good interviewer will have an armoury of other types of questions to be asked when appropriate such as:

- *Probing questions*, which ask for further details and explanations to ensure that the interviewer is getting all the facts.

- *Closed questions* to clarify a point of fact.

- *Hypothetical questions* to test how candidates would approach a typical problem.

- *Behavioural event questions* to get candidates to tell the interviewer how they would behave in situations that have been identified as critical to successful job performance.

- *Capability questions* to establish what candidates know, the skills they possess and use and their competencies – what they are capable of doing. They can be open, probing or closed but they will always be focused as precisely as possible on the contents of the person specification, referring to knowledge, skills and competences.

- *Continuity questions* to keep the flow going in an interview and encourage candidates to enlarge on what they said, within limits.

- *Play-back questions* to test understanding of what candidates have said by putting to them a statement of what it appears they have told the interviewer and asking them if they agree or disagree with the interviewer's version.

Avoid any questions that could be construed as being biased on the grounds of sex, sexual orientation, race, disability or age.

Here are 10 useful questions:

1 What are the most important aspects of your present job?

2 What do you think have been your most notable achievements in your career to date?

3 What sort of problems have you successfully solved recently in your job?

4 What have you learnt from your present job?

5 What has been your experience in...?

6 What do you know about...?

7 What particularly interests you in this job and why?

8 Now you have heard more about the job, would you please tell me which aspects of your experience are most relevant?

9 What do you think you can bring to this job?

10 Is there anything else about your career that hasn't come out yet in this interview but which you think I ought to hear?

The dos and don'ts of selection interviewing are shown in Table 17.1.

Table 17.1 The dos and don'ts of selection interviewing

Do	Don't
• Plan the interview.	• Start the interview unprepared.
• Give yourself sufficient time.	• Plunge too quickly into demanding (probing) questions.
• Use a structured interview approach wherever possible.	• Ask multiple or leading questions.
• Create the right atmosphere.	
• Establish an easy and informal relationship – start with open questions.	• Pay too much attention to isolated strengths or weaknesses.
	• Allow candidates to gloss over important facts.
• Encourage the candidate to talk.	• Talk too much or allow candidates to ramble on.
• Cover the ground as planned, ensuring that you complete a prepared agenda and maintain continuity.	• Allow your prejudices to get the better of your capacity to make objective judgements.
• Analyse the candidate's career to reveal strengths, weaknesses and patterns of interest.	• Fall into the halo effect trap (drawing conclusions about a person on the basis of one or two good points, leading to the neglect of negative indicators) or the horns trap (focusing too much on one or two weak points).
• Make use of open questions that invite people to talk.	
• Ensure that questions are clear and unambiguous.	
• Get examples and instances of the successful application of knowledge and skills and the effective use of capabilities.	• Ask questions or make remarks that could be construed as in any way discriminatory.
• Make judgements on the basis of the factual information you have obtained about candidates' experience and attributes in relation to the person specification.	• Attempt too many interviews in a row.
• Keep control over the content and timing of the interview.	

How to conduct a performance review meeting

Yearly or twice-yearly performance review or appraisal meetings are a major part of a typical performance management system. However, there has recently been a reaction against 'the annual event' approach and an emphasis on more frequent feedback through relatively informal conversations rather than an over-formalized review. Those who support the annual event procedure claim that it provides a focal point for the consideration of key performance and development issues, but it can be stressful for both parties. Formal reviews can be tricky situations and need to be handled skilfully if they are going to work. If an organization is wedded to a formal review it needs to ensure that reviewers know that to conduct a constructive review meeting they have to:

- encourage individuals to do most of the talking: the aim should be to conduct the meeting as a dialogue rather than using it to make 'top down' pronouncements on what the manager thinks about them;
- listen actively to what they say;
- allow scope for reflection and analysis;
- provide feedback that analyses performance not personality, concentrating on what individuals have done and achieved, not the sort of people they are;
- keep the whole period under review, not concentrating on isolated or recent events;
- adopt a 'no surprises' approach: performance problems should have been identified and dealt with at the time they occurred;
- recognize achievements and reinforce strengths;
- discuss any work or performance problems, how they have arisen and what can be done about them;
- end the meeting positively with any necessary agreed action plans (learning and development and performance improvement).

Providing feedback

Providing feedback to people on how they are doing is an important performance management activity. It should be given by managers informally throughout the year on appropriate occasions but it will also be the key element in a formal performance review meeting. Feedback can be positive when it tells people that they have done well, constructive when it provides advice on how to do better, and negative when it tells people that they have done badly. Feedback reinforces effective behaviour and indicates where and how behaviour needs to change.

The following are guidelines on providing feedback:

1 *Build feedback into the job.* To be effective feedback should be built into the job or provided soon after the activity has taken place.

2 *Provide feedback on actual events.* Feedback should be given on actual results or observed behaviour. It should be backed up by evidence. It should not be based on supposition about the reason for the behaviour. You should, for example, say: 'We have received the following complaint from a customer that you have been rude, would you like to comment on this,' rather than: 'You tend to be aggressive.'

3 *Describe, don't judge.* The feedback should be presented as a description of what has happened; it should not be accompanied by a judgement. If you start by saying: 'I have been informed that you have been rude to one of our customers; we can't tolerate that sort of behaviour,' you will instantly create resistance and prejudice an opportunity to encourage improvement.

4 *Refer to and define specific behaviours.* Relate all your feedback to specific items of behaviour. Don't indulge in transmitting general feelings or impressions. When commenting on someone's work or behaviour define what you believe to be good work or effective behaviour with examples.

5 *Emphasize the 'how' not the 'what'.* Focus attention more on how the task was tackled rather than on the result.

6 *Ask questions.* Ask questions rather than make statements – 'Why do you think this happened?'; 'On reflection is there any other way in which you think you could have handled the situation?'; 'How do you think you should tackle this sort of situation in the future?'

7 *Select key issues.* There is a limit to how much criticism anyone can take. If you overdo it, the shutters will go up and you will get nowhere. Select key issues and restrict yourself to them.

8 *Focus.* It is a waste of time to concentrate on areas that the individual can do little or nothing about. Focus on aspects of performance the individual can improve.

9 *Provide positive and constructive feedback.* People are more likely to work positively at improving their performance and developing their skills if they feel empowered by the process. Provide feedback on the things that the individual did well in addition to areas for improvement. Focus on what can be done to improve rather than on criticism.

10 *Ensure feedback leads to action.* Feedback should indicate any actions required to develop performance or skills.

How to conduct a discipline meeting

If you have good reason to believe that disciplinary action is necessary you need to take the following steps when planning and conducting a disciplinary interview:

1 Get all the facts in advance, including statements from people involved.

2 Invite the employee to the meeting in writing, explaining why it is being held and that he or she has the right to have someone present at the meeting on his or her behalf.

3 Ensure that the employee has reasonable notice (ideally at least two days).

4 Plan how you will conduct the meeting.

5 Line up another member of management to attend the meeting with you to take notes (this can be important if there is an appeal) and generally provide support.

6 Start the interview by stating the complaint to the employee and referring to the evidence.

7 Give the employee plenty of time to respond and state his or her case.

8 Take a break as required to consider the points raised and to relieve any pressure in the meeting.

9 Consider what action is appropriate, if any. Actions should be staged, starting with a recorded written warning, followed, if the problem continues, by a first written warning, then a final written warning and lastly, if the earlier stages have been exhausted, disciplinary action, which would be dismissal in serious cases.

10 Deliver the decision, explaining why it has been taken and confirm it in writing.

How to manage poor performance

The three major aspects of poor performance that need to be managed are incompetence (under-performance), absenteeism and poor timekeeping.

1. Dealing with under-performers

You may possibly have someone who is under-performing in your team. If so, what can you do about it? Essentially, you have to spot that there is a problem, understand the cause, decide on a remedy and make the remedy work.

Poor performance can be the fault of the individual but it could arise because of poor leadership or problems in the system of work. In the case of an individual the reason may be that he or she falls into one or more of the following categories:

- could not do it – ability;
- did not know how to do it – skill;
- would not do it – attitude;
- did not fully understand what was expected.

Inadequate leadership from managers can be a cause of poor performance from individuals. It is the manager's responsibility to specify the results expected and the levels of skill and competence required. As likely as not, when people do not understand what they have to do it is their manager who is to blame.

Performance can also be affected by the system of work. If this is badly planned and organized or does not function well, individuals cannot be blamed for the poor performance that results. This is the fault of management and they must put it right.

If inadequate individual performance cannot be attributed to poor leadership or the system of work, these are the seven steps you can take to deal with under-performers:

1 Identify the areas of under-performance – be specific.

2 Establish the causes of poor performance.

3 Agree on the action required.

4 Ensure that the necessary support (coaching, training, extra resources, etc) is provided.

5 Monitor progress and provide feedback.

6 Provide additional guidance as required.

7 As a last resort, invoke the capability or disciplinary procedure starting with an informal warning.

2. Absenteeism

A frequent people problem you probably have to face is that of dealing with absenteeism. The Chartered Institute of Personnel and Development established that absence levels in 2009 averaged 7.4 days a year per person. Your own organization should have figures that indicate average absence levels. If the levels in your department are below the average for the organization or in the absence of that information, below the national average, you should not be complacent – you should continue to monitor the absence of individuals to find out whose absence levels are above the average and why. If your department's absence figures are significantly higher than the norm you may have to take more direct action such as discussing with individuals whose absence rates are high the reasons for their absences, especially when it has been self-certificated. You may have to deal with recurrent short-term (one or two days) absence or longer-term sickness absence.

Recurrent short-term absence

Dealing with people who are repeatedly absent for short periods can be difficult. This is because it may be hard to determine when occasional absence becomes a problem or whether it is justifiable, perhaps on medical grounds.

So what do you do about it? Many organizations provide guidelines to managers on the 'trigger points' for action (the amount of absence that needs to be investigated), perhaps based on analyses of the incidence of short-term absence and the level at which it is regarded as acceptable (in some organizations software exists to generate analyses and data that can be made available direct to managers through a self-service system). If guidelines do not exist managers should be able to obtain advice from an HR specialist, if one is available. In the absence of either of these sources of help and in particularly difficult cases, it may be advisable to recommend to higher management that advice is obtained from an employment law expert.

This sort of guidance may not be available and you may have to make up your own mind on when to do something and what to do. A day off every other month may not be too serious although if it happens regularly on a Monday (after weekends in Prague, Barcelona, etc?) or a Friday (before such weekends?) you may feel like having a word with the individual, not as a warning but just to let him or her know that you are aware of what is going on. There may be a medical or other acceptable explanation. Return-to-work interviews can provide valuable information: you see the individual and find out why the time was taken off, giving him or her ample opportunity to explain the absence.

In persistent cases of absenteeism you can hold an absence review meeting. Although this would be more comprehensive than a return-to-work interview it should not at this stage be presented as part of a disciplinary process. The meeting should be positive and constructive. If absence results from a health problem you can find out what the employee is doing about it and if necessary suggest that his or her doctor should be consulted. Or absences may be caused by problems facing a parent or a carer. In such cases you should be sympathetic but you can reasonably discuss with the individual what steps can be taken to reduce the problem or you might be able to agree on flexible working if that can be arranged. The aim is to get the employee to discuss as openly as possible any factors affecting his or her attendance and to agree any constructive steps.

If after holding an attendance review meeting and, it is to be hoped, agreeing the steps necessary to reduce absenteeism, short-term absence persists without a satisfactory explanation, then another meeting can be held that emphasizes the employee's responsibility for attending work. Depending on the circumstances (each case should be dealt with on its merits), at this meeting you can link any positive support with an indication that following the provision of support you expect absence levels to improve over a defined timescale (an improvement period). If this does not happen, the individual can expect more formal disciplinary action.

Dealing with long-term absence

Dealing with long-term absence can also be difficult. The aim should be to facilitate the employee's return to work at the earliest reasonable point while recognizing that in extreme cases the person may not be able to come back. In that case he or she can fairly be dismissed for lack of capability as long as:

- the employee has been consulted at all stages;
- contact has been maintained with the employee – this is something you can usefully do as long as you do not appear to be pressing for a return to work before he or she is ready;

- appropriate medical advice has been sought from the employee's own doctor; the employee's consent is needed and he or she has the right to see the report, and it may be desirable to obtain a second opinion;

- all reasonable options for alternative employment have been reviewed as well as any other means of facilitating a return to work.

The decision to dismiss should only be taken if these conditions are satisfied. It is a tricky one and you should seek advice before taking it.

3. Handling poor timekeeping

If you are faced with persistent lateness and your informal warnings to the individual concerned seem to have little effect, you may be forced to invoke the disciplinary procedure. If timekeeping does not improve this could go through the successive stages of a recorded oral warning, a written warning and a final written warning. If the final warning does not work disciplinary action would have to be taken; in serious cases this would mean dismissal.

Note that this raises the difficult question of time limits when you give a final warning that timekeeping must improve by a certain date, the improvement period. If it does improve by that date, and the slate is wiped clean, it might be assumed that the disciplinary procedure starts again from scratch if timekeeping deteriorates again. But it is in the nature of things that some people cannot sustain efforts to get to work on time for long, and deterioration often occurs. In these circumstances, do you have to keep on going through the warning cycles time after time? The answer ought to be no, and the best approach is to avoid stating a finite end date to a final warning period that implies a 'wipe the slate clean' approach. Instead, the warning should simply say that timekeeping performance will be reviewed on a stated date. If it has not improved, disciplinary action can be taken. If it has, no action will be taken, but the employee is warned that further deterioration will make him or her liable to disciplinary action that may well speed up the normal procedure, perhaps by only using the final warning stage and by reducing the elapsed time between the warning and the review date. There will come a point, if poor timekeeping persists, when you can say 'enough is enough' and initiate disciplinary action.

KEY LEARNING POINTS

Selection interviewing

The aim of a selection interview is to provide answers to three fundamental questions: *Can* the individual do the job? *Will* the individual do the job? *How* is the individual likely to fit into the team?

A selection interview should take the form of a conversation with a purpose. It has three sections:

1 *Beginning.* At the start of the interview candidates are put at their ease.

2 *Middle.* Where interviewers find out about candidates to establish the extent to which they meet the requirements of the job.

3 *End.* Candidates are given the opportunity to ask about the job and the company. More details can be given to promising candidates, who are told what the next step will be.

Your first step in preparing for an interview is to familiarize or re-familiarize yourself with the person specification and candidate's CV, application form or letter.

The best approach to structuring the interview is one that is criteria and target based using competencies as the criteria. A biographical approach is probably the most popular because it is simple to use and appears to be logical.

The interviewer's job is to draw the candidate out at the same time ensuring that the information required is obtained. To this end it is desirable to ask a number of open-ended questions, but a good interviewer will have an armoury of other types of questions to be asked when appropriate – probing, hypothetical, behaviour event and continuity.

Performance review meetings

The performance review meeting is the means through which the five primary performance management elements of agreement, measurement, feedback, positive reinforcement and dialogue can be put to good use. A performance review meeting is a stocktaking exercise answering the questions 'Where have we got to?' and 'How did we get here?'

A constructive review meeting is most likely if the manager or team leader encourages individuals to do most of the talking and listens actively to what they say; allows scope for reflection and analysis; provides feedback; analyses performance not personality; keeps the whole period under review; adopts a 'no surprises' approach; recognizes achievements and reinforces strengths; discusses any work or performance problems, how they have arisen and what can be done about them; and ends the meeting positively with any necessary agreed action plans (learning and development and performance improvement).

Providing feedback

Providing feedback to people on how they are doing is an important performance management activity. It should be given by managers informally throughout the year on appropriate occasions but it will also be provided at a formal performance review meeting.

How to conduct a discipline meeting

If you have good reason to believe that disciplinary action is necessary you need to get all the facts in advance, plan how you will conduct the meeting, line up another member of management to attend.

Handling under-performers

There are the seven steps you can take to deal with under-performers:

1 Identify the areas of under-performance – be specific.

2 Establish the causes of poor performance.

3 Agree on the action required.

4 Ensure that the necessary support is provided.

5 Monitor progress and provide feedback.

6 Provide additional guidance as required.

7 As a last resort, invoke the capability or disciplinary procedure.

Handling absenteeism

You should continue to monitor the absence of individuals to find out whose absence levels are above the average and why. If your department's absence figures are significantly higher than the norm you may have to take more direct action. You may have to deal with recurrent short-term (one or two days) absence or longer-term sickness absence.

Handling poor timekeeping

If you are faced with persistent lateness and your informal warnings to the individual concerned seem to have little effect, you may be forced to invoke the disciplinary procedure. If timekeeping does not improve this could go through the successive stages of a recorded oral warning, a written warning and a final written warning. If the final warning does not work disciplinary action would have to be taken; in serious cases this would mean dismissal.

QUESTIONS

1 What are the aims of a selection interview?

2 What is the form of a selection interview?

3 What are the sections in a selection interview?

4 How should an interview be structured?

5 In what ways can interviews be planned?

6 What approach is required in asking questions?

7 What is an open question?

8 What is a closed question?

9 What are the key 'dos' in selection interviews? Name at least four.

10 What are the key 'don'ts' in selection interviews? Name at least four.

11 What is the purpose of a performance management review meeting?

12 What are the key approaches to conducting a performance management review meeting? Name at least four.

13 How should you provide feedback?

14 How do you deal with poor performance?

15 How should you handle absenteeism?

16 How do you handle poor timekeeping?

Learning and development skills

18

KEY CONCEPTS AND TERMS

Personal development planning   Role profile

LEARNING OUTCOMES

On completing this chapter you should be able to define these key concepts. You should also understand:

- Approaches to developing people
- Coaching
- Mentoring
- Job instruction

Introduction

A considerable amount of the responsibility for developing people rests with line managers, bearing in mind that most learning happens in the workplace. This chapter covers the many different ways in which managers can contribute to learning and development taking into account the factors affecting how people learn, as explained in Chapter 3. It starts by describing three general approaches that can be adopted: defining role profiles, induction training and personal development plans. Consideration is then given to specific L&D skills.

Defining role profiles

Role profiles set out the results that role holders have to achieve and the knowledge and skills they require, ie what they have to know and be able to do. Profiles therefore provide the basis for decisions on what people have to learn to carry out their role effectively. It is up to the manager to identify learning needs by finding out the extent to which a new starter or an existing employee has the required level of knowledge and skills and then taking steps to remedy any deficiencies.

For new starters this can be done at the induction stage when the role requirements are discussed and the extent to which the employee's existing knowledge and skills meet these requirements is assessed. For existing employees, performance management processes as described in Chapter 5 can be used to assess learning needs and produce development plans.

Induction training

Most new starters, other than those on formal training schemes, will learn on-the-job, although this may be supplemented with special off-the-job courses to develop particular skills or knowledge. As on-the-job learning can be haphazard, inefficient and wasteful, a planned, systematic approach is desirable. This can incorporate an assessment of what the new starter needs to learn, the use of designated and trained colleagues to act as guides and mentors, and coaching by team leaders or specially appointed and trained departmental trainers.

These on-the-job arrangements can be supplemented by self-managed learning in which individuals take responsibility for meeting their own learning needs, with help and guidance as necessary, offering access to flexible learning packages or providing advice on learning opportunities.

Personal development plans

Personal development plans are based on a mutual understanding of what people do, what they have achieved, what knowledge and skills they have and what knowledge and skills they need. The aims are generally to reach agreement on what is to be achieved and how, and specifically to ensure that the learning needs and actions are relevant, to indicate the time scale, to identify responsibility and, within reason, to ensure that the learning activities will stretch those concerned.

Plans are always related to work and the capacity to carry it out effectively. They are *not* just about choosing suitable courses to satisfy learning needs. Training courses may form part of the development plan, but a minor part; other learning activities such as those listed below are more important:

- coaching;
- use of a role model (mentor);
- observing and analysing what others do (good practice);
- extending the role (job enrichment);
- project work – special assignments;
- involvement in other work areas;
- involvement in communities of practice (learning from others carrying out similar work);
- action learning;
- e-learning;
- guided reading.

Coaching

First line managers, team leaders and supervisors are best placed to make a significant impact on the performance of their staff through coaching.

Coaching is a personal (usually one-to-one) on-the-job approach to helping people develop their skills and levels of competence. The need for coaching may arise from formal or informal performance reviews but opportunities for coaching will emerge during normal day-to-day activities. Managers as coaches:

- provide guidance and instruction to ensure that people acquire the knowledge and skills they need to do their job;
- make people aware of how well they are performing by, for example, asking them questions to establish the extent to which they have thought through what they are doing;
- use controlled delegation – they ensure that individuals not only know what is expected of them but also understand what they need to know

and be able to do to complete the task satisfactorily; this gives them an opportunity to provide guidance at the outset: guidance at a later stage may be seen as interference;

- use whatever situations may arise as opportunities to promote learning;
- encourage people to look at higher-level problems and how they would tackle them.

Coaching will be most effective when the coach understands that his or her role is to help people to learn and individuals are motivated to learn. The individuals concerned should be aware that their present level of knowledge or skill or their behaviour needs to be improved if they are going to perform their work satisfactorily. They should be given guidance on what they should be learning and feedback on how they are doing and, because learning is an active not a passive process, they should be actively involved with their coach, who should be constructive, building on strengths and experience.

Coaching should provide motivation, structure and effective feedback if managers have the required skills and commitment. As coaches, managers believe that people can succeed, that they can contribute to their success and that they can identify what people need to be able to do to improve their performance.

The following requirements for effective coaching were listed by Gray (2010: 379):

- establish rapport;
- create trust and respect;
- demonstrate effective communication skills;
- promote self-awareness and self-knowledge;
- use active listening and questioning techniques;
- assist goal development and setting;
- motivate;
- encourage alternative perspectives;
- assist in making sense of a situation;
- identify significant patterns of thinking and behaving;
- provide an appropriate mix of challenge and support;
- facilitate depth of understanding;
- show compassion;
- act ethically;

- inspire curiosity;
- act as a role model;
- value diversity and difference;
- promote action and reflection.

Mentoring

Mentoring is the process of using specially selected and trained individuals to provide guidance, pragmatic advice and continuing support that will help the person or persons allocated to them to learn and develop. Mentors prepare individuals to perform better in the future and groom them for higher and greater things, ie career advancement. Managers can act as mentors, or they can appoint mentors from within their department or ask the learning and development function to provide a mentor from elsewhere.

Mentoring is a method of helping people to learn and develop as distinct from coaching, which is a relatively directive means of increasing people's competence. Mentoring promotes learning on the job, which is always the best way of acquiring the particular skills and knowledge the job holder needs. Mentoring also complements formal training by providing those who benefit from it with individual guidance from experienced managers who are 'wise in the ways of the organization'.

Mentors provide people with:

- advice on drawing up self-development programmes or learning contracts;
- general help with learning programmes;
- guidance on how to acquire the necessary knowledge and skills to do a new job;
- advice on dealing with any administrative, technical or people problems individuals meet, especially in the early stages of their careers;
- information on 'the way things are done around here' – the corporate culture and its manifestations in the shape of core values and organizational behaviour (management style);
- coaching in specific skills;
- help in tackling projects – not by doing it for them but by pointing them in the right direction, helping people to help themselves;
- a parental figure with whom individuals can discuss their aspirations and concerns and who will lend a sympathetic ear to their problems.

Managers and anyone else involved in mentoring will benefit from advice on the approaches they can use and the skills they need. This advice should be available from the learning and development function, which should also monitor the effectiveness of mentors.

Job instruction

When people learn specific tasks, especially those involving basic administrative or manual skills, the learning will be more effective if job instruction techniques are used. Effective instruction follows the sequence of instruction described below.

1. Preparation

Preparation for each instruction period means that the trainer must have a plan for presenting the subject matter and using appropriate teaching methods, visual aids and demonstration aids. It also means preparing trainees for the instruction that is to follow. They should want to learn. They must perceive that the learning will be relevant and useful to them personally. They should be encouraged to take pride in their job and to appreciate the satisfaction that comes from skilled performance.

2. Presentation

Presentation should consist of a combination of telling and showing – explanation and demonstration. Explanation should be as simple and direct as possible: the trainer explains briefly the ground to be covered and what to look for. He or she makes the maximum use of charts, diagrams and other visual aids. The aim should be to teach first things first and then proceed from the known to the unknown, the simple to the complex, the concrete to the abstract, the general to the particular, the observation to reasoning, and the whole to the parts and back to the whole again.

3. Demonstration

Demonstration is an essential stage in instruction, especially when the skill to be learnt is mainly a 'doing' skill. Demonstration can take place in three stages:

a The complete operation is shown at normal speed to show the trainee how the task should be carried out eventually.

b The operation is demonstrated slowly and in correct sequence, element by element, to indicate clearly what is done and the order in which each task is carried out.

c The operation is demonstrated again, slowly, at least two or three times, to stress the how, when and why of successive movements.

The learner then practises by imitating the instructor and constantly repeating the operation under guidance. The aim is to reach the target level of performance for each element of the total task, but the instructor must constantly strive to develop coordinated and integrated performance – that is, the smooth combination of the separate elements of the task into a whole job pattern.

4. Follow up

Follow up continues during the training period for all the time required by the learner to reach a level of performance equal to that of the normal experienced worker in terms of quality, speed and attention to safety. During the follow-up stage, the learner will continue to need help with particularly difficult tasks or to overcome temporary set-backs that result in a deterioration of performance. The instructor may have to repeat the presentation for the elements and supervise practice more closely until the trainee regains confidence or masters the task.

KEY LEARNING POINTS

Defining role profiles
Role profiles describe the results that role holders have to achieve and the knowledge and skills they require.

Induction training
Most new starters other than those on formal training schemes will learn on-the-job, although this may be supplemented with special off-the-job courses to develop particular skills or knowledge.

Personal development plans

Personal development plans are based on a mutual understanding of what people do, what they have achieved, what knowledge and skills they have and what knowledge and skills they need.

Coaching

Coaching is a personal (usually one-to-one) approach to helping people develop their skills and knowledge and improve their performance. The need for coaching may arise from formal or informal performance reviews, but opportunities for coaching will emerge during the course of day-to-day work.

Mentoring

Mentoring is the process of using specially selected and trained individuals to provide guidance, pragmatic advice and continuing support, which will help the person or persons allocated to them to learn and develop.

Job instruction

When people learn specific tasks, especially those involving basic administrative or manual skills, the learning will be more effective if job instruction techniques are used. Effective instruction uses the following sequence: preparation, presentation, demonstration and follow up.

Reference

Gray, D A (2010) Building quality into executive coaching, in (eds) J Gold, R Thorpe and A Mumford, *Gower Handbook of Leadership and Management Development*, Aldershot, Gower, pp 367–85

QUESTIONS

1 What is involved in coaching?

2 What is involved in mentoring?

3 What are the four stages of instruction?

Managing
interpersonal
relationships
at work

19

Introduction

Interpersonal relationships are those that take place between people when they associate with one another at work. As covered in this chapter, they take the form of working in teams or groups, networking, communicating, being assertive, handling emotional behaviour and conflict, negotiating, handling politics, acting in a politically astute and ethical manner to secure HR objectives, and liaising with customers.

Characteristics of effective teams and team-building

Teams are essential to the effective functioning of organizations. They assemble the skills, experiences and insights of a number of people who work together to achieve a common purpose. Most formally constituted teams have an appointed leader, but informal teams can develop during the normal course of work in which leaders may emerge with the consent of the work group. It is also possible for either formal or informal teams to be self-managed.

Effective teams

In an effective team its members work together to achieve expected results. The purpose of the team is clear and its members feel the task is important, both to them and to the organization. They may not always agree on the best way to achieve the task but when they don't agree, they discuss, even argue, about their differences to resolve them.

The structure of the team is likely to be one in which the leadership and methods of operation are relevant to its purpose. People will have been grouped together in a way that ensures they are related to each other by way of the requirements of task performance and task interdependence. Job specialization is minimized, team members operate flexibly within the group, tasks are rotated among them and they are multiskilled.

The atmosphere in an effective team tends to be informal, comfortable and relaxed. The leader of the team does not dominate it, nor does the team defer unduly to him or her. The role of the team leader may be primarily to act as a facilitator – more supportive and participative than directive. There is little evidence of a struggle for power as the team operates. The issue is not who controls, but how to get the job done.

Self-managed teams

High levels of engagement and commitment and better teamwork can be achieved by a self-managed team. Such a team is highly autonomous, responsible to a considerable degree for planning and scheduling work and monitoring team performance and quality standards.

Team-building

Ten things to do to achieve good teamwork:

1 Establish urgency and direction.

2 Select members based on skills and skill potential who are good at working with others but still capable of taking their own line when necessary.

3 Pay particular attention to first meetings and actions.

4 Set immediate performance-orientated tasks and goals, including overlapping or interlocking objectives for people who have to work together.

5 Assess people's performance not only on the results they achieve but also on the degree to which they are good team members. Recognize and reward people who have worked well in teams (using team bonus schemes where appropriate), bearing in mind that being part of a high-performance team can be a reward in itself.

6 Encourage people to build networks – results are achieved in organizations, as in the outside world, on the basis of who you know as well as what you know.

7 Describe and think of the organization as a system of interlocking teams united by a common purpose. Don't emphasize hierarchies. Abolish departmental boundaries if they are getting in the way.

8 Hold special 'off-the-job' meetings for work teams so they can get together and explore issues without the pressures of their day-to-day jobs.

9 Encourage teams to socialize and provide them with facilities and even the funds to do so.

10 Use learning and development programmes to build relationships. This can often be a far more beneficial result of a course than the increase in skills or knowledge that was its ostensible purpose. Use team-building

and interactive skills training to supplement the other approaches but do not rely upon them to have any effect unless the messages they convey are in line with the organization's culture and values.

Assertiveness

Assertiveness is about expressing your opinions, beliefs, needs, wants and feelings firmly and in direct, honest and appropriate ways. It means standing up for your own rights in such a way that you do not violate another person's rights. When you are being assertive you are not being aggressive, which means violating or ignoring other people's rights in order to get your own way or dominate a situation.

Behaving assertively puts you in the position of being able to influence people properly and react to them positively. Assertive statements:

- are brief and to the point;
- indicate clearly that you are not hiding behind something or someone and are speaking for yourself by using words such as: 'I think that...', 'I believe that...', 'I feel that...';
- are not over-weighted with advice;
- use questions to find out the views of others and to test their reactions to your behaviour;
- distinguish between fact and opinion;
- are expressed positively but not dogmatically;
- indicate that you are aware that the other people have different points of view;
- express, when necessary, negative feelings about the effects of other people's behaviour on you, pointing out in dispassionate and factual terms the feelings aroused in you by that behaviour, and suggesting the behaviour you would prefer;
- indicate to people politely but firmly the consequences of their behaviour.

Interpersonal communication

People recognize the need to communicate but find it difficult. Like Schopenhauer's hedgehogs, they want to get together; it's only their prickles that keep them apart. Words may sound or look precise, but they are not. All sorts of barriers exist between the communicator and the receiver. Unless these barriers are overcome the message will be distorted or will not get through.

Barriers to communication

Hearing what we want to hear

What we hear or understand when someone speaks to us is largely based on our own experience and background. Instead of hearing what people have told us, we hear what our minds tell us they have said. We have preconceptions about what people are going to say, and if what they say does not fit into our frame of reference we adjust it until it does.

Ignoring conflicting information

We tend to ignore or reject communications that conflict with our own beliefs. If they are not rejected, some way is found of twisting and shaping their meaning to fit our preconceptions. When a message is inconsistent with existing beliefs, the receiver rejects its validity, avoids further exposure to it, easily forgets it and, in his or her memory, distorts what has been heard.

Perceptions about the communicator

It is difficult to separate what we hear from our feelings about the person who says it. Non-existent motives may be ascribed to the communicator. If we like people we are more likely to accept what they say – whether it is right or wrong – than if we dislike them.

Influence of the group

The group with which we identify influences our attitudes and feelings. What a group hears depends on its interests. Workers are more likely to listen to their colleagues, who share their experiences, than to outsiders such as managers or union officials.

Words mean different things to different people

Essentially, language is a method of using symbols to represent facts and feelings. Strictly speaking, we can't convey meaning; all we can do is to convey words. Do not assume that because something has a certain meaning to you, it will convey the same meaning to someone else.

Non-verbal communication

When we try to understand the meaning of what people say we listen to the words but we also use other clues that convey meaning. We attend not only to what people say but to how they say it. We form impressions from what is called body language – eyes, shape of the mouth, the muscles of the face, even posture. We may feel that these tell us more about what someone is really saying than the words he or she uses, but there is enormous scope for misinterpretation.

Emotions

Our emotions colour our ability to convey or to receive the true message. When we are insecure or worried, what we hear seems more threatening than when we are secure and at peace with the world. When we are angry or depressed, we tend to reject what might otherwise seem like reasonable requests or good ideas. During a heated argument, many things that are said may not be understood or may be badly distorted.

Noise

Any interference to communication is 'noise'. It can be literal noise that prevents the message being heard, or figurative in the shape of distracting or confused information that distorts or obscures the meaning.

Size

The larger and more complex the organization the greater the problem of communication. The more levels of management and supervision through which a message has to pass, the greater the opportunity for distortion or misunderstanding.

Overcoming barriers to communication

Adjust to the world of the receiver

Try to predict the impact of what you are going to write or say on the receiver's feelings and attitudes. Tailor the message to fit the receiver's vocabulary, interests and values. Be aware of how the information may be misinterpreted because of prejudices, the influence of others and the tendency of people to reject what they do not want to hear.

Use feedback

Ensure that you get a message back from the receiver that tells you how much has been understood.

Use face-to-face communication

Whenever appropriate and possible talk to people rather than sending an e-mail or writing to them. That is how you get feedback. You can adjust or change your message according to reactions. You can also deliver it in a more human and understanding way – this can help to overcome prejudices. Verbal criticism can often be given in a more constructive manner than a written reproof, which always seems to be harsher.

Use reinforcement

You may have to present your message in a number of different ways to get it across. Re-emphasize the important points and follow up.

Use direct, simple language

This seems obvious, but many people clutter up what they say with jargon, long words and elaborate sentences.

Suit the actions to the word

Communications have to be credible to be effective. There is nothing worse than promising the earth and then failing to deliver. When you say you are going to do something, do it. Next time you are more likely to be believed.

Reduce problems of size

If you can, reduce the number of levels of management. Encourage a reasonable degree of informality in communications. Ensure that activities are grouped together to ease communication on matters of mutual concern.

Handling emotional behaviour

Emotional behaviour can include aggression, withdrawal and unreasonable actions or reactions.

Aggression

If you are faced by aggression, take a breath, count up to 10 and then:

- Ask calmly for information about what is bugging the aggressor.
- State clearly, and again calmly, the position as you see it.

- Empathize with the aggressor by making it plain that you can see their point of view, but at the same time explain in a matter-of-fact way how you see the discrepancy between what they believe and what you feel is actually happening.

- Indicate, if the aggressive behaviour persists, your different beliefs or feelings, but do not cut aggressors short – people often talk, or even shout, themselves out of being aggressive when they realize that you are not reacting aggressively and that their behaviour is not getting them anywhere.

- Suggest, if all else fails, that you leave it for the time being and talk about it again after a cooling-off period.

Withdrawal

Withdrawal can take the form of lack of interest, uncooperative behaviour or refusing to take part in the work of a team, an activity or a project. If any of these happen and work is affected you have to deal with it, not by confrontation but by trying to reach agreement that something is wrong (not easy; people in an emotional state are quite prepared to believe that everyone is out of step but them) and attempting to establish the cause of the behaviour.

Almost by definition, if someone is in an emotional state it is going to be difficult to get through to them. But the attempt must be made and this is best done by being unemotional yourself and only referring to facts about the situation – what has happened or is happening. The aim is to get the person to accept that these facts are correct although there may still be a real problem that his or her view of the facts is distorted by emotions. Of course, this could apply to you and a dispassionate pursuit of the truth may result in you readjusting your views on the matter. If, and it can be a big if, you get to the root of the problem you can try to get the individual to propose what actions should be taken by him or her or by you. Try to get the person to suggest solutions; don't impose your own ideas.

Unreasonable actions or reactions

f someone seems to be acting unreasonably the first reaction of many people : 'I must make them see reason.' But you can't *make* people see reason; they ₁ve to be convinced that an alternative way of behaviour or reaction is ₂re reasonable than the one they have adopted. The best approach is the one suggested above for dealing with withdrawal. You have to question to get the facts and listen to what is said. You have to establish the reasoning behind the behaviour (assuming there is any – it could be no more than an immediate emotional reaction) so that agreement can be reached as to what can be done about it. However, if it is unreasonable and unacceptable this must be spelt out so that the individual knows what is expected and is aware of the possible consequences (eg disciplinary action) if the behaviour persists.

Handling conflict

Conflict is inevitable in organizations because they function by means of adjustments and compromises among competitive elements in their structure and membership. Conflict also arises when there is change, because it may be seen as a threat to be challenged or resisted, or when there is frustration – this may produce an aggressive reaction; fight rather than flight. Conflict is not to be deplored. It is an inevitable result of progress and change and it can and should be used constructively. Bland agreement on everything would be unnatural and enervating. There should be clashes of ideas about tasks and projects, and disagreements should not be suppressed. They should come out into the open because that is the only way to ensure that the issues are explored and conflicts are resolved.

There is such a thing as creative conflict – new or modified ideas, insights, approaches and solutions can be generated by a joint re-examination of the different points of view as long as this is based on an objective and rational exchange of information and ideas. However, conflict becomes counter-productive when it is based on personality clashes, or when it is treated as an unseemly mess to be hurriedly cleared away, rather than as a problem to be worked through. Conflict resolution can be concerned with conflict between groups or conflict between individuals (interpersonal conflict).

Handling inter-group conflict

There are three principal ways of resolving inter-group conflict: peaceful coexistence, compromise and problem solving.

1. Peaceful coexistence

The aim here is to smooth out differences and emphasize the common ground. People are encouraged to learn to live together; there is a good deal of information, contact and exchange of views, and individuals move freely between groups (for example, between headquarters and the field, or between sales and marketing).

This is a pleasant ideal, but it may not be practicable in many situations. There is much evidence that conflict is not necessarily resolved by bringing people together. Improved communications and techniques such as briefing groups may appear to be good ideas but are useless if management has nothing to say that people want to hear. There is also the danger that the real issues, submerged for the moment in an atmosphere of superficial bonhomie, will surface again later.

2. Compromise

The issue is resolved by negotiation or bargaining and neither party wins or loses. This concept of splitting the difference is essentially pessimistic. The hallmark of this approach is that there is no 'right' or 'best' answer. Agreements only accommodate differences. Real issues are not likely to be solved.

3. Problem solving

An attempt is made to find a genuine solution to the problem rather than just accommodating different points of view. This is where the apparent paradox of 'creative conflict' comes in. Conflict situations can be used to advantage to create better solutions.

If solutions are to be developed by problem solving, they have to be generated by those who share the responsibility for seeing that the solutions work. The sequence of actions is: first, those concerned work to define the problem and agree on the objectives to be attained in reaching a solution; second, the group develops alternative solutions and debates their merits; and third, agreement is reached on the preferred course of action and how it should be implemented.

Handling interpersonal conflict

Handling conflict between individuals can be even more difficult than resolving conflicts between groups. Whether the conflict is openly hostile or subtly covert, strong personal feelings may be involved. However, interpersonal conflict, like inter-group conflict, is an organizational reality that is not necessarily good or bad. It can be destructive, but it can also play a productive role.

The reaction to interpersonal conflict may be the withdrawal of either party, leaving the other one to hold the field. This is the classic win/lose situation. The problem has been resolved by force, but this may not be the best solution if it represents one person's point of view that has ignored counter-arguments, and has, in fact, steamrollered over them. The winner may be triumphant but the loser will be aggrieved and either demotivated or resolved to fight again another day. There will have been a lull in, but not an end to, the conflict.

Another approach is to smooth over differences and pretend that the conflict does not exist, although no attempt has been made to tackle the root causes. Again, this is an unsatisfactory solution. The issue is likely to re-emerge and the battle will recommence.

Yet another approach is bargaining to reach a compromise. This means that both sides are prepared to lose as well as win some points and the aim is to reach a solution acceptable to both sides. Bargaining, however, involves all sorts of tactical and often counterproductive games, and the parties are often more anxious to seek acceptable compromises than to achieve sound solutions.

Personal counselling is an approach that does not address the conflict itself but focuses on how the two people are reacting. Personal counselling gives people a chance to release pent-up tensions and may encourage them to think about new ways of resolving the conflict. However, it does not address the essential nature of the conflict, which is the relationship between two people. That is why constructive confrontation offers the best hope of a long-term solution.

Constructive confrontation

Constructive confrontation is a method of bringing the individuals in conflict together, ideally with a third party whose function is to help build an exploratory and cooperative climate. Constructive confrontation aims to get the parties involved to understand and explore the other's perceptions and feelings. It is a process of developing mutual understanding to produce a win/win situation.

The issues will be confronted but on the basis of a joint analysis, with the help of the third party, of facts relating to the situation and the actual behaviour of those involved. Feelings will be expressed but they will be analysed by reference to specific events and behaviours rather than inferences or speculations about motives.

Third parties have a key role in this process, and it is not an easy one. They have to get agreement on the ground rules for discussions aimed at bringing out the facts and minimizing hostile behaviour. They must monitor the ways in which negative feelings are expressed and encourage the parties to produce new definitions of the problem and its cause or causes and new motives to reach a common solution. Third parties must avoid the temptation to support or appear to support either of those in contention. They should adopt a counselling approach, as follows:

- listen actively;
- observe as well as listen;
- help people to understand and define the problem by asking pertinent, open-ended questions;
- recognize feelings and allow them to be expressed;
- help people to define problems for themselves;
- encourage people to explore alternative solutions;
- get people to develop their own implementation plans but provide advice and help if asked.

To conclude, conflict, as has been said, is in itself not to be deplored: it is an inevitable concomitant of progress and change. What is regrettable is the failure to use conflict constructively. Effective problem solving and constructive confrontation both resolve conflicts and open up channels of discussion and cooperative action.

Many years ago one of the pioneering and most influential writers on management, Mary Parker Follett (1924), wrote something on managing conflict that is as valid today as it was then. She said that differences can be made to contribute to the common cause if they are resolved by integration rather than domination or compromise.

Resolving conflict between team members

To resolve conflict between team members the following actions can be taken:

1 Obtain an overview of the situation from your own observations.
2 Find out who is involved.
3 Talk to each of the parties to the conflict to obtain their side of the story.
4 Talk to other members of the group to get their views, being careful to be dispassionate and strictly neutral.

5 Evaluate what you hear from both parties and other people against your knowledge of what has been happening, any history of conflict and the dispositions and previous behaviour of the people involved.

6 Reach preliminary conclusions on the facts, the reasons for the dispute and the extent to which either of the parties or both are to blame (but keep these to yourself at this stage).

7 Bring the parties together to discuss the situation. The initial aim of this meeting would be to get the problem out into the open, get the facts and defuse any emotions that may prejudice a solution to the problem. Both parties should be allowed to have their say but as the facilitator of this meeting, you should do your best to ensure that they stick to the facts and explain their point of view dispassionately. You should not even remotely give the impression that you are taking sides.

8 Try to defuse the situation so that a solution can be reached that on the whole will be acceptable to all concerned. Ideally, this should be an integrated solution reached by agreement on the basis of collaboration along the lines of 'Let's get together to find the best solution on the basis of the facts.' It may be necessary to reach a compromise or accommodation – something everyone can live with.

9 Only if all else fails or the parties are so recalcitrant in holding an untenable position that no integrated, comprise or accommodating solution can be reached should you resort to direct action – instructing one or both the parties to bury their differences and get on with their work. If the worse comes to the worst this may involve disciplinary action, beginning with a formal warning.

Handling challenging conversations

Many managers find it difficult to have conversations or hold meetings with individuals about performance or discipline issues. In advance these can look difficult and in practice they *can* be challenging if the manager wants to achieve desired changes or improvements in performance. They can be even more challenging in prospect if it is feared that unpleasantness can occur in the shape of lack of cooperation or outright hostility, or in practice when this happens in spite of efforts to prevent it. The following is a 12-point guide to handling challenging conversations:

1 Don't wait until a formal review meeting. Have a quiet word at the first sign that something is going wrong.

2 Get the facts in advance – what happened, when and why.

3 Plan the meeting on the basis of the facts and what is known about the individual.

4 Define what is to be achieved.

5 Set the right tone from the start of the meeting – adopt a calm, measured, deliberate but friendly approach.

6 Begin the conversation by explaining the purpose of the meeting, indicating to the individual what the issue is and giving specific examples.

7 Focus on the issue and not the person.

8 Ask for an explanation. Ask unloaded questions to clarify the issues and explore them together.

9 Allow people to have their say and listen to them.

10 Keep an open mind and don't jump to conclusions.

11 Acknowledge the individual's position and any mitigating circumstances.

12 Ask the employee for proposals to resolve the situation, discuss the options and if possible agree on action by the individual, the manager or jointly.

If agreement cannot be reached, managers may have to define the way forward, with reasons – they are in charge!

Networking

Networks are loosely organized connections between people with shared interests. Increasingly in today's more fluid and flexible organizations people get things done by networking. They exchange information, enlist support and create alliances, getting agreement with other people on a course of action and joining forces to make it happen.

To network effectively here are 10 steps you can take:

1 Identify people who may be able to help.

2 Seize any opportunity that presents itself to get to know people who may be useful.

3   Have a clear idea of why you want to network – to share knowledge, to persuade people to accept your proposal or point of view, to form an alliance.

4   Know what you can contribute – networking is not simply about enlisting support: it is just as much if not more concerned with developing knowledge and understanding through 'communities of interest' and joining forces with like-minded people so that concerted effort can be deployed to get things done.

5   Show interest – if you engage with people and listen to them they are more likely to want to network with you.

6   Ask people if you can help them as well as asking people to help you.

7   Put people in touch with one another.

8   Operate informally but be prepared to call formal meetings when necessary to reach agreement and plan action.

9   Make an effort to keep in touch with people.

10 Follow up – check with members of the network on progress in achieving something, refer back to conversations you have had, discuss with others how the network might be developed or extended to increase its effectiveness.

Negotiating

Negotiating takes place when two parties meet to reach an agreement on the price of something, on the terms and conditions of a contract or employment or a pay claim. Negotiation can be convergent when both parties are equally keen to reach a win/win agreement (in commercial terms a willing buyer – willing seller arrangement). It can be divergent when one or both of the parties aim to win as much as they can from the other while giving away as little as possible. This can become a zero-sum game where the winner takes all and the loser gets nothing. Negotiations in an industrial relations setting differ from commercial negotiations in the respects set out in Table 19.1. Negotiations take place in an atmosphere of uncertainty. Neither side knows how strong the other side's bargaining position is or what it really wants and will be prepared to accept.

Table 19.1 Industrial and commercial negotiations compared

Industrial relations negotiations	Commercial negotiations
• Assume an ongoing relationship – negotiators cannot walk away.	• Negotiators can walk away.
• The agreement is not legally binding.	• The contract is legally binding.
• Conducted on a face-to-face basis.	• May be conducted at a distance.
• Carried out by representatives responsible to constituents.	• Carried out directly with the parties being responsible to a line manager.
• Make frequent use of adjournments.	• Usually conducted on a continuing basis.
• May be conducted in an atmosphere of distrust even hostility.	• Usually conducted on a 'will ng buyer/willing seller' basis.

Negotiating and bargaining skills

The skills required to be effective in negotiations and bargaining are:

- *Analytical ability* – the capacity to assess the factors that affect the negotiating stance and tactics of both parties.

- *Empathy* – the ability to put oneself in the other party's shoes.

- *Interactive skills* – the ability to relate well to other people.

- *Communicating skills* – the ability to convey information and arguments clearly, positively and logically.

- *Keeping cards close to the chest* – not stating what you really want or are prepared to concede until you are ready to do so (in the marketplace it is always easier for sellers to drive a hard bargain with buyers who have revealed somehow that they covet the article).

- *Flexible realism* – the capacity to make realistic moves during the bargaining process to reduce the claim or increase the offer, which will demonstrate that the bargainer is seeking a reasonable settlement and is prepared to respond appropriately to movements from the other side.

Organizational politics

To be politic, according to the *Concise Oxford English Dictionary*, you can be sagacious, prudent, judicious, expedient, scheming or crafty. Organizational politics involves various kinds of desirable and undesirable behaviour designed to get outcomes that are sought by an individual or a group. The behaviour may consist of overt or more probably covert pressures on individuals in positions of power or on interest groups to agree to or obstruct a course of action. Influence may be exerted outside the usual channels to get things done or to undo things; for example, the opinions of committee members might be influenced by lobbying them outside the committee. This could be justified by the politician as the best ways of achieving something, but it could be undesirable if it consists of perverting the normal open and transparent processes of decision making, especially when it is perpetrated simply to pursue the organizational politician's own ends.

Political behaviour is inevitable in organizations because they consist of individuals who, while they are ostensibly there to achieve a common purpose will, at the same time, be driven by their own needs to achieve their own goals. Effective management is the process of harmonizing individual endeavour and ambition to the common good. Some individuals will genuinely believe that using political means to achieve their goals will benefit the organization as well as themselves. Others will rationalize this belief. Yet others will unashamedly pursue their own ends. They may use all their powers of persuasion to legitimize these ends to their colleagues, but self-interest remains the primary drive. These are the corporate politicians the *Oxford English Dictionary* describes as 'shrewd schemers, crafty plotters or intriguers'. Politicians within organizations can be like this. They manoeuvre behind people's backs, blocking proposals they do not like. They advance their own reputation and career at the expense of other people. They can be envious and jealous and act accordingly. They are bad news. However, it can also be argued that a political approach to management is inevitable and even desirable in any organization where the clarity of goals is not absolute, where the decision-making process is not clear-cut and where the authority to make decisions is not evenly or appropriately distributed – and there can be few organizations where one or more of these conditions does not apply.

Political sensitivity

Organizational politicians exert hidden influence to get their way, and 'politicking' in some form takes place in most organizations. If you want to get on, a degree of political sensitivity is desirable – knowing what is going on so that influence can be exerted. This means that you have to:

- know how 'things are done around here';
- know how decisions are made;
- understand the factors that are likely to affect decisions;
- know where the power base is in the organization (sometimes called the 'dominant coalition'): who makes the running, who are the people who count when decisions are taken;
- be aware of what is going on behind the scenes;
- know who is a rising star and whose reputation is fading;
- identify any 'hidden agendas': try to understand what people are really getting at, and why, by obtaining answers to the question: 'Where are they coming from?'
- find out what other people are thinking and seeking;
- network – identify the interest groups and keep in contact with them.

Dangers

The dangers of politics, however, are that they can be carried to excess, and they can then seriously harm the effectiveness of an organization. The signs of excessive indulgence in political behaviour include:

- backbiting;
- buck-passing;
- secret meetings and hidden decisions;
- feuds between people and departments;
- e-mail or paper wars between armed camps – arguing by e-mail or memorandum is always a sign of distrust;
- a multiplicity of snide comments and criticisms;
- excessive and counterproductive lobbying;
- the formation of cabals – cliques that spend their time intriguing.

Dealing with organizational politicians

One way to deal with this sort of behaviour is to find out who is going in for it and openly confront them with the damage they are doing. They will, of course, deny that they are behaving politically (they wouldn't be politicians if they didn't), but the fact that they have been identified may lead them to modify their approach. It could, of course, only serve to drive them further underground, in which case their behaviour will have to be observed even more closely and corrective action taken as necessary.

A more positive approach to keeping politics operating at an acceptable level is for the organization to manage its operations as openly as possible. The aims should be to ensure that issues are debated fully, that differences of opinion are dealt with frankly and that disagreements are depersonalized, so far as this is possible. Political processes can then be seen as a way of maintaining the momentum of the organization as a complex decision-making and problem-solving entity.

Meeting HR aims in a politically astute and ethical manner

HR practitioners are inevitably involved in organizational politics and they are more likely to survive and thrive if they handle these astutely. But they also have to behave ethically, whether they are politicking or going about their daily business of providing advice and services.

On being politically astute

Politically astute behaviour on the part of HR practitioners means that they have to identify the key decision makers when they are involved in developing new approaches and getting things done. Before coming to a final conclusion and launching a fully-fledged proposal at a committee or in a memorandum, it makes good sense to test opinion and find out how other people may react. This testing process enables them to anticipate counter-arguments and modify their proposals either to meet legitimate objections or, when there is no alternative, to accommodate other people's requirements. All this requires political sensitivity.

Ethical considerations

Making deals as described above may not appear to be particularly desirable although it does happen, and HR practitioners can always rationalize this type of behaviour by reference to the end result. This is in effect utilitarianism, as described in Chapter 8 – the belief that the greatest good to the greatest number allows people to be treated as a means to ends, if it is to the advantage of the majority. Actions should be judged in terms of their consequences. This is sometimes interpreted as supporting the dubious principle that the ends justify the means.

Politicking is unethical if it means adopting a devious approach to getting things done. For example, withholding information is not legitimate behaviour, but people do indulge in it in recognition of the fact that knowledge is power. Judicious withdrawal may also seem to be questionable, but most people prefer to live to fight another day rather than launch a doomed campaign. It may be unethical to abandon beliefs in an effort to achieve results but it is worth remembering what Benjamin Franklin said to the meeting held on 17 September 1787 in Pennsylvania State House to debate the draft constitution of the United States of America. His words were:

> For having lived long, I have experienced many instances of being obliged by better Information, or fuller Consideration, to change Opinions even on important Subjects, which I once thought right, but found to be otherwise. That people believe themselves to be right is no proof that they are; the only difference between the Church of Rome and the Church of England is that the former is infallible while the latter is never wrong.

This is a particular case. In general, ethical behaviour by HR practitioners means that HR specialists need to take account of the dignity and rights of employees when taking employment decisions. These include having clear and fair terms and conditions of employment, healthy and safe working conditions, fair remuneration, promoting equal opportunities and employment diversity, encouraging employees to develop their skills, and not discriminating or harassing employees. The ethical frameworks for judging HR practices are basic rights, organizational justice, respecting individuals, and community of purpose.

Liaising with customers

Liaising with customers, whether external or internal, is a matter of establishing their wants and needs and then meeting them. This is done in a way that will create and maintain good relationships, which for external customers results in repeat sales and an enhancement of the company's reputation in the marketplace, and for internal customers means furthering the objectives of the organization and fostering a cooperative attitude between those involved. It is necessary to define what is required from all concerned in liaising with external or internal customers, and to remember that relationships with internal customers are also important.

Defining requirements

The requirements for effectively liaising with customers can be defined in terms of attitudes, skills, knowledge and behaviours.

Attitudes

Customer service excellence is achieved by people whose attitudes can be summed up in the phrase 'put the customer first'. They must believe that they exist because customers exist and that being responsive to customer needs and expectations is a vital part of their role.

Skills

The main skills required are:

- interpersonal skills – ability to relate well to people during person-to-person contacts;
- listening skills – ability to pay attention to people, absorb what they are saying and react appropriately;
- communication skills – ability to explain matters to customers clearly and with conviction and to handle telephone conversations;
- complaints handling skills – ability to deal with complaints and handle angry customers.

Knowledge

Knowledge of the product or service offered will be required. For external customers, this could be quite advanced knowledge enabling individuals to identify and deal with faulty equipment or provide technical advice. It will also be necessary to understand the customer service systems and procedures used in the organization. For internal customers it is necessary to understand what the departments or individuals need and how to satisfy those needs.

Behaviours

When liaising with customers the behaviours required are:

- taking time to understand the specific needs, requirements and any current pressures the customer may be under;

- looking for ways to delight the customer;
- being honest about the product or service offered and what can be done to help the customer;
- generating a range of solutions to address a difficulty.

Internal customers

An internal customer is anyone who makes use of the outputs or services provided by other departments or individuals in the organization. This means everyone – all employees are customers of other employees and they all provide services to other employees. Some departments such as HR, IT and facilities management exist primarily to provide professional or technical services directly to other departments. Some departments exist to produce outputs upon which other departments rely to achieve their objectives. Research and development has to deliver products that can be promoted and sold by marketing and sales departments. Production or operating departments exist to deliver the products or services that are required by sales to meet customer demands. Marketing and sales departments produce the information on forecast demand, which enables production and operating departments to plan their activities.

It can be argued that: meeting the needs of internal customers is a prerequisite for meeting the needs of external customers. If, for example, marketing gets its sales forecasts wrong or manufacturing fails to meet the requirements specified by sales, then it is the level of service to external customers that suffers and this has a negative impact on satisfaction and loyalty.

The basic approach to creating high standards of service for internal customers is to define how the different parts of the organization interrelate and spell out who serves whom and who receives service from whom. It is then necessary to ensure that all the parties concerned know how important service to internal customers is and what is expected of them from their internal customers. This can be defined formally as a service level agreement. For example, an agreement for an HR service centre could set out standards under the following headings:

- speed of response to requests for help or guidance in areas such as recruitment, training, handling disciplinary cases and grievances, and health and safety;
- the time taken to prepare and agree role profiles, fill job vacancies or conduct a job evaluation exercise;

- the quality of candidates submitted for job vacancies;
- the proportion of discipline or grievance issues settled at the first time HR is involved;
- the number of appeals (successful and unsuccessful) against job grading decisions;
- the results of evaluations of training carried out by participants in training programmes;
- the outcome of employee attitude surveys.

These standards could be used to measure the value of the HR function.

KEY LEARNING POINTS

Interpersonal relationships
Interpersonal relationships are those that take place between people when they associate with one another at work.

Teamwork
Teams are essential to the effective functioning of organizations. In an effective team its members work together to achieve expected results. The purpose of the team is clear and its members feel the task is important, both to them and to the organization. The structure of the team is likely to be one in which the leadership and methods of operation are relevant to its purpose. The atmosphere in an effective team tends to be informal, comfortable and relaxed. The leader of the team does not dominate it, nor does the team defer unduly to him or her.

Networks
Networks are loosely organized connections between people with shared interests. Increasingly in today's more fluid and flexible organizations people get things done by networking. They exchange information, enlist support and create alliances – getting agreement with other people on a course of action and joining forces to make it happen.

Communicating
People recognize the need to communicate but find it difficult. Words may sound or look precise, but they are not. All sorts of barriers exist between the communicator and the receiver. Unless these barriers are overcome the message will be distorted or will not get through.

Assertiveness

Assertiveness is about expressing your opinions, beliefs, needs, wants and feelings firmly and in direct, honest and appropriate ways.

Emotional behaviour

Emotional behaviour can include aggression, withdrawal and unreasonable actions or reactions.

Conflict

Conflict is inevitable in organizations because they function by means of adjustments and compromises among competitive elements in their structure and membership. There are three principal ways of resolving intergroup conflict: peaceful coexistence, compromise and problem solving. Interpersonal conflict can be handled by constructive confrontation.

Handling challenging conversations

A 12-point guide to handling challenging conversations is included in this chapter.

Negotiating and bargaining skills

The skills required to be effective in negotiations and bargaining are analytical ability, empathy, interactive skills, communicating skills, keeping cards close to the chest and flexible realism.

Organizational politics

Political behaviour is inevitable in organizations because they consist of individuals who, while they are ostensibly there to achieve a common purpose, will, at the same time, be driven by their own needs to achieve their own goals.

Organizational politics involves various kinds of desirable and undesirable behaviour designed to get outcomes sought by an individual or a group.

HR practitioners are inevitably involved in organizational politics and they are more likely to survive and thrive if they handle these astutely. But they also have to behave ethically, whether they are politicking or going about their daily business.

Liaising with customers

Liaising with customers, whether external or internal, is a matter of establishing their wants and needs and then meeting them.

Reference

Follett, M P (1924) *Creative Experience*, New York, Longmans Green

QUESTIONS

1   What are interpersonal relationships?

2   What is the significance of teams in organizations?

3   What makes a team effective?

4   How can good teamworking be achieved? List at least four approaches.

5   What are networks in organizations?

6   What steps can be taken to improve networking? List at least four.

7   What are the main barriers to communication?

8   How can those barriers be overcome?

9   What is assertiveness?

10   What are the characteristics of assertive behaviour?

11   How can aggression be handled?

12   What are the three main ways of handling inter-group conflict?

13   How can interpersonal conflict be handled?

14   What is the process of negotiating?

15   What are the most important negotiating and bargaining skills? Name at least four.

16   What is the role of political behaviour in organizations?

17   What do you have to do to be politically sensitive? Name at least four actions.

18   What is politically astute behaviour on the part of HR practitioners?

19   What behaviours are required when liaising with customers?

20   What is a service level agreement?

Managing oneself

20

Introduction

Successful managers are good at managing all the resources available to them: people, money, equipment and other facilities. But they also have to be good at managing a key resource – themselves. That is what this chapter is about. The starting points in managing yourself are an understanding of individual differences as they affect your own and other people's behaviour, and an appreciation of the meaning of personality and its dimensions in terms of individual traits and types. Against this background, this chapter reviews in succession five key aspects of managing yourself: self-assessment, managing your time, the skills you need to organize yourself and your work, managing stress in yourself and others, the need for continuous personal development and, finally, how to adopt a professional and ethical approach to your work.

Individual differences

The development of HR processes, the design of organizations and the ways in which people manage others are often based on the belief that everyone is the same and will behave rationally when faced with change or other demands. But the behaviour of people differs because of their characteristics and individual differences and it is not always rational. When managing yourself it is equally important to know how you fit in with other people in all their variety so that, as necessary, you can adapt your behaviour.

The management of people and working with them would be much easier if everyone were the same, but they aren't. As discussed below, they are different because of variations in personal characteristics – their personality, abilities and intelligence, and the influence of their background. Gender, race or disability are also considered factors by some people, although holding this view readily leads to discrimination.

Variations in personal characteristics

The headings under which personal characteristics can vary have been classified by Mischel (1968) as follows:

- *Competencies* – abilities and skills.
- *Constructs* – the conceptual framework that governs how people perceive their environment.
- *Expectations* – what people have learnt to expect about their own and others' behaviour.
- *Values* – what people believe to be important.
- *Self-regulatory plans* – the goals people set themselves and the plans they make to achieve them.

These are affected by environmental or situational variables including the type of work individuals carry out; the culture, climate and management style in the organization; the social group within which they work; and the 'reference groups' individuals use for comparative purposes (eg comparing conditions of work or pay between one category of employee and another).

The influence of background and culture

Individual differences may be a function of people's background, which includes the environment and culture in which they have been brought up and now exist. Levinson (1978) suggested that 'individual life structure' is shaped by three types of external event:

1 The socio-cultural environment.
2 The roles they play and the relationships they have.
3 The opportunities and constraints that enable or inhibit them to express and develop their personality.

Differences arising from gender, race or disability

It is futile, dangerous and invidious to make assumptions about inherent differences between people because of their sex, race or disability. *If* there are differences in behaviour at work these are more likely to arise from environmental and cultural factors than from variations in fundamental personal characteristics. The work environment undoubtedly influences feelings and behaviour for all these categories. Arnold *et al* (1991) referred to research which established that working women as a whole 'experienced more daily stress, marital dissatisfaction, and ageing worries, and were less likely to show overt anger than either housewives or men'. Ethnic minorities may find that the selection process is biased against them, promotion prospects are poor and that they are subject to other overt or subtle forms of discrimination. The behaviour of disabled people can also be affected by the fact that they are not given equal opportunities. There is, of course, legislation against discrimination in each of those areas but this cannot prevent the more covert forms of prejudice.

Influences on behaviour at work

Behaviour at work is dependent on both the personal characteristics of individuals as considered below and the situation in which they are working. These factors interact, and this theory of behaviour is sometimes called 'interactionism'. It is because of the process of interaction and because there are so many variables in personal characteristics and situations that behaviour is difficult to analyse and predict. James and Sells (1981) noted the following environmental influences on behaviour:

- role characteristics such as role ambiguity and conflict;
- job characteristics such as autonomy and challenge;
- leader behaviours including goal emphasis and work facilitation;
- work group characteristics including cooperation and friendliness;
- organizational policies that directly affect individuals such as the reward system.

It is generally assumed that attitudes determine behaviour but there is not such a direct link as most people suppose. Arnold *et al* (1991) commented that research evidence has shown that feelings and beliefs about someone or something seemed only loosely related to how they behaved towards it.

Dimensions of personality

Differences in the dimensions of personality between people are significant factors in explaining behaviour. That is why personality tests are often used as part of selection procedures and various forms of personality indicators or inventories such as Myers–Briggs, the 'Big five' test and the 16PF questionnaire as described later are used in leadership and management development programmes, including executive coaching.

Personality has been defined by Huczynski and Buchanan (2007: 844) as: 'The psychological qualities that influence an individual's characteristic behaviour patterns in a stable and distinctive manner.' As noted by Ivancevich *et al* (2008), personality appears to be organized into patterns that are, to some degree, observable and measurable and involves both common and unique characteristics – every person is different from every other person in some respects but similar to others in other respects. Personality is a product of both nature (heredity) and nurture (the pattern of life experience). The dimensions of personality can be described in terms of traits or types.

The trait concept of personality

Traits are predispositions to behave in certain ways in a variety of different situations. We all attribute traits to people in an attempt to understand why they behave in the way they do. It is assumed that traits describe enduring behaviour that occurs in a variety of settings. This assumption that people are consistent in the ways they express these traits is the basis for making predictions about their future behaviour. As Chell (1987) explained, traits are used to classify people in an attempt to understand how they act. There have been a number of ways of classifying traits, as described below.

On the basis of exhaustive factor analysis (the statistical analysis of the interactions between the effects of random or independent variables) Cattell

(1946) identified 16 factors underlying human personality, which he called 'source traits' because he believed that they provide the underlying source for the surface behaviours we think of as personality. This theory of personality is known as the 16-factor personality model. Cattell also developed an instrument to measure them called the 16PF Questionnaire. The factors are:

1 Warmth.

2 Reasoning.

3 Emotional stability.

4 Dominance.

5 Liveliness.

6 Rule-consciousness.

7 Social boldness.

8 Sensitivity.

9 Vigilance.

10 Abstractedness.

11 Privateness.

12 Apprehension.

13 Openness to change.

14 Self-reliance.

15 Perfectionism.

16 Tension.

Eysenck (1953) produced a simpler model. He identified three personality traits: extroversion/introversion, neuroticism and psychoticism, and classified people as stable or unstable extroverts or introverts. For example, a stable introvert is passive, careful, controlled and thoughtful, while a stable extrovert is lively, outgoing, responsive and sociable.

A further development, based in part on the original research by Cattell was the 'Big five' classification of trait dimensions (Costa and McRae, 1992; Digman, 1990) which has become the leading model of personality traits. The 'Big five' are:

1 *Openness* – inventive/curious or consistent/cautious.

2 *Conscientiousness* – efficient/organized or easy-going/careless.

3 *Extraversion* – outgoing/energetic or solitary/reserved.

4 *Agreeableness* – friendly/compassionate or cold/unkind.

5 *Neuroticism* – sensitive/nervous or secure/confident.

However, the trait theory of personality has been attacked by people such as Mischel (1968). The main criticisms are:

- People do not necessarily express the same trait across different situations or even the same trait in the same situation. Different people may exhibit consistency in some traits and considerable variability in others.
- Classical trait theory as formulated by Cattell (1946) assumes that trait behaviour is independent of the situations and the persons with whom the individual is interacting. This assumption is questionable, given that trait behaviour usually manifests itself in response to specific situations.
- Trait attributions are a product of language – they are devices for speaking about people and are not generally described in terms of behaviour.

Type theory of personality

Type theory identifies a number of types of personality that can be used to categorize people and may form the basis of a personality test. The types may be linked to descriptions of various traits. As Huczynski and Buchanan (2007: 142) observed: 'While individuals belong to types, traits belong to individuals. You fit a type, you have a trait.'

The most familiar type theory is that of Jung (1923). He identified four major preferences of people:

1 *Relating to other people* – extraversion or introversion.
2 *Gathering information* – sensing (dealing with facts that can be objectively verified), or intuitive (generating information through insight).
3 *Using information* – thinking (emphasizing logical analysis as the basis for decision making), or feeling (making decisions based on internal values and beliefs).
4 *Making decisions* – perceiving (collecting all the relevant information before making a decision), or judging (resolving the issue without waiting for a large quantity of data).

This theory of personality forms the basis of one of the most popular personality tests – the Myers–Briggs Types Indicator. This rates personal preferences on four scales:

introvert → extroverts
sensing → intuition
thinking → feeling
judging → perceiving

Self-awareness

Self-awareness is about knowing yourself, so far as that is possible, and analysing your achievements, skills, knowledge and managerial competences. The aim is to identify strengths and weaknesses so as to make the most of the former and do what you can to overcome the latter. Drucker (1999) proposed that:

> The only way to discover your strengths is through feedback analysis. Whenever you make a key decision or take a key action, write down what you expect will happen. Nine or 12 months later, compare the actual results with your expectations.

It is also helpful to make a general assessment of yourself – your strengths and weaknesses – and conduct an overall review of how you do your job and analyse your achievements, as described below.

Knowing yourself

The question you have to answer is: 'What sort of person am I?' This is the most difficult question to answer truthfully. Try answering the self-analysis questionnaire in Table 20.1. Consider each statement under the heading 'I think I am someone who is…' and indicate in the appropriate box the extent to which you agree or disagree with it. The outcome will be a profile that you can study to identify any personality characteristics that you may need to do something about.

This analysis will help you to think about how you behave. You can't really change your personality but, given what you know about the sort of person you are, you may be able to adjust your behaviour to make it more productive and acceptable to people. However, remember what Shakespeare advised: 'To your own self be true.' Also bear in mind what Browning wrote: 'Best be yourself, imperial plain and true.' Your behaviour must be genuine not assumed, otherwise people will see through you and the relationships will simply get worse.

Job performance review

Examine your job and how you do it as follows:

1 Ensure that you are clear about what your job entails in terms of its key result areas – the most important things you are expected to do. If in doubt, ask your manager for clarification.

Table 20.1 Self-assessment questionnaire

I think I am someone who is:	Strongly agree	Agree	Neither agree nor disagree	Disagree	Strongly disagree
Outgoing, likes people	☐	☐	☐	☐	☐
Emotionally stable	☐	☐	☐	☐	☐
Easily upset	☐	☐	☐	☐	☐
Forceful, domineering	☐	☐	☐	☐	☐
Cooperative, accommodating	☐	☐	☐	☐	☐
Lively, enthusiastic	☐	☐	☐	☐	☐
Serious, introspective	☐	☐	☐	☐	☐
Imaginative, creative	☐	☐	☐	☐	☐
Prosaic, conventional	☐	☐	☐	☐	☐
Astute, diplomatic	☐	☐	☐	☐	☐
Self-assured, confident	☐	☐	☐	☐	☐
Open to change	☐	☐	☐	☐	☐
Traditional	☐	☐	☐	☐	☐
Group-orientated, a joiner	☐	☐	☐	☐	☐
Driven	☐	☐	☐	☐	☐
Relaxed	☐	☐	☐	☐	☐

2 Find out what you are expected to achieve for each of the key result areas. Expectations should be definable as objectives in the form of quantified targets or standards of performance (qualitative statements of what constitutes effective performance). Ideally they should have been discussed and agreed as part of the performance appraisal/management process but if this has not happened, ask your manager to spell out what he or she expects you to achieve.

Managing Oneself 357

3 Refer to the organization's competency framework. Discuss with your manager how he or she interprets these as far as you are concerned.

4 At fairly regular intervals, say once a month, review your progress by reference to the objectives, standards and competency headings. Take note of your achievements and, if they exist, your failures. Analyse your strengths and weaknesses. Ask yourself why you were successful or unsuccessful and what you can do to build on success or overcome failure. You may identify actions you can take or specific changes in behaviour you can try to achieve. Or you may identify a need for further coaching, training or experience.

5 At the end of the review period and prior to the appraisal discussion with your manager, look back at each of your interim reviews and the actions you decided to take. Consider what more needs to be done in any specific area or generally. You will then be in a position to answer the following questions that might be posed by your manager before or during the appraisal discussion:

- How do you feel you have done?
- What are you best at doing?
- Are there any parts of your job that you find difficult?
- Are there any aspects of your work in which you would benefit from better guidance or further training?

Analysis of achievements, skills and knowledge

An analysis of your achievements, skills and knowledge can be conducted by answering the following questions:

1 *What have I achieved so far?* Answer this question by looking back on your life and list the key events, happenings, incidents and turning points that have taken place. Whenever you have succeeded in doing something new or better than before, analyse the factors that contributed to that success. Was it initiative, hard work, determination, the correct application of skills and knowledge based on a searching analysis of the situation, the ability to work in a team, the exercise of leadership, the capacity to seize an opportunity (another and better word for 'luck') and exploit it, the ability to articulate a need and get into action to satisfy it, the ability to make things happen – or any other factor you can think of?

2 *When have I failed to achieve what I wanted?* You do not want to dwell too much on failure but it can be treated positively, as long as you analyse dispassionately where you went wrong and assess what you might have been able to do to put it right.

3 *What am I good or not so good at doing?* What are your distinctive competences? Consider these in terms of professional, technical or managerial know-how as well as the exercise of such skills as communicating, decision making, problem solving, teamworking, exercising leadership, delegating, coordinating, meeting deadlines, managing time, planning, organizing and controlling work, dealing with crises.

4 *What have been my significant learning experiences?* Recall events when you have learnt something worthwhile and how you made use of it.

5 *How well do I know my chosen area of expertise?* Have you got or are you getting the right qualifications? Have you acquired or are you acquiring the right know-how through study, training and relevant experience?

Time management

Time management is the process of making the most of a key but limited resource – the time available to carry out your work. Shakespeare's Richard II lamented: 'I wasted time, now doth time waste me.' It's a problem many people come up against. Even if we haven't been *wasting* our time most of us recognize that there is scope for managing our time more productively. To do this you need to think systematically about how you use your time. You can then take steps to organize yourself better and to get other people to help or at least not to hinder you. The first thing you need to do is to analyse your job and how you spend your time to find out where there is scope for improvement.

Analyse your job

Start with your job – the tasks you have to carry out and the objectives you are there to achieve. Try to establish an order of priority between your tasks and among your objectives. It is more difficult to do this if you have a number of potentially conflicting areas of responsibility. You have to try to reconcile these and establish priorities.

Analyse how you spend your time

Having sorted out your main priorities you should analyse in more detail how you spend your time. This will identify time-consuming activities and indicate where there are problems as well as possible solutions to them. The best way to analyse time is to keep a diary. You can do this on paper or electronically using Microsoft Outlook organizing software. Do this for a week, or preferably two or three, as one week may not provide a typical picture. Divide the day into 15-minute sections and note down what you did in each period. Against each space, summarize how effectively you spent your time by writing V for valuable, D for doubtful and U for useless. If you want to make more refined judgements give your ratings pluses or minuses. At the end of the week analyse your time under the following headings:

- Dealing with people (individuals or groups).
- Attending meetings.
- Sending and opening e-mails.
- Telephoning.
- Reading.
- Writing.
- Travelling.
- Miscellaneous administrative tasks.
- Other (specify).

Analyse also the V, D, U ratings of the worth of each activity under each heading and then consider how you can organize yourself more effectively.

Organize yourself

Such an analysis will usually throw up weaknesses in the way you plan your work and establish your priorities. You have to fit the tasks you must complete into the time available to complete them, and get them done in order of importance.

Some people find it difficult, if not impossible, to plan their work ahead. They find that they work best if they have to achieve almost impossible deadlines. Working under pressure concentrates the mind wonderfully, they say. But ordinary mortals, who work under a variety of conflicting pressures, cannot rely upon crisis action to get them out of logjams of work. For most of us it is better to try to minimize the need for working under exceptional pressure by a little attention to the organization of our week or day. At the very least you should use your diary for long-range planning, organizing your weekly activities in broad outline and planning each day in as much detail as possible. You can then use a daily organizer to good purpose.

Use your diary

Attempt to leave at least one day a week free of meetings and avoid filling the day with appointments. In other words, leave blocks of unallocated time for planning, thinking, reading, writing and dealing with the unexpected. Sit down at the beginning of each week with your electronic, desk or pocket diary and plan how you are going to spend your time. Assess each of your projects or tasks and work out priorities. Leave blocks of time for dealing with e-mails and other correspondence and seeing people. Try to preserve one free day, or at least half a day, if it is at all possible. If it helps you, record what you intend to do each morning, afternoon and, if it's work, evening.

Daily organizer

At the beginning of each day, consult your diary to check on your plans and commitments. Refer to the previous day's organizer to find out what is outstanding. Inspect your pending tray, in-tray and incoming e-mails to check on what remains and what has just arrived. Then enter or write down the things to do:

- Meetings or interviews.
- Respond to e-mails.
- Telephone calls.
- Tasks in order of priority:

  A – must be done today.

  B – ideally should be done today but could be left till tomorrow.

  C – can be dealt with later.

Plan broadly when you are going to fit your A and B priority tasks into the day. Tick off your tasks as they have been completed. Retain the list to consult next day. You can use your electronic organizer to do this, but many successful time managers are happy with a blank sheet of paper. You could use a simple form such as the one shown in Figure 20.1.

Figure 20.1 Example of a daily organizer

DAILY ORGANIZER			
Meetings and appointments	Committee/person	Where	When
To email	Person	About what	When
To telephone	Person	About what	When
To do	Tasks (in order of priority)	Priority rating* A, B or C	Approximate timing

*A = must be done today B = ideally done today C = later

Personal organizing skills

Effectiveness in a job is largely dependent on your personal organizing skills. Time management, as discussed earlier, is important but so is planning and prioritizing.

Planning

To plan you need to decide on a course of action, ensure that the resources required to implement the action will be available, and schedule and prioritize the work required to achieve an end result. The aim is to enable you to complete tasks on time by making the best use of the resources available. You need to avoid crises and the high costs that they cause; to have fewer 'drop everything and rush this' problems. Contingency or fall-back plans need to be prepared if there is any reason to believe that the initial plan may fail for reasons beyond your control.

When managers plan, they may choose certain courses of action and rule out others; that is to say, they may lose flexibility. This will be a disadvantage if the future turns out differently from what was expected – which is only too likely. You should try to make plans that can be changed without undue difficulty. It is a bad plan that admits no change.

Most of the planning managers carry out is simply a matter of thinking systematically and using common sense. Every plan contains five key ingredients:

1 *The objective* – what is to be achieved.

2 *The action programme* – the specific steps required to achieve the objective.

3 *Resource requirements* – what resources in terms of money, people, facilities and time will be required.

4 *Impact assessment* – determining the impact made on the organization by achieving the plan (assessed as costs and benefits).

5 *Consequence assessment* – anticipating any outcomes that may arise when implementing the plan.

Prioritizing

Planning involves prioritizing work, which means deciding on the relative importance of a range of demands or tasks so that the order in which they are undertaken can be determined. The fragmented nature of managerial work and the sudden and often conflicting demands made on your time mean that you will constantly be faced with decisions on when to do things, however carefully you have planned in advance. There may often be situations when you have to cope with conflicting priorities. This can be stressful unless you adopt a systematic approach to prioritization. This can be carried out in the following stages.

1 List all the things you have to do. These can be classified into three groups:
   a Regular duties such as submitting a report, calling on customers, carrying out a performance review.
   b Special requests from managers, colleagues, customers, clients, suppliers and so on, delivered orally, by e-mail, telephone or letter.
   c Self-generated work such as preparing proposals on a new procedure.
2 Classify each item on the list according to:
   – the significance of the task to be done in terms of its impact on your work (and reputation) and on the results achieved by the organization, your team or anyone else involved;

- the importance of the person requesting the work or expecting you to deliver something: less significant tasks may well be put higher on the priority list if they are set by the chief executive or a key client;
- the urgency of the tasks: deadlines and what will happen if they are not completed on time;
- any scope there may be for extending deadlines: altering start and finish times and dates;
- how long each task will take to complete, noting any required or imposed starting and completion times that cannot be changed.

3 Assess how much time you have available to complete the tasks, apart from the routine work you must get done. Also assess what resources, such as your own staff, are available to get the work done.

4 Draw up a provisional list of priorities by reference to the criteria of significance, importance and urgency listed at (2) above.

5 Assess the possibility of fitting this prioritized schedule of work into the time available. If this proves difficult, put self-imposed priorities on the back-burner and concentrate on the significant tasks. Negotiate delayed completion or delivery times where you believe this is possible, and if successful, move the task down the priority list.

6 Finalize the list of priorities and schedule the work you have to do (or you have to get others to do) accordingly.

Managing stress

People become stressed when they experience more pressure, frustration, or a higher level of emotional or physical demands than they can handle. Pressures include achieving performance expectations, meeting deadlines, coping with an excessive workload, dealing with difficult bosses, colleagues, clients, customers or subordinates, being bullied, achieving a satisfactory work–life balance (reconciling the demands of work with family responsibilities or outside interests), and role ambiguity (lack of understanding of what is expected). Pressure is fine as long as it does not build up to too high a level. Up to a point it will motivate and improve performance but it then turns into stress and results in a decline in performance, as illustrated in Figure 20.2.

The important thing to remember is that the ability to withstand pressure varies: one person's stimulating amount of pressure is another person's

Figure 20.2 How pressure becomes stress

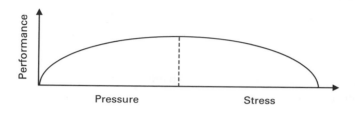

stress. This suggests that although some people may temperamentally be more prone to suffer from stress, there is some scope to manage or limit it, bearing in mind that it is often self-imposed.

Symptoms of stress

The symptoms of stress that you can observe in others or yourself include an inability to cope with the demands of the job (which creates more stress), tiredness, lethargy, lack of enthusiasm and bad temper.

Managing stress – what the organization can do

Organizations can manage stress by developing policies and processes for implementation by line managers and specialist staff. These include:

- clarifying roles to reduce role ambiguity and give people more autonomy;
- setting reasonable and achievable performance standards;
- establishing performance management processes that encourage a dialogue between managers and their staff about work and its pressures;
- giving individuals the opportunity to obtain professional counselling;
- developing anti-bullying policies and ensuring they are implemented (not easy);
- developing work–life balance policies that take account of the pressures on employees as parents, partners or carers, and which can include provisions such as special leave or flexible working hours.

Managing stress in others – what you can do

To manage stress in others you need to do the following:

- Be aware of organizational policies and procedures as set out above, and be prepared to implement them for your own staff.

- Tailor your demands on people according to their capacities – it is a good idea to agree stretching targets but they must be achievable (with effort but without undue stress) by the individual concerned.

- Look out for symptoms of stress and try to establish the cause as the basis for alleviating them.

- If an individual is under stress because of undue pressure, try to adjust demands to a more reasonable level, possibly by redesigning the job or transferring duties to someone else.

- Be prepared to listen and respond to individuals who complain of being over-stressed – you don't have to accept what they say but you should certainly hear them out.

Managing your own stress

If you feel that you are unduly stressed, here are 10 things you can do:

1 Try to establish why you are stressed – are there any specific causes or is it a general feeling that the work is getting on top of you?

2 Talk to someone about it – your boss (if likely to be sympathetic), colleagues, HR, friends, your partner.

3 If the stress is serious, ask if the organization can provide advice from a professional counsellor.

4 Discuss your workloads and deadlines with your boss to see if they can be alleviated in any way.

5 Consider whether there is scope to delegate more work to your staff.

6 Decide what is beyond your control and put it firmly to one side. Focus on what is within your sphere of influence and get on with it.

7 Take the occasional brief break in the day, if you can – relax (switch off) for a few minutes over a cup of coffee with your colleagues.

8 Don't work excessive hours unless you really have to – don't work late just to impress your manager (who wants results, not just to have you around the office) or your colleagues. Don't take work home unless this is absolutely unavoidable.

9 Consider 'mindfulness', a technique used for managing stress that involves meditation and focuses the attention of people on their current experiences.

10 Take regular exercise.

Principles of continuous professional development

Continuing professional development (CPD) is the means by which members of professional associations maintain, improve and broaden their knowledge and skills and develop the personal qualities required in their professional lives. CPD is defined as a commitment to structured skills enhancement and personal or professional competence. It is about lifelong learning and development.

As defined by the CIPD, continuous professional development is the process of consciously updating professional knowledge and improving professional competence throughout a person's working life. It is a commitment to being professional, keeping up to date and continuously seeking to improve. It is the key to optimizing a person's career opportunities, both today and for the future. It enables the integration of learning with work in ways relevant to the learner, is self-directed and contributes to the learner's development needs. The benefits to individuals include becoming better learners, profiting from learning opportunities, managing self-development, helping career advancement, and improving professional standing. The benefits to organizations include better contributions by individuals to organizational goals and objectives, improved performance for the organization, and the ability to help others learn and develop themselves to enhance their work performance and their organizational commitment.

According to the CIPD, continuous professional development should be:

- continuous – professionals should always be looking for ways to improve performance;
- the responsibility of the individual learner to own and manage;
- driven by the learning needs and development of the individual;
- evaluative rather than descriptive of what has taken place;
- an essential component of professional and personal life, never an optional extra.

Professional and ethical approaches to self-management at work

A professional approach to self-management means organizing and developing yourself to carry out your work in ways that use your expertise in providing professional advice and services. An ethical approach to self-management means that what happens as a result of your activities meets defined or generally accepted standards of behaviour. The approach should be based on self-management strategies and ethical principles, as considered below.

Self-management strategies

Self-management strategies should be based on self-assessment, which means assessing your own performance and identifying how you can improve. To assess your own performance you need to:

1 Ensure that you are clear about what your job entails in terms of the main tasks or key result areas. If in doubt, ask your manager for clarification.

2 Find out what you are expected to achieve for each of the key result areas. Expectations should be definable as objectives in the form of quantified targets or standards of performance (qualitative statements of what constitutes effective performance). Ideally they should have been discussed and agreed as part of the performance appraisal/management process but if this has not happened, ask your manager to spell out what he or she expects you to achieve.

3 Refer to the organization's competency framework. Discuss with your manager how he or she interprets these as far as you are concerned.

4 At fairly regular intervals, say once a month, review your progress by reference to the objectives, standards and competency headings. Take note of your achievements and, if they exist, your failures. Ask yourself why you were successful or unsuccessful and what you can do to build on success or overcome failure. You may identify actions you can take or specific changes in behaviour you can try to achieve, or you may identify a need for further coaching, training or experience.

5 At the end of the review period and prior to the appraisal discussion with your manager, look back at each of your interim reviews and the actions you decided to take. Consider what more needs to be done in any specific area or generally. You will then be in a position to answer the following questions that might be posed by your manager before or during the appraisal discussion:
   - How do you feel you have done?
   - What are you best at doing?
   - Are there any parts of your job you find difficult?
   - Are there any aspects of your work in which you would benefit from better guidance or further training?

This assessment should identify specific areas for development or improvement. The following 10 steps can be taken to develop yourself:

1 *Create a development log* – record your plans and actions.

2 *State your objectives* – the career path you want to follow and the skills you will need to proceed along that path.

3 *Develop a personal profile* – what sort of person you are, your likes and dislikes about work, your aspirations.

4 *List your strengths and weaknesses* – what you have done well and what you can do to build on success or develop further.

5 *List your achievements* – what you have done well so far and why you believe these were worthwhile achievements.

6 *List significant learning experiences* – recall events when you have learnt something worthwhile (this can help you to understand your learning style).

7 *Ask other people* about your strengths and weaknesses and what you should do to develop yourself.

8 *Focus on the present* – what is happening to you now: your job, your current skills, your short-term development needs.

9 *Focus on the future* – where you want to be in the longer term and how you are going to get there (including a list of the skills and abilities you need to develop).

10 *Plan your self-development strategy* – how you are going to achieve your ambitions.

Ethical principles for self-management

The ethical principles you should adopt for self-management are:

- When deciding what to do always consider the extent to which it can be justified in terms of your professional and your organization's codes of conduct and your own values on how people should be treated.

- Before doing something that affects people, review the likely consequences for them and assess whether this can be justified from the viewpoints of natural, procedural and distributive justice, as defined in Chapter 8.

- Compete fairly – manage your career in a way that does not unfairly prejudice the rights of others. Do not take advantage of the weaknesses of others, especially those with disabilities or older people.

- Do not subject people who work with you or under you to unreasonable pressure. Set fair targets to your staff – they can be demanding but they must be achievable.

KEY LEARNING POINTS

Managing yourself
The starting points in managing yourself are an understanding of individual differences as they affect your own and other people's behaviour, and an appreciation of the meaning of personality and its dimensions in terms of individual traits and types.

Personality
Personality has been defined by Huczynski and Buchanan (2007: 844) as: 'The psychological qualities that influence an individual's characteristic behaviour patterns in a stable and distinctive manner.'

The trait concept of personality
Traits are predispositions to behave in certain ways in a variety of different situations. Traits are used to classify people in an attempt to understand how they act. Type theory identifies a number of types of personality that can be used to categorize people and may form the basis of a personality test.

Self-awareness
Self-awareness is about knowing yourself, so far as that is possible, and analysing your achievements, skills, knowledge and managerial competences.

Time management
Time management is the process of making the most of a key but limited resource – the time available to carry out your work.

Personal organizing skills
Effectiveness in a job is largely dependent on how well you organize yourself. Time management is important but so is planning and prioritizing.

Planning

Planning involves deciding on a course of action, ensuring that the resources required to implement the action will be available and scheduling and prioritizing the work required to achieve a defined end result.

Prioritizing

Prioritizing work means deciding on the relative importance of a range of demands or tasks so that the order in which they are undertaken can be determined.

Managing stress

People become stressed when they experience more pressure, frustration, or a higher level of emotional or physical demands than they can handle. The symptoms of stress include an inability to cope with the demands of the job (which creates more stress), tiredness, lethargy, lack of enthusiasm and bad temper. Stress can be managed at organizational level, for individuals, and for yourself.

Continuing Professional Development

Continuing Professional Development (CPD) is the means by which members of professional associations maintain, improve and broaden their knowledge and skills and develop the personal qualities required in their professional lives.

Professional and ethical approaches to self-management

A professional approach to self-management means organizing and developing yourself to carry out your work in ways that use your expertise in providing professional advice and services. An ethical approach to self-management means that what happens as a result of your activities meets defined or generally accepted standards of behaviour.

References

Arnold, J, Robertson, I T and Cooper, C L (1991) *Work Psychology*, London, Pitman

Cattell, R B (1946) *Description and Measurement of Personality*, New York, World Books

Chell, E (1987) *The Psychology of Behaviour in Organisations*, London, Macmillan

Costa, P and McRae, R R (1992) *NEO PI-R: Professional manual*, Odessa, FL, Psychological Assessment Resources

Digman, J M (1990) Personality structure: emergence of the five-factor model, *Annual Review of Psychology*, **41**, pp 417–40

Drucker, P (1999) Managing oneself, *Harvard Business Review*, March–April, pp 66–74

Eysenck, H J (1953) *The Structure of Human Personality*, London, Methuen

Huczynski, A A and Buchanan, D A (2007) *Organizational Behaviour*, 6th edn, Harlow, FT Prentice Hall

Ivancevich, J M, Konopaske, R and Matteson, M T (2008) *Organizational Behaviour and Management*, 8th edn, New York, McGraw-Hill/Irwin

James, R and Sells, S B (1981) Psychological climate: theoretical perspectives and empirical research, in (ed) D Magnusson, *Towards a Psychology of Situations: An interactional perspective*, Hillsdale, NJ, Erlbaum

Jung, C (1923) *Psychological Types*, London, Routledge Kegan Paul

Levinson, D (1978) *The Seasons of Man's Life*, New York, Knopf

Mischel, W (1968) *Personality and Assessment*, New York, Wiley

QUESTIONS

1 What are the headings under which personal characteristics can vary?

2 What are the main environmental influences on behaviour?

3 What is personality?

4 What is the trait theory of personality?

5 What are the 'Big five' personality factors?

6 What is the type theory of personality?

7 What is self-awareness?

8 What are the key questions to be answered when analysing achievements, skills and knowledge?

9 What is time management?

10 What are the main steps required to manage time?

11 What is involved in planning?

12 What is involved in prioritizing?

13 When do people become stressed?

14 What can be done to manage the stress of others? List at least four actions.

15 What can be done to manage your own stress? List at least four actions.

16 What is continuous professional development (CPD)?

17 How should CPD take place?

18 What steps can you take to develop yourself? Name at least four.

19 What is a professional approach to self-management?

20 What is an ethical approach to self-management?

Problem solving and decision making 21

Introduction

Problem solving and decision making are closely associated processes that are a constant feature of life in organizations and elsewhere. A logical approach should be adopted, but this is not always easy – the situations where problems have to be solved and decisions made are often messy, with conflicting evidence, lack of data and political and emotional issues affecting those involved. And beware of the obvious – as H L Mencken observed, for every complex problem there is a solution that is simple, neat and wrong. But even if it is not possible to apply neat, logical and sequential methods, the principles of getting and analysing what information is available, considering alternatives and making the best choice on the evidence available (evidence-based decision making) having taken account of the likely consequences, remain the same.

Problem solving

Problem solving is the process of analysing and understanding a problem, diagnosing its cause and deciding on a solution that solves the problem and prevents it being repeated. You will often have to react to problems as they arise but as far as possible a proactive approach is desirable, which involves anticipating potential problems and dealing with them in advance by taking preventative action using the normal approaches to problem solving set out below. Proactive problem solving may require creative thinking, as considered later in this chapter.

Problems and opportunities

It is often said that 'there are no problems, only opportunities'. This is not universally true, of course, but it does emphasize the point that a problem should lead to positive thinking about what is to be done (a proactive approach), rather than to recriminations. If a mistake has been made, the reasons for it should be analysed to ensure that it does not happen again.

Improving your skills

How can you improve your ability to solve problems? There are a few basic approaches you should use.

Improve your analytical ability

A complicated situation can often be resolved by separating the whole into its component parts. Such an analysis should relate to facts although, as Drucker (1955) points out, when trying to understand the root causes of a problem you may have to start with an opinion. Even if you ask people to search for the facts first, they will probably look for those facts that fit the conclusion they have already reached.

Opinions are a perfectly good starting point as long as they are brought out into the open at once and then tested against reality. Analyse each hypothesis and pick out the parts that need to be studied and tested. Follett's (1924) 'law of the situation' – the logic of facts and events – should rule in the end and although you may start out with a hypothesis, when testing it use Rudyard Kipling's six honest serving men:

I keep six honest serving men
(They taught me all I knew)
Their names are What and Why and When
and How and Where and Who.

Being creative

A strictly logical answer to the problem may not be the best one. Use creative thinking to get off your tramlines and dream up an entirely new approach.

Keep it simple

One of the basic principles of problem solving is known as Occam's razor. It states that 'entities are not to be multiplied without necessity'. That is, always believe the simplest of several explanations.

Focus on implementation

A problem has not been solved until the solution has been implemented. Think carefully not only about how a thing is to be done (by whom, with what resources and by when) but also about its likely consequences – its impact on the organization and the people concerned and the extent to which they will cooperate. You will get less cooperation if you impose a solution. The best method is to arrange things so that everyone arrives jointly at a solution freely agreed to be the one best suited to the situation; the law of the situation again. (Further consideration to the processes of evaluating evidence and options and to the consulting skills used in problem solving is given in the next chapter.)

The 12 steps of problem solving and decision making

1 *Define the situation* – establish what has gone wrong or is about to go wrong.

2 *Specify objectives* – define what is to be achieved now or in the future to deal with an actual or potential problem or a change in circumstances.

3 *Develop hypotheses* – develop hypotheses about what has caused the problem.

4 *Get the facts* – find out what has actually happened and contrast this with an assessment of what ought to have happened. Try to understand the attitudes and motivation of those concerned. Remember that people will see what has happened in terms of their own position and feelings (their frame of reference). Obtain information about internal or external constraints that affect the situation.

5 *Analyse the facts* – determine what is relevant and what is irrelevant. Diagnose the likely cause or causes of the problem. Do not be tempted to focus on symptoms rather than root causes. Test any assumptions. Dig into what lies behind the problem.

6 *Identify possible courses of action* – spell out what each involves.

7 *Test ideas* – assess the extent to which they are likely to achieve the objectives, the cost of implementation, any practical difficulties that might emerge and the possible reactions of stakeholders. (The critical evaluation techniques described in Chapter 22 can be used for this purpose.)

8 *Weigh and decide* – determine which alternative is likely to result in the most practical and acceptable solution to the problem. This is often a balanced judgement.

9 *Decide on objectives* – set out goals for implementation of the decision.

10 *Adopt a 'means-end' approach where appropriate* – in complicated situations with long-term implications it may be useful to identify the steps required and select an action at each step that will move the process closer to the goal.

11 *Plan implementation* – prepare a timetable and identify and assemble the resources required.

12 *Implement* – monitor progress and evaluate success. Remember that a problem has not been solved until the decision has been implemented. Always work out the solution to a problem with implementation in mind.

Decision making

Decision making is about analysing and defining a situation or problem, identifying possible courses of action, weighing them up and defining a course of action. It should be a systematic and evidence-based process. Drucker (1955) produced the following words of wisdom on the subject, which have not been bettered since:

- Management is always a decision-making process. (p 310)
- The important and difficult job is never to find the right answer, it is to find the right question. (p 311)
- To take no action is a decision fully as much as to take specific action. (p 319)
- No decision can be better than the people who carry it out. (p 321)
- A manager's decision is always a decision concerning what other people should do. (p 322)

In 1967 he added:

> A decision is a judgement. It is a choice between alternatives. It is rarely a choice between right and wrong. It is at best a choice between almost right and probably wrong – but much more often a choice between two courses of action neither of which is probably more nearly right than the other. (p 120)

Decision making can be a logical process following a problem-solving, evidence-based approach but it can benefit from creative thinking. It can also benefit from involving other people. Attention has to be paid to ethical considerations and communicating the decision.

Creative thinking

Creative thinking is imaginative thinking. It produces new ways of looking at things and innovative decisions. It relates things or ideas that were previously unrelated. It is discontinuous and divergent. De Bono (1971) invented the phrase 'lateral thinking' for it and this term has stuck; it implies sideways leaps in the imagination rather than a continuous progression down a logical chain of reasoning.

Creative thinking is not superior to logical thinking; it's just different. The best managers are both creative and logical. Eventually, irrespective of how creative they have been, they have to make a decision, and logical thinking is necessary to ensure that it is the right decision. Creative thinking involves breaking away from any restrictions and opening up your mind to generate new ideas.

Breaking away

To break away from the constraints on your ability to generate new ideas you should:

- Identify the dominant ideas influencing your thinking.

- Define the boundaries (ie past experience, precedents, policies, procedures, rules) within which you are working and try to get outside them by asking questions such as: Are the constraints reasonable? Is past experience reliable? What's new about the present situation? Is there another way?

- Bring your assumptions out into the open and challenge any that restrict your freedom to develop new ideas.

- Reject 'either/or' propositions – ask, 'Is there really a simple choice between alternatives?'

- Keep on asking 'Why?' (but bear in mind that if you do this too bluntly to other people you can antagonize them).

Generating new ideas

To generate new ideas you have to open up your mind. If you have removed some of the constraints as suggested above you will be in a better position to:

- look at the situation differently, exploring all possible angles;

- list as many alternative approaches as possible without seeking the 'one best way' (there is no such thing);

- in de Bono's words, 'arrange discontinuity': deliberately set out to break the mould by such means as free thinking (allowing your mind to wander over alternative and in many cases apparently irrelevant ways of looking at the situation), deliberately exposing yourself to new influences in the form of people, articles, books, indeed anything that could give you a different insight, even though it may not be immediately relevant, switching yourself or other people from problem to problem, arranging for the cross-fertilization of ideas with other people and 'reframing' – placing the problem in a different context to generate new insights.

Team-based decision making

As Drucker (1955: 323) noted:

> People who have to carry out the decision should always participate in the work of developing alternatives… This is also likely to improve the quality of the final decision by revealing points the manager may have missed, spotting hidden difficulties and uncovering available but unused resources.

The advantages of involving teams in decision making are that more minds will be brought to bear on the problem to generate more ideas for its solution, and those taking part are likely to 'own' the solution and should therefore be more likely to welcome it and willingly take part in its implementation. Work teams can be involved in collectively dealing with problems or special problem-solving groups can be formed that can resemble the once-fashionable quality circles. Handy (1985: 160) pointed out that:

> Groups produce [fewer] ideas, in total, than the individuals of those groups working separately. So much for the stereotyping of brainstorming! But groups, though producing less ideas in total, produce better ideas in the sense that they are better evaluated, more thought through… We tend to behave more adventurously in groups than in private, where we do not have to live up to any public standard.

Group problem solving will be most effective when:

- the problem to be solved – the task of the group – is clearly defined by a briefing or by the group itself;
- the members of the group interact with one another cooperatively;
- between them, members of the group have the knowledge and skills required, including problem-solving and decision-making skills;
- the group has access to the information it needs;
- the problem-solving processes are enhanced by a skilled facilitator;
- the group is able to communicate its findings to an appropriate authority;
- the group can take part in planning and executing the decision.

You should not expect or even welcome a bland consensus view. The best decisions emerge from conflicting viewpoints. You can benefit from a clash of opinion to prevent people falling into the trap of starting with the conclusion and then looking for the facts that support it.

Ethical decision making

Answers to the following five questions should provide guidance on whether or not a proposed decision is ethical:

1 Is the proposed decision consistent with the principles of natural, procedural or distributive justice and the requirements of the organization's ethical code (if there is one)?

2 Can the decision be justified on the basis of the benefits it will provide to the organization *and* its employees?

3 Will the decision be harmful to the individual affected or to employees generally in any way, and if so how?

4 Will the decision harm the organization's reputation for fair-dealing?

5 Do the facts as established and confirmed justify the proposed decision?

Communicating and justifying decisions

Decisions affecting people should be communicated to all concerned. The communication should spell out what the decision was, why the decision was made, who made the decision, who will be affected by the decision and the right of anyone affected to raise questions or concerns about the decision.

Ten approaches to being decisive

1 *Make decisions faster* – Jack Welch, when heading General Electric, used to say: 'In today's lightning paced environment, you don't have time to think about things. Don't sit on decisions. Empty that in-basket so that you are free to search out new opportunities... Don't sit still. Anybody sitting still, you are going to guarantee they're going to get their legs knocked from under them.'

2 *Avoid procrastination* – it is easy to put an e-mail demanding a decision into the 'too difficult' section of your actual or mental in-tray. Avoid the temptation to fill your time with trivial tasks so that the evil moment when you have to address the issue is postponed. Make a start. Once you have got going you can deal with the unpleasant task of making a decision in stages. A challenge often becomes easier once we have started dealing with it. Having spent five minutes on it we don't want to feel it was wasted so we carry on and complete the job.

3 *Expect the unexpected* – you are then in the frame of mind needed to respond decisively to a new situation.

4 *Think before you act* – this could be a recipe for delay but decisive people use their analytical ability to come to swift conclusions about the nature of the situation and what should be done about it.

5 *Be careful about assumptions* – we have a tendency to leap to conclusions and seize on assumptions that support our case and ignore the facts that might contradict it.

6 *Learn from the past* – build on your experience in decision making; what approaches work best. But don't rely too much on precedents. Situations change. The right decision last time could well be the wrong one now.

7 *Be systematic* – adopt a rigorous problem-solving approach, as described above.

8 *Talk it through* – before you make a significant decision talk it through with someone who is likely to disagree so that any challenge they make can be taken into account (but you have to canvass opinion swiftly).

9 *Leave time to think it over* – swift decision making is highly desirable but you must avoid knee-jerk reactions. Pause, if only for a few minutes, to allow yourself time to think through the decision you propose to make. Confirm that it is logical and fully justified.

10 *Consider the potential consequences* – McKinseys call this 'consequence management'. Every decision has a consequence and you should consider very carefully what that might be and how you will manage it. When making a decision it is a good idea to start from where you mean to end – define the end result and then work out the steps needed to achieve it.

KEY LEARNING POINTS

Problem solving and decision making are closely associated processes that are a constant feature of life in organizations and elsewhere.

Problem solving

Problem solving is the process of analysing and understanding a problem, diagnosing its cause and deciding on a solution that solves the problem and prevents it being repeated.

Decision making

Decision making is about analysing the situation or problem, identifying possible courses of action, weighing them up and defining a course of action.

Creative thinking is imaginative thinking. It produces new ideas, new ways of looking at things and innovative decisions. The advantages of involving teams in decision making are that more minds will be brought to bear on the problem to generate more ideas for its solution, and those taking part are likely to 'own' the solution and should therefore be more likely to welcome it and willingly take part in its implementation.

Decisions affecting people should take account of ethical principles and be communicated to all concerned.

References

de Bono, E (1971) *Lateral Thinking for Managers*, London, McGraw-Hill

Drucker, P (1967) *The Effective Executive*, London, Heinemann

Drucker, P (1955) The *Practice of Management*, London, Heinemann

Follett, M P (1924) Creative *Experience*, New York, Longmans Green

Handy, C (1985) *Understanding Organizations*, 3rd edn, Harmondsworth, Penguin Books

QUESTIONS

1   What is the nature of problem solving?

2   What is the purpose of analysis in problem solving?

3   What are the key steps that should be taken in problem solving?

4   What is the nature of decision making?

5   What approach should be used to decision making?

6   What is creative thinking?

7   How can you best generate new ideas?

8   What are the advantages of involving people in decision making?

9   What are the key questions you should answer when deciding on the degree to which a decision is ethical?

10 What are the key approaches to decision making? Name at least four.

Analytical, critical and consultancy skills

22

KEY CONCEPTS AND TERMS

Analysis

Critical evaluation

Critical thinking

Evidence-based management

Fallacy

Logical reasoning

LEARNING OUTCOMES

On completing this chapter you should be able to define these key concepts. You should also understand:

- The meaning of evidence-based management
- The use of analytical skills
- The nature of logical reasoning
- The nature of critical thinking
- The nature of critical evaluation
- The skills required by external and internal consultants

Introduction

The processes of problem solving and decision making depend largely on effective analysis, critical thinking and evaluation, and the use of consultancy skills, as covered in this chapter. The basis of all these is provided by evidence-based management, as discussed below.

Evidence-based management

Evidence-based management is a method of informing decision making by making use of appropriate information derived from the analysis of policy and practices and surveys of employee opinion within the organization, systematic benchmarking and the messages delivered by relevant research. The following comments on evidence-based management were made by Pfeffer and Sutton (2006: 70):

> Nurture an evidence-based approach immediately by doing a few simple things that reflect the proper mind-set. If you ask for evidence of efficacy every time a change is proposed, people will sit up and take notice. If you take the time to pursue the logic behind that evidence, people will become more disciplined in their own thinking. If you treat the organization like an unfinished prototype and encourage trial programs, pilot studies, and experimentation – and reward learning from these activities, even when something new fails – your organization will begin to develop its own evidence base.

A five-step approach was recommended by Briner *et al* (2009: 23):

1 Practitioners or managers gain understanding of the problem or issue.
2 Internal evidence is gathered about the issue or problem leading, possibly, to a reformulation of the problem to make it more specific.
3 External evidence is gathered from published research.
4 The views of stakeholders are obtained.
5 All the sources of information are examined and critically appraised.

It should be emphasized that what is done in organizations with the evidence depends largely on the context in which it is done. Cultural, social and political factors influence perceptions and judgements and the extent to which people behave rationally is limited by their capacity to understand the complexities of the situation they are in and by their emotional reactions to it – the concept of bounded rationality as expressed by Simon (1957).

All this means that it is necessary to recognize that there are no simple solutions, no universal prescriptions, no sequences of actions that will inevitably lead to the one and only right conclusion. Short-term fixes may become long-term problems. Logical determinism – the belief that human actions can be governed by external forces in the shape of pre-scribed formulae – won't work. There is always choice. We may favour the idea of going from A to D via B and C but sometimes we have to start in the middle because our circumstances compel us to do so. We have to make the best of the situation in which we find ourselves and proceed from that point.

We need to know what that situation is – what's right and what's wrong about it. We need then to understand what can be done to address the issues emerging from the situation. We need evidence that tells us what is hap-pening within the organization, what has worked well elsewhere that may fit our requirements and what research has revealed about policies and prac-tices that will guide us in making our decisions. We need to use that evidence as the basis for our choice of the actions we intend to take. In other words, we need to practise evidence-based management using the analytical, critical thinking and consultancy skills described in the rest of this chapter.

Analytical skills

Analysis is the process of gaining a better understanding of a complex situation or problem by breaking it down into its constituent parts and establishing the relationships between them. In the Aristotelian sense it involves discerning the particular features of a situation. It requires the ability to visualize, articulate and solve complex problems and concepts and make decisions based on avail-able information. Analytical skills include the capacity to evaluate that infor-mation to assess its significance, and the ability to apply logical and critical thinking to the situation. They provide the basis for a diagnosis of the cause or causes of a problem and therefore for its solution.

Logical reasoning

If you say people are logical, you mean that they draw reasonable inferences – their conclusions can be proved by reference to the facts used to support them – and they avoid ill-founded and tendentious arguments, generalizations and irrelevancies. Logical reasoning is the basis of critical thinking and evaluation. It takes place when there is a clear relationship (a line of reasoning) between the premise (the original proposition) and the conclusion, which is supported by valid and reliable evidence and does not rely on fallacious or misleading argument. It was what Stebbing (1959) called 'thinking to some purpose'. Clear thinking is required to establish the validity of a proposition, concept or idea.

It is necessary to spot fallacious and misleading arguments. A fallacy is an unsound form of argument leading to an error in reasoning or a misleading impression. The most common form of fallacies that need to be discerned and avoided in your own or other people's arguments are summarized below:

- *Affirming the consequent* – leaping to the conclusion that a hypothesis is true because a single cause of the consequence has been observed.

- *Begging the question* – taking for granted what has yet to be proved.

- *Chop logic* – 'Contrariwise', continued Tweedledee, 'if it was so, it might be, and if it were so, it would be; but as it isn't it ain't. That's logic.' Chop logic may not always be as bad as that, but it is about drawing false conclusions and using dubious methods of argument. For example: selecting instances favourable to a contention while ignoring those that are counter to it, twisting an argument used by an opponent to mean something quite different from what was intended, diverting opponents by throwing on them the burden of proof for something they have not maintained, ignoring the point in dispute, changing the question to one that is less awkward to answer, and reiterating what has been denied and ignoring what has been asserted. Politicians know all about chop logic.

- *Confusing correlation with causation* – assuming that because A is associated with B it has caused B. It may or may not.

- *False choice* – a situation in which only two alternatives are considered, when in fact there are additional options.

- *Potted thinking* – using slogans and catchphrases to extend an assertion in an unwarrantable fashion.

- *Reaching false conclusions* – forming the view that because some are then all are. An assertion about several cases is twisted into an assertion about all cases. The conclusion does not follow the premise. This is what logicians call the 'undistributed middle'.

- *Selective reasoning* – selecting instances favourable to a contention while ignoring those that conflict with it.
- *Special pleading* – focusing too much on one's own case and failing to see that there may be other points of view.
- *Sweeping statements* – over-simplifying the facts.

Critical thinking

Critical thinking clarifies goals, examines assumptions, discerns hidden values, evaluates evidence and assesses conclusions. 'Critical' in this context does not mean disapproval or being negative. There are many positive uses of critical thinking, for example testing a hypothesis, proving a proposition or evaluating a concept, theory or argument. Critical thinking can occur whenever people weigh up evidence and make a judgement, solve a problem or reach a decision. The aim is to come to well-reasoned conclusions and solutions and test them against relevant criteria and standards. Critical thinking calls for the ability to:

- recognize problems and establish ways of dealing with them;
- gather and marshal pertinent (relevant) information;
- recognize unstated assumptions and values;
- interpret data, to appraise evidence and evaluate arguments;
- recognize the existence (or non-existence) of logical relationships between propositions;
- draw warranted conclusions and make valid generalizations;
- test assertions, conclusions and generalizations;
- reconstruct ideas or beliefs by examining and analysing relevant evidence.

Critical evaluation

Critical evaluation means not taking anything for granted and, where necessary, challenging propositions. It involves making informed judgements about the value of ideas and arguments. It uses critical thinking by analysing and evaluating the quality of theories and concepts to establish the degree to which they are valid and supported by the evidence (evidence-based) and the extent to which they are biased. It means reflecting on and interpreting data, drawing warranted conclusions and identifying faulty reasoning, assumptions and biases. The arguments for and against are weighed and the strength of the evidence on both sides is assessed. On the basis of this assessment a conclusion is reached as to which argument is preferred. Critical evaluation is required when testing propositions and evaluating the outcomes of research.

Testing propositions

Propositions based on research investigations and evidence can be tested by using the following checklist:

- Was the scope of the investigation sufficiently comprehensive?
- Are the instances representative or are they selected simply to support a point of view?
- Are there contradictory instances that have not been looked for?
- Does the proposition conflict with other propositions for which there are equally good grounds?
- If there are any conflicting beliefs or contradictory items of evidence, have they been put to the test against the original proposition?
- Could the evidence lead to other equally valid conclusions?
- Are there any other factors that have not been taken into account that may have influenced the evidence and, therefore, the conclusion?

Critically evaluating research

Putting to the test the outcomes of research, such as material published in academic journals accessed in libraries or online (eg EBSCO or Google Scholar), requires critical evaluation and the following checklist can be used:

- Is the research methodology sufficiently rigorous and appropriate?
- Are the results and conclusions consistent with the methodology used and its outcomes?
- Is the perspective adopted by the researchers stated clearly?
- Have hypotheses been stated clearly and tested thoroughly?
- Do there appear to be any misleading errors of omission or bias?

- Are any of the arguments tendentious?
- Are inferences, findings and conclusions derived from reliable and convincing evidence?
- Has a balanced approach been adopted?
- Have any underlying assumptions been identified and justified?
- Have the component parts been covered in terms of their interrelationships and their relationship with the whole?
- Have these component parts been disaggregated for close examination?
- Have they been reconstructed into a coherent whole based on underlying principles?

It is worth repeating that critical evaluation does not necessarily mean negative criticism; it means reaching a judgement based on analysis and evidence, and the judgement can be positive as well as negative.

Developing and justifying original arguments

An argument as an aspect of critical thinking consists of a presentation of reasons that support a contention. It consists of:

- a proposition or statement that expresses a point of view or belief;
- the reasoning that makes a case for the proposition or point of view;
- a discussion, the aim of which is to get the reader or listener to agree with the case that has been made;
- a conclusion that sums up the argument and its significance.

Developing an argument

An argument is based (predicated) on a premise (the proposition) that sets out the underpinning assumption. There may be more than one proposition or assumption. It could be phrased something like this: 'The argument is that A is the case. It is predicated on the assumption that B and C apply.' In a sense this suggests the conclusion the argument is intended to reach but it also indicates that this conclusion depends on the validity of the assumptions, which will have to be proved (there are such things as false premises).

Justifying an argument

The argument continues by supplying reasons to accept the proposition or point of view. These reasons have to be supported by evidence that should be based on valid research, rigorous observation, or relevant and verifiable experience, not on hearsay. It involves logical reasoning, which avoids the fallacies referred to earlier and requires critical thinking, which means coming to well-reasoned conclusions and solutions and testing them against relevant criteria and standards. It also demands critical evaluation which, as mentioned earlier, means reflecting on and interpreting data, drawing warranted conclusions and identifying faulty reasoning, assumptions and biases. Assumptions have to be tested rigorously and research evidence has to be evaluated. The checklists set out above can be used for this purpose.

Consulting skills

External management consultants providing advice and help in introducing new structures and systems and solving problems, and internal consultants who carry out a similar role within the organization, need certain skills to carry out their often demanding jobs effectively. The main skills are those concerned with:

- analysis and diagnosis;
- problem solving;
- critical thinking and evaluation;
- interpersonal relationships – establishing and maintaining productive relationships with clients;
- interviewing – obtaining information and views from people;
- persuading people to adopt a course of action;
- case presentation;
- written communications, especially report writing;
- oral communications – making presentations and leading discussions;
- facilitating meetings and group discussions;
- planning and running learning and development events;
- coaching;
- project management.

KEY LEARNING POINTS

The processes of problem solving and decision making depend largely on effective analysis, critical thinking and evaluation and the use of consultancy skills.

Evidence-based management

Evidence-based management is a method of informing decision making by using appropriate information derived from the analysis of HR policy and practices and surveys of employee opinion within the organization, systematic benchmarking and the messages delivered by relevant research.

Analytical skills

Analysis is the process of gaining a better understanding of a complex situation or problem by breaking it down into its constituent parts and establishing the relationships between them.

Logical reasoning

This involves clear thinking to establish the validity of a proposition, concept or idea.

Critical thinking

Critical thinking clarifies goals, examines assumptions, discerns hidden values, evaluates evidence, accomplishes actions and assesses conclusions.

Critical evaluation

Critical evaluation involves making informed judgements about the value of ideas and arguments.

Developing and justifying original arguments

An argument as an aspect of critical thinking consists of a presentation of reasons that support a contention.

Consultancy skills

External management consultants providing advice and help in introducing new structures and systems and solving problems and internal consultants who carry out a similar role within the organization need certain skills to carry out their often demanding jobs effectively.

References

Briner, R B, Denyer, D and Rousseau, D M (2009) Evidence-based management: concept clean-up time? *Academy of Management Perspectives*, September, pp 19–32

Pfeffer, J and Sutton, R I (2006) Evidence-based management, *Harvard Business Review*, January, pp 62–74

Simon, H (1957) *Administrative Behaviour*, New York, Macmillan

Stebbing, S (1959) *Thinking to Some Purpose*, Harmondsworth, Penguin Books

QUESTIONS

1 What is evidence-based management?

2 What does analysis involve?

3 What is logical reasoning?

4 What is a fallacy? Name three typical fallacies.

5 What does critical thinking involve?

6 What is critical evaluation?

7 What approaches can be used to test propositions?

8 How do you critically evaluate research?

9 What does argument consist of?

10 How do you develop an argument?

11 How do you justify an argument?

12 What are the key consultancy skills? Name at least four.

Information handling skills

23

KEY CONCEPTS AND TERMS

Average

Causality

Chi-squared test

Cloud computing

Correlation

Dispersion

e-HRM

Enterprise resource planning
   (ERP) system

Frequency distribution

Frequency polygon

HR information system

Human capital management

Intranet

Internal social networks

Line of best fit

Lower quartile

Mean

Median

Mode

Multi-regression analysis

Multi-variant analysis

Regression

Reverse causation

Scattergram

Self-service

Standard deviation

Statistics

Trend line

Upper quartile

Vanilla system

Variance

LEARNING OUTCOMES

On completing this chapter you should be able to define these key concepts. You should also know about:

- The meaning and purpose of information

- HR analytics

- The use of statistics
- The function and characteristics of an HR Information System (HRIS)
- Reasons for using an HRIS
- The features of an HRIS

Introduction

Information, as Drucker (1988: 46) observed, is 'data endowed with meaning and purpose'. The significance of evidence-based management, as discussed in the last chapter, is that it is based on information. Human capital management as a major HR activity is the process of informing HRM decisions by obtaining, analysing and reporting on data and information relating to employees. Evaluation of the effectiveness of learning and development and other HR activities is only possible by reference to relevant data.

HR specialists must therefore possess the knowledge required to commission and manage computerized systems to provide them and line managers with information covering such matters as employee records, absenteeism, employee turnover, rates of pay and employee benefits. Such systems also help with the administration of HR activities such as recruitment, performance management and reward. In addition, HR people need skills in using statistics to record and present information.

This chapter starts with a review of information handling skills in general, continues with an examination of the use of HR analytics and HR information systems (e-HRM) and is completed with an outline of the main statistical methods that can be used in HRM.

Handling information

To handle information it is first necessary to:

- decide what information is required for decision making and management purposes;
- identify the relevant data that is readily available and where and how it can be obtained;

- identify where any data at present unavailable can be obtained and decide whether the value of the data justifies the effort and cost of getting it;

- take steps to convert the raw data that has been made available into information that has 'meaning and purpose' in accordance with specified requirements;

- establish how best to record, analyse and present the information in ways that ensure it serves a useful purpose.

These actions inform the development of a computerized system for providing information as well as carrying out various administrative tasks, as described below. They also provide guidance on the statistical methods that can be used to analyse and present the information.

HR analytics

HR analytics use metrics (measurements) to provide the basis for assessing the impact of HRM practices and the contribution made by people to organizational performance. It is about 'data mining' – getting as much out of HR data as possible and then going on to find links, correlations and, ideally, causation, between different sets of the data, using statistical techniques.

The analytical process may involve the handling of 'big data' – very large data sets that may be analysed computationally to reveal patterns, trends and associations. The term was originated by McAfee and Brynjolfsson (2012: 63), who described it as data characterized by sheer volume, velocity (speed with which it can be collected) and variety (number of different sources, for example social media). They claimed that: 'Data-driven decisions are better decisions – it's as simple as that. Using big data enables managers to decide on the basis of evidence rather than intuition. For that reason it has the potential to revolutionize management.'

Purposes of HR analytics

As expressed by the CIPD (2015: 1):

> HR analytics enables better decision making by providing an organization with insights about the workforce and the HR policies and practices that support them. Analytics may be used to look at the traits of the workforce, in particular its human capital: the value of individual knowledge, skills and experience of individuals and teams.

The purposes to which HR analytics can be put include:

- measuring levels of engagement;
- improving employee retention rates;
- reducing absenteeism;
- evaluating the effectiveness of different sources of recruits;
- evaluating the effectiveness of learning and development activities;
- investigating the effectiveness of performance management or performance-related pay in improving performance;
- measuring the impact of organizational development interventions;
- reducing accident rates.

In each area the analysis would investigate trends and, whenever possible, the interrelationships between different types of data and between the data and performance. This evidence could be used to reach conclusions about any action required or to evaluate the effectiveness of action already taken.

There are three levels of HR analytics:

1 *Descriptive analytics*: the use of data to record a particular aspect of HR and provide information on what has been happening to, for example, labour turnover or absence rates.

2 *Multidimensional analytics*: the combination of different sets of data to establish any relationships (correlations) between them and, hopefully, indicate causation (eg that a particular HR initiative has caused an improvement in performance).

3 *Predictive analytics*: the most advanced and rare form of HR analytics is to use the data to predict trends and therefore provide guidance on future HR strategy.

CASE STUDY: Standard Chartered Bank

Standard Chartered Bank uses a human capital scorecard to analyse its data. This is produced on a quarterly and annual basis with various cuts of the same data produced for different business segments and countries, in addition to a global report. This comprises a series of slides with commentary to enable managers to understand the data.

The data is also included in twice-yearly board reviews on people strategy and forms part of the annual strategy planning process. The scorecard data is reviewed within each global business by a top team 'People Forum'. At country level, each local chief executive and his or her management committee reviews key trends in order to specify areas they need to focus on.

In addition, the Bank uses qualitative analysis to examine trends and this has led it to identify the role of the manager as mediating the relationship between engagement and performance. In turn, this has led to a focus on qualitative research to identify what raises the bank's best managers above the rest. A further example is a qualitative analysis of high performance in selected customer-facing roles to determine the key behaviours that continue to drive customer loyalty.

Using statistics

Statistics are used extensively in HR analytics to analyse and present quantitative information that can be used to guide decisions and monitor outcomes. Statistics describe and summarize data relating to a 'population', ie a homogeneous set of items with variable individual values. Statistics play a major part in the analysis of surveys and research evidence. This involves measuring frequencies, central tendencies and dispersion. Statistics also measure the relationships between variables (correlation and regression), establish the relation between cause and effect (causality), assess the degree of confidence that can be attached to conclusions (tests of significance) and test hypotheses (the chi-squared test and null-hypothesis testing). A wide variety of software is available to conduct the more sophisticated analyses.

HR professionals seldom have to use advanced statistics unless they are conducting or taking part in detailed research projects. The main statistics they will use regularly are concerned with the analysis of the incidence of events or activities (frequencies), the use of averages (measures of central tendency), how items in a population are distributed (dispersion) and the relationship between two variables (regression). But they should also be familiar with the concepts of correlation, causation and at least understand the meaning of more advanced statistical techniques used by researchers such as tests of significance, the chi-squared test and null-hypothesis testing.

Frequency

The number of times individual items in a population or set occur is represented in frequency distributions expressed in tabular form or graphically. Commonly used graphs are shown in Figure 23.1.

Figure 23.1 Examples of charts

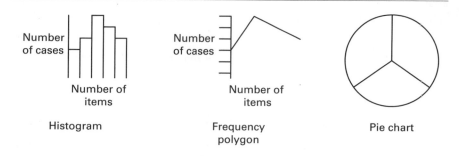

Histogram   Frequency polygon   Pie chart

Measures of central tendency

Measures of central tendency identify the middle or centre of a set of data. There are three types:

1 *Arithmetic average or mean* – the total of items or scores in a set divided by the number of individual items in the set. It may give a distorted picture because of large items at either end of the scale.

2 *Median* – the middle item in a range of items (often used in pay surveys when the arithmetic mean is likely to be distorted).

3 *Mode* – the most commonly occurring item.

Measures of dispersion

This is often useful to measure the extent to which the items in a set are dispersed or spread over a range of data. This can be done in four ways:

1 By identifying the upper or lower quartile of a range of data. The strict definition of an upper quartile is that it is the value that 25 per cent of the values in the distribution exceed, and the lower quartile is the value below which 25 per cent of the values in a distribution occur. More loosely, especially when looking at pay distributions, the upper and lower

quartiles are treated as ranges rather than points in a scale and represent the top and the bottom 25 per cent of the distribution, respectively.

2 By presenting the total range of values from top to bottom. This may be misleading if there are exceptional items at either end.

3 By calculating the inter-quartile range, which is the range between the value of the upper quartile and that of the lower quartile. This can present more revealing information of the distribution than the total range.

4 By calculating the standard deviation, which is used to indicate the extent to which the items or values in a distribution are grouped together or dispersed in a normal distribution, ie one that is reasonably symmetrical around its average. As a rule of thumb, two-thirds of the distribution will be less than one standard deviation from the mean, 95 per cent of the distribution will be less than two standard deviations from the mean and less than 1 per cent of the distribution is more than three standard deviations from the mean. Another measure of dispersion is variance, which is the square of a standard deviation.

Correlation

Correlation represents the relationship between two variables. If they are highly correlated they are strongly connected to one another. In statistics, correlation is measured by the coefficient of correlation, which varies between −1 and +1 to indicate totally negative and totally positive correlations, respectively. A correlation of 0 means that there is no relationship between the variables. Establishing the extent to which variables are correlated is an important feature of HRM research, for example in assessing the degree to which a performance management system improves organizational performance. But correlations do not indicate causal relationships: they can only show that X is associated with Y but not that X causes Y. Multiple correlation looks at the relationship between more than two variables.

Regression

Regression is another way of looking at the relationship between variables. It expresses how changes in levels of one item relate to changes in levels of another. A regression line (a trend line or line of best fit) can be traced on a scattergram expressing values of one variable on one axis and values of the other variable on another axis, as shown in Figure 23.2.

Figure 23.2 A scattergram with regression (trend) line

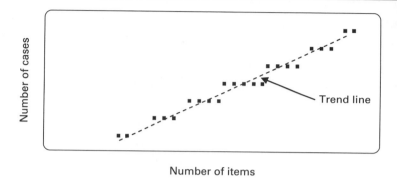

A trend line like this can be drawn by hand as a line of best fit but it can be calculated mathematically with greater accuracy. The distances of points from the trend line (the residuals) can be calculated as a check on the reliability of the line.

Multiple regression analysis can be conducted with the aid of a computer, which enables the values of additional variables to be predicted under various combinations of conditions.

Causality

Causality – determining the link between independent and dependent variables (cause and effect) – is a major issue in research, especially in the HRM field. It may be relatively easy to establish correlations in the shape of a demonstration that X is associated with Y; it is much more difficult and sometimes impossible to prove that X causes Y. There are a number of reasons for this; the two set out below are the most important.

First, complications arise because of the phenomenon of multiple causation. There may be a number of factors contributing to a result. Researchers pursuing the holy grail of trying to establish what HRM contributes to organization performance are usually confronted with a number of reasons why it has done well in addition to adopting 'best practice' HRM, whatever that is. Statistical methods can be used to 'control' some variables, ie eliminate them from the analysis, but it is difficult if not impossible to ensure that HRM practices have been completely isolated and that their direct impact on an organization's performance has been measured. Multivariate analysis is used where there is more than one dependent variable and where the dependent variables cannot be combined.

Secondly, there is the phenomenon of reverse causation when a cause is pre-dated by an effect – A might have caused B but B may have come first and be responsible for A. For example, it is possible to demonstrate that firms with effective performance management schemes do better than those without. But it might be the case that it is high performing firms that introduce effective performance management. It can be hard to be certain.

Tests of significance

Significance as a statistical concept refers to the degree to which an event could have occurred by chance. At the heart of statistical science lies a simple idea, which is that the chance or probability of various patterns of events can be predicted. When a particular pattern is observed it is possible to work out what the chances of its occurrence may be, given our existing state of knowledge or by making certain assumptions. If something has been observed that is unlikely to have occurred by chance this occurrence can be accepted as significant. The problem is that any attempt to reach general conclusions may have to rely on fragmentary data. It is usually necessary to rely on samples of the population being studied and all sampling is subject to experimental error – the result can only be expressed in terms of probability and confidence limits will have to be placed on it. These can be calculated in terms of the standard error that might be expected from a sample. A standard error is the estimated standard deviation of a sample mean from a true mean. This implies that on approximately 95 per cent of occasions the estimate of the mean provided by the sample will be within two standard errors of the true mean.

Testing hypotheses

The *chi-squared test* uses a statistical formula to assess the degree of agreement between the data actually obtained and that expected under a particular hypothesis. A *null hypothesis* is a method of testing a hypothesis frequently used by researchers in which it is assumed that there is no relationship between two or more variables. It asks the question: 'Could the hypothetical relationship have been caused by chance?' If the answer is no, then the hypothesis is worth pursuing. However, it does not prove that the hypothesis is correct; it only indicates that something is worth further investigation. It can be associated with the chi-squared test.

HR information systems

An HR information system (HRIS) is a computer-based information system for managing the administration of HR processes and procedures; 'e-HRM' is an alternative term for the use of computer technology within the HR function. Parry and Tyson (2011: 335) defined an HRIS as: 'A way of implementing HR strategies, policies and practices in organizations through a conscious and directed support of and/or with the full use of web technology-based channels.' They listed five goals for e-HRM: efficiency, service delivery, strategic orientation, manager empowerment and standardization (*ibid*: 335).

Reasons for introducing an HRIS

The CIPD (2007) survey established that the top 10 reasons for introducing an HRIS were:

1 To improve the quality of information available.
2 To reduce the administrative burden on the HR department.
3 To improve the speed at which information is available.
4 To improve the flexibility of information to support business planning.
5 To improve services to employees.
6 To produce HR metrics.
7 To aid human capital reporting.
8 To improve productivity.
9 To reduce operational costs.
10 To manage people's working time more effectively.

Uses of an HRIS

The 2007 CIPD survey found that the 10 most popular uses to which respondents put their HRIS were, in descending order:

1   Absence management.

2   Training and development.

3   Rewards.

4   Managing diversity.

5   Recruitment and selection.

6   Other (usually payroll).

7   Appraisal/performance management.

8   HR planning.

9   Knowledge management.

10 Expenses.

Features of an HRIS

The features of particular interest in an HRIS system are the use of traditional software packages, cloud computing, enterprise resource planning systems (ERPs), the intranet, internal social networks, integration and provisions for self-service.

Traditional software packages

The traditional and still most typical approach is to buy software modules from an external supplier to run in-house applications such as personal records, absence management or payroll. 'Application suites' that cover a linked set of modules can be purchased. There is a choice between buying a 'vanilla system' (ie an 'off-the-shelf' system without any upgrades) or customizing the supplier's system to meet specified business requirements. Extensive customization can make future upgrades problematic and expensive, so it is important to limit it to what is absolutely necessary.

The choice of a supplier should be made as follows:

1   Research HR software market through trade exhibitions and publications.

2   Review HR processes and existing systems.

3   Produce a specification of system requirements.

4   Send an invitation to tender to several suppliers.

5   Invite suppliers to demonstrate their products.

6   Obtain references from existing customers, including site visits.

7   Analyse and score the product against the specification.

Cloud computing

Cloud computing involves providing on-demand shared computing resources and information. Data is stored and processed in separate data centres. Services such as servers, storage and applications are delivered to an organization's computers and devices through the internet. It can replace local arrangements using bought-in software packages.

Cloud computing can be provided by an SaaS (software-as-a-service) system – an on-demand software delivery model in which users are charged for accessing and managing HR IT provision via a network. The system stores and processes data in a standardized form that can then be configured for use in the organization.

The advantages of cloud computing are high computing power – the ability to store and process masses of data – accessibility and, potentially, lower costs. A further benefit is that it is highly adaptive and changes can be made very quickly, although it may be costly to do so.

Integration

In a traditional in-house arrangement, ERPs can be used to integrate all the data processing of an organization into a unified system with the same database. HR systems are not frequently integrated to this extent although they often link payroll administration with other HR functions. Integration of the HR system with IT systems in the wider organization so that they can 'talk to one another' will enable the more effective management of HR data. However, many HR functions retain stand-alone systems because they believe integration would compromise their own system, and are concerned about the potential lack of confidentiality and the cost and possible risks involved.

Intranet

An intranet system is one where computer terminals are linked so that they can share information within an organization or within part of an organization. The scope of the information that can be shared across terminals can be limited to preserve confidentiality and this security can be enhanced by using passwords. HR intranet systems can be used for purposes such as updating personal details, online applications for internal jobs, requests for training, access to e-learning, administration of queries and communications.

Internal social networks

Internal social networks (enterprise social networks such as those provided by Yammer, Chatter and Jive) function in the same way as social networks such as Facebook. They allow people to post opinions, join in discussions and respond to questions, and are used as employee voice channels and to support social learning.

Self-service

An HR self-service system (HRSS) allows managers and employees access to information and the facility to interact with the system to input information or make choices of their own. This can operate through an HR portal (a site that functions as a point of access to information on the intranet), which may be specially designed to produce a brand image of the HR function. This is sometimes referred to as a 'business-to-employees' (B2E) portal.

For managers, self-service means that they can access information immediately. This might be HR metrics in such areas as absenteeism, personal details, performance management data, learning and development progress, and pay (as a basis for pay reviews). They can also input data on their staff. This facilitates the devolution of responsibility to line managers and reduces the administrative burden on HR. Employees can also access information, input data about themselves, request training and apply for jobs online.

e-HRM achievements

Research conducted by Parry and Tyson (2011) in 10 case study organizations established that efficiency goals were met by most of them. Service delivery improvements were generally achieved, supporting improved effectiveness of the HR function. The findings showed that a potential goal for e-HRM is to standardize operational procedures across an organization, but they noted that: 'The realization of improved efficiency and effectiveness is dependent on the design and implementation of the system, and increased effectiveness and involvement in delivering the business strategy may depend on appropriate redeployment and up-skilling of HR staff' (*ibid*: 352).

Overleaf are some case studies, as reported by Parry and Tyson (2011: 341).

CASE STUDY: AVISA

An Oracle HR system is used with extensive management self-service for performing salary changes, cost centre and allowance changes, processing leavers, updating and reporting absence, processing overtime payments and comparing performance ratings. Employee self-service is available to maintain personal details, look at payslips, request holidays and record absence. In addition, an Ask-Jeeves system to answer generic HR queries has been introduced.

CASE STUDY: BOC

BOC has used a SAP HR system since 1999 to hold HR data and allow managers to access this data via their desktop to record absence and enter bonus ratings and salary review details. The system drove the payroll process. An e-recruitment system was introduced in 2003 with a recruitment database that sat centrally and was connected to a number of different career centres. The HR intranet has also recently been relaunched.

CASE STUDY: Marks & Spencer

The range of technological HRM tools include main HRIS plus payroll and personnel data, pensions and absence management systems and an HR portal for information on policies and practices.

KEY LEARNING POINTS

The need
HR specialists must possess the knowledge required to set up and manage computerized systems to provide them and line managers with information covering such matters as employee records, absenteeism, employee

turnover, rates of pay and employee benefits. Such systems also help with the administration of HR activities. In addition, HR people need skills in using statistics to record and present information.

Handling information
To handle information it is necessary to: decide what is required; identify the relevant data that is available or can be made available; convert the raw data into information that has 'meaning and purpose'; and establish how best to record, analyse and present the information.

HR analytics
HR analytics use metrics to provide the basis for assessing the impact of HRM practices and the contribution made by people to organizational performance.

Statistics
Statistics are used to describe and summarize data relating to a 'population', ie a homogeneous set of items with variable individual values. This involves measuring frequencies, central tendencies and dispersion. They are also used to measure the relationships between variables (correlation and regression), to establish the relation between cause and effect (causality), to assess the degree of confidence that can be attached to conclusions (tests of significance) and to test hypotheses (the chi-squared test and null-hypothesis testing).

Statistics are used extensively in HRM to analyse and present quantitative information that can be used to guide decisions and monitor outcomes.

Measures of central tendency
Measures of central tendency identify the middle or centre of a set of data. There are three types: arithmetic average or mean, median and mode.

Measures of dispersion
It is useful to measure the extent to which the items in a set are dispersed or spread over a range of data.

Correlation
Correlation represents the relationship between two variables. If they are highly correlated they are strongly connected to one another.

Regression
Regression is another way of looking at the relationship between variables. It expresses how changes in levels of one item relate to changes in levels of another.

Causality
Determining the link between independent and dependent variables (cause and effect) – is a major issue in research, especially in the HRM field. It may be relatively easy to establish that X is associated with Y; it is much more difficult and sometimes impossible to prove that X causes Y.

Tests of significance
Significance as a statistical concept refers to the degree to which an event could have occurred by chance.

HRIS defined
An HRIS is a computer-based information system for managing the administration of HR processes and procedures and for providing HRM data, sometimes called 'e-HRM'.

Features of an HRIS
The features of particular interest in an HRIS system are: integration with other IT systems in the organization; provisions for self-service; and the use of traditional software packages, cloud computing, the intranet and internal social networks.

Use of statistics
The features of particular interest in an HRIS system are integration with other IT systems in the organization, use of the intranet and provisions for self-service.

References

CIPD (2015) Fact sheet: HR analytics, http://www.cipd.co.uk/hr-resources/factsheets/hr-analytics.aspx [accessed 12 November 2015]

CIPD (2007) *HR and Technology: Impact and advantages*, London, CIPD

Drucker, P (1988) The coming of the new organization, *Harvard Business Review*, January–February, pp 45–53

McAfee, A and Brynjolfsson, E (2012) Big data: the management revolution, *Harvard Business Review*, October, pp 60–68

Parry, E and Tyson, S (2011) Desired goals and actual outcomes of e-HRM, *Human Resource Management Journal*, 21 (3), pp 335–54

QUESTIONS

1 What is the meaning of information?

2 What are the purposes of HR analytics?

3 What are the main reasons for having a comprehensive HRIS?

4 What are the five most popular applications of an HRIS?

5 What is an enterprise resource planning (ERP) system?

6 What is an intranet?

7 What is self-service and why is it important?

8 What are the main considerations to be taken into account in developing an HRIS?

9 How are statistics used?

10 What use is made by HR specialists of statistics?

11 What is frequency in statistics?

12 What are the three measures of central tendency?

13 What is correlation?

14 What is causality?

15 What are the problems of establishing causation?

16 What is a test of significance?

17 How can hypotheses be tested?

Business and financial skills

24

KEY CONCEPTS AND TERMS

Absorption costing

The acid test

Activity-based costing

Balance sheet

Business model

Cash flow

Cash flow statement

Core competency

Direct costs

Earnings per share

Economic value
    added (EVA)

Gearing

Gross margin

Gross profit

Indirect costs

Key performance indicator

Liquidity analysis

Marginal costing

Net profit

Operating or trading profit

Over-trading

Price/earnings ratio

Profit before taxation

Profit and loss account

Profitability

The resource-based view

Return on capital employed

Return on equity

Standard costing

Trading statement or account

The working capital ratio

LEARNING OUTCOMES

On completing this chapter you should be able to define these key concepts. You should also understand:

- What it means to be business-like
- How to interpret a balance sheet

- How profits are classified
- The purpose of trading and profit and loss statements
- The meaning of profitability and the key profitability ratios
- How budgeting and budgetary control work
- The purpose of cash management
- Methods of costing

Introduction

To make an effective contribution HR professionals must possess business and financial skills. They need to understand what their business model is – how their organization delivers value to its customers and how the business achieves competitive advantage and makes money. They need to understand and be able to use the language of the business and, because this will generally be expressed in monetary terms, they need to appreciate how the financial systems of the business work. Equipped with this knowledge HR professionals can develop the skills needed to interpret the organization's business or corporate strategies, to contribute to the formulation of those strategies and to develop integrated HR strategies.

This requirement was spelt out by Ulrich (1997: 7) when he wrote that: 'HR professionals must know the business which includes a mastery of finance, strategy, marketing, and operations.' Research by the CIPD (2010: 5) led to the following conclusion:

> It is also evident that for some HR functions, they see HR as an applied business discipline first and a people discipline second. The ability to understand the business agenda in a deep way means that they are then able to help the business see how critical objectives can only truly be delivered if the people and cultural issues are fully factored in – insight into what it would take to truly deliver. In these places HR has a real share of voice and credibility... Where HR is grounded in the business and delivering the fundamentals well, then it is able to engage in higher value-adding 'OD' and talent-related activities that speak to the critical challenges faced in that organization.

Business skills

Business skills are required to adopt a business-like approach to management – one that focuses on allocating resources to business opportunities and making the best use of them to achieve the required results. Managers who are business-like understand and act upon:

- the business imperatives of the organization: its mission and its strategic goals;

- the organization's business model: the basis upon which its business is done (how its mission and strategic goals will be achieved);

- the organization's business drivers: the characteristics of the business that move it forward;

- the organization's core competences: what the business is good at doing;

- the factors that will ensure the effectiveness of its activities including specific issues concerning profitability, productivity, financial budgeting and control, costs and benefits, customer service and operational performance;

- the key performance indicators (KPIs) of the business (the results or outcomes identified as being crucial to the achievement of high performance) that can be used to measure progress towards attaining goals;

- the factors that will ensure that the firm's resources, especially its human resources, create sustained competitive advantage because they are valuable, imperfectly imitable and non-substitutable (the resource-based view).

Financial skills

A business-like approach means using financial skills to analyse and interpret balance sheets, cash flow and trading statements and profit and loss accounts, and to understand and make use of the financial techniques of budgeting and budgetary control, cash budgeting and costing.

Interpreting balance sheets

A balance sheet is a statement on the last day of the accounting period of the company's assets and liabilities and the share capital or shareholder's investment in the company. Balance sheet analysis assesses the financial strengths and weaknesses of the company, primarily from the point of view of the shareholders and potential investors, but also as part of management's task to exercise proper stewardship over the funds invested in the company and the assets in its care. The analysis focuses on the balance sheet equation, considers the make-up of the balance sheet in terms of assets and liabilities, and examines the liquidity position (how much cash or easily realizable assets are available) and capital structure with the help of balance sheet ratios.

The balance sheet equation

The balance sheet equation is: Capital + Liabilities = Assets. Capital plus liabilities comprise where the money comes from, and assets are where the money is now.

Make-up of the balance sheet

The balance sheet contains four major sections:

1 *Assets or capital in use*, which is divided into long-term or fixed assets (eg land, buildings and plant) and short-term or current assets, which include stocks of goods and materials, work-in-progress, debtors, bank balances and cash.

2 *Current liabilities*, which are the amounts that will have to be paid within 12 months of the balance sheet date.

3 *Net current assets (or working capital)*, which are current assets less current liabilities. Careful control of working capital lies at the heart of efficient business performance.

4 *Sources of capital*, which comprise share capital, reserves including retained profits and long-term loans.

Liquidity analysis

Liquidity analysis is concerned with the extent to which the organization has an acceptable quantity of cash and easily realizable assets to meet its needs. The analysis may be based on the ratio of current assets (cash, working capital, etc) to current liabilities – the working capital ratio. Too low a ratio may mean that the liquid resources are insufficient to cover short-term payments. Too high a ratio might indicate that there is too much cash or working capital and that they are therefore being badly managed.

The working capital ratio is susceptible to 'window dressing', which is the manipulation of the working capital position by accelerating or delaying transactions near the year end.

Liquidity analysis also uses the 'quick ratio' of current assets minus stocks to current liabilities. This concentrates on the more realizable of the current assets and so provides a stricter test of liquidity than the working capital ratio. It is therefore called 'the acid test'.

Capital structure analysis

Capital structure analysis examines the overall means by which a company finances its operations, which is partly by the funds of its ordinary shareholders (equity) and partly by loans from banks and other lenders (debt). The ratio of long-term debt to ordinary shareholder's funds indicates 'gearing'. A company is said to be highly geared when it has a high level of loan capital as distinct from equity capital.

Classification of profits

It is necessary to understand the different ways in which profits can be classified as recorded in trading statements and profit and loss accounts. There are four headings:

1 *Gross profit* – the difference between sales revenue and the cost of goods sold. This is also referred to as gross margin, especially in the retail industry.

2 *Operating or trading profit* – the gross profit less sales, marketing and distribution costs, administrative costs and research and development expenditure.

3 *Profit before taxation* – operating profit plus invested income minus interest payable.

4 *Net profit* – profit after corporation taxation.

Trading statements

Trading statements or accounts show the cost of goods manufactured, the cost of sales, sales revenue and the gross profit, which is transferred to the profit and loss account.

Profit and loss accounts

Profit and loss accounts provide the information required to assess a company's profitability – the primary aim and best measure of efficiency in competitive business. They show:

1 The gross profit from the trading account.
2 Selling and administration expenses.
3 The operating profit (1 minus 2).
4 Investment income.
5 Profit before interest and taxation (3 plus 4).
6 Profit before taxation (5 minus loan interest).
7 Taxation.
8 Net profit (6 minus 7).

Profitability analysis ratios

Profitability is a measure of the return in the shape of profits that shareholders obtain for their investment in the company. It is expressed in the following ratios:

- *Return on equity* – profit after interest and preference dividends before tax to ordinary share capital, reserves and retained profit. This focuses attention on the efficiency of the company in earning profits on behalf of its shareholders; some analysts regard it as the best profitability ratio.

- *Return on capital employed* – trading or operating profit to capital employed. This measures the efficiency with which capital is employed.

- *Earnings per share* – profit after interest, taxation and preference dividends to the number of issued ordinary shares. This is an alternative to return on equity as a measure of the generation of 'shareholder value' (what shareholders get from the company). Its drawback is that it depends on the number of shares issued, although it is often referred to within companies as the means by which their obligations to shareholders should be assessed.

- *Price-earnings (P/E) ratio* – market price of ordinary shares to earnings per share. This ratio is often used by investment analysts.

- *Economic value added (EVA)* – post-tax operating profit minus the cost of capital invested in the business. This measures how effectively the company uses its funds.

Financial budgeting

Budgets translate policy into financial terms. They are statements of the planned allocation and use of the company's resources. They are needed to: 1) show the financial implications of plans, 2) define the resources required to achieve the plans, and 3) provide the means of measuring, monitoring and controlling results against the plans.

The procedure for preparing financial budgets consists of the following steps:

1 *Budget guidelines* are prepared, derived from the corporate plan and forecasts. They will include the activity levels for which budgets have to be created and the ratios to be achieved. The assumptions to be used in budgeting are also given. These could include rates of inflation and increases in costs and prices.

2 *Initial budgets* for a budget or cost centre are prepared by departmental managers with the help of budget accountants.

3 *Departmental budgets* are collated and analysed to produce the master budget, which is reviewed by top management, who may require changes at departmental level to bring it into line with corporate financial objectives and plans.

4 *The master budget* is finally approved by top management and issued to each departmental (budget centre) manager for planning and control purposes.

Budgetary control

Budgetary control ensures that financial budgets are met and that any variances are identified and dealt with. Control starts with the budget for the cost centre, which sets out the budgeted expenditure under cost headings against activity levels. A system of measurement or recording is used to allocate expenditures to cost headings and record activity levels achieved. The actual expenditures and activity levels are compared and positive and negative variances noted. Cost centre managers then act to deal with the variances and report their results to higher management.

Cash management

Cash management involves forecasting and controlling cash flows (inflows or outflows of cash). It is an important and systematic process of ensuring that problems of liquidity are minimized and that funds are managed effectively.

The aim is to ensure that the company is not over-trading, ie that the cost of its operations does not significantly exceed the amount of cash available to finance them. The old adage is that whatever else is done, ensure that 'cash in exceeds cash out'.

Cash flow statements report the amounts of cash generated and cash used for a period. They are used to provide information on liquidity (the availability of cash), solvency and financial adaptability.

Cash budgeting

An operating cash budget deals with budgeted receipts (forecast cash flows) and budgeted payments (forecast cash outflows). It includes all the revenue expenditure incurred in financing current operations, ie the costs of running the business in order to generate sales.

Costing

Costing techniques provide information for decision making and control. They are used to establish the total cost of a product for stock valuation, pricing and estimating purposes and to enable the company to establish whether the proposed selling price will enable a profit to be made.

Costing involves measuring the direct costs of material and labour plus the indirect costs (overheads) originating in the factory (factory overheads) and elsewhere in the company (sales, distribution, marketing, research and development, and administration). Overheads are charged to cost units to provide information on total costs – this process is called overhead recovery. There are four main methods of doing this:

1 *Absorption costing* – this involves allocating all fixed and variable costs to cost units and is the most widely used method, although it can be arbitrary.

2 *Activity-based costing* – costs are assigned to activities on the basis of an individual product's demand for each activity.

3 *Marginal costing* – this segregates fixed costs and apportions the variable or marginal costs to products.

4 *Standard costing* – is the preparation of predetermined or standard costs that are compared with actual costs to identify variances. It is used to measure performance.

KEY LEARNING POINTS

To make an effective contribution, HR professionals must have business and financial skills. They need to understand what the business model is – how the organization delivers value to its customers and, in commercial organizations, how the business achieves competitive advantage and makes money.

Business skills

Business skills are required to adopt a business-like approach to management – one that focuses on allocating resources to business opportunities and making the best use of them to achieve the required results.

Financial skills

A business-like approach means using financial skills to analyse and interpret balance sheets, cash flow and trading statements and profit and loss accounts, and to understand and make use of the financial techniques of budgeting and budgetary control, cash budgeting and costing.

Interpreting balance sheets

A balance sheet is a statement on the last day of the accounting period of the company's assets and liabilities and the share capital or reserves or shareholder's investment in the company. Balance sheet analysis assesses the financial strengths and weaknesses of the company primarily from the point of view of the shareholders and potential investors, but also as part of management's task to exercise proper stewardship over the funds invested in the company and the assets in its care.

Classification of profits

It is necessary to understand the different ways in which profits can be classified as recorded in trading statements and profit and loss accounts. There are four headings: gross profit, operating or trading profit, profit before tax, and net profit.

Trading statements

Trading statements or accounts show the cost of goods manufactured, the cost of sales, sales revenue and the gross profit, which is transferred to the profit and loss account.

Profit and loss accounts

Profit and loss accounts provide the information required to assess a company's profitability. Profitability is a measure of the return in the shape of profits that shareholders obtain for their investment in the company. It is expressed in the following ratios: return on equity, return on capital employed, earnings per share, price-earnings (P/E) ratio, economic value added (EVA).

Financial budgeting

Budgets translate policy into financial terms. They are statements of the planned allocation and use of the company's resources.

Budgetary control

Budgetary control ensures that financial budgets are met and that any variances are identified and dealt with.

Cash management

Cash management involves forecasting and controlling cash flows (inflows or outflows of cash). An operating cash budget deals with budgeted receipts (forecast cash inflows) and budgeted payment (forecast cash outflows).

Costing

Costing techniques provide information for decision making and control. They are used to establish the total cost of a product for stock valuation, pricing and estimating purposes and to enable the company to establish whether the proposed selling price will enable a profit to be made. Overheads are charged to cost units to provide information on total costs – this process is called overhead recovery. There are four methods of doing this: absorption costing, activity-based costing, marginal costing and standard costing.

References

CIPD (2010) *Next Generation HR: Time for change – towards a next generation for HR*, London, CIPD

Ulrich, D (1997) Judge me more by my future than my past, *Human Resource Management*, **36** (1), pp 5–8

QUESTIONS

1 What is involved in being 'business-like'?

2 What are the essential financial skills HR professionals need?

3 What is a balance sheet?

4 What is involved in balance sheet analysis?

5 What is liquidity analysis?

6 What is capital structure analysis?

7 What are the different ways of classifying profits?

8 What is a trading statement?

9 What is a profit and loss account?

10 What are the main components of a profit and loss account?

11 What is profitability?

12 What is return on equity?

13 What is return on capital employed?

14 What are earnings per share?

15 What is the price/earnings ratio?

16 What is financial budgeting?

17 What is budgetary control?

18 What does cash management involve?

19 What does cash budgeting involve?

20 What does costing involve?

Postgraduate study skills

25

KEY CONCEPTS AND TERMS

Flash card	Quantitative research
Learning style	Triangulation
Qualitative research	

LEARNING OUTCOMES

On completing this chapter you should be able to define these key concepts. You should also know about:

- Learning styles
- Basic study skills
- Making the most of lectures
- Getting the most out of reading
- How to revise
- How to write essays and reports
- The principles of good writing
- Referencing

Introduction

Postgraduate study skills are needed by those studying for postgraduate degrees or for professional qualifications so as to be able to learn effectively. The skills are those associated with the learning acquired from lectures and reading and those concerned with accessing, evaluating and conducting research. They are linked to essay and report writing and the skills required to revise for and take examinations. Most significantly, they are an essential aspect of continuous professional development and lifelong learning. This chapter deals with the conditions required for effective learning, the study skills involved, preparing for and taking exams, and writing essays and reports.

Effective learning

Effective learning is partly dependent on the context – the quality of teaching and the educational resources available. However, it is primarily a matter of what learners do – how they make use of or adapt their learning style.

Learning styles

Learners have different styles – a preference for a particular approach to learning. Kolb *et al* (1974) identified the following learning styles:

- *Accommodators*, who learn by trial and error, combining the concrete experience and experimentation stages of the cycle.

- *Divergers*, who prefer concrete to abstract learning situations and reflection to active involvement. Such individuals have great imaginative ability, and can view a complete situation from different viewpoints.

- *Convergers*, who prefer to experiment with ideas, considering them for their practical usefulness. Their main concern is whether the theory works in action, thus combining the abstract and experimental dimensions.

- *Assimilators*, who like to create their own theoretical models and assimilate a number of disparate observations into an overall integrated explanation; thus they veer towards the reflective and abstract dimensions.

Another analysis of learning styles was made by Honey and Mumford (1996). They listed the following four styles:

1 *Activists*, who involve themselves fully without bias in new experiences and revel in new challenges.

2 *Reflectors*, who stand back and observe new experiences from different angles. They collect data, reflect on it and th

3 *Theorists*, who adapt and apply their observations in the form of logical theories. They tend to be perfectionists.

4 *Pragmatists*, who are keen to try out new ideas, approaches and concepts to see if they work.

None of these four learning styles is exclusive. It is quite possible that one person could be both a reflector and a theorist and someone else could be an activist/pragmatist, a reflector/pragmatist or even a theorist/pragmatist. It is useful for learners to identify which style or mix of styles they prefer as this will affect the way they set about learning, but they must be prepared to flex their style in different situations.

Study skills

Study skills are concerned with absorbing, classifying, evaluating and recording ideas, concepts and information and reflecting on the meaning and significance of what has been absorbed. They cover learning from lectures and reading, and revision. More pragmatically, they prepare people to pass examinations. At professional or postgraduate level it is probable, even in a taught Master's programme, that students will be left to their own devices much more than when they were taking their first degree (although undergraduates from some universities may question the extent to which they were ever *taught* a lot during their course).

It is to be hoped that students honed their study skills at undergraduate level, but they will need to exercise those skills even more effectively when they are postgraduates. Those who are studying for a professional qualification at postgraduate level such as that offered by the Chartered Institute of Personnel and Development (the CIPD) who have not attended a further or higher educational establishment will need to give careful thought to the approach they adopt. Both categories of postgraduate student need to apply study skills such as those described below.

By the time you get to a postgraduate level of studies you should have become familiar with the best ways of getting to know your subject, but it will do no harm to be reminded of the basic principles you should adopt when pursuing your studies. These are concerned with making the best use of lectures (including note taking), your reading, the information available on the internet, reflecting on what you have learnt, and revising.

Making the best use of lectures

A lecture has been defined as 'a system whereby the lecturer's notes are transferred to student's notes without passing through the minds of either' that during the lecture you should:

- Carefully track the structure of the lecture from introduction to conclusion – follow the train of the lecturer's thoughts, which should have been made clear, although this may not always be the case and you may have to work hard during or after the lecture to make sense of it.

- Listen actively – engage with the topic, relate the content of the lecture to what you already know, think about how it ties in with your experience.

- Be critical – challenge in your mind any statements or assumptions made by the lecturer and if you feel strongly about them, challenge the lecturer – politely.

- Follow the lecturer's PowerPoint slides and read the notes, but do not rely on them – do your own thinking and pay attention to your own note taking, as suggested below.

Note taking during lectures

- Do not write too much – focus on key ideas, words and phrases. You can't get everything down.

- Avoid taking detailed notes on something you could easily get out of a textbook.

- Record the key points in brief paragraphs or notes.

- Number paragraphs for easy reference.

- Record any recommendations made on further reading or references.

- If you miss something leave a space – it may be covered later in the lecture or in the conclusion and you can always refer to the lecturer's notes.

After the lecture

- Read through the notes.
- Tidy them up.
- Fill any gaps.
- Label and file the notes.
- Consider transcribing your notes onto a computer file. This is a good way of reinforcing the learning and will make them easier to access and read when using them as the basis for an essay or paper or revising. You can keep them in a portfolio alongside notes you make from your reading and any other information you need to record about your studies (some establishments require students to keep a portfolio).

Getting the most out of reading

The first thing to do is to decide what to read – there is plenty of choice. Your tutor should help by recommending key texts and referring to significant journal articles. Any good textbook will refer to supporting material. If you are studying human resource management it is obviously a good idea to read *People Management* and take a look at the information available on the CIPD website, which includes CIPD research reports and fact sheets. You should also refer to the main British HR journals to spot relevant articles and identify useful research. These include *British Journal of Industrial Relations, British Journal of Management, Employee Relations, Human Resource Management Journal* and *International Journal of Human Resource Management*. If you cannot reach them in a library, they can be accessed if you are a member of the CIPD in EBSCO on the CIPD website. You can also use Google Scholar.

In reading such material, especially those referring to current research, you should subject the contents to the tests of critical evaluation as set out in Chapter 22. Your own understanding will be increased if you analyse the positions, arguments and conclusions the author reaches to establish the extent to which they are based on sound logical reasoning.

Whatever you read, it is up to you to spot what is relevant. Lectures and general reading may help you to do this by providing the background to the subject matter, but it is ultimately up to you to extract what you think is significant in the shape of ideas, concepts, references to research, useful quotes and prescriptive material. Record these (this is the best way of concentrating the mind on complex material) or at least indicate where they can be found when wanted.

Make sure you are up-to-date with information that has appeared since your favourite textbook was published. This means collecting press cuttings, articles and in-company case studies and materials, from other organizations as well as your own.

Ensure that your notes are easily accessible when wanted for an essay or paper or for revision. They should be indexed and could be sorted in a concertina file whose compartments reflect the major content themes. Alternatively, they can usefully be stored in a computer file. They can also be recorded on flash cards – A5 index cards that contain a summary (often in bullet points) of the main points concerning a topic and which can be referred to quickly, especially if they are indexed.

Revising

Revising for an exam can be a daunting task – 'Where do I start?' 'Where do I end?' 'What do I do in between?' Answers to these questions are provided in the lists of dos and don'ts in Table 25.1. There are more dos than don'ts; revision is a positive process.

Table 25.1 The dos and don'ts of revision

Do	Don't
• Refer to the syllabus to identify the main subject areas.	• Leave revision to the last minute before the exam.
• Study previous exam papers to find out how examiners cover the syllabus and the most typical questions they ask in each area. Identify recurring questions.	• Simply keep on reading your notes – focus on the material you need to help answer exam questions.
• Define your revision priorities – draw up a list that sets out priorities, starting with the important and simple topics, continuing with the important but complex (and time-consuming) topics and finishing with the lowest priority topics – those that are complex but not vital.	• Ignore your timetable.
	• Revise your timetable unnecessarily just because you are bored with it.
	• Allow yourself to be diverted – set aside times for revision and do not permit interruptions.
	• Pile up too much revision material – concentrate on the key issues, possibly recorded on flash cards.
• Select the topics you need to revise (covering the main areas in which questions are frequently asked in examinations).	• Overdo it – there is a limit to what anyone can absorb, hence the need to pace yourself and avoid 'burning the midnight oil' spells of revision.
• As a rule of thumb, know at least 50 per cent of the content of the syllabus in detail and the rest more superficially so that if necessary you can say something sensible about any topic at all.	
• Break up what you need to revise into short, easily absorbed pieces.	

Table 25.1 Continued

Do	Don't
• Draw up a timetable, listing the topics you want to revise in order of priority.	
• Set short-term goals for revision.	
• Identify where you can find the revision material – ideally it should all be in your notes, which you may need to reduce and reclassify for ease of reading and in accordance with priorities. It can usefully include a set of flash cards covering the most important topics, providing a quick and easy way to revise key points.	
• Pace yourself – track your progress against the timetable and adjust if necessary.	
• Check your learning. Record the key things you have learnt and refer to your revision priorities and timetable to ensure that you are up to speed.	
• Work out answers to a range of questions for each topic.	
• Practise answering sample questions in each area in handwriting to check that you can produce persuasive and legible answers in the time available (this is very important). Refer to your notes and if they are not sufficiently helpful revise or expand them.	

Taking exams

The dos and don'ts for taking exams are set out in Table 25.2.

Table 25.2 The dos and don'ts of taking exams

Do	Don't
• Answer the question – this is very familiar advice but it is remarkable how in the experience of most examiners (including this one) many candidates fail to do so. • Pay particular attention to what you are asked to do in the question and do it. You will lose marks if you don't. Typically, you may be asked to: *critically evaluate* a concept, notion or idea: this means that you are expected to show that you can use critical thinking to make informed judgements about the validity, relevance and usefulness of ideas and propositions, weighing arguments for and against them, assessing the strength of the evidence and deciding which are preferable; *discuss* the key aspects of the subject, critically evaluate it and assess the implications; *refer to recent research* (recent usually means within the last five years but it can be stretched to within 10 years for important projects): you need only summarize the main messages and give the name of the researcher and the date; *refer to examples from within your own organization or one known to you*: show that you understand the practical issues by reference to actual practice; *justify*: supply evidenced reasons that support your argument; *outline*: set out the main points or general principles relating to the topic; *review*: explore the meaning and significance of a topic. • Develop your arguments logically. • Give practical examples wherever possible.	• Answer the question you would have liked to ask yourself (because you know all about it) rather than the one put by the examiner. • Spend too much time answering the questions you know about, leaving insufficient time to deal with the remaining questions. • Put down everything you know, rather than what the examiner asked you to do. • Try to get away with not providing examples or research evidence if asked to do so. • Present the examiner with undigested chunks of prose – set out each section clearly and ensure that they follow one another logically. • Produce an unstructured and confusing document – ensure that the examiner knows where you are coming from, where you are going and where you have got to. • Write illegibly – think of the examiner, who is only human and will tend to mark you down if your prose is virtually unreadable. • Rely on bullet points, simply listing headings without exploring the issue (in desperation you might use bullet points for the final answer if you are short of time but you will lose marks).

Table 25.2 Continued

Do	Don't
• Seize every opportunity to display your knowledge by citing authors, sources, research, your own organization, other organizations, case study scenarios, benchmark achievements elsewhere, etc. • Structure your answers so that your material is easy to read and easy to follow. This means: following a logical progression from introduction to conclusions, underlined side-headings to separate one part of your answer from the next (especially where a question has two or more sections); lists of itemized points; clear differentiation between your introduction and your conclusions. • Write legibly and articulately. Your presentation skills make a difference, especially at the margin.	• Deliver glib statements with no real explanation of what they mean in practical terms. • Forget that examiners prefer candidates who analyse the subject critically and conduct systematic reviews of the subject matter and its implications. • Pepper answers with dubious assumptions or grand over-generalizations that result in unconvincing arguments. • Try to get away without incorporating properly-identified evidence into material to support assumptions and views. • Simply lift standard prescriptions wholesale from textbooks and apply them without any real understanding of their meaning. • Recommend so-called 'best practice' in a few words that are insufficient to convey its real content and meaning and for use in situations for which it has no apparent relevance.

Essay and report writing

As a postgraduate student you will be required to produce essays and reports on any research projects you carry out. Report writing is also an important skill for practitioners who may be involved in dealing with a problem (troubleshooting). The approaches you should use, which are applicable to essays as well as research and business reports, are given below.

1. Define the task

Decide what you are setting out to achieve (your objective) and, broadly, how you intend to achieve it. In a research report note any basic propositions or assumptions that you are likely to put forward or adopt, or any theories or concepts that you will evaluate. Decide on a provisional title and the likely scope of the essay or report.

2. Decide what information you need

This depends on the range of subject matter to be covered and whether it is a simple essay, an extended dissertation, a research project or a business troubleshooting report. Information for academic essays and reports will be obtained from your notes, additional reading of books, journals and other sources such as e-learning material and Wikipedia, blogs, or research. Troubleshooting business reports will rely on an identification of the facts required and a systematic process of getting and analysing those facts.

3. Obtain the information

If you are a postgraduate student preparing an essay or a dissertation, trawling through your lecture and reading notes should be straightforward if you have recorded and filed them properly. Reading round the subject means a little more work. Don't overdo it – you can be confused by too much information. Information for research reports is obtained from literature reviews, surveys, interviews and the assembly of case studies.

4. Analyse the information

Reflect on the information you have obtained. Check what you have found out and decide if you have enough. Establish the extent to which it will enable you to achieve your objective and support and clarify a convincing argument. If it doesn't, get more data.

5. Plan the structure of the essay or report

It is essential to structure an essay so that the reader can follow your line of reasoning readily. You have to consider, first, how you will introduce the essay, setting out what it is about, your aim and any propositions or assumptions you are making; second, how you will present your views or evidence (this might include research findings) and develop your argument; and finally, how you will reach a conclusion.

Like an essay, a report should have a beginning, a middle and an end. If the report is lengthy or complex it will also need a summary of conclusions and recommendations. There may also be appendices containing detailed data and statistics.

Beginning

Your introduction should state why the report has been written and why it should be read. A problem-solving report should define the problem and explain the circumstances. The sources of any evidence that will be referred to in the report should be identified and details of how that evidence was obtained should be supplied. The structure of the report should be described.

Middle

The middle of the report should contain the facts you have assembled, your analysis of those facts and your observations on how they illuminate your proposition or support your argument. In a business problem-solving report the analysis should lead logically to a diagnosis of the causes of the problem.

End

The conclusions and recommendations included in the final section should flow from the analysis and diagnosis. One of the most common weaknesses in reports is for the facts not to lead on naturally to the conclusions; the other is for the conclusions not to be supported by the facts.

Summarize the facts and your observations. In a problem-solving business report in which you have identified alternative courses of action, set out the pros and cons of each one, but make it quite clear which one you favour and why. Don't leave your readers in mid-air.

The final section of a business report should set out your recommendations, stating how each of them would help to achieve the stated aims of the report or overcome any weaknesses revealed by the analytical studies. The benefits and costs of implementing the recommendations would be explained after the conclusions. A plan should be set out for implementing the proposals – the programme of work, complete with deadlines and names of people who would carry it out. The recipient(s) of the report should be told what action, such as approval of plans or authorization of expenditure, you would like them to take.

The structure of a business report given above can be used when dealing with a problem case study question in an examination.

6. Draft the essay or report

When you draft your essay or report bear in mind that the way in which you present and write it will considerably affect its impact and value. High quality content is not enough; it must be presented well.

The reader should be able to follow your argument easily and not get bogged down in too much detail. The information you provide and your ideas should be grouped together so they can be presented in separate paragraphs. Paragraphs should be short and each one should be restricted to a single topic. Headings should be placed before sections to enable the reader to follow your ideas and arguments to your conclusion. Textbooks (like this one) and business reports tend to have more headings to guide readers than essays, dissertations and journal articles. If you want to list or highlight a series of points, tabulate them or use bullet points but don't sacrifice meaning to clarity by omitting important material. Your arguments and proposition need substance; bullet points can make them look superficial.

Read and re-read your draft to cut out any superfluous material, repetition, grammatical errors or flabby writing. Ensure that the argument is clear, convincing and flows from start to finish. Reorganize the structure of the report, including how it is paragraphed and its headings, to increase clarity.

Do not clutter up the main pages of a detailed report with masses of indigestible figures or other data. Summarize key statistics in compact, easy-to-follow tables with clear headings. Relegate supporting material to an appendix.

In a long or complex report, especially a business report, it is helpful to provide an executive summary of conclusions and recommendations. It concentrates the reader's mind and can be used as an agenda in presenting and discussing the report. The abstract at the beginning of a journal article serves the same purpose.

Good writing

Table 25.3 includes some dos and don'ts of good writing.

Table 25.3 The dos and don'ts of writing

Do	Don't
• Keep language simple and direct, eg use *begin* not *initiate, buy* not *purchase, find* not *locate, go* not *proceed, use* not *utilize*. • Prefer the short word to the long. • Prefer the familiar word to the unusual or stylish. • Use words with a precise meaning rather than those that are vague. • Prefer concrete words or phrases to abstract ones, eg *This material has become scarce* rather than *The availability of this material is diminishing*. • Use active verbs where possible rather than passive ones, eg *ensure* rather than *ensuring*. • 'Use the short expressive phrase even if it is conversational' (Winston Churchill, cited by Gowers, 1962:37). • Use short sentences to help you think clearly and gain the understanding of your reader. Separate points or ideas in distinct sentences. • Remember that *each* demands a singular verb when it is the subject, eg *Each of the proposals has merit*. • Split an infinitive if it reads better. • Start a sentence with a conjunction, eg *and, but, or*, if it makes sense and reads well. But don't over-do it. • Use prepositions at the end of sentences whenever you like. • Say what you mean and mean what you say (after Lewis Carroll).	• Use more words than are necessary to express your meaning (avoid verbosity or padding). • Use jargon unless a technical term is unavoidable, in which case define it. • Use superfluous adjectives or adverbs. • Use clichés. • Write long, meandering sentences. • Write *alternatively* when you mean *alternately*. • Write *less* when you mean *fewer*. • Write *refute* when you mean *deny* or *repudiate*. • Write *mitigate* when you mean *militate*. • Write *practical* when you mean *practicable*. • Misspell eg accommodate, accessory, confident (assured), confidant (person trusted with knowledge), consensus, dependant (as a noun), dependent (as an adjective), desiccate, embarrass, liaise, stationary (at rest), stationery (paper), superintendent, underlie.

Source references

In academic essays, dissertations or reports, and in journal articles and text-books it is essential when quoting someone or referring to something they have written to give the source. The normal conventions for referencing quotes from books or articles are:

In the text of the essay or article give the name of the author or authors (if there are more than two authors give the name of the first author followed by *et al*) and then the date in brackets. If it is a direct quotation give the page number(s), eg:

Gowers (1962: 37)

If you refer to more than one publication by an author published in the same year attach a, b, etc to the name, eg:

Ulrich (1997a)

Place references at the end of the essay or article and list them by author in alphabetical order. In a book, put them either at the end of the chapter or the end of the book.

A reference to a book should state, in order, the family name of the author or authors, their initials, the date of publication in brackets, the title of the book in italics, the place of publication and the name of the publisher, eg:

Ulrich, D (1997) *Human Resource Champions*, Boston, MA, Harvard Business School Press

If the reference is to a chapter in an edited book it should look like this:

Boxall, P F, Purcell, J and Wright, P (2007) Human resource management; scope, analysis and significance, in (eds) P Boxall, J Purcell and P Wright, *The Oxford Handbook of Human Resource Management*, Oxford, Oxford University Press, pp 1–18

The page numbers of the chapter are sometimes included at the end, as in the above example.

A reference to an article should state, in order, the family name of the author or authors, their initials, the date of publication in brackets, the title of the article in plain lower case, the name of the publication in italics, the volume (which can be just the number in bold), the issue number (often in brackets and not always included, although it is helpful when tracing the article), and the page numbers, eg:

Armstrong, M (2000) The name has changed but has the game remained the same? *Employee Relations*, **22** (6), pp 576–89

If you are referencing material obtained online give the name of the author(s) or publishing institution, the date of publication and the title, quote the URL and indicate when the publication was accessed, eg:

CIPD (2015) Survey of absence management, http://www.cipd.co.uk/hr-resources/survey-reports/absence-management-2015.aspx [accessed 2 September 2016]

Note that there may be some minor variations in these styles between publishers, especially in punctuation. This also applies to academic institutions. The examples given above conform to the Kogan Page house style, which minimizes punctuation.

KEY LEARNING POINTS

Postgraduate study skills are concerned with effective learning by those studying for postgraduate degrees or for professional qualifications at that level. The skills are those associated with the learning acquired from lectures and reading, and those concerned with accessing, evaluating and conducting research.

Effective learning
Effective learning is partly dependent on the context – the quality of teaching and the educational resources available, but it is primarily a matter of what learners do – how they make use of or adapt their learning style.

Study skills
Study skills are concerned with absorbing, classifying and recording ideas, concepts and information and reflecting on the meaning and significance of what has been absorbed. To get the most out of a lecture you should track the structure of the lecture, listen actively; be critical; follow the lecturer's slides and read the notes, but do not rely on them – do your own thinking.

Getting the most out of reading
Decide what to read. Subject what the writer says to the tests of critical evaluation, and analyse the positions, arguments and conclusions the author reaches to establish the extent to which they are based on sound logical reasoning.

Revising
Lists of dos and don'ts are given in this chapter.

Taking exams
Dos and don'ts for taking exams are given in this chapter.

Writing essays and reports
The approaches to use are define the task; decide what information you need and obtain and analyse it; plan the structure of the essay or report; draft it.

Good writing
The dos and don'ts of good writing are given in this chapter.

References
In academic essays, dissertations or reports and in journal articles and text-books it is essential when quoting someone or referring to something they have written to give the source. The conventions are set out in this chapter.

References

Gowers, E (1962) *The Complete Plain Words*, Harmondsworth, Penguin Books
Honey, P and Mumford, A (1996) *The Manual of Learning Styles*, 3rd edn, Maidenhead, Honey Publications
Horn, R (2009) *The Business Skills Handbook*, London, CIPD
Kolb, D A, Rubin, I M and McIntyre, J M (1974) *Organizational Psychology: An experimental approach*, Englewood Cliffs, NJ, Prentice Hall

QUESTIONS

1 What is the significance of the concept of learning styles?

2 What are study skills?

3 How can you make the best use of lectures?

4 What are the best approaches to taking notes?

5 What should you do after a lecture?

6 How can you get the most out of reading?

7 What are the key 'dos' of revising? Name at least four.

8 What are the key 'don'ts' of revising? Name at least four.

9 What are the key 'dos' of taking exams? Name at least four.

10 What are the key 'don'ts' of taking exams? Name at least four.

11 How should an essay or report be structured?

12 What are the main points to be considered when drafting an essay or report?

INDEX

absence management 87–88
absenteeism 308–10
Adair, J 6, 11–12
Adams, J S 171, 193, 196
ADDIE model 119
Alfes, K 216, 244
analytical skills 387
appraisal interviewing 304
arguments, development and
    justification of 391
Armstrong, M 146, 213
Arnold, J 352
assertiveness 326
Atkinson, J 252–53
averages 400

Bach, S 144
Bagley, C E 166
Balain, S 213
balance sheets 415–17
Balogun, K 241
Bandura, A 43, 115, 193, 197, 232
bargaining skills 338
Barney, J 32
Bass, B M 16–17
Bauman, Z 177
Beauchamp, T L 167
Becker, B E 58
Beckhard, R 231
Beer, M 55, 233
Bennis, W G 5, 16
'Big five' personality traits 353
'big idea', the 221
Birch, P 8–9
Birdi, K S 147
Birkinshaw, J 34
black box phenomenon 139–40
Blanchard, K H 8, 34
blended learning 113
Bolden, R 122
bounded rationality 387
Bower, J I 31
Bowie, N E 167
Boxall, P 30, 32, 53, 66, 173
Brewster, C 146, 147, 150, 151, 161
Briner, R B 376
Brown, D 94, 218
Brown, S L 243

Buchanan, D A 5, 352
budgetary control 419
Burgoyne, J 6, 123
Burns, J M 16
business case 286–88
business skills 415
Butler, I 144, 243

Caldwell, R 240
Campion, M A 94–95
Carey, M R 16
Carnall, C 236
Cascio, W F 93–94
case presentation 285–86
cash management 419–20
Cattell, R B 353
causal ambiguity 139
causality 402–03
chairing meetings 291–93
challenging conversations, handling
    of 335–36
change
    models 230–33
    operational 229
    process of 229–30
    resistance to change 234–35
    strategic 228–29
    transformational 228, 239
    types of 228–29
change management
    change agents, role of 237
    change models 220–23
    defined 228
    facilitating change 243–44
    field force analysis 230
    guidelines for 237–38
    holding the gains 243
    implementing change 236–37
    influencing people 284
    leading change 242–43
    managing the transition 239–40
    overcoming resistance to change 235
Chartered Institute of Personnel and
    Development (CIPD) 18–19, 44–45,
    126, 134, 145, 160–61, 212, 217,
    256–57, 264
Chell, E 352
Clarke, N 215

Clegg, S 167, 168, 177
cloud computing 406
coaching 317–19
codes of practice (ethics policies) 163–67
codes of professional conduct 161–62
Coens, T 94
cognitive evaluation theory of motivation
        193–94
cognitive learning theory 43
Collier, J 167
Commission on the Future of Management
        and Leadership 29
commitment
    critical evaluation of the concept 204–05
    defined 202
    factors affecting 205–06
    importance of 201–03
    strategy, development of 206–07
communicating 326–29
communities of practice 114
conflict, handling of 331–35
consultancy skills 392
content theory of motivation 199
continuous professional
        development 366
convergence and divergence 151
Coopey, J 204–05
coordinating discussions 294
core-periphery model of the firm 252
correlation 401
Costa, P 353
Coster, C 173
costing 420
Crawford, E R 215
creative thinking 377–79
critical evaluation 389–91
critical thinking 389
Csíkszentmihályi, M 194, 197
Cummins, T G 238
Cunningham, I 145, 147
customer liaison 342–45

de Bono, E 377–78
Deci, E L 189, 193–94, 197
decision making
    communicating and justifying
        decisions 380
    defined 377
    ethical decision making 379
    evidence-based decision making
        374, 377
    involving people 379–80
    the steps required 376
decisiveness 380–81
delegating 280–84
dentological theory 168–69

developing people
    defined 41–42
    how people learn 42
development 108
Dickman, M 150
Digman, J M 353
Digman, L A 31
discipline meeting 306
discourse ethics 169
discretionary behaviour 171
discussions, facilitating and
        coordinating 293–94
distributive justice 171
diversity and inclusion
    achieving culture change 264
    diversity and inclusion programme,
        aim of 263
    diversity networks 266–67
    evaluating progress 267
    managing diversity 262–65
    managing inclusion 262
    policy 265–67
    rationale for management of 263
    strategy 264–65
    values 265
Dixon, N F 5, 9
Drucker, P 29, 355, 375, 377
Dyer, L 205

education defined 108
effective supervision 280
effective teams 324
Egan, G 89
e-HRM 407
Eichinger, R W 42
Eisenheim, K M 243
e-learning 117
emotional behaviour,
        handling of 329–31
emotional intelligence 10
employee communications 103
employee engagement
    and commitment 203–04, 214
    competency framework 217
    drivers of 215
    enhancing 216–17
    job engagement 212–13
    and job satisfaction 214–15
    meaning of 212–13
    measuring engagement 222
    and motivation 214
    and organizational citizen
        behaviour 214
    organizational engagement 212–13,
        220–21
    outcomes of 216

employee relations 100–01, 176
employee resourcing *see* people resourcing
employee retention 84–87
employee turnover 84–85
employee value proposition 135
employee voice 102–03, 220
employment practices, ethical
        guidelines 176
employment relationship 100
engagement *see* employee engagement
enterprise social networks 407
equity 170
equity theory 193
e-reward 95
essay writing 434–37
Estaban, R 167
ethical considerations in HR 341–42
ethical dilemmas 177–78
ethical principles for self–management 368–69
ethical standards 162–63
ethics
    ethical decisions 168
    HR frameworks 162–63
    meaning and nature of 167
    policies 163–67
evaluation of learning 123–25
evidence-based management 386–87
exams 431–23
expatriates 152
expectancy theory of motivation 42, 140,
        192–93
experiential learning theory 43
Eysenck, H J 353

facilitating change 243–44
facilitating discussions 293
Farndale, E 161
feedback 304–06
Fiedler, F E 7–8
financial budgeting 419
financial rewards 98–99
financial skills 415–20
the flexible firm 252–53
flexible hours 255
flexible working
    aim of 252
    arrangements 254–57
    facilitating flexibility 252
    functional flexibility 254
    numerical flexibility 254
    operational flexibility 254
    the significance of flexibility 251–52
    structural flexibility 254
flow theory of motivation 194
Follett, M P 375
Fombrun, C J 54–55

Foucault, M 168, 169
Frankin, Benjamin 342
Freeman, R E 169
frequency 400
Fullerton, J 263

Galpin, M 216
Gardner, H 11
George, B 13, 18
Gerhart, B 194
globalization 150–51
goal theory 43, 193
Gold, J 274
Goleman, D 4, 5, 10, 14
Graen, G 10
Gray, D A 318
Grint, K 9, 94
Guest, D E 54, 63, 136, 140, 203, 204,
        220, 223

Hackman, J R 75, 189
Hamel, G 31
Hamlin, B 234, 243
Handy, C 379
Harrison, R 108–09, 177
Hart, J 115
Harter, J K 212
Harter, S 18
Hartley, J 204–05
Harvard framework 55
Hersey, P 8, 34
Herzberg, F 191, 195
Hesketh, A 9
hierarchy of needs (Maslow) 191
high involvement management 220
Hiltrop, J M 151
Hird, M 9, 125–26
Hofer, C W 33
holding the gains 243
homeworking 257
Honey, P 426–27
hot-desking 257
House, R J 8
HR analytics 397–98
HR architecture 57–58
HR, contribution of 134–49
HR ethical considerations 341–42
HR function
    measuring the value of 59
    meeting aims in a politically astute and
        ethical manner 341
    organization of 60–61
    role of 58–59
HR, impact of 136–41
HR information systems 404–07
HR liaising with customers 345

HR partnership, role of 61
HR politically astute behaviour 341
HR professionals as change agents 240–41
HR, professionalism in 160–61
HR professional ethical standards and
        considerations 341–42, 162–63
HR's role in managing change 240–44
Huczynski, A A 5, 352
Hudson, M 146
Hughes, M 240
human resource management (HRM)
    concept of 52–53
    context of 63–64
    contextual model 55
    defined 52, 53
    ethical guidelines 172
    European model 56
    5-P model 56
    goals of 53
    hard and soft models 57
    Harvard framework 55
    HR today 66
    matching model 54–55
    meaning of 66
    models of 54–57
    philosophy of 54
    underpinning theories 54
Hunt, S 32

inclusion see diversity and inclusion
individual differences 350
induction training 316
information, handling of 396–97
instrumentality theory of motivation 190
internal customers 344–45
international HRM
    contribution of HR 152
    convergence and divergence 151
    expatriates, management of 152
    globalization 150–51
    issues 150
    policies and practices 151
interpersonal communication 326–29
interviewing, selection 79–80
Ivancevich, J M 352

Jackson, S E 55
Jenkins, M 94
job characteristics model 75
job design 74–75, 218
job engagement 212–13, 217–18
job performance review 355
job satisfaction 214–15
job sharing 257
Jones, T M 168

Jung, C 354
justice 170–71

Kahn, W A 212
Kamoche, K 32
Kandola, R 263
Katz, D 7
Kelleber, H 12
Kelley, R E 8–9
Kendall, J 146
Kep, J 241
Kessler, I 144
Kirkpatrick, D L 124
knowing oneself 344
Kochan, T a 205
Kolb, D A 43–44, 426
Kotter, J P 34, 228, 240
Kouzes, J 16

lateral thinking 377–78
Lawler, E E 134, 196, 220, 236
leader–member exchange
        theory 10
leaders
    authentic 18
    charismatic 15–16
    and followers 8–9
    good leaders 14
    qualities of 274–76
    relational 18
    roles 11–12
    transactional 17–18
    transformational 16–17
    types of 15–19
    visionary 16
leadership
    behaviour studies 7
    brand 10
    contingent leadership 7–8
    defined 4–5
    and emotional intelligence 10
    ethical 18
    leader/follower theory 8–9
    leader–member exchange
        theory 10
    and management
        compared 33–34
    path-goal model of 8
    qualities 274–76
    reality of 19
    situational leadership 8
    skills 273–74
    theories 5–7
    trait theory 6–7
leadership development 121, 123

leadership style 14–15
learning
    defined 108
    effective learning 426–27
    evaluation of 123–25
    formal and informal 111–12
    how people learn 42
    lessons from neuroscience 44–45
    the motivation to learn 42–43
    self-directed learning 112
    self-managed learning 112–13
    social learning 115–17
    styles 43–44, 426–27
    theory 43
    workplace learning 115
learning communities 116
learning and development
    components of 109
    contribution of 135–36
    defined 108
    ethical guidelines 174–75
    process of 111
    programmes 218
    role of line managers 127
learning and development (L&D) function,
    role of 125–26
learning and development (L&D)
    specialists
    role of 126–27
    ethical standards 162
learning needs, identification
    of 110–11
Lee, S 146, 147
Legge, K 54, 171, 204
Leventhal, G S 171
Levine, K J 7
Lewin, K 230
Lewis, R 217
liaising with customers 342–43
line managers, HR and L&D role of
    62–63, 127, 315
Locke, E A 214
logical reasoning 387–89
Lombardo, M M 42
Luthans, F 172–73

Macey, W H 203–04, 212, 216, 218
MacLeod, D 215
management
    defined 28
    and leadership compared 33–34
    role of management 28
    strategic 30
management development 123
management skills 279–96

managers
    characteristics needed 29
    effective managers 36
    role of 29
managing oneself 349–50
managing stress 363–65
managing within the expectations of
    the law 179
Manson, B 148
Marlow, S 149
Martin-Alcázar, F 55
Maslow, A 191, 195
Maslow's needs hierarchy 191
McRae, R R 353
measures of central tendency 400
measures of dispersion 400–01
Meindle, J R 11
mentoring 319–20
Miller, J 148–49
mindfulness 365
Minzberg, H 31, 34
Mischell, W 350
Mohrman, S A 134, 236
motivation
    defined 188
    extrinsic 189
    intrinsic 188–89
    process of 190
    theory 189–96
    types of 188–89
motivating people 276
Mount, M K 93
multiple stakeholder framework 55
multiskilling 254–55
Mumford, A 427
mutuality 203
Myers–Briggs personality test 352

Nadler, D A 236
Nanus, B 5, 16
National School of Government 162
negotiating 337–38
networking 336–37
neuroscience 44–45
Nishii, L H 263
non-financial rewards 99

Occam's razor 375
Ohio State University 5, 7–8
Oldham, G R 75, 189
online social learning 116–17
Organ, D W 214
organization design 73–74
organization development ethical
    guidelines 173

organizational citizen behaviour 214
organizational culture 141–44, 170–71
organizational engagement 213, 220–21
organizational politics 339–41
organizational transformation 238–40
organizing yourself 359–60
Osterby, B 173

Parry, E 147
partnership, HR role 61
path-goal model of leadership 8
Patterson, M G 136
Penrose, E 32
people resourcing 76–88
performance management
    ethical guidelines 175
    issues 93–95
    managing performance throughout
        the year 91
    performance assessment 92–93
    performance planning 93
    performance reviews 92
    principles of 89
    process of 89–90
    reinventing 95–96
performance review meeting 304
Perren, L 6
personal characteristics, variations in 350–54
personal development planning 113, 316–17
personal organizing skills 361–63
personality
    'big five' personality traits 353
    defined 352
    trait concept of 352–54
    type theory of 354
persuading people 284–85
PESTLE analysis 76
Petrick, J A 167
Pettigrew, A 229 , 230
Pfeffer, J 386
planning 361–62
political astuteness 341
political sensitivity 339–40
politics, organizational 339–41
poor performance, management of 307–08
Porter, L W 196
Posner, B 16
post-graduate study skills 425–26
Postuma, R A 94–95
Prahalad, C K 31
presentations 288–91
prioritizing 362–63
Pritchard, K 61–62
problem solving 374–77
procedural justice 171

professional approach to HRM 160–61
professional codes of practice 161–62
professional ethical standards in
        HRM 162–63
profitability analysis ratios 418
profit and loss accounts 418
profits 417
project management 294–96
psychological contract 100
public sector, contribution of HRM in 143–45
Purcell, J 30, 53, 63, 136, 205, 221

Quinn, J B 31, 167

ratios 418
Recruitment and Employment
        Confederation 161
recruitment and selection 77–81, 174
Rees, C 220
reference groups 351
regression 401–02
Reilly, P 218
reinforcement theory of
        motivation 43, 192
report writing 434–37
resource-based view 32
resourcing see people resourcing
reverse causation 216
reward management
    defined 97
    ethical guidelines 175–76
    financial rewards 98–99
    non-financial rewards 99
    the reward system 97–98
    total rewards 99
Reynolds, J 42, 108, 118
Robinson, D 213
role profiles, definition of 316
Royal Society 45
Ryan, R M 189, 193–94, 197
Rynes, S L 194

Saks, A M 213
Sandel, M 189
Sargeant, A 145
Schaffer, O 194
Schendel, D 33
Schneider, B 203–04
Schuler, R S 55
Scullen, S E 9
selection interviewing 79–80, 300–03
selection testing 80
self-assessment 355–56
self-awareness 355–61
self-directed learning 112

self-managed learning 112–13
self-managed teams 325–26
self-management 367–69
self-organization 359–61
self-service 407
70/20/10 model for learning and
    development 42, 115
Shields, J 194
Simon, H 387
situational leadership 8
Smallwood, N 10
SMART objectives 91
Smith, Adam 143, 177
social intelligence 11
social learning 115–17
social learning theory 43, 115, 193
social media, use in learning 114–15
source references 438–39
Sparrow, P 31, 125–26, 150, 213
Stairs, M 215
stakeholder theory 169
stakeholders 55
standard deviation 401
statistics, use of 399–404
Stavrou-Costea, E 148
Stebbing, S 388
Stewart-Smith, K 175
Stiles, P 151
Stogdill, R M 6, 7
Storey, J 53, 54, 57, 136–37
strategic capability 33
strategic change 228–29
strategic fit 32–33
strategic HRM 57
strategic management 30
strategy 30–31
stress management 363–65
Strickland, A J 30
study skills 427–30
supervision 280
Sutton, R I 386
systematic training 118–19

talent management 81–84
Tamkin, P 123–24, 274
Taylor, F W 195
Team-building 275, 325
teams 324–25
Tester, K 177
testing hypotheses 403–04
tests of significance 403
Thompson, A A 30
Thompson, M 136
Thornhill, A 241, 244
Thurley, K 231–32

time management 358–59
timekeeping, handling poor 310
trade unions
    managing with 101–02
    managing without 102
    trading statements 417
training
    defined 108, 118
    induction 316
    justification of 118
    systematic training 118–19
    training events, planning and delivery
        of 119–20
trait theory 6
transformational change 228, 239
Truss, C 144, 212
Tushman, M 236, 239
two-factor model of motivation
    (Herzberg) 191–92

Ulrich, D 10, 60, 134, 135, 150, 240,
    242–43, 244
under-performers, dealing with
    307–08
utilitarianism 169, 341–42

Vance, R J 222
Vere, D 143, 243
virtual teams, management of 34–35
voluntary sector, contribution of
    HRM in 145–48
Vroom, V 196

Walton, R E 202–03
Walumbwa, F O 18
Watkins, M 35
Watson, T J 53
Webley, S 166
Welch, J 13
Welfare, S 150
Wenger, E 115–16
Werner, A 166
Wernerfelt, B 32
West, M A 136
Whipp, R 229, 230
Winstanley, D 168, 169, 172, 175
Woodall, J 168, 169, 172
Woodward, J 234
work design 72–73
work environment 221
workforce planning 76–77
workplace learning 115
Worley, C G 238

zero-hours contracts 256–57